COMPETENCE AT WORK

COMPETENCE AT WORK

Models for Superior Performance

LYLE M. SPENCER, JR., PHD
SIGNE M. SPENCER

John Wiley & Sons, Inc.

New York • Chichester • Brisbane • Toronto • Singapore

In recognition of the importance of preserving what has been written, it is a policy of John Wiley & Sons, Inc., to have books of enduring value published in the United States printed on acid-free paper, and we exert our best efforts to that end.

Library of Congress Cataloging-in-Publication Data

Spencer, Lyle M.
    Competence at work: models for superior performance / by
    Lyle M. and Signe M. Spencer.
       p.   cm.
    Includes bibliographical references and index.
    ISBN 0-471-54809-X (cloth)
    1. Assessment centers (personnel management procedures)
  2. Executives—Rating of.   3. Employee—Rating of.   4. Performance
standards.   I. Spencer, Signe M., 1950–   II. Title.
    HF5549.5.A78S67   1993
    658.3'125—dc20   92-31255

Printed in the United States of America

10 9 8 7 6 5 4 3 2 1

To

David C. McClelland,
whose insights and methods underlie all the research presented here;

and

Capt. Dana French, USN (ret.),
whose early support for a new idea greatly advanced it;

and our daughters

Kirsta, Emily, and Julia
who cheerfully and competently managed without us the
many nights and weekends both parents worked on "the book."

Acknowledgments

This book summarizes several hundred research studies conducted over the past 20 years by many colleagues from McBer and Company, Hay Management Consultants, academic institutions, and most importantly, our clients in industry, military, government, education, health care, and religious organizations. We cannot thank by name everyone who contributed to the findings presented here, but we wish to express special appreciation to:

Our clients.

Prof. David C. McClelland, PhD.

Prof. Richard Boyatzis, PhD, whose book *The Competent Manager* summarized the findings of studies of management jobs to 1980; and who worked on versions of the Competency Dictionary, read this manuscript, and provided us with valuable criticisms and suggestions.

Murray Dalziel, PhD, and Dick Mansfield, PhD, who worked on versions of the Competency Dictionary and developed the first expert system; Dick also did most of the work on the entrepreneur competency study reported in Chapter 17.

Ron Page, PhD, who worked with us on versions of the "just-noticeable-difference" (JND) scales, and contributed ideas on job–person matching algorithms and integrated Human Resource Management Information Systems.

John Raven, PhD, with whom we have shared ideas over the years on competency measurement and teaching, and who first suggested the chemistry analogy for organizing and combining competencies.

Professors David Caldwell, PhD, and Charles O'Rielly, PhD, for information on their profile comparison method for assessing job–person matches.

Charles Bethel-Fox, PhD, who developed some of the first competency models using just-noticeable-difference scales.

Professor Kurt Fischer, PhD, for ideas on scaling cognitive competencies.

McBer research colleagues Stephen Kelner, PhD, Ruth Jacobs, PhD, Suzanne Nace, Alexandra Beal, and other coders who analyzed some 17,000 plus pages of competency models.

Hay Management Consultants colleagues Jim Bowers; Laurent Dufetel; David Fitt; Dan Glasner, PhD; Douglas O'Donnell; Michael O'Malley; and Laura Thanasse, who contributed ideas on competency-based pay.

David Hofrichter, PhD, for his succession planning case.

Hillary Pennington, President, Jobs for the Future, for data on states' competency-based human resources planning.

Jennifer Gallagher and McBer's production staff, who produced many figures and tables, and cheerfully put up with many revisions.

The United States Navy, which supported our research for 14 years.

The United States Agency for International Development, which supported our cross-cultural study of entrepreneur competencies.

The Army Research Institute, which supported research on military leaders and organizational consultants.

Kirsta Anderson, who assembled figures and tables for the final manuscript.

Our editors Donna Daniel and Michael Hamilton.

                                                          L.S.
                                                          S.S.

Preface

This book has four objectives:

1. To summarize 20 years of research using the McClelland/McBer job competence assessment (JCA) methodology. The book includes the McBer Competency Dictionary and findings from 286 studies of entrepreneurial, technical and professional, sales, human service, and managerial jobs from industry, government, military, health care, education and religious organizations.

2. To describe in detail how to conduct JCA studies.

3. To describe "state of the art" human resource management applications of JCA research: recruitment, assessment, selection, succession planning, career pathing, performance management, training and development, competency-based pay, and integrated human resource information systems.

4. To suggest future directions and applications for competency research given such human resources management issues as "information" economies, tighter labor markets for key knowledge workers, diversity, and globalization. Topics include competencies most often identified by studies as important for the future; "globalization" of the competency model data base; growing use of artificial intelligence expert systems; and societal applications of competency research methods.

The book is divided into five parts:

- *Part I* gives a brief history of the competency movement in industrial/organizational psychology and defines the term "competency."

- *Part II* lists, defines, and provides scoring criteria for the competencies that predict superior performance in most jobs. This part provides a generic competency dictionary for the 21 competencies found most often to differentiate superior from average performers in 286 studies of middle- to upper-level jobs.

- *Part III* provides instructions for designing competency studies, conducting a Behavioral Event Interview, and analyzing data to develop competency models. The actual implementation of the method requires training and practice that is beyond the scope of this book. Part III will provide an overview useful in deciding how appropriate this approach may be in a given situation.

Readers who are not primarily interested in research methods or selection interviewing may wish to skip or skim this part and go on to the generic models or research findings in Part IV.

- *Part IV* presents findings on the competencies that predict success in sales, technical/professional, helping and service, managerial, and entrepreneur jobs. To give the reader a sense of the kinds of findings that competency models may produce, the descriptions of our findings in Chapters 13 through 16 will be general and impressionistic. Chapter 17, on entrepreneurs, will present the findings of a publicly funded international study of entrepreneurs in some statistical detail.

- *Part V* describes uses of competency data in human resource management: recruiting, selection, placement, succession planning, development and career pathing, competency-based pay and integrated human resource management information systems; in society; and in the future.

This book is the first of three we plan on analysis of the competency data base. The second volume will be a detailed statistical data analysis using factor and cluster analysis techniques. The third volume will provide "programmed learning" instructions, example sets, and practice tests that readers can use to teach themselves to code competencies with acceptable interrater reliability.

We have written this book for human resource professionals, managers, and interested general readers. With the exception of Chapter 17, which presents previously unpublished data on entrepreneurs, statistics have been limited to simple means and frequencies. References are provided to orient academic readers to the relevant technical literature.

Our competency research is very much a work in process. More than 100 researchers in 24 countries are adding competency models to the data base at the rate of two a week. We have been revising the Competency Dictionary every three months to incorporate new findings. This production of new knowledge will continue and probably accelerate.

Since this first book "freezes" our findings at one point of time, November 1991, we welcome inquiries from competency researchers about our latest findings—and contributions to the competency model data base we are building. We can be reached c/o McBer and Company, 137 Newbury Street, Boston MA 02116 USA, 617-437-7080 and FAX 617-437-9417.

LYLE SPENCER
SIGNE SPENCER

Boston, Massachusetts

Contents

PART I   The Concept of Competence   1

Chapter 1: Introduction   3
Chapter 2: Definition of a "Competency"   9

PART II   A Competency Dictionary   17

Chapter 3: Developing a Competency Dictionary   19
Chapter 4: Achievement and Action   25
Chapter 5: Helping and Human Service   37
Chapter 6: The Impact and Influence Cluster   44
Chapter 7: Managerial   54
Chapter 8: Cognitive   67
Chapter 9: Personal Effectiveness   78

PART III   Developing a Model   91

Chapter 10: Designing Competency Studies   93
Chapter 11: Conducting the Behavioral Event Interview   114
Chapter 12: Developing a Competency Model   135

PART IV   Findings: Generic Competency Models   157

Chapter 13: Technicians and Professionals   159
Chapter 14: Salespeople   171
Chapter 15: Helping and Human Service Workers   185
Chapter 16: Managers   199
Chapter 17: Entrepreneurs   220

Contents

PART V   Competency-Based Applications   237

Chapter 18: Selection: Assessment and Job–Person
Matching for Recruiting, Placement, Retention,
and Promotion   239
Chapter 19: Performance Management   264
Chapter 20: Succession Planning   276
Chapter 21: Development and Career Pathing   286
Chapter 22: Pay   304
Chapter 23: Integrated Human Resource Management
Information Systems   315
Chapter 24: Societal Applications   323
Chapter 25: Competency-Based Human Resource
Management in the Future   342

Bibliography   349

Index   359

The Concept of Competence

CHAPTER

1

Introduction

David C. McClelland

In 1973, I published a paper, "Testing for Competence Rather Than Intelligence,"[1] which has been credited or blamed for launching the competency movement in psychology.[2] In this paper, I reviewed studies indicating that traditional academic aptitude and knowledge content tests, as well as school grades and credentials:

1. Did not predict job performance or success in life.
2. Were often biased against minorities, women, and persons from lower socioeconomic strata.[3]

These findings led me to look for research methods that would identify "competency" variables, which could predict job performance and were not biased (or, at least less biased) by race, sex, or socioeconomic factors. The most important of these methods were:

1. *Use of Criterion Samples.* This method compares people who have clearly had successful jobs or interesting lives with people who are less successful in order to identify those characteristics associated with success.
2. *Identification of Operant Thoughts and Behaviors Causally Related to Successful Outcomes.* That is, competency measures should involve open-ended situations in which an individual has to generate behavior, as distinguished from "respondent" measures such as self-report and multiple-choice tests, which require choosing one of several well-defined

alternative responses to carefully structured situations. Real-life and job situations rarely present such test conditions. Rather, the best predictor of what a person can and will do is what he or she spontaneously thinks and does in an unstructured situation—or has done in similar past situations.

The first tests of these methods were with U.S. State Department Foreign Service Information Officers[4] and Massachusetts human service workers.[5] The State Department study is worth recounting because it illustrates the competency identification process.

In the early 1970s, McBer and Company was approached by the U.S. State Department for help in selecting junior Foreign Service Information Officers (FSIOs). These young diplomats represent America in foreign countries. They staff libraries, organize cultural events, and give talks on America to local groups. Their real job is to get as many people as possible to like the United States and support U.S. policies. In 1970, almost all young FSIOs were white males.

Traditionally, the State Department had selected Foreign Service Information Officers through the use of a Foreign Service Officer exam. This exam was based on the skills senior officials thought a modern diplomat needed—essentially knowledge of the liberal arts and culture: American history, western civilization, English usage, and specialties such as economics and government.

The exam, however, had major drawbacks. First, because the tests required extremely high passing scores, minorities and others from less privileged cultures were much less likely to pass them. Second, a careful report prepared by Dr. Kenneth Clark found that applicants' scores on the FSIO General Aptitude Test Battery or the General Background Knowledge Test did not predict success as a FSIO, as rated afterward by performance on the job,[6] at least at the very high levels required for consideration as an FSIO appointee. How a young FSIO did on his/her feet in Ethiopia was not predicted by very high vocabulary or aptitude test scores. Given the lack of relation of scores on these tests to on-the-job success, their use potentially represented an act of illegal discrimination and handicapped the U.S. Information Service in its work since its officers did not truly represent the role of minorities in American life.

Our challenge was to answer the question: If traditional aptitude measures don't predict job performance, what does? Our approach was, first, to request a criterion sample: some clearly superior performers, and a contrasting sample of average and/or poor performers. We asked the State Department to tell us who its best junior FSIOs were and provide us with a comparison group.

The superior group was composed of superstars, the most brilliant and effective young diplomats. These people, in the eyes of their bosses, peers, and foreign clients, were the most effective representatives of the United States abroad. The average group were people who did their jobs just well enough not to get fired.

Second, we developed a technique called the Behavioral Event Interview (BEI).[7] Originally, we had hoped to observe the superior and average diplomats doing their daily work and see what the best people did that the mediocre ones did not. This approach was too expensive and impractical to try in a worldwide study. So we hit on the idea of getting people to provide very detailed, blow-by-blow accounts of what they did in the most critical situations they had been in on their jobs. The Behavioral Event Interview process gets a subject to describe three peak successes and three major failures in short-story fashion. The interviewer acts as an investigative reporter asking the following questions: What led up to the situation? Who was involved? What did you think about, feel, and want to accomplish in dealing with the situation? What did you actually do? What happened? What was the outcome of the incident? These interviews gave us several hundred short stories about the toughest situations young diplomats actually faced on their jobs in foreign countries.

The BEI essentially combines Flanagan's critical incident method[8] with Thematic Apperception Test (TAT) probes developed over 30 years in studying motivation.[9] However, whereas Flanagan was interested in identifying the task elements of jobs, we were interested in the characteristics of the people who did a job well.

Third, we thematically analyzed BEI transcripts from superior and less effective FSIOs to identify characteristics that differed between the two samples, generally behaviors shown by superior performers and not shown by average performers. Such thematic differences are typically translated into objective scoring definitions, which can be reliably coded by different observers.

BEI transcripts are then scored according to these definitions utilizing a method long used to measure motivation[10] now being called "CAVE," for content analysis of verbal expression.[11] CAVE coding enables investigators to count (measure empirically) and test statistically for the significance of differences in the characteristics shown by superior and average performers in various jobs. This method was used extensively in a subsequent study of the competencies characterizing outstanding diplomats in the regular Foreign Service.[12]

Competency characteristics that differentiated superior from average information officers included the following.

Cross-Cultural Interpersonal Sensitivity. The ability to hear what people from a foreign culture are really saying or meaning; and to predict how they will react. For example, one FSIO told the following story:

I was a cultural affairs officer in North Africa. One day I received a directive from Washington saying I had to show a certain film featuring an American politician who I knew was seen as hostile to this country's position. I knew that if I showed that film, this place would be burned down the next day by about 500 angry, left-wing students. Washington thinks the film is great, but the locals will find it offensive. What I had to figure out was how to show the film so the Embassy can tell Washington we did, and yet not offend anyone in the country. . . . I came up with the solution of screening it on a holy day when nobody could come.

This young diplomat had the social sensitivity to know how the local population would react and also knew how to handle it in his own organization.

Positive Expectations of Others.   A strong belief in the underlying dignity and worth of others different from oneself, and the ability to maintain this positive outlook under stress. For example, another diplomat told of maintaining friendships with radical student leaders who had threatened to burn down her USIA library:

> . . . despite the troubles we had with them, I never stopped liking and respecting the student leaders. They were just becoming conscious of their nationalism, and that they were going to be the leaders of a greatly changed country. I could understand that they needed to rebel against us, to stand up to us, even throw us out—even when they wanted to burn my library! So I told them that, and invited them to use our facilities to hold some of their meetings. I tried to get resident Americans here to listen, so more of them would understand. I've got good contacts with some of the student leaders now. And we haven't been burned down yet!

Speed in Learning Political Networks.   The ability to figure out very quickly who influences whom and what each person's political interests are. For example, a superior FSIO told of going to an African country and rapidly deducing that it was "the prime minister's executive assistant's mistress's nephew who called shots on petroleum policy." The FSIO then promptly managed to get invited to a party where he could meet and begin lobbying this nephew.

These three competencies, and other nonacademic skills such as the ability to generate a number of promotional ideas, appeared much more frequently in the thoughts and actions of superior FSIOs. Average performers either did not report incidents showing these skills, or they told stories in which these skills were clearly lacking. For example, average FSIOs described situations that blew up in their faces because they did not foresee the political consequences of an action (lack of social sensitivity and political savvy). Average performers' BEIs were much more likely to contain negative comments and even racial slurs about their host country's "clients."

The final step was to validate the competency model (i.e., prove that it did predict who would be a good FSIO, and that it did not discriminate unfairly on the basis of race, sex, cultural background, or irrelevant educational experiences). This was done in two ways.

First, we identified a new sample of superstar and average FSIOs. We interviewed these diplomats using the BEI method and scored their stories to see if they showed the critical competencies. Competencies that, once again, appeared more often in the stories of the best performers were considered validated, and therefore accurate, predictors of the skills needed to be a good FSIO.

Second, new kinds of tests were found to measure the competencies. For example, a good measure of empathy and social sensitivity is the Profile of Non-Verbal Sensitivity (PONS).[13] This test is a tape recording of people talking emotionally about various situations. These little snatches of emotional talk have been put through an electronic filter so that the listener can hear the emotion but not make out the words. After listening to each speech segment, the subjects are asked questions such as "Is this a man (a) talking about his divorce or (b) arguing with a subordinate?" People with more empathy can hear the difference between sorrow or hurt in the first scenario and anger or irritation in the second.

This test was given to superior and average FSIOs. Superior FSIOs scored significantly higher on the PONS because they were better able to "tune into" others' feelings. Scores on the PONS did not differ by FSIO race, sex, or educational background.

Further research using this competency assessment method led to the definition of competence and standard procedures for conducting the competency research studies described in this book.

In 1991, the competency assessment method was being used by more than 100 researchers in 24 countries. Twenty years of experience with the method have generated a worldwide competency model data base and generic competency dictionary, "just-noticeable-difference" (JND), scales for many competencies, cross-cultural comparisons, and new findings about the role of achievement motivation and information seeking in predicting job performance. These and many other innovations and applications of the competency methodology are presented in the following chapters.

The job competency movement has advanced the way in which psychologists go about their traditional task of getting the right person into the right job. Formerly, psychologists identified the tasks required for the job (as in the motor skills needed for operating a streetcar or an airplane), constructed tests to measure the skills needed to perform these tasks, factor-analyzed performance scores on those tests after making sure the scores were reliable, and then tried to match the factor scores with success on the job—without conspicuous success. In essence, traditional industrial/organizational psychology started with separate analyses of the job and the person, and tried to fit them together. This approach had its greatest success in predicting academic performance from academic-type tests, but it has proved quite inadequate for predicting performance in the high-level jobs of greatest importance to modern business.

In the job-competency approach, analysis starts with the person-in-the-job, makes no prior assumptions as to what characteristics are needed to perform the job well, and determines from open-ended behavioral event interviews which human characteristics are associated with job success. The competency method emphasizes criterion validity: what actually causes superior performance in a job, not what factors most reliably describe all the characteristics of a person, in the hope that some of them will relate to job performance.

Competencies identified by the competency process are context sensitive (e.g., they describe what successful Indian entrepreneurs actually do in their own organizations and culture, not what Western psychological or management theory say should be needed for success). Competency-based selection predicts superior job performance and retention—both with significant economic value to organizations—without race, age, gender, or demographic bias.

The competency approach provides a human resource method broadly applicable to selection, career pathing, performance appraisal, and development in the challenging years ahead.

NOTES

1. McClelland, D. C. (1973), Testing for competence rather than for intelligence, *American Psychologist, 28,* 1–14.

2. Barrett, G. V., & Depinet, R. L. (1991), A reconsideration of testing for competence rather than intelligence, *American Psychologist, 46* (10), 1012–1024.

3. Barrett & Depinet, op. cit., have questioned these findings, citing several recent meta-analytic studies showing that intelligence test scores do predict performance in a variety of jobs. In: McClelland, D. C. (in press). The knowledge testing-educational complex strikes back. *American Psychologist,* I reply, "If I would change anything in the 1973 article, it would be to describe the threshold competency issue more carefully . . . intelligence may be a threshold type of variable (but) once a person has a certain minimal level of intelligence, his performance beyond that point is uncorrelated with his ability.

   So far as I know, knowledge tests are still being used to screen out minority candidates, unfairly because of their handicapped backgrounds, who could do the job perfectly well as shown by valid competency tests, where there is absolutely no evidence that ability test scores at this high level are in any way related to superior performance in the job."

4. McClelland, D. C., & Dailey, C. (1972), Improving officer selection for the foreign service, Boston: McBer.

5. McClelland, D. C., & Fiske, S. T. (1974), *Report to the Executive Office of Manpower Affairs on validation of a human service worker test.* Boston: McBer.

6. McClelland, D. C., & Dailey, C. (1972), Improving officer selection for the foreign service, Boston: McBer.

7. McClelland, D. C., & Dailey, C. (1972), op. cit. Also see McClelland, D. (1976), *A guide to job competence assessment,* Boston: McBer.

8. Flanagan, J. C. (1954), The critical incident technique, *Psychological Bulletin, 51,* 327–358.

9. McClelland, D. C. (1989), *Human motivation,* Cambridge, UK: Cambridge University Press.

10. Atkinson, J. W. (Ed.) (1958), *Motives in fantasy, action and society,* New York: Van Nostrand.

11. Zullow, H. M., Oettingen, G., Peterson, C., & Seligman, M. E. (1988), Pessimistic explanatory style in the historical record, *American Psychologist, 43,* (9), 673–682.

12. McClelland, D. C., Klemp, G. O., Jr., & Miron, D. (1977), Competency requirements of senior and mid-level positions in the Department of State, Boston: McBer.

13. Rosenthal, R. (Ed.). (1979) *Skill in non-verbal communication,* Cambridge, MA: Oelgeschlager.

2

Definition of a "Competency"

A competency is an *underlying characteristic* of an individual that is *causally related* to *criterion-referenced effective and/or superior performance* in a job or situation.

Underlying characteristic means the competency is a fairly deep and enduring part of a person's personality and can predict behavior in a wide variety of situations and job tasks.

Causally related means that a competency *causes* or *predicts* behavior and performance.

Criterion-referenced means that the competency actually predicts who does something well or poorly, as measured on a *specific criterion* or standard. Examples of criteria are the dollar volume of sales for salespeople or the number of clients who stay "dry" for alcohol-abuse counselors.

The following sections in this chapter discuss each part of this definition: underlying characteristic, causally related, criterion-referenced.

UNDERLYING CHARACTERISTICS

Competencies are underlying characteristics of people and indicate "ways of behaving or thinking, generalizing across situations, and enduring for a reasonably long period of time."[1]

Five Types of Competency Characteristics

1. *Motives.* The things a person consistently thinks about or wants that cause action. Motives "drive, direct, and select"[2] behavior toward certain actions or goals and away from others.

Example: Achievement-motivated people consistently set challenging goals for themselves, take personal responsibility for accomplishing them, and use feedback to do better.

2. *Traits.* Physical characteristics and consistent responses to situations or information.

   Example: Reaction time and good eyesight are physical trait competencies of combat pilots.

   Emotional self-control and initiative are more complex "consistent responses to situations." Some people don't "blow up" at others and do act "above and beyond the call of duty" to solve problems under stress. These trait competencies are characteristic of successful managers.
       Motives and competencies are intrinsic *operant* or *self-starting* "master traits" that predict what people will do on their jobs long term, without close supervision.

3. *Self-Concept.* A person's attitudes, values, or self-image.

   Example: *Self-confidence,* a person's belief that he or she can be effective in almost any situation is part of that person's concept of self.

   A person's values are *respondent* or reactive motives that predict what he or she will do in the short term and in situations where others are in charge.[3] For example, someone who *values* being a leader is more likely to exhibit leadership behavior if he or she is told a task or job will be "a test of leadership ability." People who *value* being "in management" but do not intrinsically like or spontaneously think about influencing others at the motive level often attain management positions but then fail.

4. *Knowledge.* Information a person has in specific content areas.

   Example: A surgeon's knowledge of nerves and muscles in the human body.

   Knowledge is a complex competency. Scores on knowledge tests often fail to predict work performance because they fail to measure knowledge and skills in the ways they are actually used on the job. First, many knowledge tests measure rote memory, when what is really important is the ability to find information. Memory of specific facts is less important than knowing which facts exist that are relevant to a specific problem, and where to find them when needed. Second, knowledge tests are "respondent." They measure test takers' ability to choose which of several options is the right response, but not whether a person can act on the basis of knowledge. For example, the ability to choose which of five items is an effective argument is very different from the ability to stand up in a conflict situation and argue persuasively. Finally, knowledge at best predicts what someone *can* do, not what he or she will do.

5. *Skill.* The ability to perform a certain physical or mental task.

> **Example:** A dentist's physical skill to fill a tooth without damaging the nerve; a computer programmer's ability to organize 50,000 lines of code in logical sequential order.

> Mental or cognitive skill competencies include analytic thinking (processing knowledge and data, determining cause and effect, organizing data and plans) and conceptual thinking (recognizing patterns in complex data).

The type or level of a competency has practical implications for human resource planning. As illustrated in Figure 2–1, knowledge and skill competencies tend to be visible, and relatively surface, characteristics of people. Self-concept, trait, and motive competencies are more hidden, "deeper," and central to personality.

Surface knowledge and skill competencies are relatively easy to develop; training is the most cost-effective way to secure these employee abilities.

Core motive and trait competencies at the base of the personality iceberg are more difficult to assess and develop; it is most cost-effective to *select* for these characteristics.

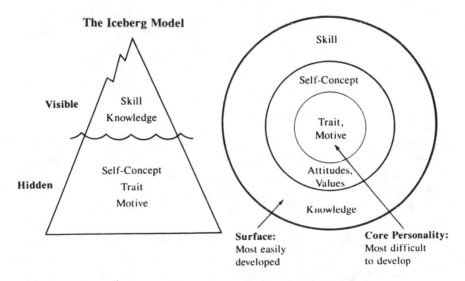

Figure 2–1   Central and Surface Competencies

Self-concept competencies lie somewhere in between. Attitudes and values such as self-confidence (seeing one's self as a "manager" instead of a "technical/professional") can be changed by training, psychotherapy, and/or positive developmental experiences, albeit with more time and difficulty.

Many organizations select on the basis of surface knowledge and skill competencies ("we hire MBAs from good schools") and either assume that recruits have the underlying motive and trait competencies or that these can be instilled by good management. The converse is probably more cost-effective: organizations should select for core motive and trait competencies and teach the knowledge and skills required to do specific jobs. Or as one personnel director put it, "You can teach a turkey to climb a tree, but it is easier to hire a squirrel."

In complex jobs, competencies are relatively more important in predicting superior performance than are task-related skills, intelligence, or credentials. This is due to a "restricted range effect." In higher level technical, marketing, professional, and managerial jobs, almost *everyone* has an I.Q. of 120 or above and an advanced degree from a good university. What distinguishes superior performers in these jobs is motivation, interpersonal skills, and political skills, all of which are competencies. It follows that competency studies are the most cost-effective way to staff these positions.

CAUSAL RELATIONSHIPS

Motive, trait, and *self-concept* competencies predict *skill* behavior actions, which in turn predict job performance *outcomes,* as in the motive/trait → behavior → outcome causal flow model shown in Figure 2–2.

Competencies always include an *intent,* which is the motive or trait force that causes *action* toward an outcome. For example, knowledge and skill competencies invariably include a motive, trait, or self-concept competency, which provides the drive or "push" for the knowledge or skill to be used.

Behavior without intent doesn't define a competency. An example is "management by walking around." Without knowing *why* a manager is walking around, you can't know which, if any, competency is being demonstrated. The manager's intent could be boredom, leg cramps, the monitoring of work to see if quality is high, or a desire "to be visible to the troops."

Action behaviors can include thought, where thinking precedes and predicts behavior. Examples are motives (e.g., thinking about doing something better), planning, or problem-solving thoughts.

Causal flow models can be used to do "risk assessment" analyses. For example, following the causal arrows in Figure 2–2, an organization that does not select for, develop, or arouse achievement motivation in its employees can expect *less* improvement in financial outcomes, productivity, and quality, and *fewer* new products and services.

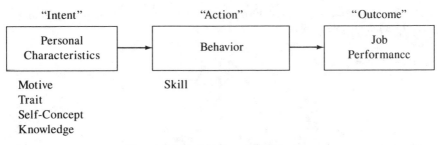

"Intent"   "Action"   "Outcome"

| Personal Characteristics | → | Behavior | → | Job Performance |

Motive   Skill
Trait
Self-Concept
Knowledge

Example: Achievement Motivation

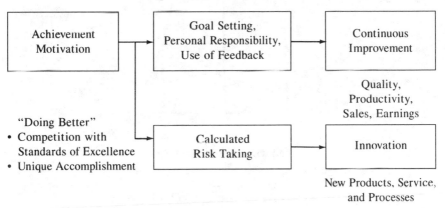

| Achievement Motivation | → | Goal Setting, Personal Responsibility, Use of Feedback | → | Continuous Improvement |

Quality,
Productivity,
Sales, Earnings

"Doing Better"
• Competition with Standards of Excellence
• Unique Accomplishment

| | | Calculated Risk Taking | → | Innovation |

New Products, Service,
and Processes

Figure 2–2 Competency Causal Flow Model

CRITERION REFERENCE

Criterion reference is critical to our definition of competence. *A characteristic is not a competency unless it predicts something meaningful in the real world.* Psychologist William James said the first rule for scientists should be that "A difference which *makes* no difference *is* no difference." A characteristic or credential that makes no difference in performance is not a competency and should not be used to evaluate people.

The criteria most frequently used in competency studies are:

■ *Superior Performance.* This is defined statistically as one standard deviation above average performance (see Figure 2–3), roughly the level achieved by the top 1 person out of 10 in a given working situation.

■ *Effective Performance.* This usually really means a "minimally acceptable" level of work, the lower cutoff point below which an employee would not be considered competent to do the job.

1 Standard Deviation (S.D.) in performance is worth 19%–120% output value-added (e.g., for high-complexity jobs 1 S.D. is worth 48% of salary).

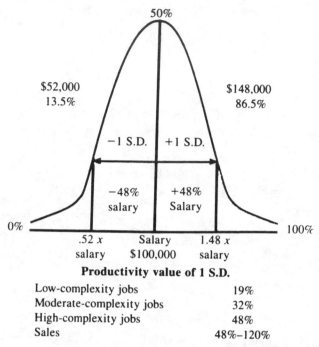

Productivity value of 1 S.D.

Low-complexity jobs	19%
Moderate-complexity jobs	32%
High-complexity jobs	48%
Sales	48%–120%

Adapted from J.E. Hunter, F.L. Schmidt, and M.K. Judiesch, "Individual Differences in Output Variability as a Function of Job Complexity," *Journal of Applied Psychology* 75 (1990), 28–42.

Figure 2–3   What Superior Performance Is Worth

"One standard deviation" is used to define superior performance for two reasons. First, many research studies have documented the economic value of this level of performance to organizations. Depending on the complexity of the job, the value of one standard deviation above the mean is 19 to 48 percent of output for nonsales jobs, and 48 to 120 percent for sales[4] (see Figure 2–3). A minimum estimate of economic value of superior performance can be calculated by taking these percentages multiplied by the average salary per year for the job. In fact, this global estimate approach seriously undervalues jobs that leverage significant revenues or assets. For example, a recent survey of 44 Southeast firms[5] found that superior salespeople (earning an average of $41,777), sold on average $6.7 million and average performers sold on average $3 million. The superior group sold 123 percent more than the average salespeople, a difference worth not 120 percent but *8,857 percent* (or 89 times) the average employee salary.

These data suggest the practical economic value of a competency model that can help a firm find even one additional superior salesperson: $3.7 million—a benefit that can justify can considerable investment in competency research.

Second, to improve performance, organizations should use the characteristics of superior performers as their "template," or "blueprint," for employee selection and development. Failure to do so is essentially to select and train to *mediocrity*—an organization's current average level of performance.

CATEGORIZING COMPETENCIES

Competencies can be divided into two categories, "threshold" and "differentiating," according to the job performance criterion they predict.

- *Threshold Competencies.* These are the essential characteristics (usually knowledge or basic skills, such as the ability to read) that everyone in a job needs to be minimally effective but that do not distinguish superior from average performers. A threshold competency for a salesperson is knowledge of the product or ability to fill out invoices.

- *Differentiating Competencies.* These factors distinguish superior from average performers. For example, achievement orientation expressed in a person's setting goals higher than those required by the organization, is a competency that differentiates superior from average salespeople.

NOTES

1. Guion, R. M. (1991), Personnel assessment, selection and placement. In M. D. Dunnette & L. M. Hough (Eds.), *Handbook of industrial and organizational psychology,* (p. 335), Palo Alto, CA: Consulting Psychologists Press.

2. The technical definition of a motive is a "recurrent concern for a goal state, or condition, appearing in fantasy, which drives, directs and selects behavior of the individual." McClelland, D. C. (1971), *Assessing human motivation,* New York: General Learning Press.

3. McClelland, D. C., Koester, R., & Weinberger, J. (1990), How do implicit and self-attributed motives differ? *Psychological Review, 96,* 690–702.

4. Hunter, J. E., Schmidt, F. L., Judiesch, M. K. (1990), Individual differences in output variability as a function of job complexity, *Journal of Applied Psychology, 75,* (1), 28–42.

5. Sloan, S., & Spencer, L. M. (1991, February 28), *Participant Survey Results: Hay Salesforce Effectiveness Seminar,* Atlanta: Hay Management Consultants.

PART

II

A Competency
Dictionary

CHAPTER

3

Developing a
Competency Dictionary

DEVELOPMENT OF THE DICTIONARY

In 1981, our colleague Richard Boyatzis reanalyzed the original data (i.e., transcripts of behavioral event interviews) from a number of competency studies of managers and found a set of competencies that consistently distinguished superior managers across organizations and functions.[1] An early attempt to scale competencies (on a conceptual rather than empirical basis) was made by Boyatzis and colleagues at McBer.[2] Encouraged by his success in identifying "generic" competencies, we decided in 1989 to look at the competencies found in all the more than 200 jobs for which competency models were available. We used the reports of the studies (referred to as "models") as the basis for our analysis. We treated each report as a qualitative study of the characteristics of superior performers in that job.

Reports of competency models (Behavioral Event Interview-based studies of the distinguishing characteristics of superior performers in a job)[3] are generally organized into *clusters* or groups of distinguishing competencies (generally about three to six clusters, similar to the clusters in the following dictionary). Each cluster contains two to five *competencies,* similar to those described in the dictionary. Each competency has a narrative definition plus three to six *behavioral indicators,* or specific behavioral ways of demonstrating the competency in the job.

Often each competency or each behavioral indicator is illustrated with a typical example drawn from the interviews of superior performers. Most reports included t-tests of statistical significance of each competency but not of the significance of each behavioral indicator within each competency.

To compare all the models, the findings needed to be translated into a "common language." This step is similar to the coding of findings for each study in a quantitative meta-analysis.

Analysis of the entire sample of competency models was based on behavioral indicators, the "lowest common denominator," or smallest unit of observation directly comparable across all models. This approach was necessary because studies developed over 20 years by more than 100 different researchers used many different names for similar competencies.

A list was made of all behavioral indicators appearing in the 286 competency models. Approximately 760 separate types of behaviors were identified. Of these, 360 indicators defining 21 competencies accounted for 80 to 98 percent of behaviors reported in each model. The remaining 400 behavioral indicators described rarely observed competencies, called "uniques" in the following discussion. The list of 360 behavioral indicators provided a preliminary dictionary.

All competency models were coded for all behavioral indicators in the dictionary. Most models contained from 50 to 150 indicators.

Using Behavioral Event Interview data, we entered 286 competency models[4] in a data base. This sample includes 187 (66%) U.S. studies and 98 (34%) studies conducted in 20 other countries or multinationally, with job incumbents in 3 to 10 countries.

Competency models in the data base include technical/professional, human service, entrepreneur, sales/marketing/trading, and managerial jobs in industry, government, military, health care, education, and religious organizations. Where several studies of a common job exist, the data base can be queried to produce generic competency models (e.g., for health care managers, high-tech salespersons, or internal trainer/consultants). Data-base queries can test similarities among different levels of a job family, different types of jobs, or job studies from different environments. For example, competencies for superior performance in similar jobs are found to be essentially the same everywhere in the world. (Chapter 17 provides comparative competency data for studies conducted in Latin America, Africa, and Asia.)

JUST-NOTICEABLE-DIFFERENCE (JND) COMPETENCY SCALES

In the coding process, we found that the same type of behavior was exhibited with more intensity, completeness, or scope in some examples than in others. For example, some Achievement stories mentioned many more action steps than others. Others addressed a larger problem (more money and jobs), or described newer, more innovative solutions to problems. We tried various means of notating the differences in intensity we found between examples of the "same" competency in different jobs. *Competency behavioral indicators appeared to have scaling properties: a clear progression from lower to higher levels on one or more dimensions.*

To clarify these competency scales, 50 verbatim examples of each competency were collected from a variety of jobs and Q-sorted by several researchers according to the extent to which they indicated more or less of the competency in question. Examples were arrayed in columns or in two dimensional grids by comparing their relative weight, or strength, adding dimensions as needed. Researchers read examples in each column and row and wrote indicators that described the similarities in examples in each column. This process produced just-noticeable-difference (JND) scales for each competency.

Competency Scale Dimensions

Because the scales were empirically derived, the underlying dimensions vary, according to the variances that we observed in the actual data (i.e., quotes from superior performers). Many competencies have more than one dimension. Typical dimensions are:

Intensity or Completeness of Action. The first or main scale of most competencies (labeled "A") describes the intensity of the intention (or personal characteristic) involved and the completeness of the actions taken to realize that intention. For example, some stories of Achievement Orientation were stronger because they involved entrepreneurial risk taking rather than just wanting to do a job well.

Size of Impact. The breadth of impact describes the number and position of people impacted, or the size of the project affected. For example, use of a competency might impact a subordinate, a peer, a boss, the CEO of the organization, or even national or international leaders. Impact can also describe the size of the problem addressed, from something affecting part of one person's performance to a project affecting the way an entire organization does business. For most competencies, size of impact (or "breadth") is the second or "B" scale.

Job size or organizational level strongly affects this dimension, and it is often more useful in comparing jobs than in comparing individuals within the same job. Some jobs afford much greater scope for impact. Nevertheless, one- or two-point differences on size-of-impact scales may distinguish superior performers. Superior performers in some jobs tackle problems slightly larger than their formal job responsibilities, whereas average performers focus on tasks slightly smaller than their formal responsibilities.

Complexity. The complexity of the behavior (e.g., taking more things, people, data, concepts, or causes into account) is the primary scale on a few competencies, primarily the "Thinking" competencies.

Amount of Effort.   Amount of extra effort or time involved in an undertaking is a second dimension for some competencies.

Unique Dimensions.   Some competencies have unique dimensions. For example, Self Confidence has a second scale, Dealing with Failure, that describes how a person recovers from a setback and avoids depressive thinking. Initiative has a time dimension: how far into the future a person sees and acts. At higher levels, superior performers see further into the future and plan or act based on their vision, for example, acting in the present to head off problems or create opportunities that may take years to realize.

Most competency definitions have two or three dimensions. For example, the definition of Achievement Orientation has three scales:

A.   Intensity and Completeness of Achievement-Motivated Action

B.   Achievement Impact (size of problem or effect on organization)

C.   Degree of Innovation

Competency examples can show any combination of strength on one dimension and low or moderate impact on other dimensions. Most of the difference between average and star performers is found in the "A" or main scale.

Competency scales have been refined and modified with input from colleagues and clients over the past two years in development of approximately 30 new competency models.

Examples in the dictionary are drawn from actual interviews with superior performers in many jobs. Details have been altered to maintain the confidentiality of the position and the speaker, and examples have been edited for clarity and conciseness, but the codable words and phrases are unaltered.

INTRODUCTION TO THE COMPETENCY DICTIONARY

Competency Clusters

Competencies have been clustered on the basis of underlying intent, which is a level of analysis between deep underlying social motives and superficial behaviors. An intent is specific to a particular circumstance and has a more ephemeral and surface quality than an underlying motive or disposition.

Competent behaviors can be driven by one or more social motives in combination. For example, intent to develop a subordinate's skill and prepare the person for promotion might be motivated by Power ("I want to have an impact on her"), by Achievement ("If she could do X, Y, and Z well, we'd save n hours or dollars"), or by Affiliation ("If I develop and promote her, she'll like me, think I'm a great boss") or a combination of these motives.

Scaling and Numbering of the Competency Levels

Each competency description is accompanied by a table containing the full scale. Scales vary in length because they are empirically derived: We found more variation in some competencies than in others. Scale levels are in order of intensity, complexity, and so on; and each level is distinguishable (by trained coders) from the preceding and following levels.[5] The numbering system is designed so that 0 is always a neutral point. Some competencies have negative points. These represent behaviors seen in average performers but not in superior performers, and which are detrimental to superior performance. Negative points are useful in development (as examples of what to avoid) and sometimes in selection (as "red flags" raising questions about the suitability of a candidate for a position in which that competency is critical).

A CAUTIONARY NOTE

The Competency Dictionary presents competencies in generic form, in scales designed to cover behavior in a wide range of jobs, and to be adapted for many applications. Several cautions are therefore in order.

1. *The Generic Dictionary Scales Are Applicable to All Jobs—and None Precisely.* Many competencies may be irrelevant to any given job. Even where a competency is critical to a job, several scale levels may be irrelevant. Effective recruitment, selection, training, and performance appraisal requires a competency study to determine the threshold and differentiating levels of each critical competency. Otherwise, the user runs the risk of selecting or training for characteristics that do not predict job performance. For example, a person may select for competency levels higher than needed, thus ignoring potentially excellent candidates in favor of overqualified candidates who may not be satisfied with the job. The generic scales speed up and add precision to competency studies, but they are not a substitute for actual research.

2. *The Scales Represent Only the 21 Most Common Competencies.* Most jobs require unusual or unique capabilities or characteristics that are poorly captured or not captured at all in the generic scales. Unique competencies range from about 2 percent to more than 20 percent of a job, depending on the position studied. The generic competency scales are best adapted for typical managerial and sales positions, least well for preschool teachers or creative scientists.

Many jobs require unique combinations of competencies used simultaneously. For example, organization development consultants use a high level of Self-Control combined with moderate levels of Conceptual or Analytical Thinking and high levels of Influence skills in leading conflict resolution sessions.

3. *Higher Levels on the Scale Are Not Necessarily Better.* The scales are arranged to reflect the intensity, completeness, or complexity of expression of each competency. In most cases, someone performing at a higher level on a scale will also be capable of the lower levels. Each job has a optimal point on each scale. A person who scores much higher than the optimal level for a job may run into as many problems as someone who scores much lower. Therefore, it is important to determine the *best* level for each job, and not to assume that a higher level will contribute to better performance.

4. *Training and Practice Are Needed to Code Behaviors Reliably.* Part II of this book is intended to give readers an understanding of the methods and findings. It is not a substitute for a full coding manual, training, and practice in application.

NOTES

1. Boyatzis, R. E. (1982), *The competent manager: A model for effective performance*, New York: Wiley-Interscience.
2. Jobs for the Future (1986), *Executive report of jobs for Connecticut's future*, Somerville, MA: Jobs for the Future. See Figure 24–1 for an example.
3. The following description applies to models created before 1991. The most recent models follow a different format incorporating ordinal scales or levels of sophistication for each competency and indicating the typical level or range of levels on each competency for both average and superior performers.
4. Another 700 competency models based on expert system analyses were examined but lacked the narrative detail needed to code for specific behavioral indicators.
5. These scales are ordinal but not interval scales. We have experience and evidence to indicate that the levels, as applied by trained coders, are in the correct order. However the distance between adjacent pairs of levels may not always be equal: For example, there may be more difference between levels 2 and 3 of Innovation than between levels 4 and 5 of Team Leadership.

4

Achievement and Action

The essence of this cluster is a bias toward action, directed more to task accomplishment than to impact on other people. However, actions to influence or lead other people to improve productivity or get better results are scored for achievement competencies as well as for Impact and Influence. While Information Seeking and Initiative can be used to support any competency or intent, these competencies combine most often with Achievement Orientation.

ACHIEVEMENT ORIENTATION (ACH)

Achievement Orientation is a concern for working well or for competing against a standard of excellence. The standard may be the individual's own past performance (striving for improvement); an objective measure (results orientation); the performance of others (competitiveness); challenging goals set by the individual; or even what *anyone* has ever done (innovation).

Other titles for Achievement Orientation include:

- Results Orientation
- Efficiency Orientation
- Concern for Standards
- Focus on Improvement
- Entrepreneurship
- Optimizing Use of Resources

The Achievement Orientation scale (Table 4–1) has three dimensions. The first dimension represents (A) *intensity and completeness of action* (ranging

Table 4–1   Achievement Orientation (ACH) Scale

Level	Behavioral Description

A. INTENSITY AND COMPLETENESS OF ACHIEVEMENT-MOTIVATED ACTION

A. −1   *No Standards of Excellence for Work.* Shows no special concern with work, does only what is required (may be preoccupied by nonwork concerns such as social life, status, hobbies, family, sports, friendships). In interviews, this may appear as an inability to give vivid or detailed stories about work, coupled with enthusiasm in describing some outside activity.

A. 0   *Focused on the Task.* Works hard, but gives no evidence of a standard of excellence for work outputs.

A. 1   *Wants to Do the Job Well.* Works toward implicit standards of excellence. Tries to do the job well or right. May express frustration at waste or inefficiency (e.g., gripes about wasted time and wants to do better) but does not cause specific improvements.

A. 2   *Works to Meet Others' Standards.* Works to meet a standard set by management (e.g., manages to a budget, meets sales quotas, quality requirements).

A. 3   *Creates Own Measure of Excellence.* Uses his or her own specific methods of measuring outcomes against a standard of excellence (not imposed by management); e.g., $ spent, grades, outperforming others, time spent, scrap rates, beating the competition, etc.; or sets goals that are vague or not really challenging. [Scoring note: goals that don't quite meet the criteria for level 5 are scored here.]

A. 4   *Improves Performance.* Makes specific changes in the system or in own work methods to improve performance. (e.g., does something better, faster, at lower cost, more efficiently; improves quality, customer satisfaction, morale, revenues), without setting any specific goal.

A. 5   *Sets Challenging Goals.* Sets and acts to reach challenging goals for self or others (e.g., "to improve sales/quality/productivity by 15% in 6 months"). "Challenging" means there is about a 50–50 chance of actually achieving the goal—it is a definite stretch, but not unrealistic or impossible. Setting and working to meet challenging goals is scored even if the goals are not actually met. [Setting less precise goals, which are "safe" and clearly not challenging does not score at all.] Or cites specific measures of baseline performance compared with better performance at a later point in time: "When I took over, efficiency was 20%—now it is up to 85%."

A. 6   *Makes Cost–Benefit Analyses.* Makes decisions, sets priorities, or chooses goals on the basis of inputs and outputs: makes explicit considerations of potential profit, return on investment, or cost-benefit analysis.

A. 7   *Takes Calculated Entrepreneurial Risks.* Commits significant resources and/or time (in the face of uncertainty) to improve performance, try something new, reach a challenging goal (e.g., starts new products or services, takes on "turn-around" operations), while also taking action to minimize the risks involved (e.g., does market research, lines up customers in advance, etc.); or in

Table 4–1 *(Continued)*

Level	Behavioral Description

Achievement for Others, encourages and supports subordinates in taking entrepreneurial risks.

A. **8** *Persists in Entrepreneurial Efforts.* Takes numerous, sustained actions over time in the face of obstacles to reach entrepreneurial goal; or successfully completes entrepreneurial endeavors.

B. ACHIEVEMENT IMPACT (applies for Achievement scores of 3 or higher only)

B. **1** *Individual Performance Only.* Works to improve his or her own efficiency through time-management techniques, good personal work methods, etc. Includes efforts to improve the personal efficiency of *one* other person (one key subordinate, secretary, etc.).

B. **2** *Affects One or Two Others.* May make a small financial commitment.

B. **3** *Affects a Work Group (4–15 People).* May achieve a moderate-sized sale or financial commitment. Works to make a more efficient system, get others working more efficiently (ACH Others), improve group performance (ACH Team).

B. **4** *Affects a Department (more than 15 people).* May achieve a major sale or comparable financial commitment.

B. **5** *Affects an Entire Mid-Size Firm. (or a division of a larger company).*

B. **6** *Affects an Entire Major-Size Firm.*

B. **7** *Affects an Entire Industry.*

C. DEGREE OF INNOVATION (applies for achievement scores of 3 or higher only).[a]

C. **0** *Does Not Do New Things.*

C. **1** *New to the Job or Work Unit.* Does things (to improve performance) that have not been done in that job before, but that may have been done elsewhere in the organization.

C. **2** *New to the Organization.* Improves performance by doing something new and different (that has not been done in the company, not necessarily new to the industry).

C. **3** *New to the Industry.* Improves performance by doing things that are unique, cutting-edge, new to the industry.

C. **4** *Transformation.* Does things that are so new and effective they transform an industry (e.g., Apple's transformation of the personal computer industry, Schockley's development of transistors, leading to the electronics industry, Henry Ford's transformation of the auto manufacturing industry). This level, by definition, is rarely seen.

---

[a]Score only for attempts to meet or exceed a standard of excellence. An innovation need not be successful to be an expression of Achievement Orientation, but it should express an intent to improve performance, make things better in some way.

from wanting to do a job well to completing entrepreneurial endeavors). The second dimension (B) represents breadth—the degree to which an enterprise is affected (from part of the individual's own work, to the way the entire organization does business). The third dimension (C) is *innovation:* How new and different the individual's actions or ideas are, in the context of the job and organization.

Common behaviors expressing Achievement Orientation include:

- *Working to Meet a Standard Set by Management* (e.g., manages to a budget, meets sales quotas or quality requirements).

- *Setting and Acting to Reach Challenging Goals for Self or Others* (e.g., to improve sales/quality/productivity by 15% in 6 months). "Challenging" means there is about a 50–50 chance of actually achieving the goal—it is a definite stretch, but not unrealistic or impossible.

- *Making Cost–Benefit Analyses.* Taking decisions, or setting priorities based on explicit considerations of potential profit, return-on-investment, or cost–benefit analysis.

- *Taking Calculated Entrepreneurial Risks.* Committing significant resources and/or time (in the face of uncertainty) to improve performance, try something new, reach a challenging goal (e.g., starts new products or services, takes on "turn-around" operations), while also taking action to minimize the risks involved (e.g., does market research, lines up customers in advance).

Achievement Orientation examples include:

I always like to see what I've done during the year for the portfolios I manage. This year I . . . measured the value added to each portfolio over the past ten years. (ACH A.3, B.1)

In March, when I interviewed for the job, we were already $350,000 in the red, and we had a business plan to make $700,000 that first year. That meant we had to make $1,050,000 in the last nine months . . . We made $1,200,000. (ACH A.3, implies A.8 also, B.5)

I weighed the cost of running the ad and considered what could come out of it in the way of business. In other words, how many leads the ad would generate, and how many would turn into clients. The ad would raise our visibility in the community and although there were no guarantees, it seemed like a good bet. (ACH A.6, B.3)

It is possible to score fairly high on the ACH without a large job. Children have been observed exhibiting ACH high levels, although with tiny impacts. People in low-level jobs, including janitors and factory workers, have been seen acting at level 4 or 5 (finding ways to improve their performance, or setting their own goals) and making cost–benefit analyses (even though they lack authority to implement their ideas):

> A shipping clerk identified that his company had sufficient Federal Express business to both get a volume discount and get a dedicated computer from the vendor to input and track shipping orders, saving $30,000. He approached the CEO on the way out the door after work and took the initiative to lobby successfully for this change by pointing out the benefits.

Quality circles are, in part, an attempt to organize and utilize the achievement motivation of low-level employees. Entrepreneurial risk taking in the lowest level employees is most likely to be seen outside of the job, in small businesses. Achievement Orientation usually refers to an individual's own performance.[1] However, it may also be expressed in terms of measuring, improving, or setting goals for the performance of other people (often subordinates or students) or for the individual's whole team. In these cases, the person's underlying need for achievement is mixed with or modified by an underlying need to influence others.

Links to Other Competencies

Effective use of Achievement Orientation (ACH A.3 and higher) usually implies the related use of:

- Initiative
- Information Seeking (especially at levels A.6 and above)
- Analytical or Conceptual Thinking and Flexibility (for Innovation, dimension C)

Optimal matching of people to job requirements for improved performance implies a combination of an Achievement A.4 (or possibly higher), high levels of Interpersonal Understanding (a balanced view of others' specific strengths and weaknesses), and a moderate level of Analytical Thinking.

CONCERN FOR ORDER, QUALITY, AND ACCURACY (CO)

Concern for Order reflects an underlying drive to reduce uncertainty in the surrounding environment. Other titles for Concern for Order, Quality, and Accuracy include:

- Monitoring
- Concern with Clarity

■ Desire to Reduce Uncertainty

■ Keeping Track

Concern for Order (Table 4–2) has a single dimension expressing the complexity of action to maintain or increase order in the environment, ranging from keeping an orderly workspace and general concern with clarity to setting up complex new systems to increase order and quality of data. It is expressed by:

■ Monitoring and checking work or information

■ Insisting on clarity of roles and functions

■ Setting up and maintaining systems of information

Concern for Order is related to Achievement Orientation expressed as concern with maintaining standards of accuracy and quality, and so on.

This scale occasionally functions as a negative predictor; in some jobs, particularly upper management positions, more Concern for Order is associated with average rather than superior performance. In these cases, the CO

Table 4–2   Concern for Order and Quality (CO) Scale

Level	Behavioral Description
−1	*Lack of Order.* Lack of concern with order, despite problems caused by disorder.
0	*Not Applicable.* Active order keeping is not needed, or is done by someone else, or a lack of concern for order is noticed but does not cause problems.
1	*Keeps an Organized Workspace.* Maintains an orderly workspace with desk, files, tools, and so on in good order.
2	*Shows a General Concern for Order and Clarity.* Works for clarity—wants roles, expectations, tasks, data crystal-clear and preferably in writing.
3	*Checks Own Work.* Double-checks the accuracy of information or own work.
4	*Monitors Others' Work.* Monitors quality of others' work, checks to ensure that procedures are followed. Or keeps clear, detailed records of own or others' activities.
5	*Monitors Data or Projects.* Monitors progress of a project against milestones or deadlines. Monitors data, discovers weaknesses or missing data, and seeks out information to keep order; general concern for increasing order in existing systems.
6	*Develops Systems.* Develops and uses systems to organize and keep track of information.
7	*Develops Complex Systems.* Puts new, detailed, complex systems in place to increase order and improve quality of data. Or deduces new needs (not having to do with order) from perceived disorder.

implies focusing on smaller issues and problems than is really appropriate for these jobs:

> I did the brief, wrote, and proofread the handouts myself to make sure they were correct. (CO 3)

> Throughout the day I checked to see how things were going. I went out and watched the mechanics to make sure no dust got on the plates. Most mechanics don't mind, but some call it "bird-dogging." But it's my job—and if I want to follow it through, I will. (CO 4)

> I spent a lot of time improving document flow and material handling. . . . I needed a system of managing the data and of information feedback. I set up a system so I could see visually where the volume of issues was for each area. (CO 6)

Links to Other Competencies

Concern for Order is related to the lower levels of Achievement Orientation, expressed as concern with maintaining standards of accuracy and quality, and so on.

Concern for Order may support some of the higher levels of Directiveness and moderate levels of Developing Others by providing accurate data for developmental feedback or for confronting performance problems or directively monitoring people's performance.

A low level of Analytical Thinking is implied in the low-to-moderate levels of CO and at least a moderate level in the highest levels of CO.

INITIATIVE (INT)

Initiative is a preference for taking action. Initiative is doing more than is required or expected in the job, doing things that no one has requested, which will improve or enhance job results and avoid problems, or finding or creating new opportunities. Other titles for Initiative include:

- Bias for Action
- Decisiveness
- Strategic Future Orientation
- Seizing Opportunities
- Being Proactive

In management positions, Initiative (Table 4–3) is expressed in terms of action taken now to avoid problems or create opportunities at some point in the

Table 4–3   Initiative (INT) Scale

Level	Behavioral Description
A.	**TIME DIMENSION**
A. −1	*Thinks Only of the Past.* Misses or fails to act on clear opportunities.
A. 0	*Not Applicable or Does Not Take Initiative.*
A. 1	*Shows Persistence.* Persists—takes two or more steps to overcome obstacles or rejection [time dimension: past assignment or task through current action]. Does not give up easily when things do not go smoothly.
A. 2	*Addresses Current Opportunities or Problems.* Recognizes and acts on present opportunities or addresses present problems (usually completed within 1 or 2 days).
A. 3	*Is Decisive in a Crisis.* Acts quickly and decisively in a crisis (where norm is to wait, "study," hope problem will resolve itself).
A. 4	*Acts Up to 2 Months Ahead.* Creates opportunities or minimizes potential problems by a unique extra effort (new program, special travel, etc.) occurring within a time frame of 1 or 2 months.
A. 5	*Acts 3–12 Months Ahead.* Anticipates and prepares for a specific opportunity or problem that is not obvious to others. Takes action to create an opportunity or avoid future crisis, looking ahead 3–12 months.
A. 6	*Acts 1–2 Years Ahead.* Anticipates situations 1–2 years ahead and acts to create opportunities or avoid problems.
A. 7	*Acts 2–5 Years Ahead.* Anticipates situations 2–5 years ahead and acts to create opportunities or avoid problems.
A. 8	*Acts 5–10 Years Ahead.* Anticipates situations 5–10 years ahead and acts to create opportunities or avoid problems.
A. 9	*Acts More Than 10 Years Ahead.* Anticipates situations more than 10 years ahead and acts to create opportunities or avoid problems.
B.	**SELF-MOTIVATION, AMOUNT OF DISCRETIONARY EFFORT**
B. −1	*Avoids Required Work.* Shirks or tries to get out of work.
B. 0	*Not Applicable or Absent.* Requires constant supervision.
B. 1	*Works Independently.* Completes assignments without constant supervision.
B. 2	*Extra Effort.* Works extra hours, nights, weekends, etc. as needed to complete work when not required to do so.
B. 3	*Does More Than Is Required.* Exceeds job description, e.g., takes on extra tasks.
B. 4	*Does Much More Than Is Required.* Starts and carries through new projects.
B. 5	*Makes Extraordinary, Heroic Efforts.* Acts without formal authority, takes personal risks, bends the rules to get the job done (emphasis must be on meeting the needs of the job, not on defiant norm breaking).
B. 6	*Involves Others.* Gets others involved in unusual extra efforts (e.g., enlists family, co-workers, community members, usually on a volunteer basis).

future. The primary Initiative scale (A) is a *time-span scale,* ranging from completing decisions made in the past (persistence or tenacity) to acting now on problems or opportunity that will not be fully realized for years to come. The second dimension (B) of Initiative involves *discretionary effort:* the extra or unrequired effort put forth to complete work-related tasks. This dimension can differentiate superior performers in virtually any job.

Routine planning ahead (making an annual business plan or budget) is *not* included in Initiative. The thinking ahead included in the Initiative scale is a spontaneous, unscheduled, perceptive recognition of upcoming problems or opportunities *and then the taking of appropriate action.* Appropriate action means, at the very least, collecting relevant information. Just thinking ahead without doing anything about it does not score, no matter how many years ahead the individual may see or how perceptive or correct he or she may be.

This time dimension of Initiative relates to work by Eliot Jacques and Gillian Stamp on the time span of discretion in managerial positions.[2] Our observation is that superior performers operate with a longer time span than do average performers in the same position.

Initiative often appears as:

- Persistence, refusal to give up when faced with obstacles or rejection
- Recognition and seizing of opportunities
- Performance of far more than the job requires
- Anticipation and preparation for a specific opportunity or problem that is not obvious to others:

We'd had a lot of valve failures in the past few years, and I began getting concerned about it. Although it wasn't directly assigned to me, I kind of dug into it. There was someone working on it, but I felt that maybe if I could give a hand or do something, together we could solve the problem. So I got together with the engineer who was working on the job and we discussed possible things we could do. (INT A.4, B.4)

I presented an idea to correct the problem to the engineer in charge of the project. He rejected my idea but didn't present any alternative. Since I had to meet a schedule, I implemented the idea, and it worked, and after that there was no argument. (INT A.4, B.5)

So what I saw coming down the line was a whole raft of these so-called sales-and-service customers saying either help us or keep your stuff, because it's no good. Of course we're going to help them. And I could see us being buried by these kinds of requests. So what I was looking for and found was a method by which we could handle that. (INT A.5)

With that sort of growth, with the number of competitors we've got , we had to do something to stay in business. So I was working on several projects to diversify our base a bit. They were projects closely akin to what we're already doing, areas where we had capability. I was trying to capitalize on our strengths. (INT A.7, B.4)

Links to Other Competencies

Initiative supports many competencies:

- Achievement Orientation
- Impact and Influence
- Relationship Building
- Technical Expertise
- Customer Service Orientation
- Developing Others
- Team Leadership

Initiative A.5 and above (recognizing and acting on future opportunities or problems) implies at least a low-to-moderate level of Analytical Thinking or Conceptual Thinking.

Information Seeking and the higher levels of Analytical or Conceptual Thinking may be considered special cases of Initiative—Intellectual Initiative.

INFORMATION SEEKING (INFO)

An underlying curiosity, a desire to know more about things, people, or issues drives Information Seeking. Information Seeking implies making an effort to get more information, not accepting situations "at face value." Information Seeking has also been called:

- Problem Definition
- Diagnostic Focus
- Customer/Market Sensitivity
- Looking Deeper

Information Seeking has a single dimension of effort (Table 4–4) expressed as how far afield the individual goes to seek information (ranging from questioning directly involved people, to doing extensive research, to getting uninvolved others to seek out information.)

Information Seeking implies going beyond routine questions. It includes:

- "Digging" or pressing for exact information or resolution of discrepancies by asking a series of questions

Table 4–4 Information-Seeking (INF) Scale

Level	Behavioral Description
0	*None.* Does not seek additional information about a situation, other than what has been given.
1	*Asks Questions.* Asks direct questions of immediately available people (or people who are directly involved in the situation even if not physically present), consults available resources. Note that even in crisis situations, superior performers take a few moments to gather all the immediately available information before taking action.
2	*Personally Investigates.* Gets out personally to see the plane, factory, ship, customer's installation, loan applicant's business, classroom, students' failing papers, or other problem. Questions those closest to the problem when others might ignore these people.
3	*Digs Deeper.* Asks a series of probing questions to get at the root of a situation or a problem, below the surface presentation.
4	*Calls or Contacts Others.* Calls on others, who are not personally involved, to get their perspective, background information, experience (this is often, but not necessarily, a form of using previously established relationships).
5	*Does Research.* Makes a systematic effort over a limited period of time to obtain needed data or feedback; or does formal research through newspapers, magazines, or other resources. [If the information is existing technical data or knowledge or the systematic effort involves taking courses, score for Technical Expertise C instead.]
6	*Uses Own Ongoing Systems.* Has personally established ongoing systems or habits for various kinds of information gathering (may include "management by walking around," regular informal meetings, etc., if these are used specifically to gather information).
7	*Involves Others.* Involves others who would not normally be involved and gets them to seek out information. [Do not score for delegating research or information-seeking to subordinates; this point is for involving people who would normally not be involved.]

- "Scanning" for potential opportunities or for miscellaneous information that may be of future use
- Getting out personally to see the plane, factory, ship, customer's installation, loan applicant's business, classroom, students' failing papers or other work-related situation:

(A commercial banking officer when a loan that he had been working for was rejected): I was just devastated. It couldn't have been worse. Of course, the customer wasn't aware of this at all. So I immediately started to find a way around this roadblock and I contacted members of the policy committee of the bank informally to determine the logical basis for this. (INFO 1)

After being told it wasn't good enough, I personally went down and inspected the plane. (INFO 2)

When _____ was coming for a major inspection, I called my friend Joe over in Kansas who had worked with _____ before, to find out what he was like, what was important to him. I found out he used to be in business, liked everything in bottom-line terms so I set up our presentation to address the bottom line. (INFO 4)

(An assistant principal phones parents regularly on a random basis to take a reading on school climate.) I said, "What I want to do is to hear your perceptions as to how your youngster is getting on in the building. Anything. teachers, courses, hallways, lunch, buses, rumors you are hearing. . . ." (INFO 6)

Links to Other Competencies

Information Seeking regarding potential future opportunities or problems supports *Initiative* A.4 or higher, depending on how far in the future the information is likely to be of use.

Information Seeking is absolutely crucial both to the higher levels of Initiative and to a number of other competencies. In fact, across a wide range of jobs, Information Seeking is one of the most prevalent characteristics of superior performers and is included in some form in most of their critical incidents.

Acquisition of (Technical) Expertise (EXP C) is a special case of Information Seeking.

Information Seeking is a prerequisite or first step for:

- Initiative
- Conceptual Thinking
- Analytical Thinking
- Interpersonal Understanding (often INFO 2—personal observation)
- Technical Expertise
- Customer Service Orientation (A.6 and higher)

and is frequently implied in

- Teamwork and Cooperation (level 4).

NOTES

1. McClelland, D. C., Atkinson, J. W., Clark, R. A., & Lowell, E. L. (1953), *The achievement motive,* New York: Appleton-Century-Crofts.
2. Jacques, E. (1989), *Requisite organization,* Arlington, VA: Cason Hall.

5

Helping and Human Service

The Helping and Human Service cluster involves intending to meet someone else's needs; attuning oneself to the concerns, interest, and needs of the other (Interpersonal Understanding) and working to meet those needs (Customer Service Orientation). This implies a stronger underlying need for Power and need for Affiliation than the other clusters.

Although Interpersonal Understanding can function independently, it is also the foundation for the higher levels of Customer Service. Interpersonal Understanding is also used to support the competencies in the Impact and Managerial clusters.

INTERPERSONAL UNDERSTANDING (IU)

Interpersonal Understanding implies wanting to understand other people. It is the ability to hear accurately and understand the unspoken or partly expressed thoughts, feelings, and concerns of others. The "others" here refers either to individuals, or classes of individuals in which all members are assumed to have much the same feelings and concerns ("my first-line supervisors felt ignored" or "The group responded enthusiastically but had some reservations about. . . .").

Cross-cultural sensitivity, which is becoming increasingly important, is a special case of interpersonal understanding, across cultural divides. It frequently includes considerable amounts of Information Seeking.

Interpersonal Understanding has also been called:

- Empathy
- Listening
- Sensitivity to Others
- Awareness of Others' Feelings
- Diagnostic Understanding

The Interpersonal Understanding Scale (Table 5–1) has two dimensions. Complexity or Depth of Understanding of Others (A) ranges from understanding explicit meanings or obvious emotions to understanding the complex, hidden reasons for ongoing behavior. Listening and Responding to Others (B), amount of effort to listen to and respond to others) ranges from basic listening to explain people's past behavior to going out of the way to help people with personal or interpersonal difficulties.

Interpersonal Understanding is often shown by:

- Perceiving the moods and feelings of others
- Using understanding based on listening and observation to predict and prepare for others' reactions
- Understanding the attitudes, interests, needs, and perspectives of others
- Understanding the causes of others' long-term underlying attitudes, behavior patterns, or problems:

Drooping mouth and sad eyes meant this guy was depressed. (IU A.1, B.1)

Countries have different customs. When you step on a ship, you're trying to be a diplomat, in a way, because you represent the U.S. government, and they represent a foreign government. So when this guy took his shoes off, I wasn't about to go in there with fishing shoes right behind him. I took my shoes off and walked on the bridge in my socks. It didn't hurt me and I think it helped me get along with the guy better. (IU A.3, B.4)

(Teacher/mentor in continuing education) It was very difficult for Mary to write her degree plan, and very painful. When you have a self-concept of being nothing, and then you start to look back over your experience and begin to realize that you really are something and can be something, that realization can be very painful. And it was painful in that way for Mary. She was looking at all she had learned and thinking "My God, I have wasted this. Is it too late?" (IU A.5, B.1)

Links to Other Competencies

Interpersonal Understanding is supported by *Information Seeking,* including observation, direct questioning, indirect information seeking (from third parties, indirect evidence), and various tactics to test one's hypotheses.

Table 5–1 Interpersonal Understanding (IU) Scale

Level	Behavioral Description

A. DEPTH OF UNDERSTANDING OF OTHERS

A. −1 *Lack of Understanding.* Misunderstands or is surprised by others' feelings or actions; or sees others primarily in terms of racial, cultural, or gender stereotypes.

A. 0 *Not Applicable.* Or shows no explicit awareness of others, but no evidence of serious misunderstandings. This level is often found in combination with Direct Persuasion (IMPACT level A-2 and 3).

A. 1 *Understands Either Emotion or Content.* Understands either present emotions or explicit content, but not both together.

A. 2 *Understands Both Emotion and Content.* Understands both present emotions and explicit content.

A. 3 *Understands Meanings.* Understands current unspoken thoughts, concerns, or feelings; or gets others willingly to take actions desired by the speaker.

A. 4 *Understands Underlying Issues.* Understands underlying problems: the reason for someone's ongoing or long-term feelings, behaviors, or concerns; or presents a balanced view of someone's specific strengths and weaknesses.

A. 5 *Understands Complex Underlying Issues.* Understands complex causes of others' long-term underlying attitudes, behavior patterns, or problems.

B. LISTENING AND RESPONDING TO OTHERS

B. −1 *Unsympathetic.* Offends others, makes them "close up."

B. 0 *Not Applicable or Makes No Attempt to Listen.*

B. 1 *Listens.* Picks up clues to others' feelings or meanings, or listens when approached by others. May ask questions confirm the speaker's diagnosis. Uses understanding to explain other's past behavior.

B. 2 *Makes Self Available to Listen.* Has "an open door," goes out of the way to invite conversations, or actively seeks to understand (often in order to influence, develop, help, or lead others).

B. 3 *Predicts Other's Responses.* Uses understanding based on listening and observation to predict and prepare for other's reactions.

B. 4 *Listens Responsively.* Reflects peoples' concerns, is easy to talk to; or responds to people's concerns by altering own behavior in a helpful responsive manner.

B. 5 *Acts to Help.* Helps people with problems presented or observed. [Scoring Note: Also consider Developing Others, Customer Service Orientation, or Know-How and Expertise. If the intent is clearly developmental, use customer service; or if the problem is technical, score the understanding on IU scale A and the action on the other competency. If the intent and context does not clearly involve one of the other competencies, score the action here. The difference between responsive action and Impact and Influence is that here the speaker does not enter the situation with his or her own agenda, but responds (flexibly) to the needs or situation of the other.]

Interpersonal Understanding forms the indispensable foundation for the higher levels of Impact and Influence and Customer Service Orientation. The effectiveness of Customer Service and of Impact and Influence is limited by the depth of accurate understanding. In the stories of superior performers, Interpersonal Understanding is woven together with Impact and Influence or with Customer Service in the same action or incident.

Interpersonal Understanding also supports Developing Others, Organizational Awareness, Teamwork and Cooperation, and Relationship Building.

Interpersonal Understanding B.4 (acts to help others) implies a moderate amount of Initiative and comes close to Influence and Impact; the difference is that in Impact and Influence the speaker has his or her own agenda in the situation, whereas here the intent is simply to be helpful or responsive, not to advance some other purpose.

Interpersonal Understanding implies the first level of Flexibility (FLX A.1) only if the speaker's own views or interests are in conflict with those of the person he or she is listening to. However, level IU B.4 (responsive action) does imply some Flexibility.

CUSTOMER SERVICE ORIENTATION (CSO)

Customer Service Orientation implies a desire to help or serve others, to meet their needs. It means focusing efforts on discovering and meeting the customer or client's needs. It is similar in depth of understanding to Interpersonal Understanding and sometimes the actions may parallel Impact and Influence, but here the focus is on first, understanding the others' needs (rather than general understanding of others' thoughts, feelings or behavior) and then doing something to help or serve the others (rather than influence them to support the performer's own agenda).

The "customer" may be an actual customer or may be end-users within the same organization. In some cases, there may be more than one group of clients. For example, teachers may show Customer Service Orientation toward students or toward parents, religious leaders toward their congregations or toward their outside ministry (the sick, the poor, orphans, etc.). In such cases, it is sometimes helpful to use two CSO scales, one for each set of clients.

Customer Service Orientation has been called:

- Helping and Service Orientation
- Focus on the Client's Needs
- Partnering the Client
- End-User Focus
- Attention to Patient Satisfaction

The Customer Service Orientation Scale (Table 5–2) has two dimensions. The first dimension (A) is intensity of motive and completeness of action, with acting as the client's trusted advisor or advocate as the complete action. A second dimension (B) is amount of effort or initiative taken on the client's behalf, ranging from actions requiring only a few extra moments to getting others to volunteer their efforts for the client's sake to extraordinary efforts (e.g., an employment agency counselor started and ran an after-hours job-applicant training program that ran 2 to 3 hours, 4 nights a week for months; a fertilizer/seed salesperson took over and ran a customer's feed store for a more than a week when the customer was suddenly taken ill and rushed to the hospital).

More typical indications of Customer Service Orientation include:

- Seeks information about the real, underlying needs of the clients, beyond those expressed initially, and matches these to available (or customized) products or services

- Takes personal responsibility for correcting customer service problems. Corrects problems promptly and undefensively

Table 5–2 Customer Service Orientation (CSO) Scale

Level	Behavioral Description
A. FOCUS ON CLIENT'S NEEDS	
A. −3	*Expresses Negative Expectations of Clients.* Makes global negative comments about clients, blames clients for negative outcomes. Includes racist or sexist comments about clients. [Scoring note: negative comments that are objectively true (i.e., "he's a criminal" about a client who went to jail for fraud) are not scored here.]
A. −2	*Expresses Lack of Clarity.* Unclear about client's need and details of own involvement. ("Wasn't quite sure what this meeting was for," "never was sure exactly what the client wanted") without taking steps to clarify the situation.
A. −1	*Focuses on Own Abilities.* Desires to show the client facts, or focuses on own or company's abilities rather than on client's needs.
A. 0	*Gives Minimal Required Service.* Gives an immediate "off the cuff" response to client's questions without probing for underlying needs or problems or getting the context of the client's inquiry.
A. 1	*Follows Up.* Follows through on client inquiries, requests, complaints. Keeps client up-to-date about progress of projects (but does not probe client's underlying issues or problems).
A. 2	*Maintains Clear Communication with Client Regarding Mutual Expectations.* Monitors client satisfaction. Distributes helpful information to clients. Gives friendly, cheerful service.
A. 3	*Takes Personal Responsibility.* Corrects customer service problems promptly and undefensively.

Table 5–2   *(Continued)*

Level	Behavioral Description

A. 4   *Makes Self Fully Available to Customer.* Is especially helpful when customer is going through a critical period. Gives customer a home phone number or other means of easy access, or may spend extra time at the customer's location. [This level may be irrelevant for some positions and critical for others, depending on the structure of the situation.]

A. 5   *Acts to Make Things Better.* Makes concrete attempts to add value to the client, to make things better for the client in some way. Expresses positive expectations about client.

A. 6   *Addresses Underlying Needs.* Seeks information about the real, underlying needs of the client, beyond those expressed initially, and matches these to available (or customized) products or services.

A. 7   *Uses a Long-Term Perspective.* Works with a long-term perspective in addressing client's problems. May trade off immediate costs for the sake of the long-term relationship. Looks for long-term benefits to the customer. May initiate actions that create visible success for a customer and then credit the customer with that success.

A. 8   *Acts as a Trusted Advisor.* Builds an independent opinion on client needs, problems/opportunities, and possibilities for implementation. Acts on this opinion (e.g., recommends appropriate approaches that are new and different from those requested by the client). Becomes intimately involved in client's decision-making process. [Effective functioning at this level depends on successful relationship building over a period of time.] May push client to confront difficult issues.

A. 9   *Acts as Client's Advocate.* Takes client's side versus own organization with long-term benefit to own organization (e.g., counsels client not to overextend on purchases (thus maintaining customer viability for the future.)); or pushes own management to resolve customer-related problems. Takes client's side in well-founded complaints regarding own company's treatment of client.

B.   INITIATIVE (DISCRETIONARY EFFORT) TO HELP OR SERVE OTHERS

B. −1   *Blocks Others' Action.* May make negative remarks about customers or resent troublesome customers.

B. 0   *Takes No Action.* May make excuses, "I couldn't take care of that because . . ."

B. 1   *Takes Routine or Required Actions.* Has an eye toward meeting the customer's needs.

B. 2   *Goes out of the Way to Be Helpful.* Takes more than routine action him- or herself (up to about twice the normal time and effort).

B. 3   *Makes a Large Extra Effort to Meet Others' Needs.* About 2 to 6 times the normal time and effort involved.

B. 4   *Involves Others in Taking Nonroutine Action to Meet Someone's Needs.*

B. 5   *Takes Extraordinary Efforts.* Uses own time or works over a period of weeks to help others; or takes on tasks or efforts that go far beyond the normal job description.

- Acts as a trusted advisor, acts on an independent opinion on client needs, problems/opportunities, and possibilities for implementation
- Works with a long-term perspective in addressing client's problems:

A client was having some difficulty getting a refund check. She came to me because she said our operations manager was rude to her. I'm sure there was just a misunderstanding because that would be very unusual behavior for him. Anyway, I apologized, helped her get the check, and sent her on her way. It only took a few minutes to straighten out the problem, and she left feeling better than when she came in. (CSO A.3, B.1)

(During a tricky negotiation for this client) When I would go to visit a friend in London, I would call the client on a Saturday and say, "How are you, Mr. C . . . how are things, what do you think of . . ." That gave him a sense that it was as if I was actually on his payroll . . . that they were the most important above all. (CSO A.4, B.2)

This particular customer was having financial problems and I had developed a close relationship with him over the years as a friend, business associate, and salesman. He valued my opinion based on this relationship. I had been working with him for several years and trying to realign his business and help him adapt to changing market conditions. He had been predominantly a wholesale operation. I convinced him that he should concentrate his efforts on retail, perhaps eliminate some unprofitable routes, streamline his business and concentrate where he could make the most profit. (CSO A.8, B.3) [Also scores for Relationship Building]

Links to Other Competencies

Customer-Service Orientation is supported by Information Seeking and Interpersonal Understanding.

Initiative is so much a part of Customer Service Orientation that the B scales (effort) of the two competencies are virtually identical. In addition, CSO A.6 and higher implies moderate levels on the time dimension of Initiative.

Achievement Orientation is often expressed in relation to the improved functioning of the customer's organization (CSO A.5 and higher).

Higher levels of Customer Service (A.6 to A.8) imply:

- Information Seeking
- Conceptual or Analytical Thinking (at least low-to-moderate levels)
- Interpersonal or Organizational Understanding (moderate-to-high levels)
- Either Technical Expertise or Business-mindedness, or both, depending on the nature and content of the product or service
- A moderate-to-high level of Relationship Building. In some strongly customer-oriented positions (such as client relationship manager) Relationship Building and Customer Service are reciprocal: Use of each competency implies and reinforces the other.

CHAPTER

6

The Impact and Influence Cluster

The Influence cluster reflect the individual's underlying concern with his or her effect on others, known as need for Power.[1] The "power" motivation that fuels effective behavior is generally influenced by consideration of the good of the organization or of others. We have not found the best performers pursuing their own status, prestige, or gain at the expense of others or of the organization. In all of the competencies, the intentions and actions that score on the positive levels must be reasonably socialized—the desired effect should be for the general good, or at least not harmful. Cutthroat competition within an organization or using influence for personal gain at the expense of the overall organization score at a negative point for Impact and Influence.

IMPACT AND INFLUENCE (IMP)

Impact and Influence expresses an intention to persuade, convince, influence, or impress others, in order to get them to support the speaker's agenda; or the desire to have a specific impact or effect on others.

The critical difference between Influence and Impact and the responsive action in Interpersonal Understanding and in Customer Service Orientation is that in Influence and Impact, the speaker has his or her *own agenda,* a specific type of impression to make or a course of action that he or she wishes the others to adopt.

Impact and Influence has also been called:

Strategic Influence

Impression Management

Showmanship

Targeted Persuasion

Collaborative Influence

Impact and Influence (Table 6–1) has two dimensions. The main dimension (A) describes the number and complexity of actions taken to influence others, ranging from a straightforward presentation to complex customized strategies involving several steps or additional people. The secondary dimension (B), considers the breadth of impact: from one other person through the whole organization to world industrial or political events.

When Impact and Influence is used on other individuals (i.e., with a small breadth) it is supported by Interpersonal Understanding. It is difficult or impossible to influence others effectively and consistently without understanding the others. Similarly, the individual needs Organizational Awareness to influence organizations effectively (IMP with a large breadth).

Common indicators of Impact and Influence include:

- Anticipates the effect of an action or other detail on people's image of the speaker
- Appeals to reason, data, facts, and figures
- Uses concrete examples, visual aids, demonstrations, etc.
- Assembles political coalitions, builds "behind-the-scenes" support for ideas
- Deliberately gives or withholds information to gain specific effects
- Uses "group process skills" to lead or direct a group:

Since you're buying one piece, why not replace the whole room? You can get a good amount of furniture for your money. As long as you're going this far you might as well do the room the right way. (IMP A.2, B.1)

When I first started that job I had very few formal qualifications. I wanted to make a very businesslike, professional impression, so no one would even question my credentials. I always wore my hair up, a very conservative suit, low heels and so on. . . . After I proved myself on the job I relaxed a bit. (IMP A.4, B.2)

I knew it would enrage two or three of the generals involved with this procurement if we sent the letters to the congressmen, but I also knew that it would stop the sole-source procurement. Sure enough, as soon as the letters hit the Pentagon, everything stopped and the word went out that everything was on hold. Of

Table 6–1   Impact and Influence (IMP) Scale

Level	Behavioral Description

A.   ACTIONS TAKEN TO INFLUENCE OTHERS

A. −1   *Personalized Power.* Cutthroat competition within the organization, concern for personal position regardless of organizational damage.

A.   0   *Not Applicable.* Or shows no attempt to influence or persuade others.

A.   1   *States Intention but Takes No Specific Action.* Intends to have a specific effect or impact; expresses concern with reputation, status, and appearance.

A.   2   *Takes a Single Action to Persuade.* Makes no apparent attempt to adapt to the audience's level and interests. Uses direct persuasion in a discussion or presentation (e.g., appeals to reason, data, larger purpose; uses concrete examples, visual aids, demonstrations, etc.).

A.   3   *Takes a Two-Step Action to Persuade.* Makes no apparent adaptation to the level and interests of the audience. Includes careful preparation of data form presentation or the making of two or more different arguments of points in a presentation or a discussion.

A.   4   *Calculates the Impact of One's Action or Words.* Adapts a presentation or discussion to appeal to the interest and level of others. Anticipates the effect of an action or other detail on people's image of the speaker.

A.   5   *Calculates a Dramatic Action.* Models behavior desired in others or takes a well thought-out unusual or dramatic action in order to have a specific impact. [Scoring Note: Threats or displays of anger do not count as dramatic actions to influence: see Directiveness level A-8].

A.   6   *Takes Two Steps to Influence.* With each step adapted to the specific audience or planned to have a specific effect or anticipates and prepares for other's reactions.

A.   7   *Three Actions or Indirect Influence.* Uses experts or other third parties to influence; or takes three different actions or makes complex, staged arguments. Assembles political coalitions, builds "behind-the-scenes" support for ideas, deliberately gives or withholds information in order to have specific effects, uses "group process skills" to lead or direct a group.

A.   8   *Complex Influence Strategies.* Uses complex influence strategies tailored to individual situations (e.g., using chains of indirect influence—"get A to show B so B will tell C such-and-such"), structuring situations or jobs or changing organizational structure to encourage desired behavior; uses complex political maneuvering to reach a goal or have an effect. [This level of complexity of action is usually associated with levels 4, 5, and 6 of Interpersonal Understanding, or with corresponding levels of Organizational Awareness.]

B.   BREADTH OF INFLUENCE, UNDERSTANDING, OR NETWORK (Own or Other Organization)

B.   1   *One Other Person.*

B.   2   *Work Unit or Project Team.*

B.   3   *Department.*

Table 6-1 *(Continued)*

Level	Behavioral Description
B. 4	*Division or Entire Mid-Size Firm.*
B. 5	*Entire Large Organization.*
B. 6	*City Governmental, Political, or Professional Organizations.*
B. 7	*State Governmental, Political, or Professional Organizations.*
B. 8	*National Political, Governmental, or Professional Organizations.*
B. 9	*International Governmental, Political, or Professional Organizations.*

course, the next thing I got was a call from General _____ who told me what my ancestry was, because, I'm sure, he had been chastised by his boss. [Dramatic action sending letters of protest to congressmen and understanding of causal chain of others' behavior, leading to predicted nasty phone call; also includes Organizational Awareness. (IMP A.5, B.8, plus IU A.4, B.1)]

I knew it was just as important to recruit his wife as to recruit him. I made sure he saw the marina, then I set out to introduce her to a couple of equestrian friends of mine. [Gets friends to impress wife so she will influence her husband to join speaker's company. (IMP A.8, B.1)]

(Consultant giving a group of directors, including a belligerent marketing director, a review of a Reduction in Force plan) I thought, well if I launch straight out and say right, one obvious area where nothing's happened is in Marketing, then there would be a thousand and one good reasons back from him why nothing had been done or why he wanted to keep it the same. So I started out by turning round on the Managing Director and said "Okay there are six of you guys and there are six secretaries and we haven't reduced those numbers any. Why haven't we reduced the numbers of your secretaries? Why haven't we started this exercise right outside your own front doors?" And that immediately wrong-footed all of them, they weren't expecting me to query their own secretaries. . . . So that gave me the opportunity, while they were still wrong-footed, to quiz in on the Marketing Department. And because the Sales Director was still smarting a bit he was not expecting the question about his Marketing Department. So, two of the other directors . . . tore into this poor guy (the Sales Director) because he hadn't got his Marketing Director to reduce the numbers in the department he held as sacrosanct. So at the end of the day we got what we wanted, but by a fairly torturous route. I enjoyed that. (IMP A.8, B.2)

Links to Other Competencies

Impact and Influence (A.4 and higher) includes Interpersonal Understanding. Effective use of influence is based on accurate Interpersonal Understanding. People do sometimes influence and intervene where they lack understanding, but the effects tend to be unpredictable, uncontrolled, and not characteristic of superior performance. Organizational Awareness is the foundation of Impact and Influence with a larger breadth of impact (high end of the B-scale) in the same way that Interpersonal Understanding is the foundation of Impact and Influence on the individual level (low end of the B-scale).

Use of Influence Strategies (IMP A.6 to A.8) implies a moderate level of Analytical or Conceptual Thinking plus some Flexibility.

Initiative frequently supports Influence, and Initiative may be taken to Impact and Influence as well as for other purposes.

Relationship Building often supports organizational-level Impact and Influence (B.3 and up), providing both information and the basis for alliances and indirect influence.

The managerial competencies discussed in Chapter 7 (Developing Others, Teamwork and Cooperation, and Team Leadership) may be considered as special cases of Impact and Influence, each expressing a different specific agenda. Directiveness is not a special case of Influence, since the intent there is generally not to influence or persuade, but rather to *impose* one's own will or wishes on others.

ORGANIZATIONAL AWARENESS (OA)

Organizational Awareness refers to the individual's ability to understand the power relationships in his or her own organization or in other organizations (customers, suppliers, etc.), and at the higher levels, the position of the organization in the larger world. This includes the ability to identify who are the real decision makers and the individuals who can influence them; and to predict how new events or situations will affect individuals and groups within the organization, or the organization's position vis-à-vis national or international markets, organizations, or politics.

This scale is parallel to the Interpersonal Understanding scale, but here the subject is organizations rather than individuals. Obviously, at least moderate levels of Interpersonal Understanding would contribute to organizational awareness, but the two characteristics are not necessarily dependent on each other. In particular, "political animals" may not listen to other people who convey information not relevant to their own agenda and are frequently accused of lacking responsive action (also known as "sensitivity to others' feelings").

This scale may refer to either to awareness and impact within the individual's own organization (coded OAI) or to awareness and impact on other organizations (customers, clients, suppliers, etc., coded OAE).

In various studies Organizational Awareness has been called:

Playing the Organization

Bringing Others Along

Awareness of Client Organizations

Using the Chain of Command

Political Astuteness

The primary dimension (A) of the Organizational Awareness Scale (Table 6–2) is complexity or depth of understanding: the number of factors the individual takes into account in understanding an organization. The depth of understanding of an organization ranges from understanding formal chain of command to understanding long-term underlying issues. The breadth dimension (B) measures the size of the organization the individual understands, and matches the breadth scale (B) used for Impact and Influence (see Table 6–1).

Typical indicators of Organizational Awareness include:

- Understands the organization's *in*formal structures (identifies key actors, decision-influencers, etc.)
- Recognizes unspoken organizational constraints--what is and is not possible at certain times or in certain positions

Table 6–2   Organizational Awareness (OA) Scale*

Level	Behavioral Description
A. DEPTH OF UNDERSTANDING OF ORGANIZATION	
A. −1	*Misunderstands Organizational Structure.* Makes blunders.
A. 0	*Nonpolitical.* Responds to explicit requests, focuses on doing his/her own job and ignores or disdains organizational "politics."
A. 1	*Understands Formal Structure.* Recognizes or describes (uses) the formal structure or hierarchy of an organization, "chain of command," positional power, rules and regulations, Standard operating Procedure, etc.
A. 2	*Understands Informal Structure.* Understands and may use informal structures (identifies key actors, decision-influencers, etc.).
A. 3	*Understands Climate and Culture.* Recognizes unspoken organizational constraints—what is and is not possible at certain times or in certain positions. Recognizes and uses the corporate culture, and the language etc. that will be best heard.
A. 4	*Understands Organizational Politics.* Understands, describes (or manipulates) on-going power and political relationships within the organization, (alliances, rivalries).
A. 5	*Understands Underlying Organizational Issues.* Understands (and addresses) the reasons for on-going organizational behavior or the underlying problems, opportunities or political forces affecting the organization. Or, describes the underlying functional structure of the organization.
A. 6	*Understands Long-Term Underlying Issues.* Understands (and addresses) long-term underlying problems, opportunities, or political forces affecting the organization in relation to the external world.

*For breadth subscale (B), see Table 6–1.

■ Recognizes and addresses the underlying problems, opportunities, or political forces affecting the organization:

(Technical Salesperson, regarding client company's handling of a proposal) I knew we would not get to see the proposal until after it was approved. They sent it up though the hierarchy of management and we didn't get to see the finished product until after the fact. It was just a policy decision on their part—they had some sensitive matters, some of their centers would be closed down completely and our new equipment installed in the computer room, so there were a lot of people whose jobs would be transferred. They also have a lot of union problems and I think they felt that the less publicity this proposal got, the better. (OAE A.3, B.3)

(Consultant describing a client organization) The new General Manager who was imported early last year, I was told was an entirely different type. The question I always ask of that position is, Is this the person's last move? I mean, have they been put aside or have they been put there to be trained for the future? This particular person is the heir apparent to the Chief Executive job so I concluded he was a very high-flyer. So I immediately knew I wanted to meet him and he was our big opportunity. I was talking to the Human Resources Manager one day, trying to position myself to meet this executive General Manager . . . (OAE A.4, B.3)

The previous procedure for _____ was perhaps less used than the one we've got now. The root cause of it (disuse of the system) was the way that the system was put together—it was one main pressure on a group of people . . . there was not much team effort because the top manager liked to impose on people, rather than letting them have a view, he imposed his own views on them straightaway. (OAI A.5, B.2)

Links to Other Competencies

A crucial support for Organizational Awareness is Information-seeking—including observation, direct questioning, indirect information seeking (from third parties, indirect evidence), and various tactics to test hypotheses.

Relationship Building is sometimes a basis of Organizational Awareness and Influence: It provides a source of information and understanding as well as the basis for alliances and cooperation in influencing.

Organizational Awareness supports the organizational levels of Impact and Influence (B.3 and up). It may also support Team Leadership and Teamwork and Cooperation.

RELATIONSHIP BUILDING (RB)

Relationship Building is working to build or maintain friendly, warm relationships or networks of contacts *with people who are, or might someday be, useful in achieving work-related goals*. Sometimes the instrumental purpose is explicit as in the examples below:

Looking to the future, probably this year and next I will be going to Maryland, because I want to develop more of a relationship with the daughter, with the idea that when she turns eighteen and receives this money she'll want to set up a trust and name us as trustee.

I cultivated the relationship with him, because I wanted to meet his boss, and down the road, shoot for the demonstration.

Sometimes the instrumental purpose is less explicit and is implied by the choice of people with whom to develop relationships. The competency of Relationship Building always includes some (possibly long-term) work-related purpose: Building friendly relationships purely for their own sake is a different competency (Affiliative Interest), which is not included in the generic dictionary.

In various models, Relationship Building has been called:

Networking

Use of Resources

Develops Contacts

Personal Contacts

Concern for Customer Relationships

Ability to Establish Rapport

Relationship Building may be expressed either within one's own organization (coded RBI) or with people from other organizations or the community (coded RBE).

Since high levels of Relationship Building are not needed in many jobs, this scale is a prime example of the statement that higher on the scale is not necessarily better. We do have several studies in which very close personal relationships with colleagues and clients characterized the best performers (e.g., client relationship manager jobs). However, mixing business and personal life successfully over the long run takes care, discipline, and subtleties beyond the scope of this book.

The primary dimension (A) of the Relationship Building Scale (Table 6–3) is the closeness or intimacy of relationships, ranging from none to formal working relationships (i.e., limited to work-related topics) to close personal friendships involving family members. The second dimension (B) describes the size or extent of the network of relationships built. This scale is the same as the Breadth scale for Impact and Influence and for Organizational Awareness (see Table 6–1). Interviews do not always give enough information to score the Breadth dimension of Relationship Building.

Typical behavioral indicators include:

■ Consciously "working at" building rapport, extending oneself to build rapport

Table 6–3   Relationship Building (RB) Scale*

Level	Behavioral Description

A. CLOSENESS OF RELATIONSHIPS BUILT

A. 0 *Avoids Contact.* Reclusive, avoids social interactions.

A. 1 *Accepts Invitations.* Accepts invitations or other friendly overtures from others, but does not extend invitations or go out of the way to establish working relationships.

A. 2 *Makes Work-Related Contacts.* Maintains formal working relationships (largely confined to work-related matters, not necessarily formal in tone or style or structure). Includes unstructured chats about work-related matters.

A. 3 *Makes Occasional Informal Contact.* Occasionally initiates informal or casual relationships at work, chats about children, sports, news, etc.

A. 4 *Builds Rapport.* Frequently initiates informal or casual contacts at work with associates or customers. Makes a conscious effort to build rapport.

A. 5 *Makes Occasional Social Contacts.* Occasionally initiates or pursues friendly relationships with associates or customers outside work at clubs, restaurants, etc.

A. 6 *Makes Frequent Social Contacts.* Frequently initiates or pursues friendly relationships with associates or customers outside work at clubs, restaurants, etc.

A. 7 *Makes Home and Family Contacts.* Occasionally brings associates or customers home or goes to their home.

A. 8 *Makes Close Personal Friendships.* Frequently entertains associates or customers at home. Becomes close personal friends with them; or utilizes personal friendships to expand business network.

*For breadth subscale (B), see Table 6–1.

- Establishing rapport easily (this may be directly observed by interviewers)
- Sharing personal information to create a common ground or mutuality
- "Networking" or establishing friendly relations with many people who may someday be called for information or other assistance:

It began as a routine conversation—how was he doing, how was I doing, because I hadn't seen him in a month or so. Then I asked if I could go into the spare-parts cabinets to look around and see what he's got. I made a list of what I needed and what he had left and he agreed to let me have the parts. (RBI A.2, B.1)

I personally made a point to talk to the head of operations who was the client, and told him that I wanted to talk to all his key players at a meeting and then I personally went around to as many people as I could find and spent 10–15 minutes bullshitting with them, telling them who I was and what we were all about. And though we had some minor problems with people during this intervention I had no major trouble with people whatsoever. (RBI A.4, B.3)

We do the entertaining thing. We had opening night at the opera last Saturday night and we had a table for 20 people and we had the best people there with their wives and husbands, so it was a 3:00 A.M. kind of deal. It was great, great exposure. (RB A.6, B.4 or higher)

I went through Ed D. the Chief Investment Officer, whom I've been very good personal friends with, and I said, "Ed, I need to make this thing go well." He got his boss in there (who normally wouldn't do this sort of thing), and it was very helpful. [This is an example of calling on an existing relationship or network. This type of example is more prevalent in the data than in this set, because these examples are often difficult to score. (RB A.8)]

Links to Other Competencies

Moderate levels of Interpersonal Understanding and Impact and Influence are implied Relationship Building, since the intent of Relationship Building is to have a general, long-term impact on others. Interpersonal Understanding is needed to understand how best to befriend someone.

A moderate level of Initiative is implied by Relationship Building (doing things today to build resources to help find future opportunities or resolve future problems.)

Once the relationships or networks are in place or ongoing, they contribute greatly to the higher levels of Impact and Influence, and especially influencing organizations.

Relationship Building is generally implied in the highest levels of Customer Service Orientation (the degree of trust involved is normally built over time, although the contacts may be formal (i.e., RBO A.2 or A.3)). Conversely, giving great customer service may be one way to start a relationship.

NOTE

1. McClelland, D. C. (1975), *Power: The inner experience*, New York: Irvington.

CHAPTER

7

Managerial

The Managerial Competencies are a specialized subset of the Impact and Influence competencies, expressing the intention to have certain specific effects. These specific intentions (to develop others, to lead others, to improve teamwork and cooperation) are particularly important for managers. They are well developed in the generic dictionary because they are so common among managers and others whom we have studied.

DEVELOPING OTHERS (DEV)

Developing Others is a special version of Impact and Influence, in which the intent is to teach or to foster the development of one or several other people. A genuine intent to foster the learning or development of the others and an appropriate level of need analysis are implied in each positive level of Developing Others. The essence of this competency lies in the developmental intent and effect rather than in a formal role. Sending people to routine training programs to meet statutory or corporate requirements (or promotions made primarily to meet business needs) does *not* express the intent to develop others and does not score on this scale. On the other hand, it is possible to work to further the development of peers, clients, and even superiors.

Behaviors similar to those in this scale, but without the intent to teach, train, or develop the other person, may be scored for Directiveness, Interpersonal Understanding, Impact and Influence, or Teamwork and Cooperation.

Developing Others has also been called:

Teaching and Training
Assuring Subordinates' Growth and Development

Coaching Others

Realistic Positive Regard

Providing Support

The primary dimension (A) of Developing Others (Table 7–1) is intensity and completeness of action to develop others, ranging from maintaining positive expectations regarding another's potential to promoting people on the basis of successful development. The second dimension (B) combines the number of people developed and their relationship to the speaker, ranging from developing one subordinate to developing a supervisor or customer to developing large groups of people at mixed levels.

Common behaviors expressing Developing Others include:

■ Expresses positive expectations of others, even in "difficult" cases. Believes others want to and can learn

■ Gives directions or demonstrations with reasons or rationale included as a training strategy

■ Gives negative feedback in behavioral rather than personal terms, and expresses positive expectations for future performance or gives individualized suggestions for improvement

■ Identifies a training or developmental need and designs or establishes *new* programs or materials to meet it

Table 7–1 Developing Others (DEV) Scale

Level	Behavioral Description
A.	INTENSITY OF DEVELOPMENTAL ORIENTATION AND COMPLETENESS OF DEVELOPMENTAL ACTION
A. −1	*Discourages.* Expresses stereotypical or personal negative expectations, resents subordinates, students, clients. Has a "pacesetter" management style.
A. 0	*Not Applicable, or Makes No Explicit Efforts to Develop Others.* Focuses on doing his or her own job well, setting a good example.
A. 1	*Expresses Positive Expectations of Others.* Makes positive comments regarding others' abilities or potentials even in "difficult" cases. Believes others want to and can learn.
A. 2	*Gives Detailed Instructions, and/or on-the-job demonstrations.* Tells how to do the task, makes specific helpful suggestions.
A. 3	*Gives Reasons or Other Support.* Gives directions or demonstrations with reasons or rationale included as a training strategy; or gives practical support or assistance, to make job easier (i.e., volunteers additional resources, tools, information, expert advice). Asks questions, gives tests, or uses other methods to verify that others have understood explanation or directions.

Table 7-1   *(Continued)*

Level	Behavioral Description

A. 4   *Gives Specific Positive or Mixed Feedback for Developmental Purposes.*

A. 5   *Reassures and Encourages.* Reassures others after a setback. Gives negative feedback in behavioral rather than personal terms, and expresses positive expectations for future performance or gives individualized suggestions for improvement; or breaks difficult tasks into smaller components, or uses other strategies.

A. 6   *Does Long-Term Coaching or Training.* Arranges appropriate and helpful assignments, formal training, or other experiences for the purpose of fostering the other person's learning and development. Includes making people work out answers to problems themselves so they really know how, rather than simply giving them the answer. Formal training done simply to meet governmental or corporate requirements does not count here.

A. 7   *Creates New Teaching/Training.* Identifies a training or developmental need and designs or establishes new programs or materials to meet it; designs significantly new approaches to teaching traditional materials; or arranges successful experiences for others to build up their skills and confidence.

A. 8   *Delegates Fully.* After assessing subordinates' competence, delegates full authority and responsibility with the latitude to do a task in their own way, including the opportunity to make and learn from mistakes in a noncritical setting.

A. 9   *Rewards Good Development.* Promotes or arranges promotions for especially competent subordinates as a reward or a developmental experience; or gives other rewards for good performance. This behavior is ranked highly because generally an individual has to have developed people well to be able to reward them for responding well.

B.   NUMBER AND RANK OF PEOPLE DEVELOPED OR DIRECTED

B. 1   *One Subordinate (or student, or counseling-type client).*

B. 2   *Several (2–6) Subordinates.*

B. 3   *Many (more than 6) Subordinates.*

B. 4   *One Peer (includes suppliers, colleagues, etc.).*

B. 5   *Several (2–6) Peers.*

B. 6   *Many Peers.*

B. 7   *One Superior or Customer (or customer-type client).*

B. 8   *More Than One Superior or Customer.*

B. 9   *Large Groups (more than 200) at Mixed Levels.*

Scoring Notes: An appropriate level of needs analysis is implied at each level: Developmental efforts are obviously inappropriate or misguided *do not count* on this scale. Developmental efforts do not have to be successful to count, but they must not be obviously inappropriate.

Sending people to routine training programs to meet statutory or corporate requirements (or promotions made primarily to meet business needs) does *not* express the intent to develop others and does not score on this scale.

■ Delegates tasks or responsibilities for the purpose of developing others' abilities:

(Noncommissioned officer, regarding his commissioned officers) I have to teach junior officers how to lead me . . . I tell them, "You're running the ship and I'm watching all this equipment for you; you've got a right to know how it's running. Ask me. And ask me to help you when I can." Pretty soon they're saying, "Chief, how's the _____ doing? Could you get it into alignment? . . . That's what I did this time." [Note that this is an example of developing one's *superiors*. (DEV A.2, B.7)]

I had immediately noticed marijuana residue in an ashtray, but I wanted my assistant to see it himself. I only stopped him if I didn't think he was going along the right lines. I really wanted him to do it on his own. I watched to see how he was going to react. (DEV A.6, B.1)

I was disturbed by the fact that the department didn't know anything about real estate law and they were asking dumb questions. As a result of that, I put together two lectures that covered about 15 clauses and said, "This is why they are there, this is what you have to do if they're not there, this is what you do if they are there." So I tried to teach them what they ought to be looking for in an instrument and whether they are complying with it. I like to continue that. (DEV A.7, B.5)

I also delegated some of the responsibility for running the Impact meeting to my assistant principal. The goals and objectives of the meeting were discussed with the assistant principal. Then the assistant principal was invited to sit in on the morning meeting, which is usually conducted by myself and/or the consultant. Then the assistant principal took over the running of the meeting and I was not present. So it was training. (DEV A.8, B.1)

Links to Other Competencies

Developing Others (A.4 and up) implies at least a moderate level of Interpersonal Understanding to recognize and respond to others' developmental needs and specific strengths.

DEV A.7 (Designing new programs and materials) implies at least a moderate level of Conceptual Thinking and may include a fairly high level, depending on the size and innovativeness of the new materials. It also implies some Innovation (Achievement Orientation C).

When developing others is not an explicit part of the job, levels A.6 and up imply moderate-to-high levels of Initiative.

DIRECTIVENESS: ASSERTIVENESS
AND USE OF POSITIONAL POWER (DIR)

Directiveness expresses the individual's intent to make others comply with his or her wishes. Directive behavior has a theme or tone of "telling people what to do." The tone ranges from firm and directive to demanding or even threatening. Attempts to reason with, persuade, or convince others to comply score as Impact and Influence, not as Directiveness. To score at the positive levels, personal power or the power of the individual's position must be used appropriately and effectively, with the long-term good of the organization in mind. Capricious or inappropriate use of positional power is *not* included in this competency, as it does not characterize superior performance.

Directiveness has also been called:

Decisiveness

Use of Power

Use of Aggressive Influence

Taking Charge

Firmness in Enforcing Quality Standards

Classroom Control and Discipline

Although Directiveness appears most clearly in boss-to-subordinate relationships, assertiveness can also be shown by nonexempt employees (e.g., a secretary making arrangements with a hotel, caterer, or supplier [DIR A.2 or A.3]; a salesperson asking assertively for a order of a specific size [DIR A.4 or A.5]).

The primary dimension (A) of Directiveness (Table 7–2) is intensity of the assertive tone, ranging from clear requests to (deliberate and controlled) displays of anger or to firing people when necessary without guilt or hesitation. The breadth dimension (number and rank of people directed) is the same as in Developing Others (see Table 7–1).

Low-level jobs may not provide opportunities for the higher levels of Directiveness. However, we have seen cases in which superior performers were occasionally highly assertive to bosses or clients, confronting them on difficult performance issues and so on. This is more acceptable when combined with high levels of Achievement Orientation (Results Orientation) or high levels of Customer Service Orientation or both.

Directiveness is not the everyday style of superior managers. It is selectively employed, with high impact, in certain situations (particularly crisis and "turnaround" situations, and when confronting poor performance that does not respond to developmental efforts).

Typical directive behaviors include:

- Confronts others openly and directly about performance problems
- Unilaterally sets standards; demands high performance, quality, or resources; insists on compliance with own orders or requests in a "no-nonsense" or "put my foot down" style

Table 7–2 Directiveness (DIR) Scale*

Level	Behavioral Description

A. INTENSITY OF DIRECTIVENESS

A. −1 *Is Passive.* Gives in to other's requests even when doing so interferes with getting the main job done. Is more concerned with being liked (or, not upsetting or angering other people) than with getting the work done properly. May be afraid to disturb or cross others.

A. 0 *Does Not Give Orders.* Or does not give directions when requested (or not required in this position). When managers exhibit this level they may be vague about requirements even when directly asked. A typical symptom is that subordinates complain that they don't know what So-and-So wants them to do.

A. 1 *Gives Basic, Routine Directions.* Gives adequate directions, makes needs and requirements reasonably clear.

A. 2 *Gives Detailed Directions.* Delegates routine tasks in order to free self for more valuable or longer-range considerations, or gives directions with very specific details. [If delegation is made for the sake of developing others' skills or knowledge, score as Developing Others. If delegation is done for the purpose of positioning oneself as leader see Team Leadership. Here the intent is generally simply to get the job done.] Superior performers sometimes show this level when they lack formal authority, but no one else is taking charge.

A. 3 *Speaks Assertively.* Firmly says "No" to unreasonable requests, or sets limits for others' behavior. May manipulate situations to limit other's options, or to force them to make desired resources available.

A. 4 *Demands High Performance.* Unilaterally sets standards; demands high performance, quality, or resources; insists on compliance with own orders or requests, in a "no-nonsense" or "put my foot down" style. This level may be found in superior salespeople, consultants, or trust officers dealing with clients.

A. 5 *Obviously Monitors Performance.* Intrusively (or publicly) monitors performance against clear standards (e.g., posts sales results next to individual goals with shortfalls circled in red).

A. 6 *Confronts Others.* Confronts others openly and directly about performance problems. [If discussion includes reassurance, positive expectations regarding future performance, or specific helpful suggestions for improvement, score as Developmental Orientation, Level 5.]

A. 7 *States Consequences of Behavior.* Uses punishment or rewards to control behavior (e.g., "If you perform well, I'll reward you, if not . . .").

A. 8 *Uses Controlled Display of Anger or Threats to Extract Compliance.* Yells or threatens, "Do that again and I'll FIRE YOU." [Do not score if anger is uncontrolled, or if speaker expresses regret or mentions negative consequences.]

A. 9 *When Necessary, Fires or Gets Rid of Poor Performers,* without undue hesitation, after appropriate efforts to get them to improve have failed and after appropriate legal procedures are followed. [Do not score if speaker expresses conflict or regret.]

*For breadth (B) subscale, see Table 7–1.

- Firmly says "No" to unreasonable requests, or sets limits for others' behavior
- Gives detailed directions, assigns tasks to get the job done or to free self for higher priorities:

Then I said, "I want this team to take care of the sand table, I want this team to write paragraph one and two, I'll write paragraph three, and I want this team to write paragraph four and five. I want you to have them done by such and such a time so I can look at them and do it. I want you to do this coordination, pick the different people to go do them." (DIR A.2, B.2).

I was very direct with him. It wasn't like I hadn't asked for the order before, but finally it came down to, "Don, I would like the order," and I had proposed a specific amount . . . ten thousand tapes. (DIR A.5, B.7)

I said: "It's been my observation that you are missing at least a day a week. That probably is very, very difficult for the students. What is the cause of the problem and what are you doing to deal with it?" (DIR A.6, B.1)

I told the people that this was not a discussion meeting . . . that I was going to tell them something, and there would be no question-and-answer period. Afterward, if they really wanted to come and talk to me individually, I would be happy to meet with them. I told them that I personally did not care how they felt about other people from a racial or personality standpoint, as long as they kept it off the plant. But when they started to bring the prejudices into the plant and it started to disrupt business, then it became my business. Their supervisor and I were not going to put up with harassment or threats. If it took sending people out the gate . . . firing them . . . then that's what we'd do. Then I left. (DIR A.7, B.3)

I set very specific performance goals for them. If the goals were consistently met, the PC was no longer in the publicly posted "dirty dozen." If the goals were not met, the PC was gone. On the other hand, I had some super producers . . . actually there was a big gap between the thirteenth and the fourteenth producers, so we had a "baker's dozen." I took them to a local club for dinner and we had a great time. [Scores DIR A.5 for intrusively monitoring; also DIR A.7 for uses reward and punishment to control performance; DIR A.9 for fires poor performers.]

I told him that I wanted to see some substantial changes. And he came back with some very self-serving unsubstantial answers to my questions. So I fired him. (DIR A.9, B.1)

Links to Other Competencies

Directiveness can be a combination of high Achievement Orientation with either a lack of skill in Impact and Influence or a specific situation in which use of those skills is not appropriate.

A moderate amount of Self-Confidence is implied in Directiveness.

Achievement Orientation may be involved in stories that invoive insisting on or enforcing high standards for performance.

Initiative A.3 (responds quickly and decisively in a crisis) frequently involves Directiveness if the situation requires more than one person's action.

TEAMWORK AND COOPERATION (TW)

Teamwork and Cooperation implies a genuine intention to work cooperatively with others, to be part of a team, to work together as opposed to working separately or competitively. The scale for Teamwork and Cooperation may be considered whenever the subject is a member of a group of people *functioning* as a team. Team membership need not be formally defined—people from different levels and departments who communicate with each other to solve a problem or complete a project are functioning as a team. A team may be anything from a 3-person, one-shot task force to the crew of a battleship.

Teamwork and Cooperation may be shown in any role within a team; the individual does not need to be a leader or in a position of formal authority. Someone who has formal authority but is acting in a participative manner or functioning as a group facilitator manner is using Teamwork and Cooperation. Many excellent executives combine Teamwork with Team Leadership.

Teamwork and Cooperation has also been called:

Group Management

Group Facilitation

Conflict Resolution

Managing Branch Climate

Motivating Others

The primary (A) dimension of Teamwork and Cooperation (Table 7–3) is the intensity and thoroughness of action taken to foster teamwork, ranging

Table 7–3 Teamwork and Cooperation (TW) Scale

Level	Behavioral Description
A. INTENSITY OF FOSTERING TEAMWORK	
A.−1	*Uncooperative.* Disruptive, causes trouble.
A. 0	*Neutral.* Neutral, passive, does not participate, or is not a member of any team.
A. 1	*Cooperates.* Participates willingly, supports team decisions, is a "good team player," does his or her share of the work.
A. 2	*Shares Information.* Keeps people informed and up to date about the group process, shares all relevant or useful information.

Table 7-3 *(Continued)*

Level	Behavioral Description
A. 3	*Expresses Positive Expectations.* Expresses positive expectations of others. Speaks of team members in positive terms. Shows respect for others' intelligence by appealing to reason.
A. 4	*Solicits Inputs.* Genuinely values others' input and expertise, is willing to learn from others (especially subordinates). Solicits ideas and opinions to help form specific decisions or plans. Invites all members of a group contribute to a process.
A. 5	*Empowers Others.* Publicly credits others who have performed well. Encourages and empowers others, makes them feel strong or important.
A. 6	*Team-Builds.* Acts to promote a friendly climate, good morale, and cooperation (holds parties and get-togethers, creates symbols of group identity). Protects and promotes group reputation with outsiders.
A. 7	*Resolves Conflicts.* Brings conflict within the team into the open and encourages or facilitates a beneficial resolution of conflicts (must involve action to resolve the conflict, not to hide it or avoid the issue).

B. SIZE OF TEAM INVOLVED*

B. 1	*Small, Informal Groups of 3–8 People.* May include social or friendship groups. [This level is infrequently scored in work situations but may be useful in selection interviewing of recent graduates.]
B. 2	*A Task Force or Temporary Team.*
B. 3	*Ongoing Work Group or Small Department.* May include a group of subordinates who are themselves department heads, if the leadership activities do not directly affect their employees.
B. 4	*Entire Large-Size Department* (approximately 16–50 people).
B. 5	*Division of Major Firm.* Or entire mid-size firm.
B. 6	*Entire Major-Size Firm.*

C. AMOUNT OF EFFORT OR INITIATIVE TO FOSTER TEAMWORK

C. 0	*Makes No Extra Effort.*
C. 1	*Takes More Than Routine Action Him- or Herself* (Up to 4 extra phone calls, conversations, or actions).
C. 2	*Takes Much More Than Routine Action Him- or Herself* (5–15 actions).
C. 3	*Makes Extraordinary Efforts* (on own time or over a period of months).
C. 4	*Gets Others to Take Nonroutine Action, Hold Extra Meetings, etc.* [Score this for peers, superiors, or people in other organizations. Do not score for delegating some personal actions to subordinates unless the subordinate's action is clearly not within their normal job description. Initiatives that involve the ordinary assistance of subordinates score at level 3, 4, or 5.]
C. 5	*Involves Others in Extraordinary Efforts.*

*Score for the size of the group directly affected by the person's cooperation or facilitation. For people in higher organizational positions, score the entire organization only when most people in the entire organization or division are affected or addressed. If the subject is working with a group of managers, count the managers themselves, not all their subordinates. When in doubt, or when the data are unclear, score level 3—Ongoing Work Group or Small Department.

from simple cooperation, doing one's share, to actions taken to build team morale or to resolve team conflict. This scale measures efforts to foster teamwork or to resolve conflicts within the team, not those to accomplish some team task or goal. The breadth (B) scale measures the size of the team (from small task forces to entire organizations) and a third dimension (C) refers to the amount of effort or initiative taken to foster teamwork.

Typical team-building behaviors include:

- Solicits ideas and opinions to help form specific decisions or plans
- Keeps people informed and up-to-date about the group process, shares all relevant or useful information
- Expresses positive expectations of others
- Credits others publicly for accomplishments
- Encourages and empowers others, makes them feel strong or important:

(At one top manager's plant, an inexperienced, first-line supervisor had mishandled an incident that occurred during an emergency situation. The manager took corrective action): I had the first-line supervisor write down everything he remembered about the incident. I talked to my boss and told him my plan. I talked to Employee Relations . . . they made some suggestions. I had my boss call the people involved . . . they came into the plant and I spoke with them. I spoke with the union president. And the speaker continued in this vein; each time a new development occurred, he informed everyone who needed to know. (TW A.2, B.4, C.2)

The area we were working in was really marshy. A thin crust of hard dirt . . . and once he got that through my head, he said, "Now that you understand the problem, you got to be more careful," and so I said, "What do you think I should do?" He said, "Well, you messed the side up, Sir. You go back and fix it." I said, "Okay." So I went back up and fixed it. [Also scores for Dealing with Failure: admits and corrects own mistakes. (TW A.4)]

I had some FCs who really exceeded their goals. I thought they had done a great job and I told them so. I also made a big to-do about it in the sales meeting. I wanted everybody to know what a good job they had done. (TW A.5)

I told the temporary operators that we had a tremendous amount of work for this shutdown. We viewed them as part of our operating area and operating unit . . . our intent was to work as a team. Any problem they had, we wanted to know about. Then my first-line supervisor and I took them on a tour of the area. (TW A.6, B.2)

In general, I was intending to build camaraderie and be somewhat social (in getting people together from different parts of the firm). (TW A.6, B.5)

Links to Other Competencies

Teamwork (A.3 and up) usually implies at least low levels of Interpersonal Understanding and of Impact and Influence.

Effective Self-confidence B (Dealing with Failure) is associated with Teamwork in a number of examples.

Teamwork may support the organizational levels of Impact and Influence (IMP B.3 and up).

Teamwork is similar in orientation to Developing Others, and they are frequently combined in models.

TEAM LEADERSHIP (TL)

Team Leadership is the intention to take a role as leader of a team or other group. It implies a desire to lead others. Team Leadership is generally, but certainly not always, shown from a position of formal authority. This entire scale, therefore, has a job-size aspect. It is often combined with Teamwork, especially by top executives and upper-level managers.

As with Directiveness, leadership must be exercised in a reasonably responsible manner: Using leadership for personal gain, for obviously unworthy ends, or in an manner contrary to the organization's purpose, *does not* score on this scale.

Leadership has also been called:

Taking Command

Being in Charge

Vision

Group Management and Motivation

Building a Sense of Group Purpose

Genuine Concern for Subordinates

The primary dimension (A) of the Team Leadership Scale (Table 7–4) is the intensity and completeness of the leadership role, ranging from simply running meetings to true charisma—inspiring and energizing others through compelling vision and leadership. The breadth (B) (size of the team) and effort/initiative (C) dimensions are the same as for Teamwork and Cooperation (see Table 7–3).

Typical leadership behaviors include:

- Informs people: Lets people affected by a decision know what is happening

Table 7–4   Team Leadership (TL) Scale*

Level	Behavioral Description

A.   STRENGTH OF THE LEADERSHIP ROLE

A. −1   *Abdicates.* Refuses or fails to lead, e.g., won't provide direction or mission statements when subordinates need them.

A.   0   *Not Applicable.* Job does not require leadership.

A.   1   *Manages Meetings.* Manages meetings—states agendas and objectives, controls time, makes assignments, etc.

A.   2   *Informs People.* Lets people affected by a decision know what is happening. Makes sure the group has all the necessary information. May explain the reasons for a decision.

A.   3   *Uses Authority Fairly.* Uses formal authority and power in a fair and equitable manner. Makes a personal effort to treat all group members fairly.

A.   4   *Promotes Team Effectiveness.* Uses complex strategies to promote team morale and productivity (hiring and firing decisions, team assignments, cross-training, etc.). [Scoring note: really complex examples, which would score for the upper half of Interpersonal Understanding and/or Impact and Influence, should also be scored on those scales.]

A.   5   *Takes Care of the Group.* Protects the group and its reputation vis-à-vis the larger organization, or the community at large: obtains needed personnel, resources, information for the group. Makes sure the practical needs of the group are met. This level is frequently seen in the military or in factory situations, but also applies to obtaining less tangible resources for professional or managerial subordinates.

A.   6   *Positions Self as the Leader.* Ensures that others buy into leader's mission, goals, agenda, climate, tone, policy. "Sets a good example" (i.e., models desired behavior). Ensures that group tasks are completed (is a credible leader).

A.   7   *Communicates a Compelling Vision.* Has genuine charisma, communicates a compelling vision, which generates excitement, enthusiasm, and commitment to the group mission. (Examples of this level are rare and are likely to be inferred from the results of activities, from reports by others, and from the interviewer's observation and impression rather than by direct quotes).

*For breadth (B) and effort/initiative (C) subscales, see Table 7–3.

- Makes a personal effort to treat all group members fairly
- Uses complex strategies to promote team morale and productivity (hiring and firing decisions, team assignments, cross-training, etc.)
- Makes sure the practical needs of the group are met. This level is frequently seen in the military or in factory situations, but also applies to obtaining less tangible resources for professional or managerial subordinates
- Ensures that others buy into leader's mission, goals, agenda, climate, tone, policy:

I organized these planning meetings, developed agendas, and asked the directors to develop their data and make presentations on their area. Then we discussed them. Everybody heard the discussions about the financial information, about the marketplace, about the engineering and manufacturing plans. The financial guy got exposed to the marketplace and vice versa. It served as a cross-education and led to more cooperation. [Also scores for Developing Others (TW A.4, B.2. C.2).]

This organization was like the New York Yankees. I had nine stars, but no team. We'd come together and agree to do something, and then everyone went back to their department and did their own thing. So I set coordination and integration as a top priority. To get people into new habits and attitudes, I'd pull teams together from R&D, from Marketing, etc., and give them some meaningful tasks that simply could not be done unless they worked closely with one another. Only after I saw that their habits and attitudes were actually changing did I begin asking the entire management group how we could bring down all the barriers that were interfering with our productivity. By that point, they were receptive. They saw the necessity for cooperation and integration and could contribute some good ideas. [Also scores for Interpersonal Understanding and Impact and Influence: Diagnoses others' long-term behavior patterns and uses a series of actions—setting up various teams and projects and later addressing the issue directly to change the situation to encourage cooperation. (TW A.5, B.3, C.2)]

We have staff in our business who are grossly underpaid for the contribution they make. I am working out a compensation schedule that allows them to share in improvements in their area. For example, if we save money in operations, then the operations people get a piece of the savings. That piece comes out of my bonus, but I feel very strongly about including them in the profit. They help create the profit so they should share in it. (TL A.3 and A.5)

Links to Other Competencies

A moderate level of Impact and Influence is implied in TL A.3 and up.

TL A.4 is high levels of Impact and Influence applied specifically to the goal of promoting teamwork and team effectiveness.

For managers, Achievement Orientation may be expressed through group achievement and then Team Leadership and Achievement Orientation may be found intertwined (e.g., a manager takes a leadership role to get the group to achieve something).

Moderate levels of Relationship Building, Organizational Awareness, and Impact and Influence contribute to effective Team Leadership. Indeed, the entire Team Leadership scale may be thought of as an elaboration of a particular form of organizational influence.

8

Cognitive

The Cognitive competencies function as an intellectual version of Initiative: the individual's working to come to an understanding of a situation, task, problem, opportunity, or body of knowledge. Like Initiative, it is most commonly thought of in relation to task orientation or Achievement Orientation, but it may also be used exclusively to support Influence and Impact or the Managerial competencies (working out complex strategies to influence others).

The Conceptual and Analytical Thinking scales measure practical or applied intelligence: the degree to which a performer does not accept a critical situation or problem at face value or as defined by others, but comes to his or her *own understanding* at a deeper or more complex level. Observation and/or information seeking are necessary prerequisites.

These scales do not directly measure basic intelligence (although a certain IQ level may be a threshold requirement for each scale level), but rather the individual's tendency to apply that intelligence usefully to work situations, to add value to his or her performance in that job. These scales measure a combination of ability and motivation.

There is a rough correlation between scores on AT and CT and job size, *for superior performers, across jobs.* Superior performers in more complex or larger jobs think about their work problems in more complex ways than superior performers in less demanding positions. They also think about larger problems, with a greater organizational impact. However, it would be perfectly possible for a superior Coast Guard boarding officer to score higher on these scales than an average bank trust officer or commercial loan officer even though the intellectual "tools of the trade" of the loan officer are far more complex than those of the boarding officer.

Winter, McClelland, and Stewart[1] developed a scoring system for essay-type responses to compare-and-contrast questions and to an analysis of arguments task requiring the subject to construct arguments for and against a controversial statement. Fischer[2] has developed a scale for measuring cognitive skills according to the number of concepts coordinated simultaneously. There is a rough correspondence between the Winter, McClelland, and Stewart scoring system, Fischer's cognitive skill levels and our own early attempts to organize all the cognitive skills into one scale. We retained separate competencies for Analytical and Conceptual Thinking because many studies found only one or the other cognitive skill.

Please note that the following examples are drawn from Behavioral Event interviews of superior performers. Thus they represent the level of complexity spontaneously expressed in conversation with an interviewer who is not a technical expert in the interviewee's field. They do not necessarily represent the highest, or most complex level at which that person could reliably perform. Analytical Thinking and Conceptual Thinking involve the same links to other competencies. These are described at the end of the section Conceptual Thinking.

ANALYTICAL THINKING (AT)

Analytical Thinking is understanding a situation by breaking it apart into smaller pieces, or tracing the implications of a situation in a step-by-step causal way. Analytical Thinking includes organizing the parts of a problem or situation in a systematic way; making systematic comparisons of different features or aspects; setting priorities on a rational basis; identifying time sequences, causal relationships or If → Then relationships.

Analytical Thinking has also been called:

Thinking for Yourself

Practical Intelligence

Analyzing Problems

Reasoning

Planning Skill

The underlying dimension of the Analytical Thinking Scale (Table 8–1) is complexity: the number of different causes, reasons, consequences, or action steps included in the analysis, ranging from simple list making to complex multilayered analyses. The second dimension (B) is breadth, or the size of the problem analyzed.

Common behavioral indicators of Analytical Thinking include:

■ Sets priorities for tasks in order of importance
■ Breaks down a complex task into manageable parts in a systematic way
■ Recognizes several likely causes of events, or several consequences of actions

Table 8–1   Analytical Thinking (AT) Scale

Level	Behavioral Description

A. COMPLEXITY OF ANALYSIS

A. 0   *Not Applicable or None.* Does each thing as it comes up, responds to immediate needs or requests; or work is organized by someone else.

A. 1   *Breaks Down Problems.* Breaks problems into simple lists of tasks or activities.

A. 2   *Sees Basic Relationships.* Analyzes relationships among a few parts of a problem or situation. Makes simple causal links (A causes B) or pro-and-con decisions. Sets priorities for tasks in order of importance.

A. 3   *Sees Multiple Relationships.* Analyzes relationships among several parts of a problem or situation. Breaks down a complex task into manageable parts in a systematic way. Recognizes several likely causes of events, or several consequences of actions. Generally anticipates obstacles and thinks ahead about next steps.

A. 4   *Makes Complex Plans or Analyses.* Systematically breaks down a complex problem or process into component parts. Uses several techniques to break apart complex problems to reach a solution; or makes long chains of causal connections.

A. 5   *Makes Very Complex Plans or Analyses.* Systematically breaks multidimensional problems or processes into component parts; or uses several analytical techniques to identify several solutions and weighs the value of each.

A. 6   *Makes Extremely Complex Plans or Analyses.* Organizes, sequences, and analyzes extremely complex interdependent systems.

B. SIZE OF PROBLEM ADDRESSED*

B. 1   *Concerns One or Two People's Performances.*

B. 2   *Concerns a Small Work Unit.* Or concerns a moderate-size sale, or one aspect of a larger unit's performance.

B. 3   *Concerns an Ongoing Problem.* May involve a moderate-size work unit, several sales, or a very large sale.

B. 4   *Concerns Overall Performance.* Involves performance of a major division of a large company or of an entire small-size company.

B. 5   *Concerns Long-Term Performance.* Relates to a major division or entire company in a complex environment (economic or demographic changes, major improvements, etc.).

*Although this scale is strongly related to job size, it is also important in considering placement, since too large a jump in problem size may overload a person's analytic or conceptual capacity.

- Anticipates obstacles and thinks ahead about next steps
- Uses several analytical techniques to identify several solutions and weighs the value of each:

Because of the massive effort that was going on in each unit, the units did not have enough supervisors to handle the work. (AT A.2, B.2)

I stayed involved with most of it because everything I heard led to another aspect of the overall problem. We had unclear sales orders and *that's why* the engineering was not complete, and *that's why* we were engineering the same day we were shipping the project, and *that's why* we were spending so much time on rework. And *that's why* our profit picture did not look good *and why* we were missing shipments. And *that's why* our customers were unhappy. (AT A.4, B.3)

I looked at the lab results on the process and noted we were above specifications. I went to the first-line supervisor and told him we had to push the temperature up to meet spec. He said, "If we live by the spec we'll overheat and shut down. Getting restarted is a lot of extra work for the operators, and then they can't meet their yearly objectives." I was trying to figure out how much of the problem was that they didn't want to put in the extra effort needed to make the product right the first time, versus how much was a genuine concern for not being able to meet their yearly objectives if they had to meet specifications. This led me to talk to Marketing. I found out we had lost a big client because of the product's meeting spec. I went to a chemist, who realized Marketing had told the client they could mix the product at different water percentages than what we had stated. What it boiled down to was: We had this one customer with a particular problem that arose for a brief part of the year. . . . was meeting the spec really worth the stress and agony we would go through in our day-to-day operation and in lower unit productivity . . . or could it be resolved out in the field? We suggested to the client that they use chilled water and fans during the two months of the year that the problem arose. (AT A.5, B.2)

CONCEPTUAL THINKING (CT)

Conceptual Thinking is understanding a situation or problem by putting the pieces together, seeing the large picture. It includes identifying patterns or connections between situations that are not obviously related; identifying key or underlying issues in complex situations. Conceptual Thinking is using creative, conceptual, or inductive reasoning to apply existing concepts (levels A.1–A.3) or to define novel concepts (levels A.5–A.7).
   Conceptual Thinking is also called:

   Use of Concepts
   Pattern Recognition
   Insight
   Critical Thinking
   Problem Definition
   Ability to Generate Theories

   In the main (A) dimension of the Conceptual Thinking Scale (Table 8–2), there are two basic issues: the complexity of the thought processes and their

Table 8–2   Conceptual Thinking (CT) Scale*

Level	Behavioral Description
A.	COMPLEXITY AND ORIGINALITY OF CONCEPTS
A. 0	*Uses No Abstract Concepts.* Thinks very concretely.
A. 1	*Uses Basic Rules.* Uses "rules of thumb," common sense, and past experiences to identify problems or situations. Sees essential similarities between current and past situations.
A. 2	*Recognizes Patterns.* Observes discrepancies, trends, and interrelationships in data or sees crucial differences between current situation and things that have happened before.
A. 3	*Applies Complex Concepts.* (e.g., "root-cause analysis," "portfolio analysis," "natural selection"); or applies knowledge of past discrepancies, trends, and relationships to look at different situations. Applies and modifies complex learned concepts or methods appropriately.
A. 4	*Simplifies Complexity.* Pulls together ideas, issues, and observations into a single concept or a clear presentation. Identifies a key issue in a complex situation.
A. 5	*Creates New Concepts.* Identifies problems and situations not obvious to others and not learned from previous education or experience.
A. 6	*Creates New Concepts for Complex Issues.* Formulates a useful explanation for complex problems, situations, or opportunities. Generates and tests multiple concepts, hypotheses, or explanations for a given situation; or identifies useful relationships among complex data from unrelated areas.
A. 7	*Creates New Models.* Creates new models or theories that explain a complex situation or problem and reconciles discrepant data.

*For breadth (B) subscale, see Table 8–1.

originality, ranging from using basic rules of thumb to creating new theories that explain complex situations. In the Conceptual Thinking scale, previously learned concepts occupy the lower portion of the scale, and original concepts the higher portion of the scale. Within each section, more complex ideas (co-ordinating more factors) are higher than simpler ideas. The second dimension (B) is breadth, or the size of the problem analyzed, and matches the breadth scale for Analytical Thinking (see Table 8–1).

Common behavioral descriptions of Conceptual Thinking include:

- Uses "rules of thumb," common sense, and past experiences to identify problems or situations
- Sees crucial differences between current situation and things that have happened before
- Applies and modifies complex learned concepts or methods appropriately
- Identifies useful relationships among complex data from unrelated areas:

I've got his number! He (commanding officer of another ship) is pulling the same trick we pulled on another ship during an exercise at _____. Is he in for a surprise! (CT A.1, B.2)

I did a force field analysis after presenting him with the data. I used that type of thought process to get into the strengths and weaknesses of the organization. [This scores for Conceptual Thinking because it is an application of a complex learned concept, even though the name of the set of interrelated concepts is "_____ _____ analysis." (CT A.3, B.3)]

I knew what was needed for this application area, and I knew what kind of a product competitors were promoting. It was hazardous. Then I knew of this other material, and I realized that this material didn't have any of the deficiencies of the other. It wasn't flammable, for example. Therefore, to me it was quite obvious that we ought to just take our material and put it into this application area. I tried it, and it worked! (CT A.6, B.4)

If you look at _____, and this group particularly, you'll find that the most successful divisions have grown from within. If you look at the divisions that have problems, you'll see several general managers who have rotated through every few years; but the most successful divisions have had long-term managers. Then there are some divisions, like ones that make a proprietary product, where it will make no difference who the general manager is unless he is completely incompetent. [Makes a model of management of successful divisions and reconciles "exceptions" as proprietary product divisions. (CT A.7, B.4)]

One top salesperson (selling large-scale projects at the highest corporate levels) used an entire 3-hour interview to explain his theory of the peaks and valleys of selling and how they related to the difference between "selling" and "partnering/ listening/serving the client's needs." He described two self-perpetuating systems, illustrated each possibility in each system with detailed stories, and then discussed how to get from one to the other. In the peaks, one makes a sale, then "all of a sudden you have the confidence, the enthusiasm, the aura of success about you that allows you to raise the interaction—the eye contact or chemistry or whatever—that allows you to take it to the next level. Part of that higher level is setting very businesslike conditions: If you hedge, if you candy-coat the tough issues, then you're not dealing in a businesslike manner with him. Then you're trying to sell him . . . ." This increased self-confidence allows the salesperson to effectively say no to unreasonable requests and even to confront the client with unresolved problems. It also allows the salesperson to recognize and take advantage of the rare exceptions to the normal procedures. And this, in turn leads to more sales, completing the system. He also described a reverse system in which loss of one sale leads to decreased self-confidence and to trying too hard, which leads to negative interactions with clients and to more lost sales. (CT A.7)

Links to Other Competencies

Analytical and Conceptual Thinking are often based on prior or concurrent Information Seeking.

They also imply a certain amount of intellectual or cognitive Initiative.

At least moderate levels of Conceptual or Analytical Thinking are necessary to support the higher levels of Interpersonal or Organizational Impact and Influence.

Conceptual and/or Analytical Thinking also support the higher levels of Customer Service Orientation and Technical Expertise, and are frequently involved in the innovative or entrepreneurial levels of Achievement Orientation.

TECHNICAL/PROFESSIONAL/MANAGERIAL EXPERTISE (EXP)

Expertise includes both the mastery of a body of job-related knowledge (which can be technical, professional, or managerial), and also the motivation to expand, use, and distribute work-related knowledge to others.

Expertise has also been called:

Legal Awareness

Product Knowledge

Expert-Helper Image

Diagnostic Skill

Commitment to Learning

There are four dimensions for the Technical/Professional/Managerial Expertise Scale (Table 8–3). Depth of Knowledge (A) is described in terms of formal educational degrees, although equivalent mastery through work experience or informal study is included at each level. Breadth (B) is the management and organization expertise necessary to manage or coordinate or integrate diverse people, organizational functions, and units to achieve common objectives. This expertise can be demonstrated in line, staff function, or team/project management roles (e.g., team/project leaders may coordinate work of others and be responsible for product delivery, schedule, and cost, but have no permanent reports).[3] Acquisition of Expertise (C) measures effort to maintain and acquire expertise, ranging from simple maintenance to extensive efforts to master new fields. The dimension Distribution of Expertise (D) is the intensity (and resulting scope) of the role of technical expert.

The Acquisition and Distribution of Expertise depend on motivation or disposition as much as on the technical knowledge involved. These two aspects of Expertise are crucial to translating technical knowledge into effective organizational results. Unless the individual has motivation to maintain and improve his or her technical knowledge, it quickly becomes outdated. Without the person's willingness to use and distribute knowledge, it is of little use to the organization.

Table 8–3 Technical/Professional/Managerial Expertise (EXP) Scale

Level	Behavioral Description

A. DEPTH OF KNOWLEDGE*

A. 1 *Primary.* Does simple, repetitive tasks that typically can be learned in a few hours to a few days. Examples: unskilled manual laborer, cleaner.

A. 2 *Elementary Vocational.* Does a variety of tasks that typically follow established sequences and require several weeks to a few months to become fully proficient. Examples: semiskilled manual laborer, entry level clerical position.

A. 3 *Vocational.* Does a variety of duties that require some planning and organizing for efficient completion; typically requires a high school education, or equivalent, and six months' to two years' experience. Examples: inventory control, technician support, secretarial work, credit and collection activities, logistics coordination, computer operation).

A. 4 *Advanced Vocational.* Does multiple, complex tasks at an advanced skill level, requiring careful planning and organizing to achieve end results. Typically requires specialized course training or job experience of about two to four years. Examples: technician, clerical supervisor, foreman.

A. 5 *Basic Professional.* Provides professional or management services (e.g., designs and implements formal programs or policies or provides leadership and expert advice to other managers and professionals). Usually requires formal education such as a college or entry level professional degree, or equivalent; or advanced vocational skills supplemented by several years' on-the-job experience. Examples: accountant, engineer, chemist, lawyer, junior manager, sales administrator.

A. 6 *Seasoned Professional.* Provides highly advanced or specialized professional or management services. Typically requires very extensive training (e.g., graduate degree: MD, JD, PhD) followed by several years of applied experience in a specialized or technical field. Examples: surgeon, tax attorney, department head, senior operational manager.

A. 7 *Professional/Specialized Mastery.* The primary result of the job is expertise or technical leadership that is considered authoritative in a technical or professional field within the organization. Examples: senior scientist, general manager, personnel director, CEO.

A. 8 *Preeminent Authority.* Nationally/internationally recognized authority in unusually complex professional or scientific field (e.g., chief scientist).

B. BREADTH OF MANAGERIAL EXPERTISE

B. 1 *None.* Individual contributor with no responsibility for coordinating or supervising the work of others.

B. 2 *Homogeneous Work Unit/Function*

Line: First-line supervisor of a work unit in which employees perform similar activities (e.g., supervisor of a production, clerical, or professional work group; area sales manager; retail store department)

Staff: Integrate related staff services (e.g., production planning, financial analysis, and planning)

Table 8–3 *(Continued)*

Level	Behavioral Description

Team/Project: Team/project leader within a homogeneous unit (e.g., lead operator, software development team leader).

B. 3 *Department/Heterogeneous/Cross-Function*

Line: Manages several work units or projects managed by subordinate supervisors (e.g., regional sales management, managing a small plant)

Staff: Manages function—finance, human resources—that impacts a business unit

Team/Project: Manages project team that includes members from several work units.

B. 4 *Several Departments/Heterogeneous Work Units*

Line: Manages a plant, district, or branch, including several departments or functions (e.g., finance, production, marketing, and human resources) managed by subordinate supervisors (e.g., district sales manager, CEO of small firm)

Staff: Integrates several staff functions (e.g., finance and administration, issues, or events that impact a business unit within a division

Team/Project: Coordinates large multidisciplinary team or projects managed by subordinate supervisors

B. 5 *Broad—Business Unit*

Line: Manages (President or General Manager) of a business unit, subsidiary within a division or group, CEO of moderate-size firm

Staff: manages function of a business, e.g., VP Finance, Marketing, Human Resources

Team/Project: manages major project or product at a business unit level coordinating R&D, production, finance, marketing, human resources

B. 6 *Broad—Division, Strategic Group of Businesses*

Line: Manages a division or group of businesses (president or executive vice president of large corporation), CEO of comparable-size firm

Staff: Corporate Headquarters or Business Development Executive Vice Presidents (EVPs) (Chief Financial, Information, etc. Officers, Marketing, Manufacturing, Human Resources, corporate strategic planning, mergers and acquisitions)

Team/Project: Manages huge ($100 + million) projects (e.g., military weapons acquisition)

B. 7 *Broad—Major Corporation CEO and COOs*

Manages large complex multi-division organization

C. ACQUISITION OF EXPERTISE

C. −1 *Resists.* Avoids adding to existing knowledge, or has "not-invented-here" syndrome. Resists new ideas, and techniques.

C. 0 *Neutral.* Is not concerned with adding to technical knowledge, but does not actively resist it either.

Table 8–3   *(Continued)*

Level	Behavioral Description
C. 1	*Maintains Current Technical Knowledge.* Makes self aware of the latest information, actively keeps skills up to date.
C. 2	*Expands Knowledge Base.* Acquires new information on smaller scale (i.e., new information on an existing project), exhibits active curiosity to discover new things, explores beyond one's immediate field.
C. 3	*Acquires New or Different Knowledge.* Makes major efforts to acquire new skills and knowledge, or maintains an extensive network of technical/professional contacts to keep abreast of the latest ideas.
D.	DISTRIBUTION OF EXPERTISE
D. −1	*Hoards.* Withholds technical knowledge, keeps technical improvements secret from colleagues.
D. 0	*Not Applicable.* Has no special knowledge to share.
D. 1	*Answers Questions.* Distributes current information in role as expert.
D. 2	*Applies Technical Knowledge to Achieve Additional Impact.* Goes beyond simply answering a question (i.e., to influence a client); or helps resolve others' technical problems.
D. 3	*Offers Technical Help.* Acts as a "floating consultant," offering personal expertise to improve performance, or resolve others' technical problems.
D. 4	*Advocates and Spreads New Technology.* Actively goes out as a technical missionary or change agent to spread new technology within the company.
D. 5	*Publishes New Technology.* Publishes articles on new technology or new methods in professional or technical journals.

*Although depth of knowledge is described in terms of formal educational degrees, equivalent mastery through work experience or informal study is included at each level.

Need for Power is likely to be the underlying motive of distribution of expertise, with personalized power at the negative, hoarding end of the scale and socialized power at the positive, sharing end.

Common behavioral indicators include:

■ Acts to keep skills and knowledge current
■ Shows curiosity by exploring beyond the immediate field
■ Volunteers to help others resolve technical problems
■ Takes courses or teaches self new subjects (related to work)
■ Actively goes out as a technical missionary or change agent to spread new technology:

Every day I try to learn something new about a product so that I always know something that no one else knows. (EXP C.1)

Somebody in the school was experimenting with an approach to language that I liked, so I went on relevant courses myself, to inform myself and read the appropriate literature. (EXP C.3)

I worked out a package on reenlistment and what I've done with it is send a copy to the Department of the Army and let them disseminate it to people who are interested in the kinds of things OE does. (EXP D.1)

I said "I'm acting as kind of a floating consultant; if any of you have problems at any point, take a break, grab me, and ask me to come down to your group." (EXP D.3)

I just love this new way to _____, make sure to introduce it to everyone, bring it up in conversations, buttonhole people to tell them about it. I caught Joe in the hallway this morning and told him all about it. And, it's so exciting, people are really starting to use this new method and it works for them! (EXP D.4)

Links to Other Competencies

Acquisition of Expertise (EXP C) is actually a special case of Information Seeking, and every level of Acquisition of Expertise implies a corresponding level of Information Seeking.

Acquisition of Expertise itself supports Distribution of Expertise (you can't distribute knowledge you don't have) and frequently (but not always) supports Analytical Thinking about technical problems, and higher levels of Achievement Orientation, especially activities involving innovation.

Distribution of Expertise (EXP D) may be used as a strategy for Impact and Influence, or to help establish Team Leadership. If the technical expertise is complex, then Analytical Thinking or Conceptual Thinking is required to support its acquisition and distribution.

Innovation (ACH C) may be involved in Distribution of Expertise, but a person can also distribute and champion innovations made by others.

NOTES

1. Winter, D. G., McClelland, D. C., & Stewart, A. J. (1981), *A new case for the liberal arts*, San Francisco: Jossey-Bass.
2. Fischer, K. W., Hand, H. H., & Russell, S. (1984), The development of abstractions in adolescence and adulthood. In M. L. Commons et al. (Eds.), *Beyond formal operations: Late adolescent and adult cognitive development*, New York: Praeger.
3. These two scales are adapted from the Hay job evaluation system. See Bellak, A. O. (1981), The Hay Guide Chart-Profile Method of Job Evaluation. In M. Rock (Ed.), *The compensation handbook* (2nd ed.), New York: McGraw-Hill. These scales are best evaluated outside the Behavioral Event Interview. They are included in the generic competencies as threshold requirements (needed for average as well as superior performance) and to facilitate comparisons between jobs for selection applications.

9

Personal Effectiveness

The Personal Effectiveness competencies share common characteristics rather than a type of intention. They all reflect some aspect of an individual's maturity in relation to others and to work. These competencies control the effectiveness of the individual's performance when dealing with immediate environmental pressures and difficulties. They support the effectiveness of other competencies in relation to the environment.

- Self-Control enables a person to maintain performance under stressful or hostile conditions.
- Self-Confidence allows a person to maintain performance against daunting challenges, skepticism, and indifference.
- Flexibility helps a person adapt his or her intentions to unforeseen circumstances.
- Organizational Commitment aligns a person's actions and intents with those of the organization.

SELF-CONTROL (SCT)

Self-control is the ability to keep emotions under control and to restrain negative actions when tempted, when faced with opposition or hostility from others, or when working under conditions of stress.

Self-Control is found most often in the low-level managerial jobs and in certain high-stress individual contributor positions. It is less often mentioned

by superior upper-level managers. This may be because executives face immediately stressful situations less often, or because by the time a person has
reached that level, Self-Control has become so ingrained that it is taken for
granted and is not entirely conscious. (The best executives don't talk about
Self-Control, they just use it).

Self-Control has been called:

Stamina

Resistance to Stress

Staying Calm

Being Not Easily Provoked

The dimension of the Self-Control Scale (Table 9-1) is intensity, and resulting scope of the control exerted, ranging from the individual's minimal control
of self by avoiding negative actions to controlling self in order to improve the
situation to controlling or calming others' reactions as well as his or her own.

Common behavioral indicators include:

- Is not impulsive
- Resists temptation to inappropriate involvements
- Remains calm in stressful situations

Table 9-1   Self-Control (SCT) Scale

Level	Behavioral Description
−1	*Loses Control.* Own emotions interfere with work effectiveness. Cites frustration and/or other negative emotions and expresses feelings inappropriately; or gets inappropriately involved personally with subordinates, peers, or clients; or "burns out" (breaks down) under stress.
0	*Avoids Stress.* Avoids people or situations that provoke negative emotions.
1	*Resists Temptation.* Resists the temptation to engage in inappropriate involvement or impulsive behavior.
2	*Controls Emotions.* Feels strong emotions, such as anger, extreme frustration, or stress; controls these emotions, but does not take constructive action.
3	*Responds Calmly.* Feels strong emotions, such as anger or extreme frustration; controls these emotions and continues discussion or other process fairly calmly.
4	*Manages Stress Effectively.* Uses stress management techniques to control response, prevent burnout, deal with ongoing stresses effectively.
5	*Responds Constructively.* Controls strong emotions or other stress and takes action to respond constructively to the source of the problems.
6	*Calms Others.* In very stressful situations, calms others as well as controlling own emotions.

- Finds acceptable outlets for stress
- Responds constructively to problems even under stress:

Some of my best friends are down in the shop, but you can't be good buddies that way and maintain credibility. (SCT 1)

I know I was getting red in the face because I was, you know, doing everything I could to restrain myself. . . . I didn't say or do a thing. (SCT 2)

I was really mad. But, you know, I had to restrain myself. I wanted to punch him in the nose. So I just said "Look, you know, this is what's happened. This is the process. This is where I think it's gone wrong. Given where we're at, how are we going to get out of this?" (SCT 5)

A boat was running around the harbor, and the crew was yelling at the boat I was on and cursing at us. I went over and said that we were going to conduct a boarding. One guy had a baseball bat; he said "We're going to kick your cans." This guy was rather large—about 6'3", and 250 pounds or so. He had two other people with him who were cursing at us and yelling. I was trying to think of a way to get on board and to calm the situation down. At that point, I left to get my side-handled baton; I was thinking it would be easier to block a blow if I had it. As we returned to do the boarding, I was talking to the people with me about how we were going to get on board. I told one person to watch the crowd so I could concentrate on the individuals on the boat. I told another person that we were going to board the boat together and I wanted him to be careful and keep alert. The man with the baseball bat kept yelling at us. I said "Calm down." I calmed myself down and tried to get him to calm down, too. And he did calm down a little bit. It ended up as a successful boarding. (SCT 6)

Links to Other Competencies

Self-Control is linked more strongly to the situation than to other competencies. It is sometimes seen in combination with Directiveness (in confronting poor performance) and with Impact and Influence or Teamwork (in directing group interactions).

SELF-CONFIDENCE (SCF)

Self-Confidence is a person's belief in his or her own capability to accomplish a task. This includes the person's expressing confidence in dealing with increasingly challenging circumstances, in reaching decisions or forming opinions, and in handling failures constructively.

Self-Confidence is a component of most models of superior performers. Whether self-confidence is an independent variable or an outcome is arguable: Is someone successful because they have self-confidence or do they have self-confidence because they are successful? Both may be the case, in a positive self-perpetuating cycle.

Self-Confidence is also called:

Decisiveness

Ego Strength

Independence

Strong Self-Concept

Willingness to Take Responsibility (Especially for B scale)

The main dimension of the Self-Confidence Scale (Table 9–2) is intensity (A) measured by how much challenge or risk the individual has the confidence to face, ranging from simple independent functioning in ordinary work situations to taking on extremely risky tasks or challenging the boss or clients. Dealing with Failure (B) is a unique dimension that combines taking personal responsibility with correctable causes of failures.

Dealing with Failure is related to learned helplessness and learned optimism described by Peterson and Seligman.[1] Seligman et al. have found that (1) external, (2) specific or limited, and (3) temporary explanations of negative events predict mental health, success in sales, and other positive outcomes. Our findings for most sales positions agree with Seligman's findings. For managers and some consultative sales positions, we separate the internal/external dimension from the other two dimensions. In management jobs, having an internal (but specific and temporary) explanatory style characterizes superior performers. The best managers see failures as due to specific, correctable mistakes that they made, and take action to avoid repetition of those mistakes or to correct the problems caused. In sales and other jobs where repeated failures or rejections are inevitable, attributing many of those failures to external factors characterizes superior performers and may protect against burnout and depression.

Frequency of explanations of negative events may also distinguish average from superior performers. Peterson suggests that the healthiest style is to make few or no attributions of any kind ("never explain").[2] In sales jobs with very high rates of rejection, superior performers simply describe unsuccessful sales attempts and then go straight on to talk about what they did next; whereas average performers keep returning to the question of why they lost that sale, offering different possibilities or repeating themselves.

Common behavioral descriptions of Self-Confidence include:

■ Makes or acts on decisions in spite of disagreement from others
■ Presents self in a forceful or impressive manner
■ States confidence in own judgment or ability
■ States own position clearly and confidently in conflicts with superiors

Table 9–2   Self-Confidence (SCF) Scale

Level	Behavioral Description

A. SELF-ASSURANCE

A. −1   *Powerless.* Asserts lack of confidence, questions own ability in a generalized way or expresses "powerlessness" or helplessness. Avoids disapproval or conflict (with detrimental impact on job performance). Has notably weak self-presentation, is "wimpy."

A. 0   *Not Applicable, or Avoids Challenges.* Defers to others. Lacks confidence.

A. 1   *Presents Self Confidently.* Makes decisions independently. Works without constant supervision.

A. 2   *Presents Self Forcefully or Impressively.* Makes or acts on decisions in spite of disagreement from others, or outside area of explicit authority. [If the others who disagree are superiors or clients, or if the action involves breaking rules in order to get the job done, score at level 5.]

A. 3   *States Confidence in Own Ability.* Sees self as an expert, compares self or own abilities favorably with others. Sees self as causal agent, prime mover, catalyst, originator. States confidence in own judgment.

A. 4   *Justifies Self-Confident Claims.* States own position clearly in conflicts. Actions support or justify verbal expression of self-confidence.

A. 5   *Volunteers for Challenges.* Is pleased or excited about challenging assignments. Seeks additional responsibility.

Expresses disagreement with management or clients tactfully or politely, states own position clearly and confidently in conflicts with superiors.

A. 6   *Puts Self in Extremely Challenging Situations.* Confronts management or clients bluntly, or chooses to take on extremely challenging tasks.

B. DEALING WITH FAILURE

B. −2   *Blames Self in a Global, Permanent Way.* Makes personal/internal explanations with a tone of "this is the way I am" as opposed to "this is the mistake I made." Any personal or internal attributions that convey a sense of helplessness, inability to change, or permanence about them score here. [Scoring note: Any indication of intention to change, strategies for change, "I'll never do that again," or "next time I'll . . . ." will disqualify an example from this category.]

B. −1   *Rationalizes or Blames Others or Circumstances for Failure.* This indicator is characteristic of superior performers in sales positions and some other jobs involving high frequency of failure. May see self as victim.

B. 0   *Not Applicable, or Not Observed.*

B. 1   *Accepts Responsibility.* Admits failures or shortcomings in a specific, nonglobal way: "I misjudged the situation."

B. 2   *Learns from Own Mistakes.* Analyzes own performance to understand failures, and to improve future performance. Explanations scoring here must be correctable: Personality characteristics such as "because I'm shy," "I'm careless" score here *only if there is explicit mention of ways to improve performance* (see Levels −2, −1, and +1 for explanations without mention of ways to improve.)

B. 3   *Admits Own Mistakes to Others and Acts to Correct Problems.*

- Takes personal responsibility for mistakes, failures, or shortcomings
- Learns from mistakes, analyzes own performance to understand failures and to improve future performance:

I think what happened (with a lost account) because the competition was so solid, we sort of lost touch with (the operations manager)—and I don't care who it is, you have to have that personal touch. The competition must have been there stroking the guy, this rep must have worked two or three years on him, along the time where we gave him the bad film deal. This guy was burned, and then I came along and I'm a nice guy and the guy likes me but he runs his numbers. I mean, anybody crunches numbers any way they want, and he crunched them against us. (SCF B.−1: A superior salesperson)

You might call me a bossy old . . . , but the staff and kids didn't know what to do, and (in that situation) I had to take over. (SCF A.2)

I had the data, knew I was right, so felt fine telling the boss she was dead wrong on this one. (SCF A.5)

The beneficiary got very annoyed with the bank and made a complaint. I was wrong. I should have followed up on it. The Operations Department should have followed up on it too, but I can't put the blame on them, because the first responsibility was with me. Since then I make sure to follow up on that sort of thing. (SCF B.2)

(Addressing boss) Well, if you're too busy to go down to the customers in the next two days, you can kiss a $150-million hardware job goodbye. (SCF A.6)

In a spectacular demonstration of self-confidence, one of our subjects interrupted the interview to say that he had to go off and finish a critical experiment, the results of which were to be reported to management 40 minutes later. When asked about the time crunch, he said, "Oh, I know it's going to work." A half an hour later, he returned and said calmly that it did work and that "it solved a big problem for management." (SCF A.6)

Links to Other Competencies

Self-Confidence and Dealing with Failure do not appear to be linked to specific competencies, but rather to support the continued and effective use of all competencies.

FLEXIBILITY (FLX)

Flexibility is the ability to adapt to and work effectively with a variety of situations, individuals, or groups. It is the ability to understand and appreciate different and opposing perspectives on an issue, to adapt an approach as the requirements of a situation change, and to change or easily accept changes in one's own organization or job requirements.

Flexibility enables the superior performer to adapt other skills and competencies to the needs of the situation. The foundation is the ability to objectively perceive the situation, including the viewpoints of others. Flexibility is also called:

Adaptability

Ability to Change

Perceptual Objectivity (especially for Level +1)

Staying Objective

Resilience

The Flexibility Scale (Table 9–3) has two dimensions: Breadth of Change (A) ranges from own opinions to adapting organizational strategy; Speed of Action (B) ranges from slow to instantaneous.

Common behavioral indicators include:

- Recognizes the validity of opposing viewpoints
- Adapts easily to changes at work
- Flexibly applies rules or procedures, depending on the individual situation, to accomplish organization's larger objectives
- Changes own behavior or approach to suit the situation:

I was disappointed, because I thought it was clear-cut from an economic standpoint. But when management disagreed, I felt there must be some reasoning behind their decision, and that we needed to look at other alternatives. (FLX A.1)

(After painstakingly negotiating an independent study program with a student) She called me up and said "I'm not going to be able to do this; I really don't think I can complete this project independently." She wondered whether she could wait and do this project in connection with a class I would be offering in a later quarter. Well, I was interested in the fact that she had identified the possible class, and that she had contacted me, and didn't just let the whole project go. So I said, "All right, we can do it that way." And the next quarter she did indeed sign up for the class. (FLX A.2, B.4)

(Partway through a sales presentation) I found that they had literally chopped out pieces of the presentation rather than bring the whole thing. So I had to start building function into the presentation right in the middle of it. They were surprised how successful we were in spite of all the disaster. (FLX A.3, B.5)

If you give him a whole lot of things that most Executive Officers (XO) have to do, he drops the ball a lot. So, that, plus taking into consideration that they have reduced the time-in-service requirements from a Second Lieutenant to First

Table 9–3   Flexibility (FLX) Scale

Level	Behavioral Description

A. BREADTH OF CHANGE

A. –1   *Counterproductively Sticks to Own Opinion/Tactics/Approach.* Despite obvious problems, retains same point of view; does not recognize others' views as valid.

A.   0   *Always Follows Procedures.*

A.   1   *Sees Situation Objectively.* Recognizes the validity of others' viewpoints.

A.   2   *Flexibly Applies Rules or Procedures.* Depending on the individual situation, adapts actions to accomplish organization's larger objectives. Pinch-hits by doing co-workers' tasks as necessary during an emergency.

A.   3   *Adapts Tactics to Situation or to Other's Response.* Changes own behavior or approach to suit the situation.

A.   4   *Adapts Own Strategies, Goals, or Projects to Situations.*

A.   5   *Makes Organizational Adaptations.* Makes smaller or short-term adaptations in own or client company in response to the needs of the situation.

A.   6   *Adapts Strategies.* Makes large or long-term adaptations in own or client company in response to the needs of the situation. (This level implies various Influence competencies, and possibly Managerial, Cognitive, or Achievement competencies.)

B. SPEED OF ACTION

B.   1   *Long-Term, Considered, or Planned Changes* (over a month).

B.   2   *Short-Term Plan to Change* (1 week–1 month).

B.   3   *Fast Change* (less than a week). This is the default score if the example has an unclear time frame.

B.   4   *Quick Changes* (within a day).

B.   5   *Instantaneous Action or Decision to Act.* "Turns on a dime."

Lieutenant to Captain, whereas, it used to take four and a half years to make Captain, it now only takes three from the time that you come into the Army. I thought about it and said, "Well, a lot of Lieutenants are going to get screwed, because they are going to make Captain and they're going to be expected to know a lot more than what they know. So I took one Platoon Leader and made him Motor Officer, which is an XO duty. I took another Platoon Leader and made him Squad Officer, which is another XO duty. Took another Platoon Leader, made him Physical Security Officer, NBC Officer, which is, again, XO's duty. And, just pretty much made the XO sort of Chief of Staff to keep touch on all these other guys. (FLX A.5, B.1)

Links to Other Competencies

Flexibility (A.1) is a prerequisite for moderate and higher levels of Interpersonal Understanding and for Customer Service when the speaker's attitudes or interests are in conflict with those of others, or when the others are from a different cultural background.

Flexibility supports effective Impact and Influence and the managerial competencies.

ORGANIZATIONAL COMMITMENT (OC)

Organizational Commitment is the individual's ability and willingness to align his or her own behavior with the needs, priorities, and goals of the organization, to act in ways that promote organizational goals or meet organizational needs. It may appear as putting organizational mission before own preferences, or before professional role priorities.

Organizational Commitment appears often in staff positions, where there may be an implicit conflict between a person's professional identity and the organization's direction. It also appears in organizations with strong missions (the military, schools).

The ability to find a new direction for an organization is not included in this competency. Creating a new vision is a unique combination of Conceptual Thinking and socialized power motivation. Implementing the new vision involves Team Leadership, the Authoritative Managerial style plus other competencies as needed.[3]

Organizational Commitment has also been called:

Businessmindedness

Mission Orientation

Vision

Commitment to the Command's Mission

The Organizational Commitment Scale has a single dimension (Table 9–4) of intensity of commitment, measured as the size of the sacrifices made for the organization's benefit, ranging from showing up on time, and dressing and behaving appropriately to getting others (usually the individual's department) to join in sacrificing their department's good for the overall organization's benefit.

Common behavioral indicators include:

- Being willing to help colleagues complete their tasks
- Aligning own activities and priorities to meet organizational needs
- Understanding need for cooperation to achieve larger organization objectives
- Choosing to meet organizational needs rather than to pursue professional interests:

Table 9–4 Organizational Commitment (OC) Scale

Level	Behavioral Description
−1	*Disregards.* Disregards or rebelliously flaunts organizational norms.
0	*Not Applicable, or Minimal Effort.* Makes minimal effort to fit in or does the minimum required to keep the job.
1	*Active Effort.* Makes an active effort to fit in, dress appropriately, and respects organizational norms.
2	*Models "Organizational Citizenship Behaviors."* Shows loyalty, willingness to help colleagues complete their tasks, respect for the wishes of those in authority.
3	*Sense of Purpose—States Commitment.* Understands and actively supports organization mission and goals; aligns own activities and priorities to meet organizational needs; understands need for cooperation to achieve larger organization objectives.
4	*Makes Personal or Professional Sacrifices.* Puts organizational needs before personal needs; makes personal sacrifices to meet the organization's needs over professional identity and preferences and family concerns.
5	*Makes Unpopular Decisions.* Stands by decisions that benefit the organization even if they are unpopular or controversial.
6	*Sacrifices Own Unit's Good for Organization.* Sacrifices own department's short-term good for long-term good of organization (e.g., volunteers cost reductions or layoffs in own group, takes on extra tasks, etc.); asks others to make sacrifices to meet larger organization's needs.

(Commanding Officer of Navy hospital) My feeling is that the active-duty military man comes first in this business—that, notwithstanding the prestigious retired people we have, my priority is the young Navy man or woman who comes in sick. He or she should receive first-class treatment. I made some efforts to change a couple of things to see that this would happen. One of the things I did was to establish a Military Medicine service, which combined the physical-examination section, the military sick call, and the immunization sections, in order to give the active population better service and to reduce the time that they spent away from work. (OC 3)

(Researcher) The three of us realized we could not spend a year in a test program, because of the business needs. For political reasons, we knew that _____ could keep the wolves away from us for three to four months. Beyond that point the justification for doing research would be outweighed by the production needs. [This, even though the researcher would have loved to do a very complete research test program. (OC 4)]

I made a rather controversial decision and I took one of our _____ people and I turned her in to a global _____ specialist. Everyone was going, "Well, why did you do that? We really don't need it." I sent her to London and this guy D.N. is saying, "Do you know how much that is going to cost you?" So she goes to London and comes back. And now she has got some credibility. This year I sent her on a month trip around the world. My people here are bitching. Yet the only place that our international effort is bearing fruit, according to _____ is here. (OC 5)

Links to Other Competencies

At the higher levels (3 and up) Organizational Commitment is supported by Conceptual Thinking (to understand and make connections to the organization's mission), Flexibility (to adapt personal priorities and strategies to fit the organization), and for levels 5 and 6, *Self-Confidence* to stick by unpopular decisions.

Levels 5 and 6 are partially related to job size: Up to that point Organizational Commitment may be shown in most positions.

Organizational Commitment generally does not support specific competencies: It makes the connection between the individual's efforts and the organization's needs.

OTHER PERSONAL CHARACTERISTICS AND COMPETENCIES

The generic competencies discussed so far cover 80 to 95 percent of the distinguishing characteristics of superior performance in most jobs studied. The remaining competencies fall into three general categories: unique behaviors expressing generic competencies; competencies we see repeatedly but not often enough to become generic competencies, and competencies that are truly unique to a specific job or type of job.

Some of the more common unique competencies are:

- *Occupational Preference.* Really enjoying one's job, getting a kick out of it
- *Accurate Self-Assessment.* Knowing one's own strengths and weaknesses and using the strengths effectively while compensating for weaknesses
- *Affiliative Interest.* Genuine interest in and enjoyment of other people (found in good teachers and client-relationship managers)
- *Writing Skills.* Ability to write well
- *Visioning.* Ability to create a new understanding of an organization's mission, think up a new vision for a group
- *Upward Communications.* Keeping one's boss informed of all important developments, bad as well as good news
- *Concrete Style of Learning and Communicating.* Learning by direct hands-on experience, communicating by provision of direct experience, demonstrations, and so on

- *Low Fear of Rejection.* Not feeling concern if others dislike him/her
- *Thoroughness.* Showing completeness and attention to detail

Some of the more unusual competencies are:

- Resists encroachment on own area of responsibility (Army Junior Officers)
- Unconflicted Use of Position and Symbolic Power: Explicitly pulls rank to overcome resistance (Army Junior Officers)
- Sets up mechanisms to obtain feedback (school principals)
- Legal Awareness: Aware of laws and the limits of legal authority, approaches boardings in a way to build an airtight legal case (Coast Guard Boarding Officers)
- Security Conscious: Aware of possible threats of robbery, takes action to secure premises (bank managers)
- Has stable relationship with an independent partner/spouse/girlfriend (deckhands on river boats)
- Sense of humor (nurses)
- Respects confidentiality of personal information (nurses, bankers)
- Dynamic Structural Visualization: Constructs and manipulates three-dimensional mental images with great detail (creative research scientists)
- Broad-Based Technical Knowledge: Draws on oddly assorted disciplines rather than a single specialty (creative research scientists).

These special, unusual competencies are very interesting, may be critical to certain jobs, and can be discovered through interviews.

NOTES

1. Seligman, M. (1991), *Learned optimism,* New York: Knopf; Peterson, C., Seligman, M. E., & Vaillant, G. E. (1988), Pessimistic explanatory style is a risk factor for physical illness: A thirty-five-year longitudinal study, *Journal of Personality and Social Psychology, 55*(1), 23–27.
2. Zullow, H. M., Oettingen, G., Peterson, C., & Seligman, M. E. (1988), Pessimistic explanatory style in the historical record, *American Psychologist, 43*(9), 673–682.
3. For more details on creating new organizational vision, see Kelner, S. P. (1992), *Visionary leadership workshop,* Boston: McBer.

III

Developing a Model

10

Designing
Competency Studies

This chapter describes three alternative methods for the design of competency studies:

A. The classic study design using criterion samples

B. A short study design using expert panels

C. Studies of single incumbent and future jobs where there are not enough jobholders to offer samples of superior and average performance

PREPARATORY WORK

Prior to beginning competency research, an organization needs to identify jobs to be studied—ideally jobs that have high value in relation to the organization's strategic plans and structure for carrying out those plans. Analysis of these factors is usually done by reviewing business plans and interviewing leadership.

Defining Organizational Strategy

This process refers to the steps an organization takes to identify its goals and critical success factors and to develop strategic plans for reaching the goals. For example, if Company X identifies strategic business unit Y as a significant source of much of the firm's future growth, the presumption is that the growth depends on the firm's ability to attract, develop, and retain innovative technical managers with entrepreneurial skills for unit Y.

Organizational Structure/Design

This factor refers to how the firm will organize itself to carry out its plans, with the emphasis on identifying critical jobs. Critical jobs are those value-added "make or break" positions held by the people who will make the biggest difference in whether the firm succeeds. Typically these are the jobs that define strategy and direction, or carry responsibility for achieving major strategic outcomes, for controlling critical resources (labor, capital, and technology) or for managing relationships with key markets or customers. Competency studies (and human resource management in general) are most cost-effective when they focus on these "value added" jobs.

This preparatory step is most critical for full-scale classic studies (Method A), which are relatively expensive. Expert panel based studies (Method B) are more suitable for analysis of large numbers of less critical jobs.

STEPS IN THE CLASSIC COMPETENCY STUDY DESIGN

This section presents the full-scale classic version of a competency study. Variations for expert panels and single-incumbent or future jobs are discussed near the end of this chapter.

Classic competency studies include the six steps shown in Figure 10–1:

1. Define performance effectiveness criteria.
2. Identify a criterion sample.
3. Collect data.
4. Analyze data and develop a competency model.
5. Validate the competency model.
6. Prepare applications of the competency model.

A full competency study takes two to three months, depending on the logistics of scheduling and conducting the Behavioral Event Interviews (BEIs), and takes about 30 person-days. A rule of thumb is to budget one and a half person-days per BEI: a half day to conduct the BEI, a half day to code it, and an additional half for concept formation, report writing, and project administration.

Step 1. Define Performance Effectiveness Criteria

The first and most important step in a competency study is to identify the criteria or measures that define superior or effective performance in the job to be studied. Ideal criteria are "hard" outcome measures, such as sales or profit data for business managers, or patents and publications for research scientists.

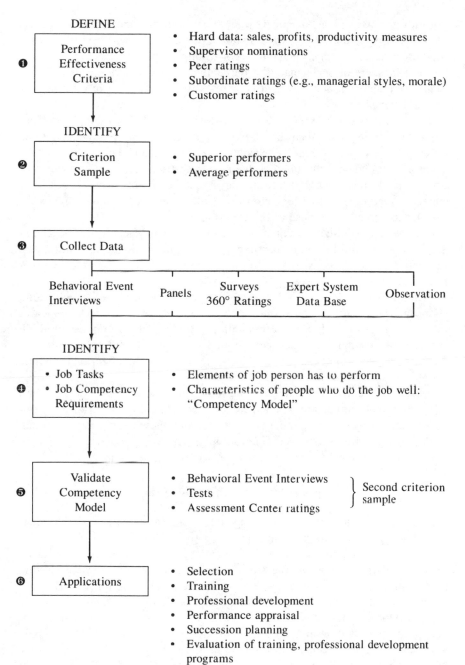

Figure 10–1 Job Competency Assessment Process

For military officers, good criteria would be unit performance outcomes, such as combat inspection scores or reenlistment rates. For human service workers, the best criteria are *client* outcomes. For example, for alcoholism counselors, the best measure of performance is percentage of clients who are still "dry," regularly employed, and have had no arrests for drunkenness in the year following counseling.

Sometimes it is necessary to develop criteria for a job. For example, to identify effective doctors, a measure of accurate diagnosis and treatment could be developed. A panel of expert physicians would evaluate the symptoms of a group of patients and formulate a diagnosis and treatment plan. A sample of doctors could then be asked to examine the same patients. The criterion for superior doctors would be how close their diagnoses and treatment plans for this group agreed with those of the experts.

Competitive simulations can also be used as performance criteria. An example would be military units participating in highly realistic war games. The leaders of units that consistently win mock battles could be considered superior officers.

If hard criteria aren't available, nominations or ratings by bosses, peers, subordinates, and/or customers and clients can be used. Research[1] indicates that peer ratings have high criterion validity, that is, they do predict hard job performance outcomes. Studies consistently show that the subordinates of superior managers report higher morale, as measured by organizational climate or job satisfaction surveys.[2]

Defining effectiveness criteria—and the *right* effectiveness criteria—for a job is extremely important. A competency model based on superior performers cannot be any better than the criteria on which these people were selected. If the wrong criteria are used (for example, personal popularity instead of performance), the model will identify the wrong competencies.

Step 2. Identify a Criterion Sample

The job effectiveness criteria or ratings developed in Step 1 are used to identify a clear group of superstars and a comparison group of average performers. A third group of poor (ineffective or incompetent) performers can also be identified if the purpose of the study is to establish competency levels that predict minimal success in a job (e.g., to set a cut-off score for hiring).

In some organizations, it is politically impossible to get a sample of people doing a poor job. Supervisors insist that "there's no such thing as a bad officer," that "poor doctors don't work at this hospital," or that they "fire people who perform badly." Sometimes it is even difficult to get people to identify average colleagues. When told "all of our people are good," the interviewer can agree gently, but say, "Yes, but some must be especially outstanding— who are the *best?*"

The hard criteria and nominations and ratings gathered in Step 1 are invaluable in identifying a good criterion sample. Nominations all but force identification of two or three top people. The best way to be absolutely sure you have identified the best superstars is to use several criteria and select only those people who are rated highly on all the criteria.

Some employees come out well on hard criteria such as sales, but are so insensitive or politically naive that they anger their managers or co-workers. Others may be rated highly on the basis of their personality but really don't like their jobs. These people are not likely to get promoted or even keep their jobs. The real superstar is someone who does well on all the hard criteria *and* who the boss perceives as a "comer" *and* who is genuinely liked and respected by co-workers, subordinates, and customers.

Sometimes the real stars are those who do well on two different criteria. For example, some Navy officers achieved high inspection scores by working their people so hard that most of them left the service as soon as the ship returned to port. During periods when the Navy has severe personnel shortages, a very important measure of a good officer is the unit retention rate— the number of sailors working for the officer who choose to stay in the service. The real mark of a superstar Navy officer is top scores on all inspections *and* a crew with high morale and retention. If an officer was high on both these measures *and* was rated highly promotable by his or her boss, the officer was put in the superstar group.

Ideally, each job study sample should include at least 20 subjects: 12 superior and eight average performers. This number permits simple statistical tests of hypotheses about competencies (such as t-tests, chi-square, ANOVA, or Discriminant Function Analysis of the difference between mean level of competence shown by superior versus average subjects). Smaller nonstatistical samples (e.g., six superior and three average performers) can provide valuable qualitative data on the expression of competencies in a given organization, such as *how* influence is used effectively in a specific job. Small samples should include two superior performers for every 1.5 average performers. A rule of competency research is "you always learn most from your superstars."

Step 3. Collect Data

Data collection methods vary according to which style of competency model is being used. Six data collection sources and methods are used to develop classic competency models: (a) behavioral event interviews, (b) expert panels, (c) surveys, (d) competency model database "expert system," (e) job function/ task analysis, and (f) direct observation. Here is a description of each collection method and its advantages and disadvantages.

Data Type (a) Behavioral Event Interviews.   Superior and average performers are interviewed using the in-depth "Behavioral Event Interview (BEI)" technique developed by David C. McClelland, a professor of psychology at Harvard University, and colleagues at McBer and Company.[3]

The BEI is derived from Flanagan's Critical Incident Method.[4] "Critical Incident" interviews ask people to identify and describe the most critical situations they have encountered on their jobs. The interviewer asks what the situation or task was, who was involved, what the interviewee did, and what the result or outcome was.

McClelland's BEI method goes beyond Flanagan's in important ways. The BEI method includes "thematic apperception test (TAT)" probes that yield data about the interviewees' personality and "cognitive style" (e.g., what they *think about, feel,* and *want* to accomplish in dealing with the situation). This enables interviewers to measure competencies such as achievement motivation or logical ways of thinking and solving problems.

Flanagan's method, like job task analysis, identifies aspects of the *job.* McClelland's BEI method identifies the *competencies* needed to do the job *well.* Asking people to focus on the most critical situations they have faced produces data on the most important skills and competencies. Interviewees tell vivid "short stories" about how they handled the toughest, most important parts of their jobs, and, in doing so, reveal their competencies to do the job.

Advantages of the BEI Method

- *Empirical Identification of Competencies Beyond or Different from Those Generated by Other Data Collection Methods.* BEI data are by far the most valuable for validating competency hypotheses generated by other methods and for discovering *new* competencies.

- *Precision about How Competencies Are Expressed.* This refers not only to the "use of influence" but to how influence is used to deal with specific situation in a specific organization's political climate.

- *Identification of Algorithms.* BEI data can show exactly how superior performers handle specific job tasks or problems. For example, the Navy wanted to help officers handle race-relations issues. The BEI method was used to ask superior and average officers to describe the toughest race relations incidents they had faced. Analysis of about 60 stories of volatile situations revealed eight specific actions superstar officers took either to avoid racial conflicts or to deal with them quickly, fairly, and effectively. These action steps could then be taught to other officers.

- *Freedom from Racial, Gender, and Cultural Bias.* The BEI approach has been adopted by many organizations because it is predictively valid without being biased against minority candidates.[5]

- *Generation of Data for Assessment, Training, and Career Pathing.* Behavioral event interviews provide very specific descriptions of effective and ineffective job behaviors that can show and teach others what to do—and what not to do—on the job. A significant by-product of these interviews is a wealth of lively short stories about job situations and problems that can be used to develop relevant case studies, simulations, and role plays for training. Interviewees' career paths can be mapped and some estimate made of when, where, and how they acquired key competencies.

Disadvantages of the BEI Method

- *Time and Expense.* A properly conducted BEI effectively takes a person-day to conduct and analyze: one-and-a-half to two hours to conduct, plus three to analyze. Transcription costs average $100.
- *Expertise Requirements.* Interviewers must be trained and "calibrated" and receive quality control feedback to get good data.
- *Missed Job Tasks.* Because the BEI focuses on *critical* job incidents, BEI data may miss less important but still relevant aspects of a job.
- *Impractical for Analysis of Many Jobs.* Labor time, expense, and expertise requirements make BEI studies impractical for analyzing a large number of jobs.

Data Type (b) Expert Panels. A panel of experts is asked to brainstorm personal characteristics employees need to perform the job at an adequate (minimally acceptable, or threshold, level) and a superior level.

These experts can be supervisors for the positions being studied, superstar performers in the job, or outside experts, perhaps human resource professionals who know the job well. (Average incumbents should not be included in these panels because, by definition, they do not know what it takes for superior performance.) The expert panel prioritizes the characteristics according to importance to job success.

Advantages of Expert Panels

- Quick and efficient collection of a great deal of valuable data.
- Panel members become knowledgeable in competency concepts, assessment methods, and variables; and their involvement can develop consensus about and support for study findings.

Disadvantages of Expert Panels

- *Possible Identification of Folklore or Motherhood Items.* Such items sound good and reflect the traditions of the organization but do not predict competent performance. For example, while senior military leaders strongly believed that "moral courage" was extremely important to be a good officer, BEI interviews indicated otherwise. In over a thousand critical incidents of Army and Navy officers, making a moral or ethical choice was mentioned only a few times. The officers did not have to face moral issues very often, did not find these decisions critical in doing their jobs, or (what the study indicated) perceived them to be *managerial* rather than moral issues. A variant of the BEI method was used to find out just what ethical and moral competencies military officers actually used. Instead of the usual procedure of letting interviewees focus on what *they* thought were their most critical job incidents, this time interviewees were asked to tell about the hardest moral or ethical decision they had to make in their career. Analysis of those incidents again showed that *management* competencies were the real issue.

■ *Omission of Critical Competency Factors for Which Panel Members Lack Psychological or Technical Vocabulary.* For example, superior furniture salespeople have a competency called "eliciting visual and tactile imagery," which means they think in terms of color (mauve, taupe, rust) and textures (nubby, silky, scratchy). They also get their customers to think in these terms and thus can steer the prospect to specific pieces of furniture. Expert panel members may not know a concept such as "eliciting imagery" and hence would miss this important competency.

Experience indicates that experts' hypotheses about the competencies needed to do a job are about 50 percent accurate, when compared with BEI data. Experts suggest competencies that are not validated by BEI data 25 percent of the time, and also miss competencies found in analysis of BEI data 25 percent of the time. For this reason, competencies are best verified by BEI or direct observation data.

Data Type (c) Surveys.   Expert panel members and others in the organization rate competency items (competencies or behavioral indicators) according to importance in effective job performance, how frequently the competency is required, and the like.

Typically, a survey focuses on specific skills one at a time and asks:

1. *How much the skill distinguishes superior from average performers.* For example, since achievement orientation distinguishes superstar from average salespeople, this would be an important competency to select for or teach potential salespeople.

2. *Whether failure is likely if employees don't have the skill.* For example, honesty and basic numeracy are important competencies for bank tellers.

3. *How reasonable it is to expect new hires to have this characteristic.* For example, specific product knowledge might be essential for a high tech salesperson, but it is not realistic to expect many applicants to have this proprietary knowledge.

4. *Whether the skill can be developed.* Achievement Orientation and initiative are hard to develop, for example, while specific product knowledge is easier to teach.

Analysis of the ratings of performance characteristics statistically provides a numerical ranking of skills according to importance in superior performance and to the likelihood that they will be priorities for human resource selection, training or job design efforts.

Guidelines for Developing Competency Survey Items

- Identify behaviors or characteristics of jobholder, not job tasks.
- Provide short, simple descriptions; no more than 100.
- Respondents should be managers of people doing the job, *superior* performers in the job, and outside experts who know the job well.

Advantages of Surveys

- This method facilitates quick and cheap collection of sufficient data for statistical analyses. Large numbers of jobs can be studied efficiently and at different times to identify trends in competency requirements.
- Filling out a survey permits many employees to have an input and builds consensus for study findings.

Disadvantages of Surveys

- Data are limited to items and concepts included in the survey and therefore often miss competencies not included by those who constructed the survey. Surveys cannot identify new competencies or provide detailed information about the nuances of competency expressed by different people in different parts of the organization. Survey data may reinforce folklore or motherhood competencies not predictive of performance.
- The method can be inefficient. Surveys often ask the same 100 questions of everyone from the CEO to the janitor, when only a subset of items is relevant to the job being studied.

Data Type (d) Computer-Based "Expert" Systems. A computerized expert system can pose questions to researchers, managers, or other experts. These questions are keyed to an extensive knowledge base of competencies identified by previous studies. The expert system manages the analysis process and provides a detailed description of competencies required for adequate and superior job performance. (The design of competency-based expert systems is discussed in greater detail in Chapter 23.)

Advantages of Expert Systems

- *Access to Data.* Access to several hundred competency studies in the data base can provide comparison data for reality-testing competencies suggested by other data collection methods (e.g., filling in competencies found in previous studies of a job when missed by a current study).
- *Efficiency.* Serving as "smart" questionnaires, expert systems quickly narrow questions to those relevant to the job being analyzed, rather than eliciting answers on all questions from all respondents as surveys do.
- *Productivity.* Expert systems analyses can provide in a hour what other competency study methods require days or weeks to produce. Expert systems do not require highly trained experts, saving labor time and expense.

Disadvantages of Expert Systems

- Data depend on the accuracy of responses to questions (i.e., expert systems are subject to "garbage in → garbage out" problems). This is also true of panels, surveys, and other data sources, but the computerized expert system may be more vulnerable when used in an unsupervised setting.
- The method may overlook specialized competencies not in the data base. Like questionnaires, expert systems can find only those competencies that have been programmed in. They cannot discover new competencies or organization-specific nuances of known competencies.
- Costs of system hardware and software may be prohibitive (although with personal computers, these costs rarely exceed three days of specialist consultant time).

Data Type (e) Job Task/Function Analysis.   Employees or observers list in great detail each task, function, or action the jobholder performs in a given period of time. Data are collected using written questionnaires, time logs, individual or panel interviews, or direct observation.

Advantages of Job Task/Function Analyses

- Produces very complete job descriptions useful for job design, compensation analysis, and by inference, some competency analysis. For example, specification of the technical tasks required in a job can be used to deduce the cognitive skills needed for the job.
- Provides data to meet Uniform Guidelines on Employee Selection Procedures regulations,[6] which some interpret to require survey information on the frequency and importance of job tasks.

■ Can validate or elaborate on data collected by other methods. Job task/function analysis can serve as a useful check of evidence from BEIs. If a job task does not show up naturally in BEI data, subsequent BEIs can ask about this task. For example, paperwork is part of a salesperson's job, but few salespeople ever mention it in their critical incidents. Superstars particularly tell stories almost entirely about *selling*. If a sales training group wanted more information about the competencies salespeople need to keep their paperwork straight, a BEI question could ask for an example of when doing—or not doing—the paperwork connected with the job made a real difference in performance.

Disadvantages of Job Task/Function Analyses

■ Provides characteristics of the *job* rather than those of the *people* who do the job well.

■ Task lists tend to be too detailed (e.g., 3,002 motions needed to drive a car) to be practical and do not separate the truly important tasks from the routine activities.

Data Type (f) Direct Observation. Employees are directly observed performing (critical) job tasks, and their behaviors are coded for competencies.

Advantage of Direct Observation

■ A good way to identify or check competencies suggested by panel, survey, and behavioral event interview data. For example, survey data suggested that military leaders who permitted "lower-level influence" had better performing units. ("Lower-level influence" means asking enlisted people for information or advice when the soldier knew more about some task than the officer.) The following direct observation of a live critical incident might support lower-level influence as a needed competency for combat leaders:

The Army trains soldiers in very realistic mock battles called "REALTRAIN" exercises. One group of soldiers attacks a hill, and another defends it. Soldiers wear clothing that changes color if they are "hit" by opponents, whose weapons fire a harmless beam of light.

Observing a REALTRAIN battles from the hill of the defending unit, one of the authors saw on one side, a lonely private muttering, "Man, we gonna get blown away, we gonna get BLOWN away."

Asked why, he said, "No one's covering my flank, this side of the hill. The enemy's gonna come right up here and wipe us out."

Asked why he didn't tell the Captain, he said, "Wouldn't do no good—that dumb SOB never listens to a word I say."

Sure enough, 30 seconds after the battle started, the attackers came right up the undefended side of the hill and "blew away" the defenders.

Observation of several incidents of this type led the researchers to conclude that receptivity to lower-level influence was a valid competency. Superstar combat leaders listened to input from their troops; "loser" leaders did not.

Disadvantages of Direct Observation

- It is expensive and inefficient. Most people experience only a few critical incidents a year on their jobs. It will take a lot of observer time to have a chance of seeing something *important*. Like job task analysis, observation risks sweeping up a lot of routine "chaff" to find a few grains of competency "wheat."

Done correctly, the BEI method gathers critical incident information equivalent to direct observation data, but much more efficiently. A 60- to 90-minute interview can produce almost as much usable data as a week of intensive observation or a year of regular work activity.

Direct observation is most efficient as a check on competency data from BEI analysis if it is clear what is to be noted. The incident regarding lower-level influence shows how it might really make a difference in combat.

Step 4. Analyze Data and Develop a Competency Model

In this step, data from all sources and methods are analyzed to identify the personality and skill competencies that distinguish superior from average performers. This process is called hypothesis generation, thematic analysis, or concept formation.

Two or more trained analysts start by laying data about superior and average performers side by side. Then they search for differences—motives, skills, or other competencies that superior people show and average performers do not or vice versa. The search is done in two ways. First, any motive, thought, or behavior that matches a definition in the competency dictionary is coded. Second, themes not in the standard dictionary are noted.

Identifying new competency themes in behavioral events is the most difficult and creative step in the analysis process.

An example is the following comments from a superior diplomat and from an average diplomat:

Diplomat A

Despite the troubles we had with them, I never stopped liking and respecting the student leaders. They were just becoming conscious of their nationalism, and that they were going to be the leaders of a greatly changed country. I could understand that they *needed* to rebel against us, to stand up to us, even throw us out—even when they wanted to burn my library! I told them that and invited them to use our facilities to hold some of their meetings. I've got good contacts with some of the student leaders now. And we haven't been burned down yet!

Diplomat B

I finally came to the conclusion that [people of country *X*] were just stupid, dumb, and unmotivated. I kept trying to schedule English classes, so these kids could learn enough to go to the United States to study, which is what they all said they wanted. But fewer and fewer showed up. So finally I canceled the classes. What can you do with people like that?

The differences are obvious. The superior diplomat expresses positive expectations and accurate empathy toward others, and the average performer does not.

These competencies predict superior performance. In the State Department study, analysts found these same negative and positive patterns in several hundred superstar and average diplomats' stories.

Analysts keep refining the definition of competencies seen in behavioral events until each can be recognized with acceptable interrater reliability. "Interrater reliability" means that two or more people can read the same story and agree on whether or not it contains a competency. Stories are repeatedly rated or scored until interrater reliability meets desired standards. Empirical coding of interviews can be done with high interrater reliability [$Rs = .80–.90$][7] and provides quantitative data that can be used in standard statistical tests of significance.

The final task is to develop a behavioral codebook that describes the competencies predictive of job performance. This codebook defines each competency and the criteria for scoring it and provides examples from BEIs of when the competency is noted or not. Competencies scaled in just-noticeably-different (JND) intervals permit precise definition of job competency requirements, as well as assessment of individuals at any level in a job family. The behavioral codebook provides the competency model for the job. This model can be used for selection, training, performance appraisal, career planning, and the like.

Step 5. Validate the Competency Model

The competency model derived in Step 4 can be validated in three ways.

First, the researcher can collect BEI data on a second criterion sample of superstar and average performers. BEI stories from the second sample are then scored to see if the competency model based on the first study predicts the superior and average performers in the second sample. This approach is called "concurrent cross-validation," meaning the competency model is tested by seeing if it predicts the performance of people in a second group at a current point in time.

Second, tests can be developed to measure the competencies described by the competency model and used to test people in a second criterion sample of superior and average performers. Alternatively, managers and other knowledgeable observers can be asked to rate and rank members of the second criterion sample on competencies using rating forms or Q-sorts. If the competency model and the tests or rating forms are valid, superstars in the second sample should get higher scores on these tests and rating forms. This is called "concurrent construct validation," meaning different constructs or measures, the competency tests, are used to predict performance of people at a certain point in time.

The third and most powerful way to validate a competency model is to select (using tests or data from BEIs) or train people using the competencies and see if these people actually perform better in the future. This is called "predictive validity" because the competency model is expected to *predict* how people *will perform*. This is what traditional education, grades, test scores and credentials do not do—predict actual job performance or success in life.

Clearly, predictive validity is the bottom line for selection or training. Employers hiring people want to use criteria that predict the people hired *will* do the job well. Trainers want to teach skills that will enable people to do the job well.

Step 6. Prepare Applications of the Competency Model

Once validated, a competency model can be used in a variety of ways. In Part V, "Applications," we show how competency data can be used to design selection interviews, tests, and assessment centers for selection, career pathing, performance management, succession planning, training and development, compensation, and management information systems.

A competency that (a) few new hires can be expected to have, (b) is likely to cause trouble if an employee lacks it, and (c) is easy to develop (e.g., specific product knowledge for a salesperson) is a priority for entry-level training.

A competency that (a) distinguishes superior from average performers, (b) can be realistically hired for, and (c) is hard to develop (e.g., achievement orientation) is a priority for selection.

A competency that (a) distinguishes superior from average performers, (b) cannot be realistically hired for, and (c) can be developed (e.g., how to introduce an innovative product) is a priority for advanced training.

A competency that (a) few new hires can be expected to have, (b) is likely to cause trouble if an employee lacks it, and (c) is hard to develop (e.g., how to operate certain highly sophisticated technical military equipment requiring a fair amount of software) suggests a need for job or tool redesign for greater "user friendliness."

A SHORT COMPETENCY MODEL PROCESS
BASED ON EXPERT PANELS

A short job competency assessment (JCA) process using primarily data from
an expert panel consists of these steps (see Figure 10–2):

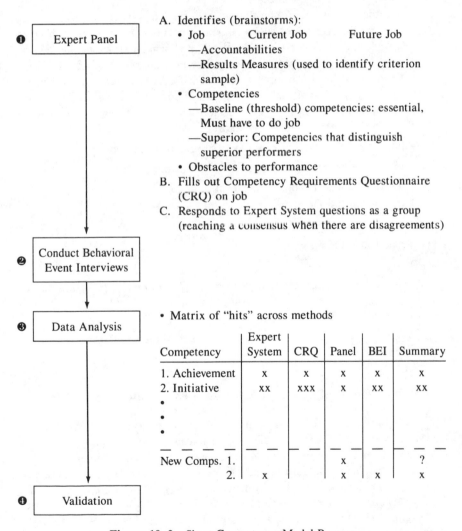

A. Identifies (brainstorms):
  • Job   Current Job   Future Job
    —Accountabilities
    —Results Measures (used to identify criterion
      sample)
  • Competencies
    —Baseline (threshold) competencies: essential,
      Must have to do job
    —Superior: Competencies that distinguish
      superior performers
  • Obstacles to performance
B. Fills out Competency Requirements Questionnaire
  (CRQ) on job
C. Responds to Expert System questions as a group
  (reaching a consensus when there are disagreements)

• Matrix of "hits" across methods

Competency	Expert System	CRQ	Panel	BEI	Summary
1. Achievement	x	x	x	x	x
2. Initiative	xx	xxx	x	xx	xx
•					
•					
•					
New Comps. 1.			x		?
2.	x		x	x	x

Figure 10–2   Short Competency Model Process

Step 1. Convene Expert Panels

For each target job or job family, knowledgeable human resource specialists, managers, and superior job incumbents identify:

a. *Key Accountabilities:* The most important duties, responsibilities, and product or service outcomes.

b. *Results measures* for these accountabilities that can be used to identify superior performers in the job.

Ideal criteria are hard outcome measures such as productivity data. In the absence of such criteria, supervisor, peer (if peers have an opportunity to observe one another's performance), subordinate (e.g., organizational climate survey) and/or customer ratings can be used. Even if a criterion sample is not identified, these data are useful for designing performance management systems and in focusing the panel on the key results outputs of the job when identifying characteristics that predict getting these results.

c. [Optional] *Career paths* that typically lead to the job.

d. *Competencies* employees need to perform the job at

    (i) a baseline or "threshold" level, and

    (ii) a superior level.

Expert panel members may also:

e. Complete a *Competency Requirements Questionnaire (CRQ),* a survey that assesses competencies required for threshold and superior performance in the job.

f. Respond as a group to questions posed by the *computer-based "expert system."*

Step 2. [Optional] Conduct Behavioral Event Interviews (BEIs)

If possible, a few superior incumbents are interviewed to confirm and provide narrative examples of competencies identified by the expert panel. BEIs are most valuable in identifying the nuances of how competencies are expressed in an organization's unique culture and context. For example, a panel, survey, or expert system can identify "Uses Influence Strategies" as a competency, but not *how, when,* or *what* an effective influence strategy looks like in this particular organization. Even one BEI can provide the richness of detail to make competencies identified "come alive" in sufficient detail to be useful for selection or training applications.

Step 3. Analyze Data and Develop a Competency Model

Data from the expert panels, surveys, expert system, and BEIs are content analyzed to identify behaviors and personality characteristics that (a) distinguish superior from average job incumbents, or (b) are demonstrated by all incumbents adequately performing the job.

Step 4. Validate the Competency Model

A competency model can be quickly validated by rating or ranking a criterion sample of superior and average performers on the competencies identified in Step 3 and confirming that superior performers are ranked higher than averages on the competencies.

Outputs of a Short JCA.   The outputs of a short JCA are one or more job description "Competency Models" that include:

a. *Purpose and Content* of the job/job family: Tasks, responsibilities, and performance measures for the job rated as to level, frequency, and importance in a form that can be used to compare the job's content with other jobs.

b. [Optional] *Career paths* for the job, with some estimate of when, where, and how key competencies for the job are developed.

c. *Competency Requirements.* The skills and characteristics required for adequate and superior performance in the job.

The short competency model process (without BEIs) can be completed in a day. Panel, survey, and expert system data are collected in the morning, analyzed in the afternoon, and a job description/competency model report prepared by the end of the day. Such models lack the richness and validation of the full job competency assessment with Behavioral Event Interviews but can provide valuable information in a short time.

STUDYING FUTURE JOBS OR SINGLE-INCUMBENT JOBS

Special challenges are posed in determining the competency requirements for *future* jobs and *single incumbent* jobs where there may be only one incumbent or the job being defined does not yet exist. How can competencies for these jobs be determined?

Future Jobs

Three approaches for studying future jobs (in inverse order of desirability) are (a) expert panel "guesstimates," (b) extrapolation from job elements with known competency correlates, and (c) sampling employees doing analogous jobs now.

Expert Panels.   An expert panel analysis of future jobs is similar to that described for the Short Competency Model Process. Experts first list the accountabilities, results measures and competencies of the most similar current job(s) in the organization, then identify accountabilities and competencies likely to be required by the *future* job(s). Experts can even construct critical incident scenarios for future jobs by imagining typical situations a person in the future job might face and then identifying competencies needed to deal with these situations effectively.

Extrapolation from Known Job Element ↔ Competency Correlates.   Elements or accountabilities for some future jobs may include competencies already identified by previous competency research. Competency models for a future job can be assembled from these elements. For example, a U.S. telecommunications firm needed a model for senior marketing representatives capable of winning European government and community officials' approval for telecommunication equipment to be sold in the European Common Market. With no overseas personnel or experience, the firm had no superior or average performers to study.

An analysis of this future "technical ambassador" job indicated it will combine elements of diplomatic and high-tech sales jobs. Competency models already exist for both diplomats and high-tech salespeople. From the diplomatic model, competencies for the "technical ambassador" job included "cross-cultural interpersonal sensitivity," "overseas adjustment" (adaptability, liking for novelty, resistance to stress caused by living overseas), and "speed of learning (foreign) political networks" from the diplomatic model; from the high-tech sales models, competencies included "achievement orientation" and "consultative selling skills."

Analysis of Analogous Present Jobs.   The best way to identify competency requirements for future jobs is to (a) study superior performers in similar jobs now, then (b) use labor economics studies to extrapolate how many people will be employed in these jobs, hence need the requisite competencies, at future points in time.

For example, "knowledge engineers" (persons who debrief human experts and translate their expertise into artificial intelligence "expert system" computer programs) now represent fewer than 1 percent of employees in data processing but are expected to make up 20 percent of data processing jobs after the year 2000. A competency study might show superior "knowledge engineers" have both higher level cognitive competencies such as pattern recognition, conceptualization, and analytic thinking (the ability to recognize and state problem-solving algorithms used by human experts in computer programmable "if → then" rules) *and* the interpersonal interviewing skills needed to establish rapport with and debrief subject matter experts.[8] These findings suggest selection and training criteria for EDP personnel to be hired and developed over the next decade.

Even if an organization lacks people with the competencies needed to do a future job, people may be doing the job in another organization. For example, a sleepy neighborhood thrift institution wanted to become a marketing-oriented commercial bank. Its existing branch managers were kindly sixtyish gentlemen who stamped little old ladies' passbooks and chatted about grandchildren. The thrift wanted marketing-oriented branch managers who would sell savings customers additional financial services (i.e., grab the little old lady and sell her a trust for her grandchildren).

The thrift did not have anyone with the competencies of an aggressive, cross-selling branch manager. So it gave a grant to a banking industry association, which then hired a consulting firm to study superior branch managers in banks that the thrift had identified as the best marketers in its area (i.e., the superstars of its future competitors).

A final question on competency analysis of future jobs is whether characteristics that predict superior performance in 1990 will still predict superior performance in 2001. Coding of historical data sources[9] and longitudinal studies in the U.S. Navy between 1976 and 1987[10] suggest that, while the *behavioral indicators* (e.g., "uses computer to conduct factor analyses") for competencies may change, the underlying competencies (e.g., "conceptual thinking") do not. Achievement Orientation has the same predictive accuracy for economic activity in Greece in 300 B.C. and in many cultures in 1991, although business practices have obviously changed. Random passages of Caesar's *Gaulic Commentaries,* ca. 30 B.C., coded for leadership and management competencies shown by contemporary superior military officers, rate Caesar a "high superior" despite obvious changes in military technology. Competency models are dynamic in the sense that, although the way tasks are carried out is likely to change, core motivational, interpersonal, and cognitive competencies that predict success remain the same over time.

Competency Studies of Single-Incumbent Jobs

Competencies for single-incumbent jobs can be determined by assembling data from key people (dependencies) who interact with the person in the job. A model was created for the Vice President of Human Resources of a certain hospital. This position was empty; the incumbent had been fired. Competencies for this job were identified by conducting BEIs with superiors (the hospital's CEO and directors), peers (other functional and operating vice presidents), key subordinates, and customers (union leaders and prominent members of the community who dealt with human resource issues with the hospital). Respondents were asked to identify critical incidents in which they had seen previous VPs of human resources be particularly effective or ineffective. If they could not think of incidents involving a previous job incumbent, respondents were asked for incidents involving any health care VP of human resources.

For example, asked to cite an instance of effective performance, after a long pause, the CEO said:

> Well, there was this very tense meeting with the nursing staff, who were about to go out on strike . . . X (the previous HR VP) came in and cracked a joke. Everyone laughed, and that sort of broke the ice . . . the meeting was less tense after that.

Asked for examples of ineffective performance, the CEO immediately remembered two incidents:

> The worst thing I ever saw X do was his absolutely disastrous presentation at our top management "vision for the future" retreat. Everyone was supposed to present where he or she thought we should be going in the next 10 years, based on labor force demographics, economic, technological, industry, market, etc. trends. X was the kind of person who lives in the "now"—I don't think he could think as far ahead as next week. So he had his staff write a speech for him—but he didn't bother to read the speech before trying to give it! He embarrassed himself—and all of us. And then, when he got negative feedback, his response was to go back and punish his *staff* for writing a lousy speech!

> Another embarrassing incident: The daughter of one of our Directors, a very important man in this part of the state, sent in a job application. Human Resources apparently lost it. Then, to make it worse, she called a number of times—and no one returned her phone calls! It came to my attention when her father called *me*. That's not what, or how, you want to hear about how your HR group is doing business.

Asked for critical incidents involving any health care HR VP he had seen as particularly effective, the CEO said:

> The best one I know—the head of a university health system—really thinks ahead and has pulled off some really incredibly innovative staffing. He couldn't get enough qualified nurses here, so he thought of recruiting from *Indian* medical and nursing schools: He found he could get first-rate people who thought a chance to come to the United States and make $12,000 a year was a "died and gone to heaven" opportunity. He even worked a deal with Immigration to get them green cards (U.S. residency and work permits) by lobbying local congressional representatives that only this way would they get better care for their elderly constituents . . ."

It is not hard to identify competencies important to the CEO (or other respondents) from these critical incidents: strategic thinking, concern for impact, presentation skills, customer service orientation, quality concern, innovativeness, political influence skills. Reasonably complete and accurate competency studies can be prepared using the Short Competency Model Process and modified BEIs with key dependencies of a job, even if it is a single-incumbent job—and empty.

NOTES

1. Lewin, A. Y., & Zwany, A. (1976), *Peer nominations: A model, literature critique, and a paradigm for research,* Springfield, VA: National Technical Information Service; Kane, J., & Lawler, E. (1979), Methods of peer assessment, *Psychological Bulletin, 85,* (3), 555–586.
2. Caldwell, D. F. (1991, April 12), *Soft skills, hard numbers: Issues in person–job/person–organization fit,* Paper presented at the Personnel Testing Conference of Southern California Spring Conference. Ontario, CA.
3. McClelland, D. (1976), *A guide to job competence assessment,* Boston: McBer.
4. Flanagan, J. C. (1954), The critical incident technique. *Psychological Bulletin, 51* (4), 327–358.
5. Austin, A. W., Inouye, C. J. & Korn, W. S. (1986), *Evaluation of the CAEL Student Potential Program,* Los Angeles: University of California, Los Angeles.
6. Uniform Guidelines on Employee Selection Procedures, (1978), *Federal Register, 43* (166), 38290-38309.
7. Boyatzis, R. (1982), *The competent manager,* New York: Wiley. Also see data on reliability of interview coding in Chapter 18.
8. McGraw, K. L., & Harbison-Briggs, K. H, (1989), *Knowledge acquisition: Principles and guidelines,* Englewood Cliffs, NJ: Prentice Hall.
9. McClelland, D. C. (1976), *The achieving society,* New York: Irvington; Zullow, H. M., Oettingen, G., Peterson, C., & Seligman, M. E. (1988), Pessimistic explanatory style in the historical record, *American Psychologist, 43,* (9), 673–682.
10. McBer (1987). *A history of the U.S. Navy Leadership and Management Education and Training Program,* Boston: McBer.

11

Conducting the Behavioral Event Interview

This chapter explains how the Behavioral Event Interview (BEI) method differs from traditional interviewing methods and provides step-by-step instructions on how to conduct a BEI.

The Behavioral Event Interview is the heart of the Job Competency Assessment process. BEI data are the richest source of hypotheses about competencies that predict superior or effective job performance. To do competency research, it is essential to know how to conduct and analyze a BEI.

In addition, properly conducted BEIs can be used as psychometric tests to assess competencies for selection and other human resource applications (see Chapter 18).

TRADITIONAL INTERVIEWING METHODS

Traditional interviewing methods do not work well to identify competencies. Numerous studies have shown that unstructured, nonbehavioral selection interviews have little power to predict who will do a good job.[1] Standard interview probes such as "Tell me about your background," "What are your strengths and weaknesses?" "What jobs have you liked and not liked?" are ineffective for two reasons.

First, most people don't *know* what their competencies, strengths and weaknesses, or even their job likes and dislikes really are. It's not unusual to find that managers who earnestly believe their greatest strength is "dealing with people" are disliked and distrusted by their co-workers. Artists who say they "hate business" and think selling is "degrading" can become first-rate salespeople—if they are high in achievement motivation. Harvard psychologist Chris Argyris has shown that people's "espoused theories of action" (what they *say* they do) bear no relation to their "theories in use" (what they *actually* do).[2]

Second, people may not reveal their real motives and abilities. Most interview questions are "leading" and most people can give the "socially desirable" answer: what they think the interviewer wants to hear. As a result, people's self-reports of background, strengths, and preferences do not provide reliable information about their competencies.

The basic principle of the competency approach is that *what people think or say about their motives or skills is not credible.* Only what they actually *do,* in the most critical incidents they have faced, is to be believed. The purpose of the BEI method is to get behind what people say they do to find out what they *really* do. This is accomplished by asking people to describe how they actually behaved in specific incidents. The following interview examples may help explain this difference.

Example 1

Most managers in industry have been told for years that they should be "Theory Y, democratic-participative" leaders. They should listen, let subordinates participate in decisions, and manage by consensus. This is their espoused "theory of action," how they think they manage. An interview with a manager might go:

SALES MANAGER: I manage participatively, I get my people together, share information with them, and get their inputs. That's what makes a good team!

INTERVIEWER (using the BEI method): Can you tell me about a specific incident in which you managed participatively?

SALES MANAGER: Well, sure. Sales were really down in our Northwest region. I got all the sales data, broken down by district, went out there and called a meeting. I told all my district managers, "These results speak for themselves. They're terrible. And they're going to change, or there are going to be a lot fewer people sitting around this table the next time I call this meeting. The ball's in your court. How are you going to fix it?"

INTERVIEWER: Is this an example of your "participative" management?

SALES MANAGER: Well, yes. I had a meeting, didn't I? I gave them all the information I had, and the responsibility to act on it.

In fact, this manager's approach is anything but participative. He tries to motivate his subordinates by threatening them.

Example 2

In the military, the espoused theory of management is just the opposite. Leaders are expected to be authoritarian, to give direct orders that are immediately obeyed. An interview with a military officer might go like this:

NAVY OFFICER: When you take over a command, you have to step on them hard right off the bat. It's like a kindergarten: If the teacher doesn't show who's boss the first day, the kids won't respect her and she'll never have any control of the class. So I come in tough. I scare them— and punish anyone who doesn't get the message. I think if you don't create a little bit of fear, you'll never get any respect.

INTERVIEWER (using the BEI method):   Can you give me a specific example of a time you used this approach?

OFFICER: Sure. When I took over here, the ship had just come out of a major overhaul in the yard. It was still torn up something terrible, dirt and debris everywhere. As weapons officer, I've got 33, maybe 34, spaces to maintain. I only had four men, and the skipper was on my tail to get everything shipshape in a couple of weeks for a major inspection. My guys were working 16 hours a day, down on their hands and knees in 100 degree heat, scraping and painting. They were totally demoralized—they thought it was hopeless.

INTERVIEWER: What did you do?

OFFICER: Well, I called a meeting and explained Maslow's hierarchy to them. You know, about how you have to do the low-level scut work before you can get to the high-level work that makes you feel proud about yourself. I explained the problem and said we needed a plan. I asked them if they had any ideas. One of my chiefs said he knew where there were some other sailors from another department who weren't doing anything who we might steal. Which I did. We got a realistic plan together which I sold to the skipper. Also I pitched in myself—showed 'em I wasn't too proud to do some work. You gotta be visible. Once they got about 3–4 spaces cleaned up, they saw it wasn't hopeless and morale starting going up. It's sky high now—and we maxed the inspection!

INTERVIEWER: That's an example of "stepping on them hard right off the bat?"

OFFICER: Sure the hell is. They knew who was boss from the moment I arrived.

In fact, this officer's management style, if not participative, is hardly the authoritarian approach he says he uses.

In both examples, what the person *thinks* his managerial style is is almost the opposite of how he actually behaves. The traditional interview probes ("Tell me how you manage") do not produce useful information. By asking for an actual incident and very detailed example of real behavior, the BEI method gets much closer to the truth.

Traditional Interview Strategies and Their Problems

The Fact Finder.   The fact finder asks for specific information about people's background. Typical probes are "What was your college grade point average?" "How many people did you manage?" "What type of course did you design?"

The problem with facts of this type is that they say little about a person's motives, values, self-concept, or cognitive skills. They reveal nothing about why the person received good or bad grades, what motivates him or her, or how he or she behaves in critical situations. Fact-finding probes control the responses of the interviewee. These may be data, but they are not about many important competencies.

The Therapist.   The therapist asks about people's underlying feelings, attitudes, and motives. Typical probes are "tell me about yourself . . ." followed by "reflections" of what the interviewee is saying: "So in that situation you felt . . ."

Data from therapist interviewers depend very much on the therapist's interpretation of the interviewee's reactions, and these interpretations are notoriously unreliable. "Feeling" data usually say little about what a person can do or actually does. A person might feel negatively about a task but do it well because he or she is high in achievement motivation, or is highly skilled. Another person may feel great about a task and his or her ability but, in fact, lack both motivation and skill for that task. From a competency assessment standpoint, the feeling may be irrelevant. The competencies are the achievement motive and the skill—and the therapist will miss these.

The Theorist.   The theorist asks people for their espoused beliefs or values, about how they do things. Typical probes are "*Why* did you . . . ?"

The problem with this approach is that it gets theories or after-the-fact rationalizations of why a person *thinks* he or she did something, not actual behavior. As shown in the preceding examples, people's theories about what they do often bear scant relation to their actual behaviors or competencies. Whenever someone starts with "My general approach to management (or anything else) is . . ." be *very* skeptical; ask for a specific example.

The Fortune-Teller.   The fortune-teller asks people what *they would* do in future (or hypothetical) situations. Typical probes are "What would you do *if* . . ." The fortune-teller is the theorist projected into the future. People's beliefs about what they *think* they *would* do are as unreliable as their theories about why they did things in the past. Smart interviewees say what they think the fortune-teller wants to hear.

The Salesperson.   The salesperson tries to win people to his or her point of view by asking leading questions. A typical probe: "Don't you think this is the best way to do it?" Leading questions put words in other people's mouths. Data obtained in this way will reflect what the interview*er* believes or would do, not how the interview*ee* can or will behave.

The Behavioral Event Interview is designed to avoid these traditional interview problems.

HOW TO CONDUCT THE BEHAVIORAL EVENT INTERVIEW[3]

The objective of the BEI is to get very detailed behavioral descriptions of how a person goes about doing his or her work. The interviewer asks other questions, but these are either designed to set the stage or to lead people to provide critical-incident "short stories." The interviewer's job is to keep pushing for complete stories that describe the specific behaviors, thoughts, and actions the interviewee has shown in actual situations.

Because most personnel professionals have been trained in one of the traditional approaches, the BEI may not be as easy as it sounds. Interviewing habits can be hard to break, particularly for psychologists and others trained in counseling methods.[4]

Preparing for the BEI

The following guidelines will help interviewers prepare to do a BEI:

1. *Know Who You Will Be Talking To.* Learn the name of the person to be interviewed and how to pronounce it correctly, his or her job title and something of what the job involves, and what the person's organization does.

Interviewers should *not,* however, know whether the person they are interviewing is rated as a superior or average performer. This can bias the interview. If the person is known to be a superstar, you may ask leading questions that give them an unequal opportunity to say how good they are. If they have been identified as average, you may not interview them with equal interest or support and thus limit their opportunity to provide useful data.

2. *Arrange a Private Place and 1½–2 Hours of Uninterrupted Time for the Interview.* The interview should not take place where others can overhear you. It may be best for the interview to be away from the interviewee's office and interruptions from the telephone or visitors.

3. *Arrange to Tape Record the Interview.* Whenever possible, tape-record and make transcriptions of a BEI. Besides being much less work for the interviewer, BEI transcripts are invaluable for capturing the exact nuances of interviewees' motives and thought processes. Interviewer notes often miss rich details that can help identify competencies. Notes tend to be more the *interviewer's* version of the facts than the interviewee's. BEI transcripts can also provide a valuable source of training materials, such as case studies, role plays, and simulations.

When interviewer, respondent, and transcription time are taken into account, each BEI represents an investment of several hundred dollars. It is well worth your while to use a good tape recorder, with fresh batteries and tapes. Check it before the interview and then test with the interviewee to be sure it is operating correctly. Labeling of tapes on the spot can prevent mix-ups later.

4. *Know What You Will Say.* Memorize the scripts provided in the following sections for each step of the Behavioral Event Interview. Interviewers have found that preparing a prompt to remind them of what to say at each step is very helpful in learning to do a BEI and in summarizing data.

Behavioral Event Interview Outline

BEIs contain five steps. Most of the interview should focus on Step 3—the Behavioral Events themselves. The steps are as follows:

1. *Introduction and Explanation.* Introducing yourself and explaining the purpose and format of the interview.

   Optional 1a. *Career Path.* Asking about the interviewee's education and previous work experiences.

2. *Job Responsibilities.* Getting the interviewee to describe his or her most important job tasks and responsibilities.

3. *Behavioral Events.* Asking the interviewee to describe, in detail, the five or six most important situations he or she has experienced in the job—two or three "high points" or major successes, and two or three "low points" or key failures.

4. *Characteristics Needed to Do the Job.* Asking the interviewee to describe what he or she thinks it takes for someone to do the job effectively.

5. *Conclusion and Summary.* Thanking the interviewee for his or her time and summarizing key incidents and findings from the interview.

Description of BEI Steps

Here are detailed objectives and statements or questions that can serve as a script for each step of the BEI. Pointers on techniques and dealing with problems are provided for each step.

Step 1. Introduction and Explanation.   The real purpose of this step in the BEI is to establish a sense of mutual trust and good will between yourself and the interviewee so he or she is relaxed, open, and ready to talk to you. Specific objectives are:

1. *Put the Interviewee at Ease.* Introduce yourself in a low key, friendly way.

2. *Motivate the Interviewee to Participate.* Explain the purpose and format of the interview. Most people want to know why they are being interviewed and what the responses will be used for. You can say:

> The purpose of this interview is to (or more personally, "I've been asked to try to") find out what it takes to do your job. The way we do this is by asking people like you—the ones who are actually doing the job—how you do it. You have been selected by (the organization, your supervisor, etc.) as someone who can tell me what I need to know about the kind of work you do. Since you are the obvious expert about what it takes to do your job, all I will do is ask you some questions about how you do your work. The best way we have found to do this is to ask you to describe some of the most important incidents you have encountered on your jobs—what the situations were and what you actually did.

Alternatively, you can give the interviewee a printed outline of the BEI and say:

> I will be asking you about your duties and responsibilities; and about some "critical incidents:" some "high" or success incidents, and some "low" or failure incidents you have had on your job in the past 12 to 18 months. We've found it helpful to give you a few minutes to reflect and jot down your most important responsibilities and some critical incidents on this outline.
> I'll give you a few minutes to think while I set up.

Busy yourself getting your notes and tape recorder ready to avoid giving the interviewee the idea you are impatiently standing over him or her. When he or she looks up from the outline, continue:

3. *Emphasize the Confidentiality of the Responses.* Explain how the data will be used and who will see it. You can say:

> Everything you say in this interview will be kept strictly confidential and will not be shared with anyone else in your organization. Your data will be transcribed "blind"—without your name or anyone else's attached—and included with data from everyone else we are interviewing.

4. *Get Permission to Tape-Record.* You can say:

> With your permission, I would like to record the interview so I can pay more attention to you and not have to take so many notes. Again everything you say will be kept confidential. But if there is anything you want to say off the record or don't want me to record, just let me know and I'll turn off the tape.

Pause briefly, to see if there is any objection, then say immediately, enthusiastically:

Okay, I'll start the tape and we can begin.

Almost everyone gives this permission and soon forgets the tape recorder.

Pointers on Technique

- Establish trust with another person by openly explaining who you are, what you are doing and why, and then asking the person's help. If you are open, informal, and friendly, the interviewee is likely to respond in kind.

- Asking someone for his or her views minimizes the status differential between the interviewee and you as the "expert researcher." Taking the role of an "inquirer" and being genuinely interested will establish your respect for the interviewee's knowledge and the value of what he or she has to say. Treating the interviewee as an expert on his or her job is empowering—it makes him or her feel strong, safe, and in control. Most people find it rewarding to talk about themselves, their jobs, what they know well.

Problems and Dealing with Them

- The interviewee is nervous or concerned about why he or she was "singled out" to be interviewed.

To deal with this, repeat the purpose of the interview, emphasizing that it is to get data about the *job,* not to evaluate the interviewee personally. Reassure the person that he or she is only one of many people being interviewed. Empower the interviewee by acknowledging his or her expertise.

Optionally, depending on the interviewee's curiosity, you can say:

This is part of a research program that should lead to better selection and training for the job. If we can identify the skills and abilities you use to do your job, we can better select and train people for jobs like yours.

- The interviewee is worried about confidentiality or is uncomfortable with the use of a tape recorder.

To deal with this, repeat the promise of confidentiality and what will be done with data from the interview. Emphasize that the tape recorder is only to help you take notes. Offer to turn it off if the interviewee requests.

You can say:

Everything you say will be kept strictly confidential. Your interview data will be put together, without your name attached, with data from everyone else we will be talking to. The tape recorder is just to help me take notes. If there is anything sensitive you want to say "Off the record," I'll turn the recorder off.

Optional Step 1a. Career Path. The objective of this step is to identify "feeder" jobs, education, and life experiences that may have developed the interviewee's competencies to do his or her present job. These data can be helpful in designing career paths and succession planning systems.

This fact finding can also be a low-threat way of encouraging the interviewee to start talking specifically about what he or she actually does on the job or has done in his or her career. Occasionally interviewees will mention a major event in the past that they feel has had a major influence on their personality or life. You may want to ask more about this event, using it as a critical incident.

Specific questions would focus on *educational background, major jobs* before the current job and their most important *responsibilities,* and how the interviewee got the *current job.*

Pointers on Technique

- Keep this part of the interview brief (5–10 minutes).
- Focus the interviewee on talking about his or her job experience.
- Look for thoughts about career goals and directions and patterns of behavior in the way the person has made career choices.
- Focus on the person's current job.

Step 2. Job Responsibilities. Specific questions in this section are directed at what the person actually *does* and with whom on his or her current job.

1. "What is the title of your present job?"
2. "Whom do you report to?" Note the supervisor's title and/or position. You can say, "I don't need his or her name, just his or her title."
3. "Who reports to you?" Note the titles or positions of the interviewee's direct reports. Again you can say that you don't need names, just subordinates' positions.
4. "What are your major tasks or responsibilities? What do you actually do?" If the person has difficulty listing major job tasks or responsibilities, you can phrase the question even more specifically.
5. "For example, what do you do in a given day, week, or month?"

Pointers on Technique

- Spend no more than 10 to 15 minutes on this part of the interview.
- "Train" the person to focus on specific job behaviors.

You can do this by asking clarifying questions and by asking for specific examples. For example, a police captain may say, "Well, I supervise the lieutenants." So you ask him or her to explain a little more what he or she means by "supervise," and what actually is involved in the supervising. The response may range from reading reports written by subordinates to working with them in critical situations.

Similarly, if a staff person says, "I prepare long-range strategic plans," you should ask what he or she does to prepare a plan. Again, responses might range across tasks requiring very different skills, from reading technical reports to interviewing top executives.

- Get people to clarify buzzwords.

Often in the course of describing their work, interviewees will use technical jargon and acronyms or say things that puzzle you and that you want clarified. For example, an aircraft radar technician says, "I repair 102DZ FCS 'black boxes.'"

Always ask the meaning of anything you don't understand: "What is a 102DZ FCS 'black box'? What does 'FCS' mean?" "Naive" interviewers often elicit better data because they draw people out when they ask many questions.

- Ask for moderate detail so that you're clear about how much time the person spends on what activities.

- Listen for possible incidents you may want to ask the interviewee about if he or she has difficulty coming up with critical incidents.

- Use the interviewee's description of job tasks and responsibilities to provide a "natural" transition to describing a critical incident.

Interviewees often start telling a critical incident on their own: "I handle all the plant's maintenance crises—for example, just last week . . ." Interviewees usually mention some responsibility that suggests a natural lead-in to a critical incident. A statement such as "The hardest thing I have to do is be the person who says 'no' to budget requests . . ." offers you a natural opening to ask, "Can you give me a specific example of a time you said 'no' that you think was particularly hard?"

Problems and Dealing with Them

- The interviewee continues listing too many tasks or responsibilities.

To deal with this, you can interrupt the interviewee and ask for a specific example. You can say, "Could you choose one of your most important tasks or responsibilities and give me a specific example of how you handled it?" Or more specifically, "You mentioned that you have to make all the tough hiring decisions. Can you think of a particularly tough decision you had to make, and tell me about it?"

Step 3. Behavioral Events. The central objective of the BEI is getting the interviewee to describe in detail at least four and preferably six complete stories of critical incidents. Some respondents provide as few as four incidents, and others as many as ten. This section should take up the bulk of the interview time and should provide specific details. A good rule of thumb is that you have sufficient detail if you could stage a videotape (with voice-over for the interviewee's thoughts) of the incident without having to invent much of it.

If the interviewee's description of job responsibilities has not naturally led into describing an event, you can say:

> Now, I'd like to get a complete example of the kinds of things you do on your job. Can you think of a specific time or situation which went particularly well for you, or you felt particularly effective . . . a high point?

To get a complete story, you want the answers to five key questions:

1. "What was the *situation?* What events led up to it?"
2. "*Who* was involved?"
3. "What did you (the interviewee) *think, feel,* or *want* to do in the situation?" Here you are particularly interested in the person's perceptions and feelings about the situation and people involved in it.
    - How was the person thinking about others (e.g., positively or negatively?) or about the situation (e.g., problem-solving thoughts?)?
    - What was the person *feeling* (e.g., scared, confident, excited?)?
    - What did the person *want* to do—what motivated him or her in the situation (e.g., to do something better, to impress the boss)?
4. "What did you actually *do* or *say?*" Here you are interested in the skills that the person showed.
5. "What was the outcome? What happened?"

Pointers on Technique—Do's

- *Start with a Positive Event.* Most people find it easier to tell about their high points or successes, times they felt effective. Telling how he or she has done something well tends to empower a person, making him or her feel more confident and ready to talk.
- *Get the Story in Proper Time Sequence.* Try to get the interviewee to begin at the beginning and take you through the story as it unfolded. Otherwise you may get confused about what happened and who did what. This may be difficult, because the interviewee will usually start by remembering the outcome of an event. Think of a time line running

from a starting point to a conclusion point. Do not proceed until you are clear about those two. You can say:

That's exactly the kind of incident I'm looking for. Now could you walk me through it, starting at the very beginning, and continuing to the end, so that I can understand what happened, in what order?

Fill in all the gaps in the narrative by asking the interviewee for the data you need to get a complete story.

If the interviewee gives you a complex incident, ask about the most important or memorable subincidents within it. For example, if he or she says, "Over the past three years I 'blue-skyed', sold, spec'd, developed and installed a $50 million inventory control system in our 90 offices worldwide," you can ask:

What was the single most important step in the overall project? What stands out for you as being most memorable?

The response will likely be: "The presentation I made to the Board of Directors where I asked for the $50 million!"

When the interviewee identifies a critical subincident, continue by asking the BEI questions: "What led up to that presentation . . ." and so on.

■ *Ask Questions That Shift the Interviewee into Discussing an Actual Situation.* Focus the interviewee on real past occurrences rather than on hypothetical responses, philosophizing, abstractions, and espoused behaviors.

> Always probe espoused and hypothetical responses by asking for a *specific example.* For example, if the interviewee says: "I'm a participative manager . . . ," immediately ask for an example of when he or she managed someone participatively. If the interviewee begins a sentence with "Usually I . . ." or "Generally . . . ," immediately ask for an example of when he or she *did* that or of what he or she actually *did* do in the incident. If the interviewee says, "If they'd refused to go along with me, I'd have . . . ," immediately ask for an example of what he or she did when a person or group *refused* to go along.

> Probe for specifics. In doing a BEI, be an investigative reporter, continuously probing for *facts:* "*Who* said that? *Where* did this happen? *How* did you 'convince' her? *What happened* then?" Asking for time, place, and mood often helps the interviewee recall the episode, since usually all the person has left in mind is some memory of how it all turned out, which he or she told you first anyway.

> Keep your probes short—no more than 6 to 10 words—and in the *past* tense. Often, all you need to ask is "*Who* did that?" "*What* happened?" "*How* did you do that?" "*When* did you do it?" or "What was going

through your mind *at that time?*" Use "why" carefully: It often elicits a person's theory about a situation, not what he or she actually did. Similarly, questions in the present ("What *do* you do in that situation?" and future ("What *will* you do next time?") invite hypothetical responses. Questions longer than a sentence tend to confuse and block interviewees or become leading questions, which bias their responses.

Probe the "royal 'we'" by asking "*Who,* specifically?" to find out what the person him- or herself did. Interviewees will often say things like "So then *we* went straight to the top with it and sold the boss." You should immediately ask "Who is 'we'? *Who* went? What was your role/part in it? What exactly did *you* do"? (e.g., to prepare the report, make the presentation)?

Ask interviewees to re-create what people said in situations in "dramatic dialogue" form, like the script of a play:

He said:

She replied:

He then said:

You can ask:

"What did you actually say to him?"

"How did he respond/react to that?"

"What did you say then?"

If the interviewee says he/she can't remember the actual words, say: "Just give me the flavor of it. What *sort of thing* did you say?" Getting interviewees to re-create the dialogue almost always triggers recall of actual behavior.

■ *Probe for Thoughts behind Actions.* Probe for thought processes in technical problem solving, pattern recognition, strategic planning. In "knowledge worker" jobs, 75 percent or more of the job is *thinking.* Even in simple jobs, much behavior is "covert." For example, an auto mechanic tightens nuts when mounting wheels. The important part of this task is knowing *when the nut is tight enough.* Good mechanics will have an algorithm or rule: "Tighten the nut finger-tight, then a further three-quarters of a turn with a wrench. A quarter-inch less and the nut loosens, a quarter of a turn too far and its threads are stripped—and the wheel falls off the car." Good competency research identifies these algorithms. You can ask:

"How did you know to do that? That that was the case?"

"How did you reach that conclusion?"

"What were you thinking at the time?"

In the future, competency research is likely to increasingly resemble "knowledge engineering": the process of identifying human experts' thinking to develop computer expert systems.[5]

■ *Reinforce the Interviewee for Useful Responses.* Be appreciative of good incidents, detailed descriptions of behavior, and so on. Some people need a lot of encouragement and stimulation to really get into the process of telling a good story. Be sure that you are continually giving the interviewee plenty of reinforcement for what he or she is telling you. You can laugh with the interviewee, even tell stories of your own, if necessary, to keep the flow of talk informal and pleasant. Constantly reinforce him or her for the help he or she is giving in clarifying what goes on in this job. You can nod and smile, continually say, "um, hum" or "That's exactly the kind of incident or detail I'm looking for."

By continual reinforcement, you can "train" the interviewee to provide information in critical-incident form. By the end of the first incident most interviewees catch on to what you are after. This makes subsequent incidents easy to get.

■ *Understand That the Interview May Be an Emotional Experience for the Interviewee.* Talking about critical successes—and particularly failures—may arouse strong feelings in a person. Often an interviewee will say, "You know, I never really stood back and looked at the whole experience this way before." If the person is becoming emotionally involved, you may need to stop probing and sympathize with or just listen respectfully until the interviewee calms down.

Pointers on Technique—Don'ts

■ *Avoid Questions That Shift the Interviewee into Abstractions.* Hypothetical responses, philosophizing, and espoused theories do not serve the purpose of the Behavioral Event Interview. Present, future, and conditional tense questions are particularly dangerous. For example:

Present tense "why" questions: "Why *do* you do that?"

A better probe: "What was going through your mind when you *did* that?"

Hypothetical questions: "What *could* you have done?"

A better probe: "What *did* you *do?*"

Espoused theory or value questions: "What is your *usual* approach?" "How do you *generally* interview somebody?" "What do you look for when selecting someone?" "How do you deal with problems in the service area?" "How do you discipline people?"

A better probe: In every case you should ask for an *actual incident*: "Tell me about someone you had a particularly good or bad interview with." "Can you give me an *example* of someone you disciplined—what led up to the situation? Who was involved?"

■ *Don't Use Leading Questions or Jump to Conclusions.* Don't put words (yours) in the interviewee's mouth. For example, if you ask, "So you tried to *influence* her . . . ," you are prompting the interviewee to tell you about his or her motivation or skill in using power. In the actual incident, the interviewee may not have thought of or wanted to influence someone else at all. Your leading probe may bias the interview data by introducing a competency the interviewee doesn't really have. Similarly, jumping to a conclusion by saying to the interviewee "so you succeeded in selling the prospect" may lead the person to tell you what you want to hear and give you an outcome to the incident that didn't happen. Don't assume you know what is happening, or who is involved, unless the interviewee specifically states it. When in doubt, probe!

■ *Don't "Reflect" or Paraphrase What the Interviewee Says.* Although "nondirective" counselors are trained to use this technique, using a reflective statement (e.g., "So you tried to help him?") at best doesn't get you any additional information and at worst may be a leading question. It is better to respond with a noncommittal "um, hum" and then to ask an investigative question (e.g., "*How,* exactly, did you do that?").

The only exception to this rule is in dealing with an interviewee who is emotionally upset. In this case, you may need to reflect in a "therapeutic" manner until the person is ready to continue. Try to shift the interviewee from talking about his or her present feelings to what he or she felt at the time of the incident:

INTERVIEWEE: Everyone was attacking me . . .

INTERVIEWER: How *did* you feel at that point (in the incident . . .)?

■ *Avoid Probes That Restrict the Interviewee's Domain of Subjects.* For example, avoid this kind of statement: "Tell me about a critical incident in which you *had to deal with a people problem.*"

In competency research studies where the BEI is used for hypothesis generation (to identify competencies important to doing a job), it is better to cast the widest net possible (i.e., ask simply for "a critical incident" without restricting the incident to "dealing with people"). What interviewees choose to talk about is what is salient to them; what they consider "critical" is an important clue to their competencies. Often superior and average interviewees' choice of critical incidents is so different it sounds as if they were in different jobs. For example, average salespeople talk about keeping their paperwork straight; stars talk about client contacts. Average operations managers talk about interpersonal conflicts; stars talk about planning. Average chief engineers talk about solving engineering problems; stars talk about influence strategies and organizational politics. (An exception to this rule is the "focused" BEI used to assess specific competencies for selection, discussed in Chapter 18.)

Getting Additional Behavioral Events. Once the interviewee has described the first critical incident, the objective is to get four or five more. Make the transition to the second incident by reinforcing the person for the story he or she has just told.

You can say, "That's exactly the kind of incident I'm looking for. . . Can you think of another time or situation on the job when things went particularly well or were particularly difficult?" (This gives the interviewee the choice of telling either a positive or negative experience). If you specifically want a failure or low-point incident, you can say, "That helps me understand much better what you do in your job. Now, can you think of an instance in which you feel you *weren't* as effective as you could be, when things *didn't* go well, when you were particularly *frustrated*—a real low point?"

If the interviewee balks, you can add, "We're interested in your worst experiences, the toughest situations you've had to face, because these are things we would want to prepare anyone coming into this job to face."

Asking for particularly "tough" or "frustrating" experiences is a useful indirect way of getting ineffective or failure incidents.

When the interviewee comes up with a specific event, you again want to get a complete story, using the key probes:

"What was the *situation?*"

"*Who* was involved?"

"What did you *think* about, *feel, want* to accomplish?"

"What did you *do* or *say?*"

"What was the *outcome*—what happened?"

Pointers on Technique

- *Stay with One Situation at a Time.* Don't let the interviewee change the topic or go on to a new incident until you have a complete behavioral event.

- *Look for Patterns.* As the interviewee tells you additional incidents, you are learning things about him or her. You should ask questions that will verify or double-check inferences you are beginning to draw about his or her competencies. For example, if several of an interviewee's incidents deal with conflict situations, you can be on the alert to probe how the person feels about, views, and deals with others in conflicts.

Problems and Dealing with Them

- *The Interviewee Can't Think of a Specific Event.* Occasionally you will run into someone who blocks when you ask for an example of something that went particularly well or poorly. The interviewee just can't seem to think of anything important. He or she may begin to get frustrated or annoyed about not being able to do what you want. In this case you should use other approaches to get the interviewee to talk.

Things you can do:

Tell about an experience of your own in behavioral-event story form to illustrate the kind of material you want.

Give an example of a good behavioral event from someone else you have interviewed with which the interviewee can empathize (but be careful not to lead the interviewee too much).

Refer back to something the interviewee mentioned earlier in the interview (e.g., when listing responsibilities or in the context of another interview). You can say:

Earlier you mentioned you have to discipline people . . .
I'd like to come back to something you said earlier. Could you tell me more about that?

Ask, "Is there anything else you do in your job?," "Was there anything else you did during that time?," or "Do you work with anyone else?" When the interviewee recalls something, let him or her describe it in general terms for a few moments, then zero in by asking, "Could you give me a specific example?" or "Could you tell me about a specific time when you did that/dealt with that person?"

Remain silent. The interviewee will usually break the silence with new material.

Continue to Step 4 and ask "What do you think it takes to do this job? What would you look for if you were going to hire someone to do what you do?" When the interviewee mentions something (e.g., "integrity" or "I have to be good with figures"), immediately ask for an example: "Can you think of a situation on the job that called for integrity/using figures?" Continue with the critical-incident format.

- *Vagueness.* The interviewee talks on and on about his or her philosophy of how to do the job, how he or she usually handles problems, remaining abstract or discussing *hypothetical* situations without telling you what he or she *actually did* in a *specific, real* situation. Here you must "downshift" the interviewee out of abstraction and get him or her to focus on and tell you about a concrete event:

    INTERVIEWEE: I believe in treating subordinates with respect.

    INTERVIEWER: Can you think of a specific time you treated a subordinate with respect? (or) Can you think of a particular subordinate you treated that way?

- *The Interviewee Is Concerned about Confidentiality.* He or she "clams up," becomes evasive or hostile, or refuses to answer because of not wanting to reveal confidential material about himself/herself or others. Reassure the interviewee and provide him or her with a way to continue telling the incident without loss of crucial details but also without violating confidentiality concerns. You can say:

> I don't need any names. Just tell me what happened, (or) It's okay to disguise the organization and people's names; I'm only interested in what basically happened and your part in it.

Listen respectfully to the person's concerns about the interview, sympathizing or reflecting what he or she is feeling, as you would with an interviewee who becomes emotional. When the person has gotten his or her feelings out, continue the interview by asking him or her to pick up where he or she left off.

■ *The Interviewee "Runs Away" with the Interview.* Especially dominant and articulate interviewees—super-salespeople and top managers—often present a barrage of very persuasive talk. They go on and on with grand generalizations about the state of business or the world, their philosophy of management, and the like. All this is, of course, useless from a BEI standpoint. Things you can do:

> Interrupt the interviewee. Be very direct about what you want. You can say, "I need for you to tell me about a *specific incident* you were *personally* involved in, something that *actually happened*. I need you tell me it in 'short-story' fashion. Specifically, I need to know what the *situation* was, *who* was involved . . . (state each of the key BEI probes)." Keep interrupting (nicely) until the interviewee focuses on a single incident.

> Ask for examples (see suggestions for dealing with vagueness, above).

■ *The Interviewee Asks You for Advice.* The interviewee may try to get your feedback or your conclusions (e.g., "Have you ever been in a situation like that? What should I have done? How do you think I handled it?"). *Don't get sucked in.* Anything you say is likely to elicit hypothetical responses ("What could have been done") or turn into an abstract bull session. Try to turn the interviewee's question back into another incident: "Have *you* ever encountered that problem before? How did you deal with it that time?"

Step 4. Characteristics Needed to Do the Job.   This step has two objectives:

1. *To get additional critical incidents* in areas that may have been overlooked.

2. *To leave the interviewee feeling strong and appreciated* by asking for his or her expert opinion.

What to say:

The final thing I'd like to ask you is what characteristics, knowledge, skills, or abilities you think are needed to do your job. If you were hiring or training someone to do your job, what would you look for?

This question appears to ask for the very hypothesizing that the BEI method tries to avoid. In fact, it is a strategy to get additional critical incidents that may shed light on some of the organization's espoused or folklore values.

If an interviewee mentions a characteristic you would like to follow up, you can usually get the interviewee to give you a critical incident by asking for an example of when he or she used it on the job. For example, if the interviewee says, "In this job, you've got to stay cool under pressure," you can ask, "Can you think of a particularly pressured time on the job when your being able to stay cool—or your losing your cool—made a real difference?" Continue with the standard critical-incident probes.

Pointers on Technique

- Use the "characteristics" question to get additional incidents if the interviewee has not been able to come up with 5 or 6 incidents before this point.

- Reinforce the interviewee for whatever characteristics he or she gives you, in order to end the interview on a positive note. You can be particularly appreciative, saying "That's *very* interesting. That's exactly the kind of thing we're finding from all the interviews we are doing," and so on.

Problems and Dealing with Them

- *The Interviewee Can't Think of Any Knowledge or Skill Characteristics Needed to Do the Job.* If you have enough incidents, terminate the interview at this point. If not, continue to probe by encouraging the interviewee. You can say, "What do you think you know, what skills do you have, that enable you to do the job well?"

- *The Interviewee Gives Vague, General, or "Off-the-Wall" Characteristics.* Ask for a specific example of how the interviewee has actually used the characteristic, or how it has made a difference, on the job. Often you will find that what the person means by the characteristic is very different from what it sounds like.

Step 5. Conclusion and Summary

Conclusion.   Conclude the interview by thanking the interviewee for his or her time and the "valuable information." You may need to "cool out" the interviewee by sympathizing with his or her situation; for example, if the person is in a job he or she doesn't like or clearly isn't doing very well. Attempt to leave the interviewee feeling as strong and valued as possible.

Summary Write-Up.   After the interview is over it is a good idea to sit down quietly for an hour and summarize what you have learned. If there is time, this is the best point to write up the entire interview, while your memory is still fresh. This may include a brief characterization of the person you have just interviewed. Use the write-up to define things about which you are still unclear. Note any hypotheses you may have about competencies needed to do the job, so that you can check them in later interviews.

Summarize the data from the interview.

1. *Introduction and Description of Duties and Responsibilities.* Fill in the interviewee's name, job, title, and so on. List the job responsibilities in outline form. Add any examples given for each task or responsibility in narrative form. Write everything in the first person, as if the interviewee were talking, and use the words of the interviewee as much as possible.

2. *Behavioral Events.* Check the tape recorder to be sure you have all the data. If the tape recorder has failed, write up the behavioral events *immediately* following the interview; dictate them, if possible. The longer you wait, the less you will remember, even with the best notes. Treat each event as if it is a good story that you want to tell, including the answers to the key BEI questions:

What led up to the situation?

Who were the people involved?

What did the interviewee think, feel, want to do in the situation? What did the interviewee actually do?

What was the result?

Again, use the interviewee's words as much as possible.

3. *Performer Characteristics.* List the performer characteristics in outline form. Write the examples given for each performer characteristic in narrative form. Use the interviewee's words as much as possible. Write up the additional behavioral events that come from "Performer Characteristics," as in Step 2.

4. *Summary and Interpretation.* In this section, record miscellaneous observations: themes in the interview, your impressions, opinions, and tentative conclusions. These notes will help you identify competencies when you analyze your BEI data. Note the following, if relevant, along with whatever other observations that seem applicable:

- The physical appearance of the interviewee and his or her office (e.g., neat/messy).
- The conversational style of the interviewee.
- Words and phrases that the interviewee used repeatedly.

- How the interviewee made you feel (e.g., uncomfortable/ relaxed), and what he or she was doing to have this effect.
- Any difficulty you had getting the interviewee relaxed or able to talk about high and low points.
- The way in which the interviewee handled subordinates in your presence.
- The kinds of materials the interviewee pulled out for you to look at.
- The interviewee's conclusions about events and people.
- How the interviewee seems to handle different situations in similar ways.
- Anything that seemed to be missing or out of place in the interviewee, compared with other people in the same job whom you have interviewed.
- Any probes that had interesting results.

Feel free to characterize the interviewee in your best "personality assessment" style; give an example that illustrates your conclusion.

Try to determine which competencies the person demonstrated in the interview that tell you something about how he or she works.

The next chapter will show how to analyze BEI data to identify the competencies people need to do a job well.

NOTES

1. Mayfield, E. C. (1964), The selection interview: A re-evaluation of published research, *Personnel Psychology, 17*, 239–249.
2. Argyris, C., & Schon, D. A. (1974), *Theory in practice: Increasing professional effectiveness,* San Francisco: Jossey-Bass.
3. Based on McClelland, D. C. (1976), *Guide to behavioral event interviewing,* Boston: McBer; McBer. (1981, 1992), *Interviewing for competence.* Boston: McBer.
4. Most people can, however, learn to do BEIs well enough to do JCA research. This takes two days of intensive training, with coaching and feedback from a certified BEI instructor. Instruction and certification in Behavioral Event Interviewing are available from McBer and Company, 137 Newbury Street, Boston, MA 02116, 617-437-7080, and Hay/McBer offices in 30 countries.
5. See the inquiry strategies discussed in McGraw, K. L., & Harbison-Briggs, K. (1989), *Knowledge acquisition: Principles and guidelines.* Englewood Cliffs, NJ: Prentice-Hall. Interesting examples of "inquiry strategies" to identify thought processes are found in Jean Piaget's classic works [Piaget, J. (1965), *The child's conception of the world,* Totowa, NJ: Littlefield, Adams]; Chris Argyris's "action science" [Argyris, C., Putnam, R., & Smith, D. M. (1987), *Action science,* San Francisco, CA: Jossey-Bass]; Lev Landa's "algorithmization" methods [Landa, L. (1974), *Algorithmization in learning and instruction,* Englewood Cliffs, NJ: Learning Technology Publications]; and in modern cognitive psychology, e.g., Perkins, D. N. (1981), *The mind's best work,* Cambridge, MA: Harvard University Press; Perkins, D. N. (1986), *Knowledge as design,* Hillsdale, NJ: Lawrence Erlbaum. All involve analysis of people's "thinking out loud" while they perform behaviors, solve problems, or recall experiences to identify cognitive competencies.

12

Developing a
Competency Model

This chapter describes how to develop a competency model from Behavioral
Event Interview (BEI), survey, panel, expert system, and observation data.

ANALYZING BEHAVIORAL EVENT INTERVIEW DATA

Research to develop competency models is a "discovery of grounded theory"
approach.[1] To discover competencies, we work backward from the criterion—
superior or effective performance in a job—to identify the characteristics of
people who perform at these levels.

Two "thematic analysis" methods are used to identify competencies in BEI
data: (1) coding interview transcripts for known competencies, using the
Competency Dictionary; and (2) conceptualizing new competency themes
from interview narratives. Thematic analysis is the most difficult and creative
part of the competency analysis process.

Thematic Analysis

Thematic analysis is the process of identifying themes or patterns in raw data.
This ability is itself two levels of the competency Conceptual Thinking:

- Use of Concepts (CT A.1 to A.3) is the ability to recognize or apply a
  concept *already known* from previous study or research. An example of
  Use of Concepts is the ability to code BEI transcripts for competency

levels described in the Competency Dictionary provided in Chapters 3 through 9.

■ Concept Creation (CT A.4 to A.7) or "Conceptualization" is the ability to *recognize a pattern* and *invent a new concept* to make sense of raw data. For example, consider the following brief incidents in the life of Bill:

1. As a boy, Bill was always taking apart mechanical things and fixing them.
2. Bill was captain of his high school baseball team.
3. Bill dropped out of school and joined the Navy because he was "tired of school."
4. Bill was rated the top mechanic in his work group. Co-workers looked to him for direction and help.
5. Bill turned down a promotion and left the Navy because he didn't want to attend a required advanced technical training school.

What do these five incidents tell us about Bill?

There seem to be certain patterns or themes in Bill's life. Data (shown in italic at left) from Bill's critical incidents suggest the three themes on the right:

Incident	Supporting Data	Theme
1	Bill was *always taking things apart and fixing them.*	Bill likes and is good with mechanical things.
4	Bill was rated the *top mechanic.*	
2	Bill was *captain* of his baseball team.	Bill is a leader.
4	Co-workers *looked to him for direction and help.*	
3	Bill *dropped out of school* because he was *"tired of school."*	Bill doesn't like formal schooling.
5	Bill *didn't want to attend a required school.*	

Identifying these themes is an example of thematic analysis conceptualization: You have to recognize or invent concepts such as "good at mechanical things" or "doesn't like school" to make sense of Bill's data. Knowing these themes could help you make better personnel decisions concerning Bill. For example, you would probably not recommend him for an advanced computer programming course but might consider him for promotion to foreperson of a maintenance work crew.

Identifying Competencies: *What* to Look For

One systematic way to organize a thematic analysis of competency data is to look at how superior and average people answer each of the key questions in BEIs.

1. *Situation.* Do superiors and average talk about different kinds of things in their BEIs? Do they focus on different parts of the job?

Example: *salespeople, bank trust officers*

Superiors talk about *selling*.	Averages talk about *administration* — keeping paperwork straight.
I saw the annual review meeting as a chance to *sell* more services.	I was really concerned that all *preparations* for the annual review meeting were *right*—people had travel *arrangements*, etc.

Self-concept competencies are often indicated by the way people think about their jobs (e.g., "I am a salesman" vs. "I am an administrator").

2. *Who Is Involved.* Are there differences in the way superiors and averages see their involvement with people or equipment? Do they regard others positively or negatively?

Example: *computer programmers*

Superiors talk about *clients' needs* (user orientation).	Averages talk about *machines*, not people (hardware orientation).
I heard *him* saying *he needed* all the data in a simple format that could fit on one page.	The *HP3000/30's* BASIC compiler was too slow, so I went directly to a *machine* language routine.

Example: *alcoholism counselors, diplomats, consultants*

Superiors express *positive regard* and *expectations* for clients.	Averages express *negative* sentiments toward clients.
She was having a bad time, but I knew she was a *strong person* who was *going to get it together*.	Face it—we get the real *dregs* here—there's *not much we can do for them*.

3. *Thoughts.* Are there differences between superiors and averages in the way they think, use concepts or knowledge, make sense of complex data, remember details, organize things in logical order?

Example: *consultants*

Superiors are high in *Conceptual Thinking:* They see themes and patterns in complex data.	Averages cannot make sense of complex data.
We had about 40 flipcharts with maybe 500 observations—*I cooked these down to the five key problems* the workgroup was facing.	We got the survey data back in a six-inch printout, *hundreds of* pages of *statistics. I couldn't make any sense of it,* so we ended up junking it.

Example: *manufacturing managers, military officers, pilots*

Superiors are high in *attention to detail:* They think in checklists and are able to tick off numerous items involved in planning tasks; they are also high in *logical thought* prioritizing tasks in order of importance and scheduling them in logical order.	Averages talk about tasks in vague, general terms, appear overwhelmed by detail, and do not prioritize or schedule tasks by detail, or in logical order.
There were *20 steps* required to get the aviation fuel-pumping system ready for inspection: (1) . . . , (2) . . ." [names all twenty]. *I prioritized* them and got two crews working on the toughest. Also, I saw several steps could be worked on at the same time, so I *laid out a schedule* that got everything done in the shortest time.	I'm in a continual state of crisis management. There's no way to plan ahead, so I just *deal* with things *on a day-to-day basis.*

Conversely, superior creative people think divergently, not logically.

Example: *creative designers*

Superiors overflow with ideas in a somewhat breathless, random order.	Averages think *logically, convergently;* they go by the book.
Wow—once I started visualizing it—painted green, covered with velvet, with a built-in vibrator, etc.	I know there are three basic shapes for that dress—I've got the design handbook right here.

4. *Motivation.* Do superiors and averages talk about *wanting* different things? Do they see situations in different terms?

Example: *small-business entrepreneurs*

Superiors think about *achievement,* doing better against goals.

Averages think about *power,* influencing others, enhancing their status.

I *set my goal* at 110% of quota, for the *challenge*—last year I'd made quota, and just doing that again didn't seem like much fun.

I knew the way to *impress* the competition was to put on a splashy show with a big booth at the trade fair, so I did it, even though I couldn't really afford it.

Conversely, superior managers think about *power,* not individual achievement (doing a task themselves) or affiliation (getting people to like them).

Example: *managers, military officers*

Superiors think about *influencing others* to get jobs done.

Averages think about wanting to be liked or wanting to do a job well themselves.

I pulled out all the stops—I wanted to *persuade* them to work overtime to get the job done. *I appealed to their pride* but included a veiled *threat* about how we'd all be out of a job if we lost the contract.

I couldn't ask him to stay—it was his kid's birthday. You just *get yourself disliked* that way. I said the hell with 'em. I *could do it faster and better* myself than if I had to tell them how to do it.

5.   *Feelings.* Do superiors or averages differ in their feelings or how they express or control their feelings?

Example: *managers, military officers*

Superiors show high *emotional self-control.*

Averages do not control their emotions.

I knew I was getting upset, so I want out for coffee and walked around until *I calmed down.* When I went back to the meeting, I was calm and collected.

I blew my stack, pounded on the desk and told him to get the hell out.

6.   *Actions.* Do superiors or averages *do* different things or show different skills in dealing with similar situations or people?

Example: *entrepreneurs, managers, superstars* in almost every field

Superiors are *proactive:* take *initiative*—nonroutine action to accomplish objectives or solve problems—and *persist* (try two or more action steps to overcome obstacles) when blocked.	Averages are *reactive:* tend not to take nonroutine actions, and give up rather than persist when blocked.
She wanted a transfer—she was a good kid and I wanted to keep her. *I called Personnel;* they said "no way." I called Corporate; they said the same. *I kept submitting the request.* Then I remembered I had a friend in Texas who had some clout at Corporate and who owed me one. *I called him,* and he pounded it through.	I sent the request through channels. Personnel said no. I patiently explained to her that there wasn't much I could do—it was out of my hands.

Example: *human service workers*

Superiors show interpersonal *listening* skills, especially *accurate empathy,* sensitivity to and understanding of others' feelings.	Averages do not understand, pick up on, or show sensitivity to others' feelings.
He seemed *upset—I could see he was hurting.* I made myself available to be talked to.	Damned if I know what was going on with him—some people just can't hack it, I guess.

7.   *Outcomes.* Do superiors and averages produce different *outcomes?*

Example: *consultants, managers*

Superiors achieve outcomes for their organizations (socialized power) and/or use power in a way that empowers others.	Averages achieve outcomes for themselves, using power in a way that makes others feel the consultant or manager is strong.
I set it up so they all got the credit—it really motivated the team, and our unit did quite well.	I made sure I got the juiciest assignment, did it well, and got the kudos. The others were envious, which is their problem.

8.   *Other Characteristics.* Traits or competencies not expressed in the BEI may be apparent to the interviewer, including:

a. *Physical Appearance.* Do superiors and averages *look* different, dress differently, and appear to have "charisma" or "command presence" versus a lack of impact?

Example: *diplomats, police captains*

Superiors have "command presence" —are large, imposing, impeccably dressed, distinguished looking.	Averages do not impress by appearance.

b. *Physical Setting, Materials, Props.* Do superiors and averages differ in those surroundings under their control, such as offices, resources, accessories?

Example: *manufacturing managers, military officers*

Superiors displayed many planning devices: "to do" lists, tickler (follow-up and monitoring) forms and files, PERT charts, etc.	Averages did not display planning devices.

c. *Articulateness/Conversational Style/Verbal Fluency.*

Example: *senior government officials, college deans, and presidents*

Superiors were charming, spontaneous, easily and persuasively told detailed, colorful stories, and seemed to enjoy conversation.	Averages had trouble talking, remembering and telling incidents, were vague, hemmed and hawed, and appeared uncomfortable in conversation.

Interestingly, in one study of public utility forepeople, articulateness was negatively associated with performance. The forepeople who "talked a good game" turned out to be the averages.

As these examples illustrate, thematic analysis is a continual comparing and contrasting of superior and average performers. Any difference may suggest a competency.

It may be helpful to organize observations of differences into general categories, such as these three:

■ *Cognitive/Intellectual.* Skills involved in creating, getting, or using information; learning from experience; objectively analyzing data; or thinking through alternatives for action. Use of concepts, conceptualization, analytic thinking, logical thought, and divergent thinking are cognitive/intellectual competencies.

- *Interpersonal.* Skills involved in communicating with, understanding, and influencing others, such as accurate empathy, positive regard and expectations, articulateness and public speaking ability are interpersonal competencies.

- *Motivational.* The needs or drives that cause people to want and do different things; achievement, affiliation, and power motives; and emotional self-control, are motivation competencies.

The preceding competencies illustrate *what* to look for in thematic analysis. These examples provide a number of concepts that can be used diagnostically in analyzing BEI transcripts.

Precise definition of competencies still requires considerable conceptualization ability. Subtle nuances in what a competency means or how it is expressed are critical in identifying what it really takes to do a job well.

For example, superior performers in a job may appear to be more persistent than average performers. However, it is important to define the kinds of persistence involved. Does the persistence derive from a motivational need for power—the desire to influence people or be right? Or is it a kind of orderliness that insists on picking up loose ends? Or is it simply a liking for routine, for doing things in a standard way? This deeper level of analysis is absolutely essential to identifying correct competencies.

It is also important to distinguish the degree or strength of the competency required. Some competencies are curvilinear: Having too little of the competence causes a person to fail, but having too much also predicts failure. For example, a certain level of clerical skill is needed to be an effective social worker. Too little competence in filling out forms means clients won't receive their welfare payments. But social workers with too much interest in form processing spent too little time with clients to serve them effectively and were seen as cold and bureaucratic. Identifying the right degree of administrative skill in this case is critical to understanding what is needed to be an effective social worker.

Identifying Competencies: *How* to Look

The following team approach has been found to help researchers in identifying competencies. This approach consists of three analysis and four validation steps:

Analysis Steps

1. *Form the Analysis Team.* Ideally, a competency thematic analysis team should include at least four persons who conducted the BEIs for the study. If fewer interviewers were used, noninterviewers experienced in thematic analysis may also be suitable. Interviewers are preferred because the very experience

of interviewing and observing subjects in their work settings makes team members more sensitive to the nuances, language, and culture of the people and job being studied.

2. *Individual Analysis of Interviews.* Analysis team members work in pairs. Each analyst receives BEI transcripts for a mix of four to six superior and average interviewees drawn from a sample of half of the interviews conducted (but at least 10). Analysts should receive some of their own interviews and some done by other team members. This minimizes analyst bias yet ensures a variety of analyst perspectives.

Working independently, each analyst reads each assigned transcript and identifies competency themes. Good practice is to underline *everything* in an interview that might suggest a competency theme. Any competency recognized from the competency dictionary is noted, or coded, on the margin of the transcript opposite the words underlined. The analysts use their own words for themes and/or the abbreviation for the competency and its level.

A high-tech method of coding uses a word processor with multiple windows. The transcript is in one window and the competency dictionary in another. Examples of competencies can be copied from the transcript to the dictionary to provide custom examples of each competency level coded. The dictionary itself can be customized by tailoring the definitions of competencies and competency levels to describe the data being coded.

Table 12–1 illustrates a "first cut" analysis of an incident from a study of college teachers. Note themes that seem to be emerging: "sees student problems" and "sensitivity to student feelings."

"Sensitivity to student feelings" is a version of Interpersonal Understanding, which includes competencies such as accurate empathy and nonverbal sensitivity known to predict success in a variety of human service jobs. "Linking academic assignments to student interests," however, is new: a competency unique, perhaps, to the job of teaching. Identifying this competency in

Table 12–1   Coding/Thematic Analysis of a BEI Transcript

Incident	Analyst Notes
Interviewee p. 9	
I had this one student, a black woman, who was <u>struggling.</u> She had a <u>real desire to learn</u>—I mean, she was really hanging in there. But she had <u>difficulty articulating.</u> One of the requirements of my course was a <u>position paper. I figured that was going to be a real problem for her.</u> We were out on this field trip, and I saw she was alone. So <u>I sidled up to her,</u> as unobtrusively as I could, and said a couple of little amenities:	Sees student problems (IU A3) Positive expectations, regard (DEV 1) Sees student problems (IU A3) Sees student problems (IU A3)

Table 12–1 *(Continued)*

Incident	Analyst Notes
"How's it going, Maggie?" "How do you feel?" "What's your reaction?" And she said, "It's funny that you asked because that meram grass that you pointed out really brought back some memories that I'd just as soon forget."	Invites student to talk (INFO 1, IU B2)
Now, meram grass is that razor-edged grass that grows in sandy areas and is one of the initial pieces of vegetation that holds the sand down. So one thing that this told me is that she had learned the name of meram grass! But the way she said it was with such a depth of feeling that I couldn't help but say, "Well, if you don't mind telling me, what was the memory?" And she said, "The way it grows reminded me of the cottonfields back home in Mississippi; I remember my mother picking cotton until she could hardly straighten up and I remember being brought into the fields as a kid to help pick the cotton and that's the reason I left, trying to prove myself, by coming to Chicago."	Sensitive to student feelings (IU A1) Notices when student learns something Notices, is sensitive to student's feelings: Accurate empathy (IU A2) Invites student to talk about feelings (INFO 1, IU B2)
Well, that kind of hit me, and I said, "Well, have you decided what subject you are going to take for the position paper?" She said, "No, I'm really worried about it." Now, she never would have told me she was worried about it. So I said, "Why don't you take this subject of meram grass and relate it back to cottonfields and relate that to change, because you're not in cottonfields now, but your mother was, and that's change, that adaptation, that's growth, development." Well, her eyes opened up like silver dollars and she said, "Oh, I am glad you said that, that sounds good." And she ended up doing that, and she did it extremely well.	Sensitive to student feelings (IU A2) Invites student to talk about feelings (INFO 1, IU B2) Sensitive to student feelings (IU A2) Links academic assignments to student's experience (IU B4? DEV 6?); UNIQUE: makes assignment meaningful Sensitive to student feelings (IU A3, B3) "Empowers" student—makes her feel strong (DEV 5) Positive regard/notices when student does well (DEV 1)

(Thematic Analyst's first cut noting all themes from a college teacher that might suggest competencies of a critical incident.)

raw critical incident data is an example of Concept Creation. If validated, it might become a known competency concept usable in other thematic analyses. For example, effective managers might be found to sound out subordinates' feelings, then assign them tasks on the basis of their emotions or interests.

An incident, action, or sentence may be coded for more than one competency. For example, "I *convinced* them to *do better*" is coded for both Impact and Influence and Achievement competencies. Specific words relating to each competency coded should be underlined. Superior performers' stories often include competency "molecules"—several competencies used together to accomplish a task or deal with a difficult situation. These combinations should be described in the competency model. Competency combinations, or algorithms, provide important information about how superior performers get better-than-average results and are very helpful when applying the model for development or performance improvement.

Competencies are coded each time they appear, providing data on frequency as well as the scale level. For example, a difference between average and superior salespeople is the frequency with which they spot and seize opportunities. Average performers may tell of one or two such instances in a two-hour research interview, while superior performers tell of six or eight. The scale level or coding of each of these stories may be the same, but the higher frequency of the behavior leads to improved results.

Competency themes are summarized on a Theme Log on 5" × 8" cards, or, if a word processor is used, directly as edits to the dictionary. The page number of the transcript on which evidence for the theme is found is noted opposite the theme. Tick marks are used to note how often the theme is expressed. Page numbers with the best examples of each theme should be circled (or copied to the dictionary). When each analyst has read the four to six BEI transcripts initially assigned, he or she trades transcripts with the analyst he or she is paired with and individually analyzes each new transcript in the same way. This process generates the largest possible number of competency concepts using the perspectives of all team members.

Analysts should also note algorithms: superior performers' rules of thumb, behaviors, or strategies for handling important job tasks or situations. Algorithms are not competencies, but are usually evidence of two or more competencies used together or in a sequence.

An algorithm can range from the simple—"turn the nut finger-tight, then a further three-quarters turn with a wrench"—to the complex (a flow chart of steps required to perform a difficult operation).

Table 12–2 shows the interpersonal and cognitive competency differences between a superior and an average technician who repairs high tech equipment:

- *Interpersonal Competencies.* The average repair technician first looks at the machine. The superior technician first interviews the operator of the broken machine, tactfully, taking care to talk in operator rather than

Table 12–2   Competencies of High-Tech Repair People

Average	Superior
Step N: Diagnosis	
• Look at machine	• Interview key operator:
	Speak operator language
	Interact tactfully: "Cool out" (positive regard, accurate empathy)
	"Inquiry Strategy": Cues associated with malfunction ("clank," "puff of blue smoke")
	Listen accurately:
	a. Identify key words
	b. Respond positively
Step K: Fix	
• Linear search sequence	• Try quick fixes (hypotheses)
	• Half-split search sequence
Step X: Leave-Taking	
• "Good-bye"	• Teach key operators:
	How to avoid problem
	How to fix problem

technical language and to sympathize with the operator who is frantic at not being able to get his or her work done. The best repair technicians use an inquiry strategy of questions to elicit facts associated with the machine's breakdown that might help diagnose the problem.

After fixing the machine, the average repair technician says good-bye. The superior technician stays to teach the operator how to avoid the problem in the future and/or how to fix it him or herself.

■ *Cognitive Competencies.* The average technician uses a linear search sequence, that is, starts testing at the first point the machine could malfunction, then point 2, then point 3, and so on, until the problem is found. The superior technician uses If → Then hypotheses to deduce problems from the pattern of malfunction symptoms, then tries quick fixes. Often this enables the technician to jump to the correct solution and avoid a lengthy diagnostic testing session. When the best technicians do diagnostic testing, they use a "split half" search sequence: that is, they start in the *middle* of the machine's operating cycle, and test forward and back. This narrows their search by half of the possible malfunction points. They then test the half of the system that has the malfunction, cutting their search in half again. This process leads to the problem geometrically and much more efficiently than a linear search.

Figure 12–1 shows a cognitive-affective algorithm for superior versus average "cold call" salespeople. All cold callers meet with frequent rejection. Average performers feel helpless (affect), think about how hopeless or bad their job, company, product, or service is (cognition), and respond with "flight" behavior (e.g., go home early and have a couple of stiff drinks to avoid their feelings of rejection). Superior performers feel *nothing* (report no affect whatsoever when rejected), think about how to solve the problem ("I could say I was calling from inside using the prospect's first name, and get around the secretary"), then respond with goal-oriented behavior: "So I did 1, 2, 3 . . ."

Algorithms can be used to construct specific tests, such as for Self-Confidence B (Dealing with Failure: absence of fear of rejection and depressive explanatory style). Algorithms are most useful for developing training to teach new hires or average employees the behaviors of superior performers (e.g., efficient trouble-shooting or "overcoming call reluctance" training—essentially cognitive therapy for depression—for cold callers).

3. *Thematic Analysis Team Definition of Competencies.* The analyst team meets in daylong sessions to discuss and document competency themes identified by individual analysis of the transcripts. Each analyst in turn describes the themes he or she found. Each theme discussed should be characteristic of the superior performers as a group (positive themes), characteristic of the average performers as a group (negative themes) or characteristic of all performers (threshold themes). Themes suggested by team members should be stated in specific behavioral terms. Evidence for the themes should be read from the transcripts and/or posted on flip charts.

Unique competencies, those not found in the generic dictionary, are discussed and then either added to the competency dictionary as a customized level of a known competency or as a new competency. New competencies may be presented as simple presence/absence behavioral indicators or, preferably,

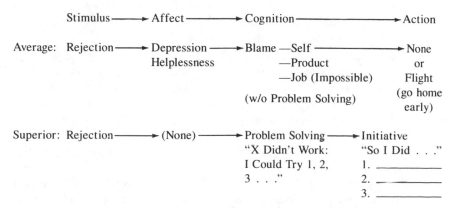

Figure 12–1 Self-Confidence in "Cold Call" Selling

in the form of just-noticeable-difference scales similar to those in the competency dictionary (see instructions for developing JND scales in Chapter 3, Developing a Competency Dictionary).

Analyst team members then "boil down" the group competency themes into the smallest number of competency clusters that can include all themes found. Usually individual analysts will have used different words to describe themes and/or conceptualized unique competencies in somewhat different ways. The real task of the analysts' competency definition meeting is to argue out and agree on the best words or labels to describe each competency cluster and theme.

Judgment, experience, and understanding of the client are needed to weigh and integrate data coded against a generic dictionary. Questions to consider include:

- Are the data believable? Check any unusual or missing values.

- Are certain competencies combined in patterns? For example, all or most analytical thinking in a sales model may be about Impact and Influence or Organizational Awareness, but this is very different from a technical model where most analytical thinking is about technical issues.

- Which competencies are most important? The degree of importance is a combination of a competency's frequency, the consequences of its absence, benefits of its presence, and its future necessity, given the company's strategic direction. Some thought about the outcomes of the incidents in which competencies were displayed or missing is helpful.

- Is there a pattern to how the competency occurs? Is it present in most of the superior performers, or just a few? Is it absent in most average performers, or only some of them?

- Which competencies and which levels contain most of the data? Irrelevant or rarely seen competencies or levels should be omitted. Long "laundry lists" of competencies are less useful than shorter, better focused lists of the most essential items. A good rule of thumb is Miller's "magical number 7 plus or minus 2."[2] Efficient competency models list the five to nine most important competencies.

- How does the competency play out in the job being studied? Does Initiative consist of both "seizing opportunities" and "preventing problems" or is it mostly "preventing problems?" Similar questions should be considered for each competency and the behavioral indicator rewritten to reflect how it is displayed in the job. For example, Table 12–3 presents a Competency Model developed for college teachers. Note that the competencies in this model look quite different from the generic scales. Generic dictionary scale level descriptions are written to cover as many different jobs as possible. These definitions cannot give the precision and direction essential to a model that is to be used for development or performance improvement.

Table 12–3 Competency Model of Effective Teachers and Mentors in
Nontraditional Degree Programs

Competencies	Indicators
1. Student-Centered Orientation	
a. Has Positive Expectations of Students	(+) Positive regard: expresses view that average students are capable; identifies and affirms others' capabilities
	(+) Expresses view that students are capable of change
	(+) Permits student-initiated modifications of the learning contract when they are consistent with the student's learning objectives
	(−) Negative regard: expresses view that students are stupid and incapable of change; treats students with disdain; identifies students' weaknesses without suggesting ways to help
	(−) Expresses negative stereotypes of others, their personality or potential
b. Attends to Students' Concerns	(+) Is accessible: makes self available to students of average ability as well as to those of superior ability
	(+) States awareness of students' feelings
	(−) Does not recall details of "high" and "low" points in dealing with individual students
	(−) Puts own concerns, well-being, or objectives before students' interests
	(−) Identifies with standards of elite or traditional institutions

The results of the analysis team are summarized in a Competency Model, as shown in Table 12–3. Competency codebooks are organized by competency clusters, competencies, and behavioral indicators. Competency level behavioral indicators, with examples, provide the criteria for coding the presence of a competency in a BEI transcript.

Validation Steps.   If the competency model is to be used for research or selection, additional validation steps can be used to refine the Competency Model Dictionary and develop interrater reliability.

4. *Preliminary Testing of the Competency Coding System: Individual Coding.* Analyst team pairs receive copies of the codebook and copies of BEI transscripts not previously coded. Each analyst codes the transcripts assigned to him or her, indicating the competency abbreviation from the codebook after each note in the transcript as shown in Table 12–1.

5. *Analyst Team Meets to Reconcile Coding.* Analyst team pairs meet to discuss their coding, reconcile differences, and agree on coding for each interview transcript. This process results in further refinement of the Competency Codebook. For example, the criteria for recognizing when a competency is present are refined to increase coder reliability. The draft codebook is revised to include these refinements.

6. *Statistical Analysis of Preliminary BEI Sample.* Interview coding is analyzed statistically to see (a) if coders have reached an acceptable level of interrater reliability, and (b) which themes best distinguish superior from average

Table 12–4   Statistical Analysis of the College Teacher Competencies

Competency	Competency Strength		Significance* (t-test)
	Study Sample ($n = 16$)	Control Sample ($n = 14$)	Total Sample ($n = 30$)
1. Student-centered orientation			
a. Has positive expectations of students	3.8	−2.9	4.91**
b. Attends to students' concerns	3.7	−2.5	3.99**
2. Humanistic-learning orientation			
a. Values the learning process	3.8	0.9	4.28**
b. Views specialized knowledge as a resource	0.8	−0.3	3.51**
3. Creating a context conducive to adult learning			
a. Works to understand students' frames of reference	3.3	1.1	3.48**
b. Works to establish mutuality and rapport	2.6	0.4	3.24**
c. Holds students accountable to their best learning interests	1.9	−0.4	4.43**
4. Grounding learning objectives in an analysis of students' needs			
a. Actively seeks information about students	3.6	0.9	3.97**
b. Diagnoses	4.3	1.3	3.96**
c. Prescribes action	3.8	1.1	3.53**
5. Facilitating the learning process			
a. Links pedagogy to students' concerns	3.9	1.6	3.03**
b. Structures processes to facilitate students' active learning	4.3	0.7	4.80**
c. Adapts to situational demands	1.3	0.1	3.33**
d. Responds to nonverbal cues	1.8	0.5	2.25**

*One-tailed probabilities: **$p < .01$.

performers. Themes present in both superior and average performers are identified as threshold competencies.

Steps 5 and 6 may be repeated several times until Competency Codebook definitions are detailed enough to establish interrater reliability and to differentiate superior from average performers.

7. *Coding the Remainder of the BEI Sample.* The revised codebook is validated by scoring applied to the remainder of the BEI transcripts (i.e., transcripts not considered in Steps 1–5). Two members of the core interview team will ordinarily be selected to code these interview transcripts. Coders independently score these transcripts blind (i.e., they do not know whether the transcript they are scoring is that of a superior or average performer). They meet only to discuss problem cases or examples that are difficult to code.

8. *Final Statistical Analysis.* Statistical analyses are performed on the scores given to the BEI transcripts in the validation sample to see if the codebook competencies really distinguish superiors from averages. Table 12–4 shows a statistical analysis for college teachers. Data from all interviews are then analyzed together to further refine and cluster the competencies.

9. *Preparation of Final Competency Codebook for the Job.* The final Competency Codebook is prepared. It contains precise definitions of each competency with detailed rules and examples of scoring from BEI transcripts.

ANALYZING PANEL, SURVEY, EXPERT SYSTEM AND OBSERVATION DATA

Panel, survey, expert system, and observation data are used to confirm findings from the BEI analysis and add (selectively) any competencies missed. Table 12–5 shows a spreadsheet matrix of competencies by data sources. Competencies identified by each data source are ranked high (3), medium (2), low (1), or absent (0) in importance for predicting average and superior performance in a job. Data sources can be weighted according to the researchers' confidence in the data collection method used in the study. For example, in Table 12–5, BEI data are weighted 2; Panel data, 1.5; and Survey and Expert System data, 1. The spreadsheet can be used to calculate an overall score for each competency, from 0 (not present) to 1.00 (present and rated "high" in importance by all data sources), and sort competencies needed for adequate and superior performance in descending order of importance. Analysts' highest confidence can be placed in those competencies that all data sources indicate are important to doing a job well.

Discrepancies in data from various data sources provide useful information. For example, the expert system may indicate that a competency *should* be present but is *not* found in an organization's BEI, panel, or survey data. As the expert system references a data base of all previous analyses of similar jobs in

Table 12–5 Spreadsheet: Integration of Competency-Model Data

Competency	BEI		Survey		Panel		Expert System		Summary		
Range	L = 1, H = 3		L = 0, H = 1.0		0, L = 1, H = 3		0, L = 1, H = 3		L = 0, H = 1.0		
Average or Superior	A	S	A	S	A	S	A	S	A	S	
WT	2	2	1	1	1.5	1.5	1	1	16.5	16.5	DIVISOR
Ach Drive	2	3	0.611	1	1	3	3	3	0.536	1.00	
Initiative	1	3	0.72	0.85	2	3	1	3	0.498	0.934	
Order & Org	1	2	0.44	0.2	2	1	1	2	0.430	0.453	

other organizations, this means that even the client organization's superior performers lack a competency that other superior performers—probably in competitive organizations—have. This is valuable competitive intelligence for the client organization: it will need to select for or train the missing competency to remain competitive.

If Panel and Survey data—the organization's best estimate of a job's requirements—indicate a competency is important, but it does not appear in BEIs of superior performers, it may be an espoused competency not actually needed to do the job well, a competency that will be needed in the future, or a competency suppressed by the organization's management or culture. In these cases, the expert system can act as a tiebreaker. If it indicates the competency is needed to do similar jobs, the competency should be considered for future selection and training. If evidence suggests that organizational factors are suppressing one or more needed competencies, management training and organizational development interventions may be indicated. If not required, the competency is an espoused value in the organization but not actually needed for effective or superior performance.

RECOMMENDED FORMAT FOR
COMPETENCY MODEL REPORTS

Following a brief description of the study method, competencies should be presented by cluster. Competencies can be clustered in any of several ways. Options include:

- By *dictionary cluster.* As in Chapters 3 through 9: Achievement-related, Power-related, Cognitive, Interpersonal (affiliation), Self-Management.
- By *job task* or responsibility. For example, a first-level supervisor model clustered competencies in terms of managing self, one other person, and groups:

    Cluster 1. Manages Self (*n* Ach, cognitive problem-solving style—competencies internal to the person, not involving others)

    Cluster 2. Manages *An*other (coaching, 1-on-1 influence, and interpersonal skills)

    Cluster 3. Manages Other*s* (group influence skills)

- By *logical sequence in time.* For example, successive steps in "consultative selling": a logical sequence of first getting data, then putting data together in meaningful patterns, and so on:

    Cluster 1. Consultative selling

    Competency 1. Gathers information from many and varied sources (Information seeking, Initiative)

    Indicator 1. Calls x friends in industry every 2 weeks to ask "what's new?"

    Competency 2. Identifies new market needs/opportunities (Conceptualization, Pattern Recognition)

Ideally, each competency should be scaled in JND intervals, with a behavioral indicator definition for each level *and* one or more examples of the competency level from BEI data, with words scored underlined or highlighted. The importance of examples cannot be emphasized too highly. Verbatim examples make the competency model "come alive." Examples convey the nuances of *how* a competency is used for a job in an organization's unique culture and environment. Anecdotes that illustrate how superior performers handle the most difficult situations on their jobs provide compelling material for communicating study findings and for training.

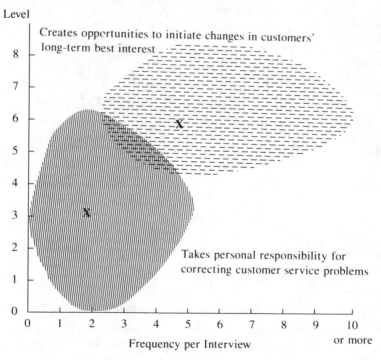

Figure 12–2   Difference Between Superior and Average Total Quality Managers

Graphs or tables can be used to show how competencies of superior performers differ from those of averages. A spreadsheet like that shown in Table 12–5 can be used to compare competencies identified by different data collection methods. Figure 12–2 shows the differences between superior and average "total quality" program managers on both level and frequency of Customer Service Orientation.

Additional data analyses that can add value include:

- A Job Responsibility by Competency matrix showing which competencies are needed to do each part of the job. The relation of competencies to job behaviors and results can also be shown in a "causal flow" model like that shown in Table 2–2. Competency by Job Responsibility figures can be used for risk assessment: the consequences in job performance if a competency is missing.

- Algorithms, or specific rules of thumb or tricks of the trade that superior performers use to get results. (Algorithms used by high tech repair people can be seen in Table 12–2.)

- Obstacles to improved performance such as organization management, structure or cultural factors that may suppress expression of competencies in current or future jobs. Competency studies, especially BEI data, provide a wealth of information for organizational diagnosis. If these data suggest the need for management, structure, or organization development changes, these problems should discussed in the report.

Competency reports should conclude with recommendations for human resource applications that can add value to the organization. Examples of selection, performance management, succession planning, development, compensation, and information systems uses of competency data are provided in Part V.

NOTES

1. See Glaser, B. & Straus, A. (1967), *The discovery of grounded theory*, Chicago: Aldine; Straus, A., & Corbin, J. (1990), *Basics of qualitative research: Grounded theory procedures and techniques*, Newbury Park, CA: Sage.

2. Miller, G. A. (1956), The magical number seven, plus or minus two: Some limits on our capacity for processing information. *Psychological Review, 63*, 81–97.

Findings: Generic Competency Models

13

Technicians
and Professionals

INTRODUCTION TO CHAPTERS 13 THROUGH 17

Most of the original models specified only those behaviors that distinguished superior from average performance. The behaviors and characteristics discussed were more common in superior than in average performers. The absence of a characteristic from a model may mean either that the characteristic was irrelevant to the position or that it was a minimum requirement, found in all jobholders. Usually we have some sense of which is the case, based on the reading of average transcripts and on the panel discussions that preceded many models.

Since most recent models specify the characteristics of average (threshold, minimum-required, typical) performance as well as superior performance, this source of uncertainty will be eliminated in the future.

The generic models will not fit any specific position well, but are intended to form a basis for comparison between groups. Generic models are also used to provide a comparison with new models (i.e.,"this job is different from the usual sales manager position in this way"). The comparison of models of a number of similar positions from different companies and different years also provides a way to validate the results. If the same qualities are found to characterize superior first-level supervisors in a wide variety of situations, we can feel confident of the validity of those findings.

PROCEDURE FOR CODING MODELS

The original competency models were each organized into 3 to 6 clusters containing 12 to 27 competencies, each with 3 to 7 behavioral indicators plus examples (quotes from interviews), descriptions and explanations. Some models had many examples and much explanation while others had little or no explanation, description, and/or examples.

The existing competency models were coded to a list of 350 generic behavioral indicators. These indicators were then matched to the Just-Noticeable-Difference scales given in Part II. A team of trained coders, each a specialist in one cluster of competencies, also coded the entire models (behavioral indicators, commentary, examples, etc.) directly to the generic scales. These coded (renotated) models were then ready to be compared with each other. In renotating the original competency models, the following procedures were used:

- The behavioral indicators, examples, and descriptions were all coded for all competencies. The title of the original competency was used as a clue to the intent of the writers of the model, but not as a restriction. A competency called "Group Management," which included indicators from the Leadership scale would be coded for both competencies. A single behavioral indicator might be coded for two competencies: "Seeks others' ideas and input in order to improve team productivity" would be coded for both Teamwork ("Seeks others' inputs . . .") and for Achievement Orientation (". . . in order to improve team productivity"). Achievement Orientation was coded both for personal productivity and for efforts to improve team, group, or others' performance. The final coding manual distinguished between personal and other-oriented (socialized) Achievement Orientation.

- The entire coding manual was divided into five sets of related competencies, coded by someone who specialized in that set. This allowed greater accuracy and also increased the frequency count of coding since specialists noted low levels of a competency in stories with a main theme showing a higher level of another competency.

- The original competency was the unit used to record the renotated behaviors. Each behavioral indicator was recorded only once per original competency (although if a behavioral indicator appeared in more than one original competency, it was recorded again). Thus if the same behavior was listed as an indicator, was described, and then showed up in two examples, all in the same original competency, it would still only be listed once. This rule compensated for the differences in detail in the reports. (Even with this rule, some models had 2 or 3 times as many observation points as others). It also made coding more reliable.

INTERPRETATION OF THE FREQUENCY OF INDICATORS

Most original competencies, when coded to the generic lists, contained elements from several generic competencies. Because of this and because each scale level (behavioral indicator) was coded for each original competency in which it appeared, a given indicator or scale level may not appear at all or may appear many times in the coding of a model. One or many of the scale levels (behavioral indicators) of a given competency may be coded for a model. In addition, the model writers tended to try to arrange their competencies so that there were roughly even numbers of examples for each competency. If most of the examples were about thinking, there would be several cognitive competencies with fine distinctions, while all the influence efforts might be lumped together in one competency. If a job is mainly about relationships with clients, there might be two or three competencies that would fit the generic Customer Service Scale (i.e., "Focusing on Client's Needs," "Partnering with the Client," and "Adding Value to the Client System"). These factors mean that the number (frequency) of indicators or scale levels for a certain competency gives an indication of the importance of that competency for superior performance in that job.

The discussions of specific job types in the following chapters are based on analysis of generic behavioral indicators and scale levels of a number of models for each category. In these analyses, all indicators from all relevant models were added together and *percentages* of the sum total were used for the frequency counts. Richer models, from which more detail was available, had more generic behavioral indicators and received relatively more weight than sparser models. This weighting seemed appropriate since we have more confidence in the accuracy of the reading of models rich in examples and description.

Use of percentage of the model as the measure of frequency makes comparison of models of varying levels of detail easier, but it partly obscures the comparison between simple and complex jobs, where one job may actually require more competencies than another job. In this case, the percentage frequency of other competencies will be forced down as additional competencies are included.

Although in the following chapters we use frequency of indicators as a stand-in for the importance of the competency, in actual practice the importance of a competency is a combination of frequency with professional judgment regarding:

- The negative consequences attendant on the lack of the competency
- The importance of the benefits of using the competency in this job
- The future requirements of the job, given foreseeable changes in the work environment and in the company's strategic direction

Technical/professionals are defined as individual contributors whose work involves the use of technical (as opposed to human services) knowledge. Jobs studied include software developers, engineers, applied research scientists, and a technical job in a bank trust department.

Technical/professionals deal primarily with problems concerning machines, numbers, or physical processes, rather than with interpersonal processes and problems. Given this focus, it is intriguing that fully one-quarter of the distinguishing characteristics fall into the interpersonal and managerial clusters. The best "hard science" technical/professionals use interpersonal skills and teamwork to accomplish their technical jobs.

GENERIC MODEL FOR INDIVIDUAL CONTRIBUTORS

Since this model includes a wide range of knowledge workers, its primary use is to contrast the competencies of the knowledge worker in general with those of the manager, human services professional, salesperson, and so on.

Competencies are discussed in the descending order of importance in distinguishing superior technical professionals (see Table 13–1). Within each competency, specific typical behaviors are also described in descending order of importance. "Importance" is measured by the frequency with which the competency appeared in a group of models of technical/professionals.

Achievement Orientation

Achievement Orientation is the single most frequent distinguishing characteristic of superior technical contributors. The main focus is on measuring performance or outcomes against a standard of excellence (ACH A.3) and on improving outcomes or performance in some way (ACH A.4):

> Part of an engineering job is making forecasts, and something that I've always attempted to do is go back and find out how accurate I was in my forecasts. And you can check reality, or actual, versus your forecast, or prediction. If the actual is something different from my prediction, I've always made an effort to go back and find out why. Because maybe I can learn to make better predictions in the future.

Meeting specific standards, including deadlines (ACH A.2), is also common. Some positions include setting challenging but achievable goals (ACH A.5). Sometimes these goals are highlighted by friendly competition such as bets on who will meet a challenging goal first, and a few include cost–benefit analyses (ACH A.6). One drilling engineer devised a procedure that decreased the time spent at the well site from 10 days to 3:

> I felt very effective there. We saved a hundred thousand dollars per well—four wells: that costs a half a million dollars. You're saving 20 percent of the whole cost. We have done probably 20 wells so far. We saved about $2 million.

Table 13–1   Generic Competency Model
for Technical Professionals

Weight*	Competency
XXXXXX	*Achievement Orientation* Measures performance Improves outcomes Sets challenging goals Innovates
XXXXX	*Impact and Influence* Uses direct persuasion, facts, and figures Gives presentations tailored to audience Shows concern with professional reputation
XXXX	*Conceptual Thinking* Recognizes key actions, underlying problems Makes connections and patterns
XXXX	*Analytical Thinking* Anticipates obstacles Breaks problem apart systematically Makes logical conclusions Sees consequences, implications
XXXX	*Initiative* Persists in problem solving Addresses problems before asked to
XXX	*Self-Confidence* Expresses confidence in own judgment Seeks challenges and independence
XXX	*Interpersonal Understanding* Understands attitudes, interests, needs of others
XX	*Concern for Order* Seeks clarity of roles and information Checks quality of work or information Keeps records
XX	*Information-Seeking* Contacts many different sources Reads journals, etc.
XX	*Teamwork and Cooperation* Brainstorms, solicits input Credits others
XX	*Expertise* Expands and uses technical knowledge Enjoys technical work; shares expertise
X	*Customer Service Orientation* Discovers and meets underlying needs

*"Weight" refers to the relative frequency with which each competency distinguishes superior from average performers. See p. 160, "Interpretation of the Frequency of Indicators."

For scientists and research professionals, a strong desire for innovation—trying new and different (better) ways to do things is critical (ACH C.2-4):

> . . . I worked all day and some progress was made, but that's not exciting to me. What's exciting is doing something new in the lab—something that leads to new science.

Impact and Influence

The competency of Impact and Influence is one of the most frequently mentioned distinguishers of superior technical/professionals. Technical/professionals primarily use Direct Persuasion (IMP A.2), supported by data, concrete examples or demonstrations, facts and figures, and graphic presentation:

> Management was looking for unprofitable services to eliminate and they came to the conclusion that one of the things they wanted to eliminate was the _____ services. I was able to put together an analysis that showed that this service was in fact extremely profitable. So I presented my analysis to the controller's department of the bank, which verified its accuracy, and top management was able to reach the same conclusion that I had.

Superior technical professionals tailor their comments or presentations to the anticipated reactions of the audience (IMP A.4):

> When I was planning the presentation, I knew it was for a management meeting, so I made it a broader view. I did not want to delve into the actual data and calculations I had generated, but rather give conclusions and key evidence.

They are also concerned about the impact of their ideas and about establishing professional credibility. In the interviews, the superior software engineers sometimes expressed an explicit concern with image. For example, a software engineer who had been involved in a project that took longer than expected voiced concern about how his boss perceived him. Describing another situation, when he had been delayed by an overloaded time-sharing system, this software engineer again expressed this concern.

More subtle influence strategies were rare in this group. Most of the content of Influence and Impact centered around technical issues: which ones had highest priorities, how they should be addressed, and presenting findings.

Conceptual Thinking and Analytical Thinking

These two competencies combined would be the most frequent distinguisher of technical/professional stars. The cognitive competencies were more frequently mentioned in this group of jobs than in many others. Within this group, the variety and strength of the cognitive competencies is related to the degree of research-science orientation in the position.

Technical professional jobs need both logical, deductive Analytical Thinking and Conceptual Thinking: Analytical Thinking appears most often as breaking tasks into component parts in a rational, systematic manner:

> . . . So we had the bearing problem. We made a list of about 20 things we thought it could be and set out to try to solve them, and we basically went through the list and started with the easiest things first. We got down to about 5 items fairly quickly and kept hashing over what could be wrong on a technical basis and then we got down to 2 items that I could think it could be. It was very specific decision making—let us get everything out and then go through it.

Analytical Thinking also appears as anticipating and planning for obstacles or seeing the implications or consequences of situations:

> The process of selling a customer on your interpretation of his need is basically being able to think at a lower level than he's been thinking, to raise the soft technical questions or issues about his problem. You're solving his problems in ways that make your job easier. You collect that information together and write bullets on a piece of paper and say, "These are the reasons, right here. . . ." [Also scores for Impact and Influence].

The more inductive Conceptual Thinking is equally important: seeing connections and patterns that others don't see; condensing large amounts of information in a useful manner; identifying key actions to take to resolve a murky situation; identifying underlying problems:

> One morning I was sitting here thinking of graphite and its properties. I got to thinking about the dry weather. Don't ask me why those two thoughts went through my mind except that it was hot in here. I began to think about moisture, dryness, and graphite and the way I began to put it together was relating it to a far removed phenomenon. I began to think about the flying fortresses of World War II that flew at great heights, where gun turrets and electrical systems were going out. It was the brushes on the generator burning out and was an emergency situation. So sitting here that Saturday morning, tying moisture and graphite together, I thought maybe there are other effects of moisture on graphite . . . (when I don't have a solution for a problem) I turn on the computer in the mind and let memory discs spin for awhile.

Conceptual Thinking also involves putting together information from different areas (an unusual or nonroutine application of a principle or procedure):

> We ran what's called a _____. It's common in gas wells but nobody that I knew had ever done it before on an oil well. It seemed like the concept was the same, to try to determine what the maximum bottom-hole pressure was, and try to determine what the producing bottom-hole pressure was.

The Analytical type of thinking may predominate in terms of frequency but not, perhaps, in terms of importance. In both cases most examples are found near or just above the middle range of the scales. Most of the content is technical, although a few examples included organizational or political effects.

Initiative

Initiative appears as Tenacity or Perseverance in sticking with a difficult problem until it is completed (INT A.1, B.2-3):

> I still remember in the afternoon my co-worker and I were talking. We just got so worked up. He had some material, I had a blender and we said, "By God, let's just go out and squeeze some of that stuff!"

This enthusiasm for the experiment and the reward in the immediacy of feedback explains some of the conceptual designer's persistence in solving problems:

> We tried about 50 different ways of doing it. Three worked. You could just smell it was going to work. It was just a matter of which way.

Initiative is also a matter of taking advantage of present opportunities or addressing present problems before being required to do so (INT A.2), and of acting on future opportunities or problems (INT A.4-5):

> We had a dust problem for a number of years. I had heard about it in my previous position, and I felt strongly about doing something about it. Though I tried my best, I knew I didn't have the expertise—I needed someone outside to help me, give me a recommendation. I did that and it worked. We reduced the dust by at least 50 to 90 percent.

Initiative is mostly found in terms of going beyond the required or expected effort to get the job done, although a few models mention exceeding formal authority to accomplish a task:

> I presented an idea to correct the problem to the engineer in charge of the project. He rejected my idea but didn't present any alternative. Since I had to meet a schedule, I implemented the idea, and it worked, and after that there was no argument.

In addition, many models mentioned taking on tasks clearly outside their job description. Superior researchers think about work-related problems off the job and coming up with solutions at odd times and places.

Self-Confidence

Self-Confidence is the main personal characteristic of superior Technical Professionals. It is most often seen as:

- Confidence in one's professional judgments (SCF A.3).
- A preference for or enjoyment of difficult challenges in the professional field. (SCF A.4) Most of the models' self-confidence seemed related to professional or technical skills, judgment.
- Actively seeking independence and responsibility in one's professional work. (SCF A.5):

When asked, "Can you do it?" he responded, "I don't see why not. We have three weeks!" (Another team had tried unsuccessfully to solve this problem for 6 months.)

When I first came here, my boss talked to me and he was real concerned that I was going to be a staff-operations engineer—I was going to be at a level with others who have been with the company a long time and are very knowledgeable and I was basically a rookie. He was concerned with whether I'd be able to handle that. Of course, me being just totally self-confident and thinking, "No problem at all—I'm really going to enjoy it," and I said it would be no problem (and it worked out fine).

Superior Technical Professionals show a wide variety of other qualities of personal maturity such as Flexibility and Ability to learn from mistakes, but not in a strong or consistent pattern.

Interpersonal Understanding

Interpersonal Understanding appears as fairly basic sensitivity to the attitudes, interests, and feelings of others (IU A.1 to 3). It is used to tailor and adapt presentations (and informal communications) and sometimes to help understand customer or end-user needs:

This driller had worked on these rigs for 30 or 40 years. You don't walk out to a person like that and tell him how to drill unless you want to climb out of a mud pit.

Concern for Order and Quality

Concern for Order, Accuracy, and Clarity was found more often than in most jobs (about 5% of the indicators). It was mostly focused around clarity for the sake of communication and/or future reference. A general concern for order and clarity of roles, expectations, and tasks, predominated in most models (CO 1 and 2):

I had been working with the production geologists who are responsible for the well, and I asked them if they had put together a testing program yet. They said, "Well, not specifically." As part of my experience in this business, I had seen it's always good to get things down very explicitly in writing—I guess as in any highly technical position. So I just said to them, "Well, do you want me to put one together?" And they said, "Yeah, go ahead." So I basically dwelled on my overseas experience and I put together a step-by-step basis what it took to test that well.

Double-checking information or accuracy and monitoring the quality of data were also found in most models (CO 4–5). Some models included designing new systems to increase order or improve the quality of data (CO 6). This level was found most often in computer and software professionals:

My role in the test program was to plan, establish, execute, and complete the program, then write a report that summarized all the activity. I have seen a lot of things not get documented. People in the future don't benefit from the knowledge gained, because it stays in somebody's head, and often that person is no longer available.

Information Seeking

Information Seeking among technical professionals appeared across the whole range from asking questions to extensive research and involving others who would not normally be involved. It was closely linked to networking among researchers.

Teamwork and Cooperation

Teamwork and Cooperation is by far the strongest "managerial" competency among technical professionals. Much technical work is done in teams or involves close coordination with other areas. The ability to foster a spirit of cooperation by genuinely soliciting others' input (TW 4) and by crediting and empowering others is important. (TW 5):

Well, I know all the field people and I would go down there and ask them how this equipment is working right now. I'm friends with all of them. We'd just have a friendly dialogue. The people we've got in most of these areas have been there for some time. They've got a lot of experience with that equipment. . . . Most of the foremen have been there for some time. . . . Between the foreman and the pumper, and maybe the local mechanic, you're going to be able to tell right away where the problems are and what would happen if you were to change anything.

Expertise

Technical Expertise appears frequently in computer and software professionals. Technical knowledge is implicit in many analytical thinking, initiative, and achievement examples. Broad-based technical knowledge (including some knowledge of more or less peripheral topics (e.g. software engineers who know a lot about hardware) seems associated with innovative solutions.

The best technical professionals are distinguished by their willingness to use technical knowledge to help others solve problems (EXP D.2), and by enthusiasm for the technical aspects of the work (a unique technical expertise indicator):

> I guess the fun part of the business for me is the logical part. I love looking at well logs. It goes back to when I was a kid. I loved looking at road maps, and a good part of this job is dealing with charts on walls, thickness maps, and pressure data.

They also actively maintain and expand technical knowledge through journals, conferences, courses, and informal means (EXP C.2-3).

Customer Service Orientation

Customer Service Orientation is expressed (especially by the best information systems professionals) in taking care to identify the real needs of end-users, and focusing work on solutions that address internal "customers'" needs (CSO 6):

> I work closely with the managers in terms of fitting the program to meet their needs.

Other Competencies

Superior Technical Professionals show a wide variety of other qualities of personal maturity such as *Flexibility* and ability to learn from mistakes, but not in a strong or consistent pattern.

Directiveness/Assertiveness is mentioned more than half the models, generally as stating one's position or limits forcefully (DIR 3-4). This characteristic seems related to Self-Confidence rather than to managerial skills per se.

Team Leadership, Developing Others and conflict resolution (TW 7) appear strongly in a few technical professional models, and not at all in the others. These are competencies specific to certain situations or organizations rather than characteristic of the profession as a whole. When *Developing Others* does appear, it covers the whole range, including voluntarily setting up classes to teach technical background or skills to others (DEV 6 and 7).

Relationship Building or networking with professional colleagues (often outside the organization) was emphasized in some models and not mentioned in others. It appears that the more scientific research-oriented models focused more on networking and on brainstorming with colleagues:

> So I went about this by determining through the scientific grapevine and by calling up Phillip C. and Andy J. to determine what type of work they were

doing in this area and what their interests were. I then thought about the type of experiments I know how to do, and what would be of interest.

These findings are consistent with research that shows superior professionals are "high communicators"[1] in "invisible colleges"[2] (networks) in their fields.

More applied technical/professionals may network with internal line colleagues. In both cases, a flow of information (rather than favors or influence) is the primary intent of networking.

MANAGERS OF TECHNICAL/PROFESSIONALS

These managers look much like other managers. Moving from a technical professional position to a managerial position requires development of interpersonal and managerial competencies, especially Interpersonal Understanding, Impact and Influence, and Teamwork and Cooperation.

Achievement Orientation and Technical Expertise need to be shifted from personal use and "socialized" or shifted toward supporting others. A danger for new technical or research managers, like new sales managers, is that they will retain too much of their role as an individual contributor. For example, average research managers "take over" projects when there are difficulties, rather than use their expertise to think of the questions that will guide and inspire their subordinates to solve the difficulties themselves.

NOTES

1. Shapero, A. (1989), *Managing professional people: Understanding creative performance* (pp. 137 ff.), New York: Free Press; Pelz, D. C. & Andrews, F. M., (1976), *Scientists in organizations* (pp. 35–53), Ann Arbor, MI: Institute for Social Research, University of Michigan.

2. Crane, D. (1972), *Invisible colleges,* Chicago: University of Chicago Press.

14

Salespeople

Competencies of superior salespeople vary according to the length and complexity of the sales cycle, the characteristics of the company and the region, the product, and the type of customer.

Sales positions can be placed on a continuum representing the length and complexity of the sales cycle (the time and number of interactions between initial contact and completion of the sale). For example, telemarketers work on an extremely short cycle (much less than an hour), while consultants, bank trust officers, and "client relationship managers" are long-cycle salespeople.

The characteristics of short, intermediate, and long-cycle sales positions are listed in Table 14–1. The models considered include:

- *Short-Cycle Sales.* Telemarketers and retail.
- *Intermediate-Cycle Sales.* Nontechnical repeat sales to businesses: coatings and chemicals, textbooks, advertising space, retail products to be sold by the client.
- *Long-Cycle, Technical Sales.* Computers, computer systems, other complex business machinery, consulting interventions.
- *Financial Sales.* Insurance, stockbrokers, bank trust officers, other bank salespeople selling financial instruments.

Customers may range from individuals (retail sales) and small businesses to large corporations or government agencies. The size of the sale in our sample ranges from a few hundred to millions of dollars.

Competencies of superior salespeople are described in descending order of frequency in the generic model shown in Table 14–2.

Table 14-1   Characteristics of Short and Long Sales Cycle Positions

Short Cycle	Intermediate	Long Cycle
Most retail positions	Some retail, much business sales	Complex sales to business
Single buyer	Usually a single buyer or small group	Many purchasing influences
Personal impact only, or very small business impact	Small-to-moderate impact on business	Large impact on client's business
Short interactions, usually one-time	Repeated brief interactions, often on a regular basis	Long-term, complex relations; close involvement in client decisions and implementation
Very many customers	Many customers	Fewer customers
Small $ per sale	Moderate $ per sale	Very large $ sale
Very frequent rejection	Varied amount of rejections	Less frequent rejection
Varied products, not customized, simple installation	Other vendors offer similar products; not technically complex	Complex technical products; may be customized, installed, and supported.

GENERIC MODEL OF SALESPEOPLE

The most important competency clusters for salespeople are the Achievement and Action cluster and the Interpersonal Impact and Influence cluster. These two clusters are mentioned with roughly equal frequency and both are essential to success in sales. Although there are more indicators and examples for Impact and Influence, Achievement Orientation is actually equally important. In recent studies of salespeople including large numbers of average performers, average-performing salespeople lacked Achievement Orientation more than they lacked Impact and Influence.

Impact and Influence

Influencing Others—namely to buy one's product—occupies the bulk of the salesperson's time and therefore the largest share of behavioral indicators. In some superior salespeople, the Impact and Influence competency may function at the skill level, and may actually be driven by an underlying Achievement motive. Salespeople who are desire to meet challenging goals learn to influence others effectively.

Most of the influence strategies are relatively straightforward.

Table 14–2   Generic Competency Model for Salespeople

Weight	Competency
XXXXXXXXXX	*Impact and Influence* Establishes credibility Addresses customer's issues, concerns Indirect influence Predicts effects of own words and actions
XXXXX	*Achievement Orientation* Sets challenging achievable goals Uses time efficiently (Improves customer's operations) (Focuses on potential profit opportunities)
XXXXX	*Initiative* Persists, does not give up easily Seizes opportunities (Responds to competitive threats)
XXX	*Interpersonal Understanding* Understands nonverbal behavior Understands others' attitudes, meanings Predicts others' reactions
XXX	*Customer Service Orientation* Makes extra efforts to meet customer needs Discovers and meets customer's underlying needs Follows up customer contacts and complaints (Becomes a trusted advisor to customers)
XXX	*Self-Confidence* Confident in own abilities Takes on challenges Optimistic style
XX	*Relationship Building* Maintains work-related friendships Has and uses networks of contacts
XX	*Analytical Thinking* Anticipates and prepares for obstacles Thinks of several explanations or plans
XX	*Conceptual Thinking* Uses rules of thumb Notices similarities between present and past
XX	*Information Seeking* Gets information from many sources
XX	*(Organizational Awareness)* Understands functioning of client organization
Threshold	*Technical Expertise* Has relevant technical or product knowledge

*"Weight" refers to the relative frequency with which each competency distinguishes superior from average performers. See p. 160, "Interpretation of the Frequency of Indicators."

Note: Items in parentheses are relevant only to some sales positions.

Strategies Common to All Sales Positions

- Concern with establishing credibility or making some other specific type of impression (including the use of details of dress, language, surroundings, etc., to make an impression; IMP A.4). This competency is particularly crucial when selling across cultures (e.g., Americans selling in Asia), but also appears in a smaller way within cultures:

Sometimes you deal with factory people, where if it means taking your jacket off and rolling up your sleeves, you do it. I would go in without the briefcase and the flair, and say, "Hey, how ya doin' today? Want a hotdog from the vendor across the street? Let's go out and get it together." As far as dress, I know that if I'm going to call on the man in the jeans and the flannel shirt, I won't wear my three-piece blue suit, but play the middle-of-the-road.

- Understanding and addressing the customer's most important issues and concerns (this is where interpersonal understanding comes especially into play; IMP A.4):

I wanted [the customer] to buy ten times more than he normally buys, but I thought he could do it because I was going to get co-op money, and I would run demos and guarantee displays. I had all the bases covered to ensure that the sell-through would be good to eliminate the account's concern of too much inventory. [also shows moderate levels of ACH].

- Using experts or other third parties to influence the customer (IMP A.7):

The next time I came to visit him, I brought my District Manager and a marketing specialist with me to let him know that, hey, we're taking this guy seriously. He smiled a little and later admitted that he was pulling my chain by not giving me the time that I wanted to meet with him. But because I had brought these other people with me, it showed that our company was really interested in his business and from then on he took me seriously and we were able to sit down and talk.

- Selecting and screening the information to be given (not mentioned in the financial models and might be counterproductive or unethical in financial settings; IMP A.7):

She said, "I want that machine out now." Instead of trying to challenge her, I said, "Okay, let me go back to Service" and I told them exactly what I was going to do. I said, "I'm going to take care of it for you." Sometimes that means that you're going to get the current machine fixed, rather than get a new machine. But they liked to hear that I was going to take care of the problem.

- Understanding how others perceive the salesperson, predicting the effect of specific actions or statements (IMP A.4):

I think people want to hear "systems"; they don't want to hear, "Equipment is nice," but rather "How can this system help you?" So we started talking about that. I also don't like to bring out brochures at this point, because then they get involved in the brochure and aren't listening.

Long-Cycle Sales

■ Using data and information effectively, including preparing carefully before a presentation (IMP A.3 or IMP A.6 if customized to the specific audience):

I prepared what I was going to say beforehand. I discussed the steps in our presentation with my manager and the [technical specialist]. I took notes. I tried to anticipate their questions. I made a list of all the contacts in this part of the country. I included whom to contact in credit, how to place orders, and so forth.

■ Pointing out the benefits to the customer of the proposal. This behavior may well be a baseline requirement in other sales, but may be neglected by average technical salespeople in their enthusiasm for the technical details of their product:

I pointed out the advantages of the product . . . . We cut replenishing rates, which is cutting dollars—we cut dollars off the product for them. It's much cheaper to run than the old product, and I pointed out, "Hey, you know, we lowered the rates this much" and said, "That's going to mean half the price." He looked at me and said, "Wow." I also said, "On top of that, the wash rates are reduced by two thirds and that's a lot of water" and told him how many gallons a minute it would be. So he was very impressed with that.

■ Using dramatic actions or demonstrations to make a point. There is a theatrical flair to the presentations or demonstrations of many of the best technical salespeople (IMP A.5):

I spent almost a whole day trying to fix [the piece of equipment] with bits and pieces I had secured locally, and finally the motor burned up and we had to get another portable mixer from another plant. . . . One thing I want to point out was that they were actually amazed that a ABC Person would roll up his sleeve and dig in, get dirty, and work on somebody else's equipment. It really didn't have anything to do with the ABC part. They really didn't consider it my responsibility and they appreciated all these things. They had no idea they could get this much support from ABC [also demonstrates Customer Service].

■ Customized influence strategies for a particular situation:

I just sat there and took really detailed measurements of the space where the machine would be set up and showed them, "You could move it over here by 'x' inches—that'll be great. And you know, this way you'll have a good user traffic flow." He's going to have all this extra space where the old machine used to be.

The influence and impact competency seems to be especially important for sales to businesses (running 22%–29% of the indicators) and somewhat less of a differentiator for financial and retail sales (12%–17% of these models).

Corporate Sales (Intermediate and Long-Cycle).   These models include Organizational Awareness (irrelevant to retail sales) as a basis for broad-impact Influence Strategies. Depending on the decision-making structure of the clients, organizational awareness can represent as much as 16 percent of the differentiators of superior performance. Clients whose decision-making bodies are complex committees such as schools or school districts buying textbooks require the most organizational awareness from their salespeople:

> I developed a hierarchy of people within the account to determine who we should be selling [the product] to. It evolved very quickly that an executive VP who was relatively new on the board was really a rising star and a "favorite son" of the president of the corporation. He was really the decision maker: He had carte blanche from the president so the decision went no higher. We found that fostering a relationship with him was very much to our benefit—and I think in essence was the key to the sale.

Achievement Orientation

Although mentioned less frequently than Impact and Influence, Achievement Orientation may be even more important for superior performance. Studies involving measures of underlying motives (e.g., Picture Story Exercise) rather than job-related thoughts and behaviors have emphasized the importance of the need for Achievement in salespeople.[1]

Achievement Orientation starts with self-management (ACH B.1) for all types of salespeople: setting challenging but achievable goals for oneself (usually higher than those set by management) (ACH A.5) and using one's time efficiently (ACH A.4, B.1). Enjoying competition is mentioned in a few sales models:

> I can do better than _____ to help the customer.

> It was really a game as to whether I could make my letters look better than the investment advisor's letters.

Retail Sales.   Superior salespeople may shift unlikely prospects to other salespeople and are concerned about using their time productively (ACH A.4):

> When business is slow, I straighten up the displays, brush up on product knowledge, write thank-you notes.

Intermediate and Long-Cycle Sales. Achievement Orientation, a higher percentage of the model than that for retail sales, focuses on improving the customer's operation (ACH A.4, B.2-3) as well as on personal efficiency, and includes results orientation, cost benefit analysis, and sometimes calculated risk-taking (especially for those salespeople in a position to engineer deals):

> I could go into a million X stores from here to eternity and get all the pats on the back that I want, but I can really move the needle with an account like [a major store chain]. That was where the business was. It's always easy to run into places where there's-Joe-and-Shirley-and-you-have-a-cup-of-coffee; but that wasn't the real challenge [results-orientation, focus on potential profit].

> I would say I have probably saved six or seven hours in their day, doing what they were doing. That's a lot of matching and sorting that they did with the _____ system but didn't have to do with ours, so she loved it.

Long-Cycle Sales. Focusing efforts or making decisions based on the greatest bottom-line (profit) potential (ACH A.6):

> The point is, you don't take an arbitrary stand. The way I figure it, if we have a program or policy and the customer wants something different and is willing to take personal responsibility for the action and protect the bank, if we are going to make money, then we should do it [also shows flexibility].

Initiative

Initiative in salespeople often takes the form of Tenacity and Persistence: trying again and again, (perhaps in different ways), putting in long hours, not giving up in the face of rejection (INT A.1, B.2+):

> I can tell you, I do not work an eight-hour day. I was up at two o'clock this morning finishing up my proposal—I'm calling stores during the day and preparing my programs and presentations at night.

> I saw the guy an average of once every 10 days to the point where he got sick of answering my calls.

Intermediate and Long-Cycle Sales. Initiative includes seizing opportunities, taking immediate action to deal with competitive threats, and generally doing more than the job requires (INT A.2-4, B.2+). One trust officer even managed to sell an account to his doctor while hospitalized with a serious illness; another, at the end of our interview, asked the interviewer if *he* had a will—to this officer *everyone* was a potential client:

> So I said to him [the owner of the store], "Even though you have a photofinishing counter, why not put a display up by the cash register to give your customers a second chance to buy film?" People come into a grocery store, not

usually looking for photographic products and so they might not always go to
the photo counter. But when they're passing through checkout, they might just
as well think: "Why don't I pick up a roll?"

Interpersonal Understanding

Interpersonal Understanding (the ability to understand the attitudes, interests,
needs, and perspectives of others and to interpret their nonverbal behavior) is
an important part of all sales models. It is the essential underpinning of both
Impact and Influence and of Customer Service Orientation. Understanding is
used to explain and to predict others' behavior (IU B.1 and 3) to influence or
serve them better:

> From the looks they were giving each other, I knew that I was on the verge of
> losing them. (IU A.1)

Long-Cycle Sales.   In some major sales, the superior salesperson needs to
coordinate the efforts of a number of people (technical experts, credit and
finance people, etc.) as a team. In these cases, the ability to match colleagues
to clients, using sensitivity to the style of both client and colleagues, distinguishes superior performers.

Customer Service Orientation

Customer Service Orientation, ranging from prompt and courteous service to
taking a role as a customer's advisor in important decisions, is a small (around
5%–6%) but essential part of the sales models. The essence of customer service is taking the time to uncover the customer's real needs and match them to
the products or services (CSO A.6) and making an extra effort to meet the
customer's needs (CSO A.4, B.2+):

> It was important that the new equipment worked out, so I stayed at the account,
> just as my customer-support reps did, to be sure that the people were being
> trained correctly and to be sure that they welcomed the change of equip-
> ment . . . that I personally was there to facilitate the change. And the account
> really appreciated that.

> When we decided to get out of stock transfers, I personally called on all the
> large customers. I decided that some of the people are going to want me to make
> recommendations to them for transferring so I visited several New York banks
> and a couple in Philadelphia and evaluate all of them and make recommenda-
> tions. Most of the accounts accepted my recommendations. We also devised a
> computer program to assist in the conversion.

Long-Cycle and Technical Sales.   The superior salesperson takes a role as
a trusted advisor to the client (CSO A.8). Obviously, to carry this role over

time, one must have a knowledge of both the product and the customer's business. In some cases, this role extends to upholding the customer's side on well-founded complaints against the salesperson's company or to advising the client not to place an order larger than they could comfortably carry (CSO A.9):

> This particular client was having financial problems and I had developed a close relationship with him over the years as a friend, business associate, and salesman. He valued my opinion based on this relationship. I had been trying to realign his business and help him adapt to changing market conditions. He had been predominantly a wholesale _____. I convinced him to concentrate his efforts on retail, perhaps eliminate some nonprofitable routes, streamline his business and concentrate where he could make the most profit.

Self-Confidence

Self-Confidence (at the level of expressed confidence in one's own ability and a confident attitude toward new challenging situations) is the dominant personal characteristic for salespeople. It seems to be most critical in those models where technical expertise is least important:

> I'm the best _____.

> Suddenly I found myself as the account manager of one of the world's largest banks! Another computer company was also trying to get into this bank for the first time. It was a bit overwhelming, but I looked at it this way: I'll give it my best shot, and maybe get a real sense of accomplishment.

Dealing with Failure (a subscale of Self-Confidence) describes the individual's way of explaining and understanding defeats, failures, and rejections and is a part of many, but not all, sales models. All types of salespeople tend to explain rejections in "optimistic" ways: as something short-term and limited in scope. Salespeople give a mix of internal explanations (it is something I did or did not do) and external explanations (the competition got there first, the customer didn't listen . . .). Internal explanations by superior performers are usually accompanied by plans for improvement.

Very Short-Cycle Sales (with Frequent Rejections). The superior performers show little concern or feeling about the rejections and use mostly external explanations (SCF B.1) when they make any explanation at all. The frequency of any explanation at all in star performers is low. Average performers, in contrast, go on and on about different possible reasons for losing each sale:

> They didn't understand my presentation because they were idiots . . . pearls before swine.

I think what happened [with a lost account] was because the competition was so solid, we sort of lost touch with the operations manager—and I don't care who it is, you have to have that personal touch. The competition must have been there stroking the guy, this rep must have worked two or three years on him, along the time where we gave him the bad film deal. This guy was burned, and then I came along and I'm a nice guy and the guy likes me but he runs his numbers. I mean, anybody crunches numbers any way they want, and he crunched them against us.

Intermediate to Longer-Cycle Sales and Consultants.   The balance shifts toward an equal mix of external and internal explanations (taking responsibility) as the sales cycle lengthens. Taking responsibility seems to go with a trusted, advisory relationship to the client.

Financial Salespeople.   An internal, taking-responsibility explanatory style (similar to that of managers) characterizes the best financial salespeople:

The beneficiary got very annoyed with the bank and contacted X and made a complaint. I was wrong. I should have followed up on it. The Operations Department should have followed up on it too, but I can't put the blame on them, because the first responsibility was with me. Next time I'll follow up on that sort of thing.

Relationship Building

Relationship Building is traditionally thought of as a main part of sales. This is true for certain types of sales, particularly those selling mature or commodity-type products. Highly technical sales or consultative sales depend less on Relationship Building and more on Customer Service or Technical Expertise. It includes building rapport (RB A.4):

I was talking to a customer of mine and said that if you spill wine on Herculon it'll come right off. He said he made wine of his own at home, so we talked about wine making for a while.

Sometimes, it includes extensive networking (RB B.3 and higher):

I tried to meet as many people as I could. Just by showing up—talking to the print shop guys, other contacts. Asking to talk to people in Purchasing. Being introduced. One person will introduce you to another person who will introduce you to another person . . . that's how business happens.

Maintaining and calling on business-related friendships are also involved:

I went through Ed D., the Chief Investment Officer, whom I've been very good personal friends with, and I said, "Ed, I need to make this thing go well." He got his boss in there (who normally wouldn't do this sort of thing), and it was very helpful.

Intermediate Sales Cycles, with Repeat Sales.   These positions depend most heavily on personal relationship building with buyers:

> What I've been doing in the past six months is contacting this guy again, I've invited him to a baseball game, sat with him at the luncheon . . . just trying to be pals with him. I didn't talk with him about anything about his equipment or his job . . . just wanted to be his buddy.

Analytical Thinking

For long-cycle technical and financial sales, analytical thinking may involve technical processes, solving problems, or improving processes for the customer. Otherwise, the content is generally about how to understand and influence the client. Most examples also contain Impact and Influence, Organizational Influence, or Customer Service Orientation. Analytical Thinking by salespeople is generally at a basic-to moderate level of complexity. Typical indicators are:

- Making inferences about customer's preferences or considerations:

> . . . he was very resistent. However the recording sheets intrigued him. "Could I get a pad of these?" he asked. I thought to myself, "Well at least I know he wants something from us. . . ." I said "No, not really, these come with the service, but let's think what more [we] could do for you." We went on to talk about X and eventually he says, "Well, if I bought N_____, then I couldn't . . ." "Hold on," I thought, "He's already talking about N_____ even though I haven't mentioned it specifically. He must really want to buy."

- Anticipates and prepares for obstacles (generally other people's reactions):

> I knew it was going to be a difficult call, so I went in there right from the beginning with my benefits statement, my dollar amounts, the dead-net cost of the _____, my advertising schedule, and the full program on board.

Long-Cycle and Technical Sales.   More complex reasoning, taking several factors into account, is used both for solving technical problems and for devising influence strategies:

> Some of the suggestions I made were incorporated into the design. . . . I convinced them if they increased the size of the tanks at the higher level, they wouldn't have to install another tank at the lower level. I first had to sell the ideal to two supervisors and then convince the manger of he regional plant that it would be more cost-effective. . . .

Conceptual Thinking

Conceptual Thinking is most often found at the basic levels: using rules of thumb, recognizing patterns or consistencies in their interactions (CT A.1):

> These guys, all they're interested in is price and when you can deliver. You don't want to spend the first 15 minutes shooting the breeze with them if they've only got 5 minutes. So, instead, I come in with the price lists and I'm saying, "Here's what I can do for you this week. How many do you want to order?" and then I'll write it up. In and out in 5 minutes.

Intermediate and Long-Cycle Sales.   These positions require recognizing key actions to resolve a problem or conclude a negotiation (CT A.4):

> At that point I suggested that he approach this other finisher, the logic being that he could actually play one against the other. If the large X finisher knew he was negotiating with the other outside finisher, he would be in a better position to demand more money for his business.

Although the bulk of sales examples are at the low-to-moderate levels of complexity, some high-level sales executives have built very complex theories of sales cycles or very complex strategies to influence client organizations.

Information Seeking

Information Seeking about the products, the customers, potential customers, their needs, and about the competition is a part of every sales model:

> Every day I try to learn something new about a product so that I always know something that no one else knows.

> He's a very unassuming guy—he keeps a very low profile. But I found out that he has a stock portfolio of about $400,000; he's got $200,000 cash in CDs; and he also owns a number of rental properties.

Long-Cycle Sales.   Superior long-cycle salespeople are more likely to ask direct questions and "dig" beneath the obvious (INFO 3), perhaps because their clients have more incentive to dissemble, or have more deeply hidden needs:

> I sat down with him one evening and discussed the workflow in his plant. I asked him to outline how many _____ he makes in a typical day, typical week, typical month—to make these extensions—and asked him what his goals and expectations were in terms of growth. We outlined what that would translate to in the subsequent months and years ahead. We then looked at how this growth would impact on his current processing facilities, his equipment, and his plan. It became very evident, once I took his numbers, that he was going to be very much

in a productivity squeeze, as related to _____, if he was as successful as he was hoping to be.

Technical Expertise

Short-Cycle (Retail) Sales.   Expertise is seen as seeking out extra product knowledge (EXP C.1).

Intermediate (Nontechnical) Sales.   Technical know-how is not listed as distinguishing superior performers. This doesn't mean that a certain level of expertise (at least product knowledge) is not needed to maintain a sales position, but only that, given the required baseline, more technical knowledge is not what makes the difference between average and star performance.

Long-Cycle (Technical) Sales.   Technical Expertise is a threshold requirement. While this knowledge and the willingness to use it to help others solve their problems is useful in establishing credible relations and in supporting an advisory role with the client, in itself Technical Expertise was not credited with distinguishing much between superior and average performers.

The managerial competencies are generally not relevant to sales, with the exception of Directiveness and Assertiveness.

Directiveness and Assertiveness

Short and Intermediate-Cycle Sales.   Interestingly, this competency did *not* distinguish superior salespeople in the less technical corporate sales positions. It is possible that in those positions the average performers are sufficiently direct (the stereotype of the aggressive salesperson).

Long-Cycle and Financial Sales.   Superior salespeople are more able to say no to unreasonable customer requests and to close in a direct and assertive manner (DIR A.4–5, B.7). Superior consultants may also directly confront the client about performance problems (DIR A.6, B.7):

> (A trust officer describes how he confronted a decedent's children, who continually failed to reply to letters of inquiry about the assets in the estate) Finally I just sent them all registered letters and told them I was expecting them to be at the bank at a certain time and date, and if they didn't show up we would have no alternative but to take them to court. And they did all show up, with their lawyer and accountants.
>
> I said, "Frank, I need these orders back, signed; and if you expect to put the system in by the end of the year, this is the date I need the order on." I asked him flat out, "When do you expect you will be able to do this?"

And he said, "We've got to go to our management. . . . It should take two to three weeks to get an answer."

I said, "In two and a half weeks I'll be back, and we will sit down and talk about it."

SALES MANAGERS

Sales manager models look more like other managers than like salespeople. This is partly because reasonable competence as a salesperson is usually a prerequisite for sales manager positions; thus the characteristics of the superior salesperson are more or less taken for granted in the sales manager position. The sales manager models, then, represent the *additional* competencies needed for success as a sales manager.

Slightly more and slightly higher levels of both Achievement Orientation and Interpersonal Understanding are needed in moving from a sales to a sales manager position.

Achievement Orientation needs to be refocused from personal performance to group performance with more emphasis on the bottom line. An example, from several high-level sales manager models, is focusing developmental efforts and support on the higher performing salespeople because they will give the best return for the effort.

Interpersonal Understanding now applies primarily to the manager's relationship with his or her salespeople and the understanding needs to be somewhat deeper than it was with customers.

All the other competencies decrease somewhat in importance, to make way for the managerial cluster, which becomes the most important.

Developing Others by sales managers focuses on coaching—giving feedback, suggestions, support, and encouragement. Positive expectations of the salespeople are often expressed.

Teamwork focuses on general morale, teamwork and team spirit, giving credit to others, etc. While one model included several indicators of conflict resolution, most did not mention conflict.

The weight is mostly on Developing Others and on Teamwork and Cooperation, with little leadership and a bit more directiveness than for salespeople. The managers' Directiveness is focused on confronting performance problems, with occasional need to fire poor performers.

NOTES

1. McClelland, D. C., Atkinson, J. W., Clark, R. A., & Lowell, E. L. (1953), *The achievement motive,* New York: Appleton-Century-Crofts; McClelland, D. C. (1976), *The achieving society,* New York: Irvington.

CHAPTER

15

Helping and Human Service Workers

Each of the jobs in this chapter focuses on interventions that help people, rather than on business outcomes or technical processes. The positions studied include nurses, physicians, teachers at all levels from preschool to college, organizational-effectiveness consultants (internal to the organization), and alcoholism counselors. This is a rather wide range of jobs with many differences within the group both in professional knowledge and in specific competencies. For example, helping and human service worker jobs divide into two groups: those that emphasize caring for others and those that emphasize influencing others. Superior people in the "caring" helping and human service jobs are likely to have a "helping" motive profile: moderate Achievement, higher Affiliative, and moderate Power motivation.[1] "Influencing" helpers—teachers, clergy, and social workers—are more likely to have low-moderate Achievement, high Affiliative, and even higher Power motives.[2]

Nevertheless, a generic model of the entire helping group can illustrate how the range and focus of competencies for this general type of job differs from other broad types of work such as management, sales, and technical professionals.

Although none of the personal effectiveness competencies (Self-Control, Self-Confidence, Flexibility, Organizational Commitment, and assorted unique personal maturity competencies such as Accurate Self-Assessment, and Occupational Preference) by itself was most important, the Personal Effectiveness cluster contains about a quarter of the behavioral indicators for human services professionals overall. In contrast, in other generic models, the Personal Effectiveness cluster represents around an eighth or less of the model and is one of the smaller clusters, rather than the largest cluster. This emphasis makes some sense in that these people are using themselves, their responses, attitudes, beliefs as an integral tool in their work.

The importance of the managerial competencies of Developing Others, Teamwork and Directiveness was intriguing, since none of the jobs included in this sample involved formal managerial responsibilities (studies of nurse supervisors were excluded, for instance). In a sense, teachers, nurses, and counselors do "manage" their students or patients. No managerial indicators were found in the physician's model.

The Achievement and Action cluster is observed less frequently for human service professionals than for many other types of work. Our sense is that in this case it is because these competencies are not greatly used rather than because they are threshold requirements.

GENERIC MODEL OF HELPING AND
HUMAN SERVICE PROFESSIONALS

Competencies of superior helping and human service workers, in descending order of importance, are listed in Table 15–1 and discussed next. Indicators are discussed in descending order of frequency.

Impact and Influence

Although Impact and Influence is the largest single competency here, as in the sales models, in this model it represents a relatively small proportion of the indicators (around 10%, compared with around 20% of the model for Salespeople).

Table 15–1   Generic Competency Model for Helping and Service Workers

Weight	Competency
XXXXX	*Impact and Influence* Establishes credibility Tailors presentation, language to audience Individual influence strategies Uses examples, humor, body language, voice
XXXXX	*Developing Others* Innovative teaching methods Flexible response to individual needs Belief in students' potential
XXXX	*Interpersonal Understanding* Takes time to listen to others' problems Is aware of others' moods and feelings, understands body language Aware of others' background, interests and needs May understand long-term situations in depth

Table 15–1 *(Continued)*

Weight	Competency
XXX	*Self-Confidence* Confident in own abilities and judgment Takes responsibility for problems, failings Questions, gives suggestions to their superiors
XXX	*Self-Control* Keeps own emotions from interfering with work Avoids inappropriate involvement with clients, etc. (Stress-resistant, has stamina, humor)
XXX	*Other Personal Effectiveness Competencies* Accurate Self-Assessment, learns from mistakes Occupational Preference: finds work enjoyable Organizational Commitment: aligns self with mission Affiliative Interest: genuinely likes people Positive Expectations of others
XXX	*Professional Expertise* Expands and uses professional knowledge Physicians more complete, extensive medical knowledge
XXX	*Customer Service Orientation* Discovers and works to meet underlying needs Follows through on questions, requests, complaints
XXX	*Teamwork and Cooperation* Solicits input, credits, and cooperates with others
XXX	*Analytical Thinking* Sees causal relationships, inferences Systematically breaks apart complex problems
XX	*Conceptual Thinking* Recognizes patterns, uses concepts to diagnose situations Makes connections, theories Simplifies, clarifies difficult material
XX	*Initiative* Does more than is required in job (Responds quickly, decisively in a crisis)
XX	*Flexibility* Adapts style, tactics to fit the circumstances
XX	*Directiveness/Assertiveness* Sets limits, says no when necessary Confronts problem behavior

*"Weight" refers to the relative frequency with which each competency distinguishes superior from average performers. See p. 160, "Interpretation of the Frequency of Indicators."

Note: Items in parentheses are relevant only to some helping and service workers.

Human service professionals use many interpersonal influence methods, depending on the situation. The most common are:

- Working to establish credibility, to get others to trust one's ability and judgments (consultants and physicians; IMP A.4)
- Using subtle, individualized influence strategies that may involve parents, other students, or rewards systems (consultants, some teachers, and nurses; IMP A.7)
- Tailoring language to the audience (teachers and consultants; IMP A.4)
- Using concrete examples or demonstrations to explain (teachers and nurses; IMP A.2):

I asked him, "Do you want to be a hose man all your life? If you want to do anything else in the fire department, you are going to need a degree, and the skills you will learn in this program will be helpful to you." He didn't see how anything he would be studying in this curriculum would be of use in the fire service. For economics, I explained that what was going on in the economy affected the funding of public service and reminded him that the fire-prevention program in the school had been canceled because the funding was withdrawn. I said, "You need to know why that happens. You also need to understand the relationship between social issues, government, and how government works in private enterprise."

[Giving subordinate feedback to a manager] So I went through all the points, all the questions for her, and showed her what the responses were, and the things that were most problematic were how she treated and interacted with people. . . . I thought very carefully about how much do I put in—so I don't make her too defensive and turn her off but yet communicate to her what the issue is.

Other communication strategies such as dramatic gestures, voice modulation, humor, and touch are used as appropriate.

Developing Others

Developing Others was the most frequent managerial competency. Although one would expect to find this for teachers, the best nurses also displayed large amounts of Developing Others (directed mostly toward patients or patients' families, occasionally to other nurses). Both teachers and nurses displayed the full range of developmental skills. Alcoholism counselors and organizational consultants also displayed developmental efforts toward their clients; such efforts constituted about 1 out of every 20 indicators.

[Military organizational consultant] When we sat out there, I sat down and coached the Chief. Since I knew he was the focus, I gave him some pointers on what he should say so that he wouldn't close the discussion down.

The special qualities of Developing Others shown by the best teachers were innovative programs or ways of teaching (DEV A.7), flexibility in allowing students to use individualized ways to learn or to meet requirements. More often, the distinction lies in the teacher's belief in the students (DEV A.1), and the way these positive expectations shape the teacher's feedback to the student and the effort the teacher is willing to make:

> Whether they pass [a required exam] or not, students often don't know what their problems are. So I invite anyone who has taken the test into my office and I sit down with the exam, and I tell them where they have done well and what they need to work on.

> [To a student suffering from writer's block, who had finally turned in a paper after several months of counseling sessions:] It was only one paragraph. It was supposed to be three pages, but it was so good I decided I would accept it. I told him that. And I explained, "It's short, but it's very good." It had coherence and unity, and there were no grammatical or stylistic problems.

In contrast, average performers express negative expectations, which then justify making less effort (DEV A.1):

> He (the client) was a very confused man. I never met anyone who was so bad. He couldn't sort out problems; he seemed to have had no problem-solving techniques; he was a rambler. A lot of it was he was trying to bullshit me and was using that with other people, too, and I came close to giving up on the guy just in an interview.

Interpersonal Understanding

Interpersonal Understanding (Empathy) is related to Affiliative Interest[3] and is an important part of helping and service as well as being the foundation of customer-service orientation and of influence and impact.[4] The most frequent indicators are:

- Taking time to listen to others' problems (personal as well as work-related; IU B.2)
- Being aware of others' moods and feelings (IU A.1)
- Being aware of other's background or frame of reference and its impact on their attitudes, needs, and interests (IU A.4):

> Drooping mouth and sad eyes meant this guy was depressed.

> [An analogy describing a new consultant's thoughts and feelings] He had some apprehensions about what he was doing when it came time to get into the water drill; he really wasn't sure whether the swimming lessons were going to fully equip him to do the cross-channel marathon.

The way the others in the room straightened up in their chairs, I knew he was the one in charge. I knew he would be the one making the decision about the future of our project.

Sometimes interpersonal understanding encompasses an in-depth analysis of someone's ongoing situation (IU A.5):

[Teacher/mentor in continuing education] It was very difficult for Mary to write her degree plan and very painful. When you have a self-concept of being nothing, and then you start to look back over your experience and begin to realize that you really are something and can be something, that realization can be very painful. And it was painful in that way for Mary.

Self-Confidence

Excellent Human Service professionals:

- Present themselves in a confident, impressive manner (SCF A.1-2)
- Express confidence in their abilities and in their viewpoint, decision, or judgment (SCF A.3)

Half the models included indicators or examples of

- Challenging, questioning, or offering suggestions to one's boss or other "superior" (SCF A.5–6):

I very simply told the general that if anyone was going to write a concept paper, it was going to be me. He said, "Sounds fine to me."

[A U.S. Army consultant who felt he was not getting the real information about what was bothering a superior officer confronting him] He proceeded to go through a series of things that he felt were bothering him and as I looked at him I burst out laughing at one of the cases and said, "General, that just sounds like bullshit."

Half the models had indicators or examples including an internal (taking responsibility) style of explanation for negative events (SCF B.1-3). No models showed superior performers blaming others or circumstances for their failures:

I had done nothing whatsoever at the onset to gain any commitment from the client to go through the four-step process. The failure was totally my fault, you know I'll accept all the blame.

Self-Confidence was especially important for physicians, perhaps because of the weighty decisions they must make. Self-Confidence was least important for teachers.

Negative indicators, which are characteristic of average but not superior performance, included focusing on one's own internal reactions in a crisis or anticipating and preparing for failure.

Self-Control

Self-Control is critical to human service workers as they face crises, angry or upset clients, and temptations to become personally involved with clients or students. Excellent human services personnel do not let their own emotions interfere with their performance, but respond constructively to the situation (SCT 5). Again this competency was most important for the medical workers (physicians, nurses, alcoholism counselors) who face the most severe stresses:

> He tried to tear down my abilities. I ignored the hostility and asked him, "Why is it you're here?"

> [In this negative example, a consultant lost his temper with his peers and as a result severely damaged his relationship with them.] So I just finally blew up; I got very angry and said, "There is no teamwork here, we're not doing anything at all. Everybody is going their own way."

Other Personal Effectiveness Competencies

Accurate Self-Assessment. Although the human service professionals do not allow their emotions to interfere with their performance in crises or under day-to-day stresses, they do not ignore their own feelings. They examine their own experiences, beliefs, reactions, and mistakes in order to learn from them (found eight times in eight models):

> The lesson I learned was that I should have had other people deal with him sooner . . . I ain't God.

> . . . and it was the first time that I had worked with an all-female organization and it was very difficult at first because I was looking around and was distracted by all the women there. I was not thinking about what I was really supposed to be doing. It was an education in how to work with women.

They identify their own weaknesses and shortcomings in order to seek assistance in those area or to otherwise prevent those weaknesses from hindering their work.

Occupational Preference and Organizational Commitment. Intrinsic enjoyment of their work and a strong commitment to the process of learning and to the mission of their school characterized the best teachers:

It's really a joy to work with students who are beginning to get past the kinds of things that have been hanging them up!

That was a very special moment for me. Here was a woman who is very bright, very capable, could easily sail through our program and get nothing out of it but the degree. She came in saying, "I have a husband, a family, all I want is a college degree." But she was able to go beyond what she thought she would get from our program . . . it taught her to see herself as someone who knows something and who is able to share the knowledge with others. That was great!

Affiliative Interest.[5]   Teachers and nurses are, so far, the only models in which genuine, noninstrumental, affiliative interest (Positive Affiliation)[6] characterizes superior performance. Many other models have elements of an altruistic interest in other people, but in other positions the intrinsic interest in others is molded to serve some instrumental purpose (making networks of useful contacts, influencing others to some work-related purpose). In other positions, too, much interest in other people may distract one from the main function of the position or may make it difficult to set limits, refuse requests, and so on.[7]

In teaching, nursing, and counseling, helping others is the point of the job, and a genuine valuing of other people characterizes the best performers. Although sometimes affiliative interest leads teachers or others to establish personal relationships with students or clients outside the professional setting, most often it is expressed by an awareness of the progress of the individuals after the teaching or other professional role has concluded:

He went on to finish college at _____ and is now working at a Legal Services office with the poor and the homeless.

Now she's about to graduate from _____ with honors.

Average performers, in contrast, convey a definite lack of personal interest in their clients or students.

Closely related to Affiliative interest is expressing Positive Expectations of Others even in difficult cases. In almost every model of human services professionals, the most effective performers express positive expectations. This attitude is included in the Developing Others and Customer Service Orientation scales. Here, it seems to go beyond those specific circumstances, and to express a more generalized attitude:

[Regarding a student who spent months in turmoil and confusion regarding the program's expectations] Oh, I've always felt good about John. I didn't agree that he was hopeless. But then, one of the reasons I do this work is that I don't feel anyone is hopeless.

Less effective professionals are likely to write off at least some of their students or clients (sometimes with ethnic, racial, or sexist slurs):

> . . . The situation was hopeless. It was obvious that he hadn't understood any of the materials, and I told him that I could see nothing we could do about it. I doubted whether he could write about this subject analytically. I suppose I could have argued that I was expecting him to think like a Westerner and he wasn't a Westerner.

These positive or negative expectations are subtly conveyed to the students or clients and may account for a significant part of the effectiveness of the professional in the "Pygmalion effect" of self-fulfilling prophecies.[8] Because of the powerful effect of the teacher's expectations on the learning of the student, positive expectations are the base level of the Developing Others scale.

Professional Expertise

Expertise made up one-fifth of the physicians model. This was one of the rare instances in which superior performance was largely characterized by more and better technical knowledge. The best physicians simply know and remember more and thus have more resources to draw on in making a diagnosis. They also maintained and expanded that knowledge base.[9] Keeping up to date on technical knowledge and going out of the way to share it also characterized nurses, alcoholism counselors, consultants, and—to a smaller degree—teachers. Some of the best demonstrate and share their expertise by publishing articles.

Customer Service Orientation

The helping and service competencies overall were surprisingly low—only a little higher than in sales models and about twice as frequent as in managers. The low frequency may be due to a combination of factors. Minimal levels of customer service may be a threshold requirement (taken for granted) and therefore not included in the models. Also, up to 8 percent of the behavioral indicators for these models were coded as Uniques not found in the generic list. Many of these unique competencies, for example, teachers' concern for making academic material relevant to students, might be considered as specialized versions of Customer Service Orientation.

Customer Service Orientation is most often displayed as

- Probing to discover the client/patient/student's underlying needs and matching available or customized services to that need (CSO A.6). This was particularly common in consultants and teachers.
- Following through to ensure that promises are kept and questions or complaints are resolved (CSO A.1)

- Operating with a long-term view of the relationship and the other's needs (CSO A.7):

> I was constantly trying to get clear with the general manager whether he should take a fairly directive role, a very strong leadership role or a more low-key role. We settled on taking a lead role in kicking it [an organizational intervention] off and then becoming a small group member rather than spending a great deal of time trying to influence the whole group.

> . . . . my role is to come up with recommendations that are implementable in the client's organization as well as technically correct.

> The reader was too advanced for him—so I gave him a reading list of books that I liked and could read when I was at his reading level.

> I said to him, "That's a problem . . . let's look at how we're going to deal with this project proposal . . . Did you talk to the people on your supervisory board who have to make a decision on this?"

The positive expectations of others discussed under Other Personal Effectiveness Competencies are a crucial support for Customer Service Orientation.

Teamwork and Cooperation

Teamwork and Cooperation was important for consultants and for teachers of younger children (who cooperate with parents, other teachers, and other professionals). It did not distinguish superior medical professionals. Conflict resolution (TW A.7) is important in some consultant positions, not in others. Some teachers use a participative teamwork style of interaction with students (TW A.2–5).

Concern to help children and the desire to develop their own skills led teachers into mutually beneficial dialogue with other professionals (TW A.1) such as speech therapists and psychologists:

> I was very pleased to have a chance to meet with the speech therapist working with Joey. I explained what I have been doing to try and help Joey; what I think Joey is capable of doing; what I've seen him accomplish. And he told me what he's trying to do. He went over all the things he noticed, in case I hadn't. And so we're working together on that.

Analytical Thinking

Among these models there is a wide range in the frequency and complexity of analytical and conceptual thinking. We think this variation is largely due to the variation in the cognitive requirements of this group of jobs. Analytical Thinking appears as:

- Identifying causal relationships, or using inference chains
- Breaking a large problem apart into manageable pieces in a systematic manner

Counselors thought analytically about their clients, linking client characteristics to the strategies most likely to help individual clients:

He's willing to do whatever *you* want him to do . . . really a lack of self-motivation. So some contracts would help him to make some movements.

Teachers thought about the connections in the subject matter and how to get those across to the students:

The goal of the essay in the book was to think about punctuation differently and the discussion evolved into why they were so reticent to talk about punctuation at all, which I then connected to how they were taught grammar originally, which then got to the idea that if these guys know so much about writing, how come the grammar books are so awful? So poorly written?

Conceptual Thinking

Physicians and organizational consultants and, to a lesser extent, nurses use Conceptual Thinking—the recognition of patterns and the use or invention of concepts—to understand or diagnose situations:

There were a couple of people who . . . were unwilling to own their own behavior and their own responsibility for anything being different than it was right now, or than it always had been" and in that size organization that was enough to block any effective work.

I could see they didn't want to do it because they were really fearful of getting involved in this because they felt that these two people were ahead of them, would hold it against them. So it was a lot of fear of some sort of reprisals. I could tell this from the little laughter that broke out every once and a while and a few comments they made . . . No one said, "Hey, I'm afraid to do this," but there were definitely indications that there was some fear [also includes Interpersonal Understanding].

Teachers, especially at high school and college levels, use conceptual thinking to make connections between course work and their students' lives and to make complex material clear and vivid.

Initiative

Initiative—going beyond the job requirements and tackling problems before they become urgent or inescapable—characterizes counselors, teachers, and some nursing jobs. Responding immediately and actively to crises is more characteristic of physicians and teachers of very young children. However, overall initiative represents less than 5 percent of the behavioral indicators in these models.

Flexibility

Flexibility was critical for teachers and organizational consultants, less so for alcoholism counselors and nurses, and did not appear in the physician's model. Flexibility typically appears as:

- Seeing situations objectively, recognizing the validity of other viewpoints (FLX 1)
- Adapting one's style or role to fit the needs of the situation, or changing one's tactics to fit the circumstances (FLX 3). This level often supports Impact and Influence efforts:

With this sort of person, I used humor, I've even given her one of the badges that you give the children . . . I wouldn't do this with some other of the parents [also can be coded for Influence Strategy].

[A number of top-notch military organizational consultants recognize that if materials are ever going to get to the eyes of the commanding officer, they had better meet military standards] We talked about a number of opportunities to introduce technology—a better way of work—at least what we thought was a better way to work. I was able to get the concept into a very traditional-looking concept paper. I use all the traditional staff techniques and approaches to get my foot in the door.

Directiveness/Assertiveness

Directiveness/Assertiveness ran around 3 percent to 5 percent of the models for most human service professionals, but was 11 percent for alcoholism counselors. Directiveness is more frequent in less skilled teachers: The best teachers are so compelling and/or have established their boundaries so well that they don't focus on directiveness. Organizational consultants, teachers, and nurses all:

- Set boundaries and expectations (DIR A.4)
- Say no when necessary
- Tell people directly what to do on occasion (DIR A.2-3)
- Confront misbehavior or other violations of their expectations (DIR A.6):

"I feel frustrated and embarrassed to have to say this, but it looks to me that there has been collusion between the two of you on this exercise. As the instructions explicitly stated, you were not to get any help other than from a librarian." They finally admitted to having collaborated and I told them, "This is not acceptable. You both have to go back and start over."

Frequently, teachers set boundaries through rules. These clearly establish, especially for younger children, appropriate classroom behavior. When a child breaks a rule, superior teachers will explain the consequences of their actions (DIR A.7):

> You know you are not allowed to walk around the room during nap time and if you try that, the work-study people may be angry. When I come back, if you're in the middle of a tantrum, I'm going to let them [work-study people] handle it. I'm not going to get involved." That's just what happened.

A unique directive skill used by teachers is redirecting the child's attention toward a more constructive activity.

Achievement Orientation

Achievement Orientation is a very small portion of the superior human service professional's profile (less than 3% of the indicators). When it appears, it is usually shown either as a concern for standards of performance such as setting specific goals for students' learning or as innovation—finding creative new ways to teach. It is stronger in teachers and in consultants in a business environment and appears in some nurses. It was absent in the military models of human services (although present in other military models).

MANAGERS OF HUMAN SERVICES

The shift from individual contributor to manager in human services requires the addition of different competencies just as the same shift in other fields does.

While the human services individual contributor models are low in Achievement Orientation and Initiative, their managers need as much of these competencies as do other managers. Achievement Orientation and Team Leadership, two of the least significant competencies in the models of human services individual contributors, are two of the more important competencies in their managers and will need to be found or developed.

Human services individual contributors often show several managerial competencies in relation to students, clients, or patients; managers must shift these competencies toward their subordinates and must add Team Leadership and a little more Directiveness. Similarly, Interpersonal Understanding shifts toward subordinates.

Customer Service Orientation and the Personal Effectiveness Cluster shrink in importance though not in level of sophistication, possibly because a reasonable mastery of these competencies may be assumed in those who are promoted to human service management positions.

Organizational Awareness and Relationship Building are added to the managerial models.

NOTES

1. Kolb, D. A., & Boyatzis, R. E. (1970), On the dynamics of the helping relationship, *Journal of Applied Behavioral Science, 6*(3), 267–289.
2. Winter, D. G. (1973), *The power motive* (p. 106 ff.), New York: Free Press.
3. Kelner, S. P. (1991), *Interpersonal motivation: Positive, cynical and anxious,* unpublished doctoral dissertation, Boston University.
4. Carkhuff, R. R. (1973). *The art of helping,* Amherst, MA: Carkhuff Associates. Also see Carkhuff, R. R., & Berenson, B. G. (1976), *Teaching as treatment,* Amherst, MA: Human Resource Development Press.
5. Boyatzis, R. E. (1972), A two factor theory of affiliation motivation, unpublished doctoral dissertation, Harvard University.
6. Kelner, S. (1991). Interpersonal motivation: Positive, cynical and anxious, unpublished doctoral dissertation, Boston University.
7. Boyatzis, R. E. (1973), The need for close relationships and the manager's job, Boston: McBer.
8. Rosenthal, R., & Jacobson, L. (1968), *Pygmalion in the classroom,* New York: Holt, Rinehart & Winston. Also see Livingston, J. S. (1969, July–August), Pygmalion in management, *Harvard Business Review,* 81–89.
9. The physician's model was for acute care physicians in a hospital setting. Doctors in family practice or in other specialties might need additional competencies, such as interpersonal understanding and caring ("bedside manner"), self-confidence, and accurate assessment of their own limits to make timely referrals to specialists.

CHAPTER

16

Managers

Managerial jobs are the largest group of jobs studied with Job Competency Assessment (JCA) methods. Because of their prevalence and importance, managerial jobs have received relatively more attention in competency work than other types of jobs.

Managerial jobs may be grouped according to a number of dimensions:

- *Level.* From first-line supervisor to executive
- *Function.* Production, sales, marketing, finance, engineering, human resources
- *Industry or Environment.* Military, health care, education, manufacturing

Boyatzis wrote an exhaustive reanalysis of the original data from the early JCA studies of managers,[1] with detailed comparisons of managers of different functions and in different sectors. In this chapter, as in the preceding chapters, we analyze the existing models rather than the original data. Although our findings are substantially similar to those of Boyatzis, there are some variations due to the different levels of analysis and also to our inclusion of new data.

Superior managers of all types and levels share a general profile of competencies. Managers of all types are also more like each other than they are like the individual contributors they manage (salespeople, factory workers, human service professionals, technical professionals).

This chapter presents a generic competency profile derived from models of the entire range of managers. This generic profile fits all managerial jobs reasonably well but none precisely.

Figure 16–1 shows the overall frequency of competency clusters in managers, compared with the frequencies in three types of individual contributors.

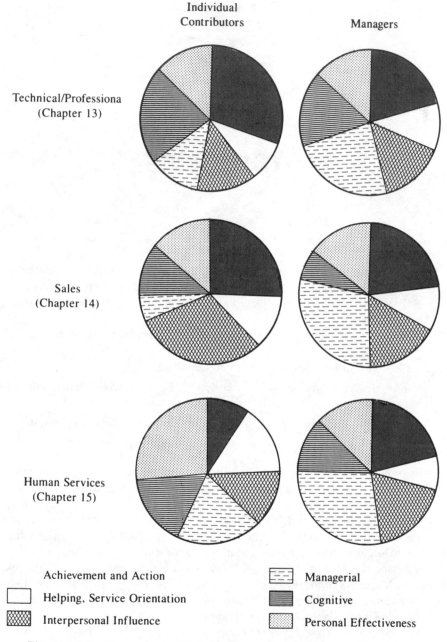

Figure 16–1 Comparison of Relative Frequencies of Competency Clusters in Three Types of Individual Contributor Jobs and in Their Managers

Even at this simple level of analysis, the similarities between levels of managers and the differences between managers and other types of jobs are apparent.

After the generic managerial profile, we will consider each dimension (level, function, and environment) and discuss differences between the various subgroups and the generic profile. We will not repeat the entire generic managerial model for each grouping but will look at the variations on that basic theme. Managers of research and technical services, of salespeople, and of human services (education and health care) were contrasted with their respective subordinates at the end of each chapter on individual contributors.

Although all models of managers look similar, this is *not* an argument for the "all-purpose, can manage anything" image of the manager. The technical and contextual knowledge of the function and business being managed is *a necessary threshold for reasonable performance managing that function.*[2] However, more of those same competencies do not distinguish superior performance as a manager.

GENERIC MANAGERIAL MODEL

The generic managerial model (Table 16–1) is based on 36 different managerial models, covering a wide range of levels (first-line supervisors to general managers) in a range of functions (production, sales, marketing, human services, educational, etc.) and environments (military, educational, health care, industry, financial services, etc.). The generic model highlights the similarities between all the managerial jobs and provides the background against which the special characteristics of different levels, functions, and environments stand out. This model is not intended to be applied to any particular job.

Table 16–1   A Generic Competency Model of Managers

Weight	Competency
XXXXXX	*Impact and Influence*
XXXXXX	*Achievement Orientation*
XXXX	*Teamwork and Cooperation*
XXXX	*Analytical Thinking*
XXXX	*Initiative*
XXX	*Developing Others*
XX	*Self-Confidence*
XX	*Directiveness/Assertiveness*
XX	*Information Seeking*
XX	*Team Leadership*
XX	*Conceptual Thinking*
Base Requirements	*(Organizational Awareness and Relationship Building)*
	Expertise/Specialized Knowledge

Competencies and indicators or levels within each competency are listed by frequency, with the most frequent or important first. Even though Impact and Influence is the largest single competency, the two largest clusters (each accounting for about a quarter of the behavioral indicators and examples) are the Achievement and Action competencies and the Managerial competencies.

Impact and Influence

The best managers use reasonably well-socialized Impact and Influence to improve the functioning of the company, *not* for personal gain at all costs.

Impact and Influence are most often seen as:

- An expressed concern with personal impact—working to establish credibility or to make some other specific impression on others
- Calculating the effect of specific words or actions on others. Occasionally, concern with the company's reputation distinguishes superior managers, but mostly it is their personal credibility or a specific impression they wish to convey (IMP A.4–6):

Sometimes I try to give the impression of skepticism without saying, "No." I do it consciously. I wouldn't want to create an attitude around here of "anything goes" or that it's duck soup to get my approval, because then people who've worked hard wouldn't think I recognized the challenge in what they were attempting. I like them to have a sense, when it's over, that I have gone into it somewhat skeptically and that they've proven to me that they can really do it. So I say things and give them certain looks at times—I kid them a lot: "How much is that going to cost? Can we afford it?" or "Isn't that too ambitious?" I never do it in a way that says you can't do it, but just enough so that they get the sense of having to prove something to me.

Various means of Direct Persuasion are popular among superior managers (IMP A.2 and A.3):

- Using data or other information
- Pointing out the benefits to the others
- Using concrete examples, visual aids or demonstrations
- Appealing to reason or logic
- Various unique persuasive techniques:

I told him this is what we need, we can't do everything that we'd like without it, that you're the bottleneck, that these analytics you're not doing are doing anyone any good if you keep them a secret [appeals to the common good].

Adapting either the content or the style of one's presentation to the specific audience (IMP A.4 to A.6) also implies a moderate level of Interpersonal Understanding:

> I helped rewrite the report at the last minute. It was just too complex. We were only going to have the attention of the senior managers for 40 minutes and it was just too complicated for the audience as it was written.

More complex influence strategies (IMP A.7 or 8) are relatively rare among managers, showing up in less than half the models as:

- Using experts or other third parties
- Doing things to make others feel ownership of one's own solutions:

> I talked to them about possible suggestions they might have for me hiring people. And they gave me a whole bunch of names. So it wasn't a big shock to them that I was out looking, because they were making contributions to that effort. I did all that because I wanted them again committed to the change.

Achievement Orientation

For managers, Achievement Orientation encompasses measuring performance, improving efficiency or effectiveness, setting goals, and calculating cost and benefits for their subordinates or team, as well as for themselves personally. Most examples involve other peoples' performance in some way. For managers to be effective, much of their Achievement Orientation needs to be socialized or spread to include their team or subordinates, and thus to include an element of need for Power (Impact and Influence cluster).

Excellent managers most frequently measure their (or their subordinates' or groups') results and they think and talk about these measurements (ACH A.3).

> I felt good about helping him succeed—I knew I had some part in making him a success: I didn't make him a high producer, but I gave him the proper direction, the proper vehicle. The first year he did about $100,000, the second year it was up to $400,000 and this year it will be close to $800,000. That's starting from zero.

Virtually all managerial models cite superior performers as finding better, faster, more efficient ways of doing things (ACH A.4):

> When I took over the division, we had four basic product models in 12 variations, covering a fairly narrow span of the market. I reduced the number of models to 3 and the variations to 8, making the biggest one bigger and the smallest one smaller. We had fewer inventory problems, less fuel-production problems, and we covered a broader segment of the market.

and as setting specific, challenging goals (ACH A.5):

> I was convinced that this type of account was good for the branch, so I decided to promote it. I wanted to have more accounts than any other branch. This was a stretch, but not impossible—we proved that, because we did it.

Some, but not all, models of managers cited making cost-benefit analysis (ACH A.6), taking calculated entrepreneurial risks (ACH A.7 and 8), and concern for innovation (ACH C.2 and up):

> Space on the platform was extremely costly—about $300,000 per square foot. By changing the chemical solution used in the pumping system, the whole scope of the pumping system and the money involved were reduced by a factor of 10. I'm a shareholder and it's just one instance where the company I'm a part owner in was able to avoid spending somewhere in the order of a million dollars.

> I weighed the cost of running the ad and considered what could come out of it in the way of business—how many leads the ad would generate and how many would turn into clients. The ad would raise our visibility in the community, and although there were no guarantees, it seemed like a good bet.

Achievement orientation, along with good depth of Interpersonal Understanding, enables managers to make optimal job–person matches to improve performance (ACH A.4):

> I picked a woman to be the faculty leader in preparing for the accreditation review who was creative, expansive, outgoing, held in high regard by her colleagues, respected in the county, and hardworking. She would give hours and hours of her time to see that she carried off any delegated assignment. I knew that if she led the effort, she'd do an outstanding job.

Teamwork and Cooperation

Teamwork and Cooperation or participative management is the most often mentioned managerial competency. It is often shown toward one's subordinates as a group or team but may also be used with peers or superiors:

- Superior managers solicit the input of others and involve others in issues that may affect them (TW A.4):

> I made it very plain that there was no standardized way of doing it, and I invited them to explore their own methods of presenting their thoughts.

> Others wanted help on the form the planning should take, which was what I was trying to avoid, because I wanted them to identify their own scheme.

- Giving credit or recognition and encouraging and empowering the group (TW A.5) is also important:

I always post our test results on the bulletin board, draw a line of where we are and put in a little "Bravo, _____, _____ and _____."

Later I got into special training of minority workers who had never worked before . . . most of them learned and . . . showed the LMN how to create a good work atmosphere.

- Working to improve group spirit and morale, to develop teamwork and cooperation (TW A.6), is fairly frequent:

When I came on board, there were actually POs wandering around who didn't know who their bosses were. I immediately organized things so that everyone knew who he reported to, emphasized the chain of command . . . morale and performance both improved.

- Resolving conflicts (TW 7) is very strong in some models, and virtually absent in others, depending on the situation and demands of the specific position. Generally, positions requiring negotiating show Level 7.

Analytical Thinking

Thinking logically and sequentially is an important characteristic of superior managers at all levels. Managers think analytically about influence, technical difficulties, and about achievement-related issues. The most frequent indicators were:

- Sees implications or consequences of a situation or information (If _____, then _____)
- Analyzes situations systematically to determine the causes or consequences
- Anticipates obstacles realistically and plans ways to deal with them
- Thinks ahead about the steps in a process, analyzes what is needed to accomplish a task or goal:

We wanted to see if we could develop the design and development process for X. So I got that unit manager to put down on paper all the things that he had been doing in the past couple of years on several models. Then I got some cooperation out of marketing and I said to the appropriate Product Planning Manager, "Check these things over and see if these are the things you observed; if not, what other things did you see happen?" Then I got the quality control guy in manufacturing and said, "You look at the same list and see if these are the things that you recall." Then the advanced manufacturing engineer got them. Then I spent some time writing it up and went to the department staff and said, "I would like to have a task force of these people. . . . I will volunteer the _____ and have him lead it, but I want to end up with a document that describes our development process and how the work is authorized to be done."

Initiative

Initiative is most frequently seen in going beyond the job requirements to seize an opportunity or prepare for a future problem or opportunity (INT A.4 and up).

> I wanted to hire people who were financial-planning types, because of the new marketing effort. So I searched them out. I found out who the best people were and took them to lunch, for drinks, whatever—and got seven really good producers [also includes Information-Seeking and Relationship-Building].

Initiative in addressing current situations takes the forms of

- Seizing opportunities as they arise (INT A.2)
- Handling crises swiftly and effectively (INT A.3)
- Exceeding the bounds of one's formal authority, (INT B.5):

> There was a lack of understanding at the top as to exactly what our product line was and what our technical capabilities were. So when I heard some of top management was coming to look at our operation, I thought, "Great! This is a golden opportunity to show what we're contributing and what we can contribute to the company." So we worked hard on our presentation [also scores for Concern with Impact].

Tenacity and persistence in completing a task or reaching a goal and willingness to work long hours as needed also characterize superior managers (INT A.1, B.2):

> I had a cab pick me up at 5 o'clock on Monday mornings and I caught the 6 o'clock flight out. And I was in the office at 7:30. I flew home early Fridays.

Developing Others

Developing Others, the second most frequent distinguishing managerial competency, is similar in tone to Teamwork. Both competencies imply or state positive expectations of others.

- Giving constructive feedback (DEV A.4)
- Reassurance or encouragement after difficulties (DEV A.5) covered more than a third of the examples:

> I started holding performance appraisal reviews every month after I'd gotten that month's reports. During individual conferences, I asked my people how

they thought they were doing, and said how I saw it. Then I asked them what their objectives were for the next month and told what my expectations were—you know, straight management by objectives. It was amazing, no one had ever told them what their jobs were, what we wanted, or how they were doing. Once they knew, we started getting super performance [also scores for setting objectives, ACH A.3].

- Coaching by giving instructions, suggestions, explanation, and other support (DEV A.2 and 3) was the next most common style of developing others:

He had a tendency of staying right up there in the front of the room, almost hanging onto the blackboard or his desk. There were students in the back of the room half asleep. I asked him, "What about some quality attention to them?" I told him to try making himself mobile: "Get around to all the students. It keeps them on their toes."

- Giving specific developmental assignments or training (DEV A.6) was also characteristic of superior managers in many models. This training was not routine or required training, but was geared to the developmental needs of the person or position:

All she had been doing was shuffling papers— you know, somebody wanted some numbers, so she'd go generate some numbers. She had never seen a whole project; it was always little bits and pieces. So I had a project that I had just started that I thought would be a good project for her to take over. I turned it over to her and told her to feel free to come any time she had a question in order to help her get a larger sense of the process and begin to learn to manage a project.

Self-Confidence

In superior managers, Self-Confidence appears fairly evenly up the scale and includes:

- General confidence in one's ability and judgment (SCF A.1–3)
- Enjoying challenging tasks (SCF A.4)
- Directly questioning or challenging the actions of a superior (SCF A.6):

Hey, give us a shot, give us a chance, let us go attack the cost question. We're not going to be able to do it with the current design, it's too expensive and we know what the limitations are. We're going to have to look at it entirely new, but until I look at it, I don't know.

I was very happy to take it on. I felt confident I could take the mess and put the thing together . . . you know do a first-rate job.

Dealing with Failure (SCF B) is mentioned in only about a third of the models of superior managers. When it is mentioned, it is always an "internal" style:

- Taking personal responsibility for failures or problems (SCF B.1)
- Usually with the intention of improving performance in some way (SCF B.2)

In some examples, superior managers take personal responsibility for problems or failings that an observer might feel are not truly the manager's fault:

He flunked the exam because I overworked him. I just wasn't thinking.

My subordinate's presentation to upper management went poorly because I misjudged the audience [and gave him bad advice].

Interpersonal Understanding

Interpersonal Understanding appears most often as:

- Understanding the attitudes, interests, needs and perspectives of others
- Interpreting nonverbal behavior, understanding the moods and feeling of others
- Knowing what motivates others
- Understanding both the strengths and limitations of others
- Understanding the reasons for others' behavior

While Interpersonal Understanding is sometimes used on its own, it more often supports Impact and Influence, or the managerial competencies. In the following example, a manager uses Interpersonal Understanding to improve someone's performance:

As a trainee he was awful—he wasn't a salesperson. But he was good with details, so I thought he would be good on staff. I felt he was frustrated and needed to succeed at something, but I also knew that his ego would be bruised. . . . I knew that if I made him a sales assistant, some people in the office would think that I was unfair—and he probably would be upset, because it would be an admission that he couldn't make it as an _____. I figured that despite the initial discomfort, most people would see it was the best solution, including the personnel in question. He is now doing great and is in the place he should be, job-wise (IU A.4, B.5).

It was a very difficult situation—his wife was terminally ill and it was a great strain. I did everything I could to make it easier for him—it is impossible to expect anyone to be able to concentrate with something like that happening. . . . I knew he felt bad that he wasn't pulling his weight, but that once this was past he would be all right. When he came back, he proved me right. (IU A.4, B.4)

Directiveness/Assertiveness

Directiveness is a less frequent distinguishing characteristic and is probably used by superior managers less frequently than Developing Others, but it is very important in certain situations. The most common levels are:

- Assertiveness in setting limits, saying No when necessary (DIR A.3) and
- Setting standards, demanding performance (DIR A.4):

My predecessor hadn't established any discipline about meetings. The first few meetings I held, people straggled in late and weren't prepared—they hadn't finished their reports or gotten their thoughts straight. So when it happened a third time, I put my foot down. I said, "Ladies and gentlemen, I can't accept this situation. I'm postponing this meeting for two days. Be on time and be prepared or there'll be hell to pay."

- Confronting others' performance problems in a clear and direct manner distinguishes superior managers in about half the models (DIR A.6):

The current distributor in this state was not getting the job done, and this had traditionally been a very strong market, so I had a knuckle-rapping session with the distributor in which I made it clear that we expected the job to get done well, that we were going to get it done, that we wanted to get it done with them but we expected them to do their part well.

- The ability to fire poor performers when necessary for the good of the company appears less often than one might think.

In some cases, it appears that average managers are more likely to depend on directiveness than superior managers but to do it less skillfully.

Information Seeking

Information Seeking characterizes managers as well as many other jobs. Frequently information is sought to diagnose problems or identify future opportunities. Specific types of information seeking are:

- Systematic information gathering (INF 5)
- Seeking information from many sources (INF 4)
- Physically getting out to see or touch the situation (INF 2)

Often the information-gathering is integrated into a larger incident:

> Something was amiss, so I began to pull some of their reports and to ask them how they did the problems. I discovered that they couldn't divide because they couldn't multiply.

Systematic information seeking is often informal in nature:

> [An assistant principal makes it a practice to telephone students' parents on a random basis to take a reading on school climate.] "What I want is to hear your perception as to how your youngster is getting on in the building. Anything. Teachers, courses, hallways, lunch, buses, other kids. Rumors you're hearing . . ."

Team Leadership

Team Leadership is a small differentiator of superior managers; less than 5 percent of the indicators relate to it.
The most common indicators are:

- Setting and communicating high standards for group performance (which also has some socialized achievement orientation) (TL A.6)
- Standing up for the group in relation to the larger organization: obtaining needed resources for the group (TL A.5)

Conceptual Thinking

Conceptual Thinking in managers appears as:

- Seeing connections or patterns that are not obvious to others
- Noticing inconsistencies or discrepancies not obvious to others
- Rapidly identifying key issues or key actions in complex situations
- Using vigorous, original analogies or metaphors

Superior managers think about process and business decisions and also about influence strategies:

> When you look out in that office, if you see nothing but people talking on telephones, then you aren't seeing it. You've got to see channels of distribution, pipelines, and when you start thinking of it that way, then you start thinking of more efficient way to deliver what we deliver, because that's all we are, we're a big pipeline. You just can't screw around with one part of this office without thinking about the whole office, or the whole account at the other end, all the ramifications. Before you make a move out there, you have to think it all the way through.

Organizational Awareness and Relationship Building

Organizational Awareness and Relationship Building each get less than 3 percent of the total indicators, although each is at least mentioned in most managerial models.

Concern for Order

Concern for Order is an infrequent differentiator of superior performance as a manager. In some models, it is a negative indicator: Average performers use it more heavily than stars.

Technical Expertise

Although more Technical Expertise or other specialized knowledge is not usually a differentiator of superior managers and executives, this is not to say that the technical background and context of a manager's functioning is unimportant. In fact, it is the basis of the judgments that inform the use of competencies. Thus technical or business know-how is often buried in other competencies, as shown in the following examples.

Judgment as to what actually is a challenging but achievable goal and what is a moderate risk depends on a combination of underlying Achievement Orientation and contextual knowledge (partly technical, partly general business, partly specific to the organization):

> Certainly the idea to improve _____ did not originate with me, but we really had not developed a plan on how we were going to improve it. . . . I got behind and pushed it . . . gave certain people a little push in the right direction, to get it done.

Developing Others depends on possessing a mastery of the material and/or techniques to be taught, especially since most of the differentiating developmental activity involves providing informal instruction, not sending people away to a formal training program:

> I was able to give this group an impression of what to expect from a people point of view—which I think is critical—and then from a process point of view and, thirdly, from a lack-of-technology point of view. Because X-making is still pretty much of an art form.

Similarly, effective Team Leadership is partly dependent on establishing credibility, difficult to do if you don't know what you are talking about.

Impact and Influence strategies often also depend on background knowledge or on the reputation for knowledge:

> I had to reassess my working relationship with the associates here—how I was interfacing with them. Being with a company for many years you develop a

certain rapport, a certain credibility and if you're new in a company you don't have it. . . . a discussion with my boss who said I wasn't coming across as being supportive. And then it dawned on me that it was just that what I was saying was not necessarily being taken as words of wisdom, because I had no real credibility here yet.

Even though special or technical expertise is a threshold requirement, it can become "too much of a good thing" when managers depend on it too heavily. In this case, average managers tend to retain too much of the role and function of the people they manage. Average sales managers tend to take over critical sales and spend too much time dealing directly with customers rather than coaching, supporting, and leading their salespeople. Average research managers tend to try to solve technical problems themselves, rather than stimulating their subordinates to do so.

MANAGERS BY ORGANIZATIONAL LEVEL: FIRST-LINE SUPERVISORS, MIDDLE MANAGERS, AND EXECUTIVES

Managers are commonly divided into three levels: first-line, middle, and upper management.

There are two versions of first-level supervisors, one for people supervising hourly-wage employees (bank tellers, factory workers, soldiers) and another for people supervising exempt technical and professional employees (salespeople, researchers, teachers, technicians, computer programmers).

"Middle managers" comprise all managers that fall between first-level supervisors and executives.

"Executives" have:

- Titles like "General Manager," "Commanding Officer," "Director," "Vice President"
- Two of more layers of managers below them
- Responsibility for a large, multifaceted division within a very large organization

Executives in our sample are generally not chief executive officers (CEOs), but have executive responsibility for units the size of a moderate-size company. Our sample includes executives from financial, manufacturing, military and health-care organizations.

First-Line Supervisors

First-Line Supervisors are divided into supervisors of hourly wage employees and supervisors of technical and professional workers because interesting differences appear between these groups. Supervisors of hourly employees show much stronger dependence on the managerial competencies and slightly more of the achievement and action cluster, while the supervisors of technical and professional employees used the helping and service, the impact and influence, and the personal effectiveness competencies more often than the supervisors of hourly wage employees.

Supervisors of Hourly Workers. The superior first-level supervisors of hourly employees showed a heavier concentration on the managerial cluster, especially Developing Others. Developing Others seems to be similar in range of scale levels to the generic managerial model but is mentioned more as distinguishing superior supervisors. Possibly average first-line supervisors do not develop their people very much. The content of the first-level supervisor's developmental efforts tends to be very specific and technical (how to fill out this form, install that part, do this task efficiently, etc.) and the teaching style is very concrete. Team Leadership and Teamwork and Cooperation are both somewhat stronger differentiators of superior performance in first-line supervisors than they are in the generic managerial model.

The Achievement and Action cluster appeared somewhat less frequently for first-line supervisors than for managers overall. Achievement Orientation was mentioned only about two-thirds as often as in the overall model and was found at a slightly lower level, more toward measuring and improving performance.

Concern for Order—seen as monitoring and checking up on employees' work—characterizes superior first-level supervisors, though it is not a significant component of other models of superior managers.

Information Seeking, while mentioned in most models, covers less than 2 percent of the indicators and seems less important for superior performance in these jobs than in most other jobs.

Supervisors of Technical and Professional Workers. Supervisors of technical and professional workers look very much like the generic middle manager in the competency profile. The "hidden" or threshold need for technical expertise is especially high in this group. At least a reasonable technical competence is implicit in many of the examples of developing, giving feedback, influencing, and leading from this group of models. Indeed, it is difficult to imagine doing an excellent job of managing researchers without a technical understanding of their work or of managing salespeople without first being a successful salesperson. However, the competencies that distinguish the best managers are not additional technical proficiency, but rather the additional managerial competencies.

Achievement Orientation is less frequently mentioned as distinguishing superior technical/professional first-line managers. This is interesting since some of the jobs supervised are strongly distinguished by Achievement Orientation (salespeople, researchers and computer software people) while other models barely mention it (teachers and other human services workers). In both cases, Achievement Orientation is about 5 percent to 8 percent of the distinguishing characteristics of superior *managers,* compared with more than 11 percent for managers overall.

In the case of the managers of high Achievement Orientation jobs (sales, technical professionals), a certain level of Achievement Orientation appears to be a threshold characteristic. Even average sales and technical managers are generally recruited from the ranks of excellent salespeople or technical professionals and would be likely to have rather high levels of Achievement Orientation. On the other hand, human service workers rarely mention achievement-related themes, so for their managers, Achievement Orientation would represent an added competency.

The other competencies in this cluster (Initiative and Information Seeking) appear at about the same frequencies as in the generic managers model.

Superior managers of professionals are more often distinguished by Developing Others, Interpersonal Understanding, and Customer Service Orientation. These competencies appear in much the same form as in the generic managerial model, but somewhat more frequently. Organizational Commitment is mentioned more often for these supervisors than for most managers, and Self-Confidence is mentioned somewhat less frequently than is usual for managers.

Middle Managers

The profile for middle managers is similar to the overall profile for managers (see Figure 16.1). This is both because the profiles form a continuum, with middle managers in the center (executives and first-level supervisors differ from middle managers in opposite ways) and because our sample contained more middle management positions than either executive or first-line positions.

Executives and General Managers

Executives have more indicators per model than other managers (an average of 89 versus 71 for middle, 61 for first-line supervisors). They appear to have more different competencies and indicators overall (a wider repertoire of skills) and also appear to combine their competencies in more complex ways and in more intricate combinations. Executives appear to use more different competencies per incident than first-line supervisors.

Executives are higher on the size of impact scales and some additional competencies come into play.

Top-performing executives are characterized by socialized Achievement Orientation, Organizational Awareness, and Relationship Building more often than are most managers. Their models focus less on the Managerial and Personal Effectiveness competencies. Since executives demonstrate more competencies overall, we do not feel that this represents a lessening of the need for personal maturity and managerial skills at the higher levels of management, but rather that competencies in other areas are added.

Some competencies, such as Concern for Order and Self-Control, are virtually absent from the executive models. We do not feel that these qualities are lacking in superior executives, but that they have been mastered to such an extent that they are taken for granted and are no longer discussed. Average executives may tend to focus on these competencies to a greater extent than do the best executives.

The largest competency cluster for executives is Achievement and Action, and the most frequent single competency for executives is Achievement Orientation. In addition to mentioning Achievement-related themes much more often than most other managers, top-performing executives also show a higher scale level. They are more likely to talk about taking calculated entrepreneurial risks, supporting new ventures or new ideas, and calculating the costs and benefits of a decision than are middle managers or supervisors. Achievement-related themes pervade the best executives' discussion of how they influence, develop, or lead others. They use cost–benefit arguments to convince others as well as to make their own decision, they set challenging goals for others, and they support others' innovation or entrepreneurial ideas. The best executives also show Information Seeking and Initiative more often than middle managers, and generally look and act ahead in a somewhat longer time frame.[3]

Relationship Building, developing and using a network of contacts (both inside and outside the organization) is mentioned in all the executive models. In some cases, extensive community involvement or leadership characterizes the top executive. This seems to vary according to the organization and the community.

Organizational Awareness becomes more important and is mentioned more frequently at the executive level. It is found in relation to the executive's own organization (using organizational politics as a means to influence and lead the organization) and vis-à-vis outside organizations (clients, regulatory agencies, etc.).

The most common executive-level indicators of Influence and Impact are using subtle strategies to influence others and working to establish the *organization's* credibility or reputation.

Directiveness is mentioned as distinguishing superior executives more frequently than it is in the generic managerial model. It is mostly seen as telling people directly what to do, setting expectations and limits, and confronting performance problems directly. Appropriately firing poor performers who fail to improve is also mentioned in several models as distinguishing superior executives from average ones.

MANAGERS BY FUNCTION

Each function model will contain managers of that function at all levels and will be compared with the overall generic model. Only those clusters and competencies that showed noticeable variations from the generic manager model will be discussed. Competencies not discussed in this section were essentially similar to the generic model described earlier.

Sales Managers

Sales managers' people represent their means of production. Therefore, their focus must be more heavily on people, and the bulk of the problems they address involve developing and motivating their people individually and as a team.

Developing Others appears about twice as often in models of superior sales managers as in models of other managers and is tied with Impact and Influence for most frequent competency. It is mostly focused at the individual coaching end of the scale, with particular emphasis on giving encouragement and rewards and on reassuring and giving helpful suggestions for future improvement (DEV A.5). This may be a response to the frequent rejection that salespeople experience.

Teamwork and Cooperation is seen with the same frequency as in other models of managers, but is focused somewhat higher on the scale: promoting teamwork and good morale, crediting and empowering others (TW A.5 and A.6) rather than soliciting input from others.

The Helping and Service Cluster, both Interpersonal Understanding and Customer Service Orientation are more frequent than usual for managers. Interpersonal Understanding is important to support the Developing Others and Impact and Influence competencies. Even though the best sales managers deal less often with customers than do salespeople, they still show more Customer Service Orientation than the average manager.

Cognitive competencies are a much *smaller* portion of the distinguishing characteristics of sales managers than of most other managers.

Marketing Managers

The managerial cluster is much smaller in the marketing managers than in any other group of managers; all the other clusters are somewhat larger, except the helping/service cluster. The marketing managers look more like individual contributors than like most managers. Perhaps they tend to function that way—focusing more on pace setting for a small team than on leading and coaching their people.

Although all these positions have titles of Manager and have subordinates, the focus of the job seems to be more on the activities and functions of marketing as a process than on the management of the subordinates. The subordinates in these departments seem to function as assistants or colleagues to the manager rather than as his or her main focus of attention.

There was an interesting pattern of consistencies in the Unique competencies in this group. The following unique competencies were each found repeatedly:

- Stamina and tolerance for stress and long hours
- Enthusiasm for the product and/or concern for the product's image
- Information seeking regarding the activities of competitors
- Focus on deadlines, meeting deadlines, sometimes making compromises to meet deadlines
- Concrete, "hands-on" learning style

Research and Development Managers

Research and Development (R&D) managers have two basic tasks: to nurture and support their team of individual contributors, giving technical guidance where needed; and to focus their group's efforts on serving the end-users or internal clients' needs. The differences between R&D managers and other managers make sense in light of this concept of their role: The biggest difference is the addition of Customer Service Orientation and Technical Expertise.

Customer Service Orientation appears much more frequently here than in other managers and is especially strong for those managing software-development projects, where user-friendliness is a major issue. Other R&D managers also show concern for the internal client or the ultimate market. Generally customer service orientation is at the level of discovering the clients' real needs and matching development efforts to those needs. Interestingly, the manager's customer service orientation is much higher than the individual technical contributor's: It is as though the manager takes on this role for his or her department.

Technical Expertise also is mentioned much more frequently for R&D managers than for others. Although the best managers avoid pacesetting by taking on too many projects individually, they do use their technical knowledge not only to establish credibility but also to help their subordinates work through difficult problems or to provide fresh technical insights. Average managers overuse technical knowledge to complete technical tasks themselves; superior managers use it to provide perspective, to ask the right questions, or to suggest useful new resources or approaches that help subordinates successfully complete projects.

In the managerial cluster, Teamwork and Cooperation is more frequently mentioned than usual, while Directiveness is seen less often. Teamwork is most often seen as encouraging initiative and participation by others and as giving credit or recognition for others, encouraging or empowering them. In other words, the Research manager supports the self-confidence of the researchers, both individually and as a team.

Flexibility in adapting managerial strategy to the demands of the situation and in recognizing the merits of opposing viewpoints contributes to the effectiveness of the technical and teamwork competencies.

Organizational Commitment supports service to internal clients by aligning the manager's own actions with the organization's goals.

Achievement Orientation appears about half as often in these models as in other manager models. However, superior research and technical individual contributors are high in Achievement Orientation, and in general, research managers are drawn from the ranks of superior researchers. Hence, Achievement Orientation may be missing from the managers' models because it is present in the average managers as well as the stars and therefore does not distinguish superior performance. New models specifying average as well as superior performance will confirm or disprove this explanation.

Production Managers

Production managers, who cover the entire range from first-line to general managers, look much like the generic model of managers, with somewhat less emphasis on Impact and Influence.

There are some interesting subtle differences within the Managerial cluster. Developing Others and Directiveness represent a somewhat smaller than usual portion of the superior production managers models, while the Team competencies represent a larger proportion of the model. Teamwork and Cooperation is mentioned more than twice as often as Team Leadership. In Teamwork and Cooperation, keeping people informed, clear, and up to date appears very frequently as an indicator. The production manager seems to function as the team's informational clearinghouse, soliciting input and dispensing up-to-date information. Impact and Influence is a smaller than usual portion of the superior production manager's model, whereas Achievement Orientation and Initiative appear with slightly greater frequency and slightly higher levels. There is greater than usual emphasis on measuring performance in financial terms and on making cost–benefit analyses.

MANAGERS GROUPED BY ENVIRONMENT

Managers in Human Services: Schools and Hospitals

Models of managers of human services (principals and other educational administrators, medical supervisors, and commanding officers of navy hospitals) look very much like other models of middle managers. They include more indications of

- Conceptual Thinking
- Team Leadership
- Organizational Commitment

than most other middle-manager positions, possibly because they are somewhat less likely to have many layers of upper management above them and therefore take on some of the responsibilities and characteristics of executives.

Managers in the Armed Forces

Military managers (line officers at a variety of levels and functions) basically resemble civilian managers, but the Managerial cluster contains a larger proportion of the indicators and examples (about a third of the observed differentiators, compared with a quarter in the civilian sector). All the managerial competencies are more frequent in the military, but Developing Others and Team Leadership show the sharpest difference. A lot military effort is devoted to informal as well as formal training. (Military instructors were not included in this sample.) Leadership is also especially important in the military and combines setting standards and policy, and demanding high performance with providing for the team's needs (sometimes physical needs for food, sleep, etc.) and treating everyone fairly. These two themes of leadership (demanding and caretaking) are closely interwoven in the military examples.

Self-Confidence is mentioned less often in military than in civilian models. Perhaps the greater formal structure (reflected in slightly higher Organizational Awareness with strong emphasis on formal structure and rank) relieves some of the need for personal Self-Confidence by providing more organizational or structural support. Self-Confidence appears as a "can-do" attitude and as a willingness to question or offer suggestions to a superior officer, rather than in the civilian forms of general statements of confidence in personal ability or judgment.

Concern for Order and Quality appears almost twice as often as in civilian models. Checking on others' work and keeping clear, detailed records distinguish star military officers.

NOTES

1. Boyatzis, R. E. (1982), *The competent manager: A model for effective performance.* New York: Wiley.
2. Kotter, J. (1982), *The general managers,* New York: Free Press.
3. Jacques, E. (1989), *Requisite organization,* Arlington, VA: Cason Hall.

C H A P T E R

17

Entrepreneurs

Numerous studies over the past 25 years have shown the relationship between achievement motive thoughts, entrepreneurial behaviors and success in starting and growing businesses.[1]

When the competency methodology described in this book was developed in the early 1970s, it seemed likely that other competencies besides achievement motivation would be found to predict entrepreneurial success.

In the fall of 1983, the United States Agency for International Development (USAID) funded a cross-cultural study to identify *"personal entrepreneurial characteristics"* (PECs),[2] that is, competencies that predict business formation and success within and across cultures. The study's objective was to replicate and extend earlier achievement motivation research using the new competency assessment methodology.

An additional objective was to *develop* and validate practical, cost-effective *assessment methods* for selecting potential entrepreneurs and those already in business who would be most likely to use scarce resources such as education and credit effectively to generate economic growth, including income, jobs, capital investment, tax revenues, as well as the secondary "multiplier effects" that successful small businesses produce in their communities.

The USAID study provides a generic, cross-culturally valid competency model for entrepreneurs and serves as an example of a large competency study with extensive statistical validation analyses.[3]

THE CROSS-CULTURAL ENTREPRENEURSHIP COMPETENCY STUDY

A criterion sample of successful and less successful entrepreneurs was identified in three developing countries in Latin America (Ecuador), Africa

(Malawi), and Asia (India). The samples were identified by seeking nominations from a variety of knowledgeable sources, including banks, chambers of commerce, ministries of trade and finance, trade organizations, and so on, within each country.

Researchers interviewed 12 superior and 12 average entrepreneurs in manufacturing, marketing/trading, and service businesses, for a total of 72 in each country and 216 in the full sample. Each entrepreneur had to be an owner or partner in the business, involved in starting the business, and in business at least three years.

Each entrepreneur was interviewed for two to three hours in the appropriate native language. Entrepreneurs were first asked a standard set of questions about their personal background and business.

Background questions included:

Years of education

Work history

Other experiences relevant to present business

Number of other businesses started

Father's and mother's education

Number of other family members who own businesses

Regular business activities

Number of hours worked in a typical week and whether this is more or less than the hours worked previously as someone else's employee

Business data included:

Products and services

How long the entrepreneur has owned the business

Sales volume in the past year

Change in sales volume over the past three years

How much the business earned in the past year

Change in business earnings over the past three years

Changes in products or services over the past three years

Locations of business facilities

Major equipment owned or leased

Number of employees and their jobs

Financing sources

The Behavioral Event Interview method was then used to obtain a detailed account of how the entrepreneur started the business and four other key situations (high points and low points) experienced in running the business.

Half of the interviews were tape-recorded, translated, and transcribed, and analyzed to identify competencies that distinguish superior from average entrepreneurs. This preliminary competency model was validated by systematically coding the remaining transcripts for each competency. The final competency model for entrepreneurs is shown in Table 17–1.

Several statistical analyses were used to identify the competencies that best distinguished superior from average entrepreneurs.

Table 17–1   Generic Entrepreneur Competency Model

I.   ACHIEVEMENT

   1. *Initiative*
      a. Does things before being asked or forced to by events
      b. Acts to extend the business into new areas, products, or services

   2. *Sees and Acts on Opportunities*
      a. Sees and acts on new business opportunities
      b. Seizes unusual opportunities to obtain financing, land, work space, or assistance

   3. *Persistence*
      a. Takes repeated or different actions to overcome an obstacle
      b. Takes action in the face of a significant obstacle

   4. *Information Seeking*
      a. Does personal research on how to provide a product or service
      b. Consults experts for business or technical advice
      c. Seeks information or asks questions to clarify a supplier's needs
      d. Personally undertakes market research, analysis, or investigation
      e. Uses contacts or information networks to obtain useful information

   5. *Concern for High Quality of Work*
      a. States a desire to produce or sell a top or better quality product or service
      b. Compares own work or company's work favorably to that of others

   6. *Commitment to Work Contract*
      a. Makes a personal sacrifice or expends extraordinary effort to complete a job
      b. Accepts full responsibility for problems in completing a job for customers
      c. Pitches in with workers or works in their place to get job done
      d. Expresses a concern for satisfying the customer

   7. *Efficiency Orientation*
      a. Looks for or finds ways to do things faster or at less cost
      b. Uses information or business tools to improve efficiency
      c. Expresses concern about costs vs. benefits of some improvement, change, or course of action

II.   THINKING AND PROBLEM SOLVING

   8. *Systematic Planning*
      a. Plans by breaking a large task down into subtasks
      b. Develops plans that anticipate obstacles
      c. Evaluates alternatives
      d. Takes a logical and systematic approach to activities

Table 17–1 *Continued)*

---

9. *Problem Solving*
    a. Switches to an alternative strategy to reach a goal
    b. Generates new ideas or innovative solutions

III. PERSONAL MATURITY

10. *Self-Confidence*
    a. Expresses confidence in his or her own ability to complete a task or meet a challenge
    b. Sticks with his or her own judgment in the face of opposition or early lack of success
    c. Does something that he or she says is risky

11. *Expertise*
    a. Had experience in the same area of business
    b. Possesses strong technical expertise in area of business
    c. Had skill in finance before starting business
    d. Had skill in accounting before starting business
    e. Had skill in production before starting business
    f. Had skill in marketing/selling before starting business
    g. Had skill in other relevant business area before starting business

12. *Recognizes Own Limitations*
    a. Explicitly states a personal limitation
    b. Engages in activities to improve own abilities
    c. States learning from a past mistake

IV. INFLUENCE

13. *Persuasion*
    a. Convinces someone to buy a product or service
    b. Convinces someone to provide financing
    c. Convinces someone to do something else that he or she would like that person to do
    d. Asserts own competence, reliability, or other personal or company qualities
    e. Asserts strong confidence in own company's products or services

14. *Use of Influence Strategies*
    a. Acts to develop business contacts
    b. Uses influential people as agents to accomplish own objectives
    c. Selectively limits the information given to others
    d. Uses a strategy to influence or persuade others

V. DIRECTING AND CONTROLLING

15. *Assertiveness*
    a. Confronts problems with others directly
    b. Tells others what they have to do
    c. Reprimands or disciplines those failing to perform as expected

16. *Monitoring*
    a. Develops or uses procedures to ensure that work is completed or that work meets standards of quality
    b. Personally supervises all aspects of a project

Table 17–1 *(Continued)*

VI. ORIENTATION TO OTHERS

    17. *Credibility, Integrity, and Sincerity*
        a. Emphasizes own honest to others (e.g., in selling)
        b. Acts to ensure honesty or fairness in dealing with others
        c. Follows through on rewards and sanctions (to employees, suppliers)
        d. Tells customer he or she cannot do something (e.g., complete a task) even if it means a loss of business

    18. *Concern for Employee Welfare*
        a. Takes action to improve the welfare of employees
        b. Takes positive action in response to employees' personal concerns
        c. Expresses concern about the welfare of employees

    19. *Recognizing the Importance of Business Relationships*
        a. Sees interpersonal relationships as a fundamental business resource
        b. Places long-term good will over short-term gain in a business relationship
        c. Emphasizes importance of maintaining cordiality or correct behavior at all times with the customer
        d. Acts to build rapport or friendly relationships with customer

    20. *Provides Training for Employees*

VII. ADDITIONAL COMPETENCIES

    21. *Building Capital* (Malawi Only)
        a. Saves money to invest in business
        b. Reinvests profits in business

    22. *Concern for Image of Products and Services* (Ecuador Only)
        a. Expresses a concern about how others see his or her product, service, or company
        b. Expresses awareness that clients spread knowledge of the product or company by word of mouth

T-Tests

Significant differences were obtained for the following competencies:

I.   Achievement

    1. Initiative

    2. Sees and Acts on Opportunities

    5. Concern for High Quality of Work

    6. Commitment to Work Contract

    7. Efficiency Orientation

II.   Thinking and Problem Solving

    8. Systematic Planning

    9. Problem Solving

V.   Directing and Controlling
     15. Assertiveness
     16. Monitoring
VI. Orientation to Others
     19. Recognizing the Importance of Business Relationships

Significantly, there are no differences between superior and average entrepreneurs on background and demographic variables, and only two minor differences between countries (Building Capital in Malawi and Concern for Image in Ecuador).

Regression Analyses

Competency Effects.   A stepwise multiple regression of competencies against entrepreneur criterion rating found three competencies to be significant: 19 recognizes the importance of business relationships; 2, sees and acts on opportunities; and 16, monitoring.

Country Effects.   To see if competencies differed by culture, dummy variables for country were added to list of predictors. Inclusion of country variables did not affect either competencies or the multiple R.

Entrepreneur Background and Business Effects.   Multiple regressions were conducted with various combinations of background and business variables with competencies. None of these variables affected the three competencies or the multiple R.

Discriminant Function Analyses

A discriminant function analysis was conducted to test whether the 20 competency scores could differentiate successful from less successful entrepreneurs. The discriminant analysis program selected variables by minimizing Wilks' lambda. This stepwise procedure stopped after 10 competency scores were entered into the analysis. At this point, the canonical correlation was .50 ($p < .0002$). When the results of this program were used to assign sample entrepreneurs to successful and less successful groups, 81.4 percent of the less successful group, 65.2 percent of the successful group, and 72.7 percent overall were correctly classified.

Further discriminant analyses were conducted to see if entrepreneur background information would add to the competency scores' ability to predict successful performance. The results obtained did not differ significantly from those using the competency scores alone. The results of these discriminant analyses indicate the competencies and not the entrepreneur background variables differentiate successful from less successful entrepreneurs.

Factor Analyses of Competency Scores.   Several factor analyses were conducted on the competency scores. An initial analysis of competency raw scores revealed four factors with eigenvalues greater than 1. Subsequently, analyses were run to extract 2, 3, and 4 factors.

If a cutoff criterion of .5 is used, Factors I and II include the following competencies:

Factor I

Achievement

    1. Initiative

    3. Persistence

Thinking and Problem Solving

    9. Problem Solving

Personal Maturity

    10. Self-Confidence

    12. Recognizes Own Limitations

Influence

    13. Persuasion

Factor II

Achievement

    5. Concern for High Quality of Work

    6. Commitment to Work Contract

    7. Efficiency Orientation

Thinking and Problem Solving

    8. Systematic Planning

Personal Maturity

    10. Self-Confidence

Directing and Controlling

    16. Monitoring

Factor I suggests a action-oriented, analytical, dominant (confident and persuasive) personality, and Factor II, strong achievement motivation with implementation skills: planning to achieve goals and monitoring to get feedback on progress toward goals.

Successful entrepreneurs showed significantly more of both competency factors (Action-oriented, Dominant: $t = 3.52$; $p = .001$; Achievement-oriented: $t = 2.63, p = .010$).

Conclusions

1. *Differentiation.* Personal entrepreneurial competencies differentiate successful from less successful entrepreneurs. Seven competencies in four clusters in the entrepreneurship competency model were significant in most of the statistical analyses:

Achievement

    1. Initiative

    2. Sees and Acts on Opportunities

    3. Persistence

    5. Concern for High Quality of Work

Personal Maturity

    10. Self-Confidence

Controlling and Directing

    16. Monitoring

Orientation to Others

    19. Recognizing the Importance of Business Relationships

2. *Identification.* The competency assessment method does identify characteristics besides achievement motivation associated with entrepreneurial success, specifically:

- *Thinking and Problem Solving* (cognitive competencies). Systematic Planning and Problem Solving

- *Personal Maturity* (or self-concept traits). Includes self-confidence

- *Influence* (associated with power motivation). Persuasion and business relationship building

- *Directing and Controlling.* Includes monitoring (of work outcomes)

The competency assessment method used in the cross-cultural study does, however, strongly confirm David McClelland's original findings on the relationship of achievement motivation to entrepreneurial success.

3. *Background Information.* Entrepreneur background and demographic data do not distinguish superior from average entrepreneurs. Entrepreneurship is an "equal opportunity" career.

4. *Consistency of Characteristics.* Competencies of successful entrepreneurs are essentially the same in the three different countries. A finite set of characteristics or traits appear to predict entrepreneurship across cultures. These characteristics are not strongly affected by the entrepreneur's background, expertise, or business experience.

DEVELOPMENT OF
ENTREPRENEUR ASSESSMENT METHODS

Four criteria were used to select competencies for which assessment methods would be developed:

1. Evidence that the competency differentiated successful from less successful entrepreneurs.
2. Evidence that the competency occurred with sufficient frequency to justify assessing its presence in existing or potential entrepreneurs.
3. Opportunity for demonstration of the competency before starting the business or attaining a managerial position
4. Content validity of the competency and its behavioral indicators as skills needed in starting or running a business.

Assessment methods were developed for the following competencies:

Initiative
Sees and Acts on Opportunities
Persistence
Information Seeking
Concern for High Quality of Work
Commitment to Work Contract
Efficiency Orientation

Systematic Planning
Problem Solving
Self-Confidence
Persuasion
Use of Influence Strategies
Assertiveness

In addition, achievement motivation was assessed as an underlying personality trait distinct from its behavioral expression in competencies such as Initiative, Sees and Acts on Opportunities, Persistence, Information Seeking, Concern for High Quality of Work, Commitment to Work Contract, and Efficiency Orientation.

Objectives for development of the assessment methods included:

1. Provide a valid summary score predicting entrepreneurial success to aid in making decisions about the allocation of resources, namely, who should receive money or training to start or grow a business.
2. Provide data on specific competencies for use in entrepreneurship training programs where feedback to individuals on their strengths and weaknesses on specific competencies is useful in identifying priorities for development.
3. Resistance to faking and social desirability (likely when candidates know that the results of a test will be used to decide who will receive a loan or other valuable resources).

4. Applicable and acceptable to diverse populations in all cross-cultural settings.

5. Ease of administration and scoring: Methods should be usable with illiterate populations by assessors without high levels of skill in interviewing or psychological assessment.

Some of these objectives conflict. Respondent measures, such as paper and pencil tests in which people choose their answers from several provided alternatives, are easy to administer and score but subject to faking and social desirability effects. Operant measures that provide a consistent stimulus and require the person taking the test to generate a unique response are less easily faked but more difficult to administer and score.

Assessment methods with different formats were developed to determine which might prove both valid and practically useful. All methods were designed for oral administration to illiterate respondents. These methods are described in the following sections.[4]

Information Interview

Separate information interview protocols were developed for established entrepreneurs and those preparing to start a business. Both forms included background questions about the entrepreneur: educational and technical training, previous business and entrepreneurial experience, age, marital status, occupations of parents, entrepreneurial activity by other family members, pre-start-up acquaintances with entrepreneurs, and reasons for starting the business.

The Information Interview for existing entrepreneurs also included questions on sales, profits, income, number of employees, and the entrepreneur's rating how well his or her business is doing compared with the previous three years. These data provided measures of business success to validate the assessment methods.

The information interview takes about 30 minutes to administer.

Focused Interview

The focused interview, a simplified version of the Behavioral Event Interview used in the research phase of the project and described in Chapter 11, asked respondents to describe what they had done in five previous situations: a time when they had "accomplished something on your own," "had to get somebody to do something," and "had difficulty getting something done."

Specific follow-up questions are provided for each of these main probes to ensure that interviewers elicited enough information to score the targeted competencies. After probing for details of the interviewee's behavior and thoughts in each situation, the interviewer used a checklist to note the number of situations in which the person presented evidence of each competency.

The advantages of the focused interview are its high validity and resistance to faking and social desirability effects. Its disadvantages are difficulty in administration and scoring. The interview must be individually administered and scored, a process that takes a full hour. Administration and scoring require some training. Inaccurate scoring is a potential threat to the validity of the test.

SYMLOG (Systematic Multiple Level Observation of Groups) Scoring of the Focused Interview

Following the Focused Interview, interviewers completed an additional Scoring form, SYMLOG,[5] based on their interaction with the interviewee. The SYMLOG scoring form requires the interviewer to rate how often the interviewee expressed each of 26 concerns. These concerns are scored for three underlying personality dimensions: Power (dominant vs. submissive), Affiliation (friendly vs. hostile or aloof), and Achievement (task-focused vs. emotional). The SYMLOG Power and Achievement dimensions resemble closely the "Achievement" and "Action-oriented, dominant" factors found by the research study to characterize more successful entrepreneurs.

A special SYMLOG rating form was developed for this project. Statements were designed to reflect concerns that might be expected to emerge in the incidents or behavior recounted during the Focused Interviews. For example, the first three statements were:

1. Power, status, making a lot of money
2. Being popular, liked, and admired
3. Active teamwork toward common goals

After conducting the Focused Interview, the interviewer rated how often (rarely, sometimes, or often) the interviewee expressed each of the 26 concerns.

The Symlog Rating Form takes only about 10 minutes to complete and score.

Self-Rating Questionnaire

The Self-Rating Questionnaire consists of 70 items describing typical behaviors. Respondents are asked to rate how well each statement describes them on a 5-point scale from "very well" to "not at all." Of these items, 65 are based on the 13 core competencies targeted for assessment. For example, one item in the Initiative Scale requires rating this statement: "I do things before it is clear that they must be done." The remaining five items form a social desirability scale that is used to correct for some people's tendency to rate themselves overly favorably. Like the Focused Interview, the Self-Rating Questionnaire provides scores on each of the targeted competencies.

The primary advantage of the Self-Rating Questionnaire is that it is easy to administer and score. It can be administered in 30 minutes to a group of individuals.

The main disadvantage of the Self-Rating Questionnaire is its susceptibility to social desirability and faking effects; it is unlikely to be useful in situations where the test outcome determines who gets a loan or admission to a desirable training program. This instrument is better used in entrepreneurship training courses to help participants identify their own training needs.

The Business Situations Exercise

This 52-item questionnaire contains brief descriptions of 20 situations that an entrepreneur might face. Following each situation are several items, each consisting of a pair of alternative thoughts or actions. For example, a sample situation, followed by one item, would be:

> You have visited a potential customer to see if he has a need for the service you offer. The potential customer tells you very bluntly that he doesn't think you can provide what he wants.
>
> 1. Which would you do?
>   a. Tell the person that your service can precisely meet his needs and how this is so.
>
>   *or*
>
>   b. Thank the person for his time and indicate that you hope to be of service in the future.

Respondents select the alternative that more closely describes what they would do in this situation. For each item, one of the alternatives is based on use of a targeted competency. The Business Situations Exercise provides a profile of scores on the 13 targeted competencies.

In its written form, the Business Situations Exercise is easy to administer and score. It can be administered in group settings in 35 minutes. Unlike the other instruments, it can measure an aptitude for competencies that the person has had limited opportunity to demonstrate in real-life situations.

Disadvantages of the Business Situations Exercise include faking, social desirability, and reading or listening burdens on the test taker. When the test is administered orally, test takers must remember the situation and both alternatives to make a meaningful choice for each item. Finally, the decision-making process in the hypothetical situations is artificial, since the information about each situation is limited to two or three sentences.

The Picture Story Exercise

The Picture Story Exercise is a six-picture Thematic Apperception Test (TAT) that measures three basic motives: Achievement, Affiliation, and Power.

Respondents are asked to look briefly at each picture and then to write (or tell) a brief story based on the picture. Projective tests assume the stories that people write reflect their own underlying motivations.

Respondents' stories were coded using a simplified scoring system[6] similar to that developed for the Focused Interview. Interviewers checked whether or not nine themes (behaviors or thoughts), three associated with each of the three motives, were present in each story. The scores for each motive are summed across stories to yield overall scores for Achievement, Affiliation, and Power.

A two-hour practice session was conducted to test whether naive persons could be trained to use this coding system reliably. Four coders achieved satisfactory intercoder reliability and agreement with expert coders.

The Picture Story Exercise is relatively easy to administer and score. With literate subjects, it can be administered in written form, although it must be individually scored. It is less testlike than the other measures and therefore potentially more fun to complete. Since the "correct" answers are not obvious, effects due to faking and social desirability are lessened.

Disadvantages of the Picture Story Exercise include the training required to achieve reliable scoring and its susceptibility to situational influences. Achievement Motivation scores are likely to be elevated in situations that test takers perceive as competitive.

Validation Samples

Assessment methods were piloted in Malawi and India, revised, and then used in a more extensive validation study in India.

Pilot Assessment Method Validation Study. The assessment methods were piloted on 45 successful and 45 less successful entrepreneurs not interviewed in the initial research; 30 start-up entrepreneurs in business for less than six months, and 30 potential entrepreneurs—persons who had expressed an interest in starting a business but had not yet done so—in Malawi and India. The pilot validation sample was to be divided equally among manufacturing, marketing/trading, and service businesses.

The Focused Interview differentiated successful from less successful entrepreneurs in both Malawi and India. All competencies observed in each interview were summed to total score. In Malawi, the mean score for the successful entrepreneurs was 17.5, compared with 14.0 for the less successful group. In India, the mean total score for the more successful group was 39.5, compared with 24.8 for the less successful group. The more successful group scored higher on 12 of the 13 competency scores.

SYMLOG Ratings also differentiated superior entrepreneurs in both Malawi and India. In Malawi, Achievement scores were higher for the successful group (6.0 vs. 4.0), as were Power cores (5.3 vs. 4.4), while Affiliation scores were lower (0.25 vs. 1.8). Superior Indian entrepreneurs scored higher on all three Symlog rating scores (6.40 vs. 3.75 for Achievement, 8.20 vs. 3.75 for Affiliation, and 6.40 vs. 2.50 for Power).

Picture Story Exercise scores were slightly higher for the more successful entrepreneurs in Malawi (3.0 vs. 2.0 for Achievement, 3.0 vs. 2.7 for Affiliation, and 2.8 vs. 2.0 for Power). In India, entrepreneurs essentially rejected the PSE, refusing to tell stories or take the test instructions seriously.

The Self-Rating Questionnaire of the Business Situations Exercise proved difficult to administer and inconclusive: No difference was found between the successful and less successful entrepreneurs on these respondent measures in Malawi or India.

Final Assessment Method Validation Study. Revised versions of the Information Interview and the Focused Interview were administered to 28 potential entrepreneurs and to 92 existing entrepreneurs in manufacturing businesses. (The Self-Rating Questionnaire, Business Situations Exercise, and Picture Story Exercise were dropped.)

Sample. Criteria were established for three sample groups: successful, average, and potential entrepreneurs. Average and successful entrepreneurs had to have started and be involved in running a manufacturing business that had operated for 3 to 10 years.

To be designated as successful, an entrepreneur had to be nominated as outstanding by at least two different organizations knowledgeable about entrepreneurs in the geographical areas where interviews were being conducted. Nominating organizations included state development and private banks, entrepreneur training institutes, chambers of commerce, and government invest ment and extension service organizations. Average entrepreneurs had to be known by at least one of these organizations but not nominated as outstanding. Potential entrepreneurs were persons without previous entrepreneurial experience who had demonstrated an interest in starting a business by applying for a loan or by enrolling in an entrepreneurship training program.

To test the accuracy of nominations as a criterion variable, a factor analysis of entrepreneurs' business variables was conducted. This produced four factors with eigenvalues greater than one, three of which seemed robust. Factor 1 represented recent sales; Factor 2, recent profits; and Factor 3, sales and profits in the second year of the business (if the business had been in existence for more than four years). Factor scores were computed on these factors and entered into a two-group MANOVA (multivariate analysis of variance). This analysis produced a highly significant difference between the two groups of entrepreneurs (Wilks' lambda = .692; $p = .0002$). The simultaneous contrasts indicated that the two groups were significantly different on Factor 1 and Factor 2 ($p < .01$ in each case) but that the groups did not differ on Factor 3 ($p = .14$).

A total of 46 average and 46 successful entrepreneurs were interviewed. The interviews were conducted in Hindi, English, or another language spoken by both the interviewer and the entrepreneur. Interviewers did not know whether they were assessing superior or average entrepreneurs.

The successful and average groups of entrepreneurs were compared on personal background and business variables assessed in the Information Interview and on the competency scores and SYMLOG motive scores measured in the Focused Interview. The most important finding was that the successful entrepreneurs expressed significantly more competencies in the Focused Interview, and higher achievement and power motivation on SYMLOG coding of the Interview.

T-tests and chi-square analyses found few differences among the groups on personal background or demographic variables. Successful entrepreneurs were higher on a social class index constructed from some of the background variables, but this social class difference did not account for the competency differences between the successful and average groups.

Analyses of Differences on the Competency Scores

The means and standard deviations for the two groups were calculated on each of the 15 competencies. More successful entrepreneurs were significantly higher than averages on 8 of the 15 competencies:

Competence	Probability Level
Sees and Acts on Opportunities	.035
Persistence	.007
Information Seeking	.000
Concern for High Quality of Work	.054
Commitment to Work Contract	.050
Systematic Planning	.005
Self-Confidence	.025
Use of Influence Strategies	.014

A MANOVA showed a highly significant difference between the more and less successful entrepreneurs (Wilks' lambda = .638; p = .001). A discriminant analysis performed on the data produced a significant function (lambda = .638; p = .0013). Information Seeking and Systematic Planning showed discriminant function coefficients greater than .4.

Analyses of Relationships Among the Competency Scores

A factor analysis of the competency assessment scores yielded four factors with eigenvalues greater than one. A scree test indicated that only the first three of these were robust. Using a criterion of a factor loading of .5 or greater, and placing a competency in the factor on which it demonstrates the higher loading if the .5 criterion is met more than once, the three factors were defined as:

Factor 1

Initiative

Sees and Acts on Opportunities

Concern for High Quality of Work

Commitment to Work Contract

Efficiency Orientation

Problem Solving

Self-Confidence

Monitoring

Concern for Others' Welfare

This factor accounts for 36 percent of the variance, contains 9 of the 15 competencies, and seems to represent a proactive concern for quality and standards.

Factor 2

Persistence

Assertiveness

Use of Influence Strategies

This factor accounts for an additional 13 percent of the variance and seems to represent a persistent concern for influencing others.

Factor 3

Systematic Planning

Persuasion

This factor accounts for an additional 8 percent of the variance and seems to center on Systematic Planning.

A two-group MANOVA test of differences between the two groups of entrepreneurs on the three factors proved highly significant (Wilks' lambda = .715; $p = .00001$).

Analysis of SYMLOG Scores

Successful entrepreneurs were significantly higher on Power and Achievement SYMLOG scales. A two-group MANOVA of these data provided additional support for this finding (Wilks' lambda = .832; $p = .0012$).

Conclusions

1. *Validation.* The entrepreneurship competency model developed in Phase I of the project is validated by Focused Interview and SYMLOG rating data collected on a second criterion sample. Eight of the fifteen competencies assessed distinguished superior from average entrepreneurs at statistical levels of significance.

2. *Acceptability.* The Focused Interview and SYMLOG ratings, although requiring some training to administer, are the most acceptable and effective methods for assessing entrepreneurial competencies.

The two respondent instruments, the Self-Rating Questionnaire and Business Situations Exercise, did not differentiate superior from less successful entrepreneurs and proved lengthy and difficult to administer. The Picture Story Exercise TAT also failed to distinguish superior entrepreneurs and was rejected by the Indian sample.

NOTES

1. See McClelland, D. C. (1976), *The achieving society* (Chapters 6–8), New York: Irvington; McClelland, D. C., & Winter, D. (1971), *Motivating economic achievement,* New York: Free Press; or literature review in Spencer, L. M. (1986, April 1), *An update on achievement motivation theory and entrepreneurship,* paper presented at the Séminaire Entrepreneurship, École des Hautes Études Commerciales, L'Université de Montreal. Boston: McBer.

2. Mansfield, R. S., McClelland, D. C., Spencer, L. M., & Santiago, J. (1987), *The identification and assessment of competencies and other personal characteristics of entrepreneurs in developing countries,* Final Report: Project No. 936-5314, Entrepreneurship and Small Enterprise Development, Contract No. DAN-5314-C-00-3065-00. Washington, DC: United States Agency for International Development; Boston: McBer.

3. This chapter is abstracted from reports prepared by Richard Mansfield EdD, and statistical analyses conducted by Joseph DuCette, PhD; in Mansfield, R. S., McClelland, D. C., Spencer, L. M., & Santiago, J. (1987), *The identification and assessment of competencies and other personal characteristics of entrepreneurs in developing countries.* Final Report: Project No. 936-5314, Entrepreneurship and Small Enterprise Development, Contract No. DAN-5314-C-00-3065-00. Washington, DC: United States Agency for International Development; Boston: McBer.

4. Methods and instruments, with detailed instructions for administration and scoring, appear in Appendix A ("Manual for Selection and Impact Measures," McBer, August 1985) to the Mansfield, et. al. Final Report op. cit.

5. Based on an instrument developed by Harvard Professor R. F. Bales for the assessment of interpersonal behavior. See Bales, R. F., & Cohen, S. P. (1979), *SYMLOG,* New York: Free Press.

6. For scoring instructions for Achievement and Affiliation motivation, see Atkinson, J. W. (ed.). (1958), *Motives in fantasy, action and society,* Princeton, NJ: Van Nostrand; for power motivation scoring, Winter, D. G. (1973), *The power motive,* New York: Free Press.

Competency-Based Applications

18

Selection: Assessment and Job–Person Matching for Recruiting, Placement, Retention, and Promotion

DEFINITION

Selection is the process of matching people and jobs, either people outside the organization (recruiting and new hire selection) or inside (placement and promotion).

COMPETENCY-BASED SELECTION

Competency-based selection methods are based on the following hypothesis:

> The better the fit between the requirements of a job and competencies of the jobholder, the higher job performance and job satisfaction will be.[1]

Successful job–person matching therefore depends on (1) accurate assessment of individual competencies, (2) competency models of jobs, and (3) a method of assessing the "goodness of fit" between a person and a job. The development of competency models has been described in Part IV. This chapter discusses the assessment of individual competencies and methods for testing the match between people and jobs.

ORGANIZATION ISSUES

The following issues suggest a need for competency-based selection:

- *Poor Performance or Productivity in a Critical Job.* If a firm's sales staff is being outsold or its service quality is not on a par with its competitors, the perception may be: "Our *people* aren't as good—we need better people."

    Competency-based selection can be a way to gain competitive advantage. The market for human talent is imperfect. A firm that knows how to assess competencies effectively can, for example, hire "underpriced" but highly entrepreneurial MBAs from lesser known business schools. These MBAs may offer better value for money than higher priced graduates of Harvard, Stanford, or Wharton. Here competency-based selection is analogous to buying low-priced stocks of small companies with major growth potential before their value is recognized by the market.

- *High Turnover/Poor Retention.* This is usually due to a high failure rate among new hires. For example, turnover rates in retail and insurance sales frequently exceed 50 percent per year. It is very costly to keep bringing in new people, training them, and then having them fail or quit because they are unhappy in their jobs.

    Competency-based selection increases performance and also decreases turnover rates. High job performance and satisfaction in turn predict retention because (a) good performers need not be fired, and (b) satisfied employees are less likely to quit.[2] People well matched to their jobs intrinsically enjoy their work more, which produces a better organizational climate.

- *Succession Planning.* There may be an organizational need to identify new hires with the potential to become future managers or leaders.

- *Long Learning Curve Times.* A lengthy training period may transpire before new hires become productive (defined as the average productivity of experienced job incumbents). Competency-based selection can cut new hire learning curve periods by 33 to 50 percent. New hires with the competencies to do a job become fully productive faster.

- *Equal Opportunity for Nontraditional* (nonyoung, nonwhite, and nonmale) *Candidates.* In times of shrinking labor pools and changing demographics, competency-based selection does not discriminate on the basis of age, race, or sex.

- *Organizational Change.* Any change in an organization—globalization, privatization, growth, cultural change, or downsizing—involves shifting people out of some jobs into others that they must be able to do.

    Globalizing organizations need to know which employees have the competencies to perform in foreign environments. Privatizing agencies need to know which government bureaucrats have the competencies to become entrepreneurs in a free market. Growing firms need to know whom to hire to sustain growth. Changing organizations need to know which employees have the competencies to adapt and be successful in their future structure and culture. For downsizing firms, the question is who should be retained—which employees have the competencies to do the "leaner and meaner" jobs that remain.

■ *Determining Training Needs at Entry.* A gap between the competencies needed and what the organization can hire for indicates the training new hires will need.

STEPS IN DEVELOPING
A COMPETENCY-BASED SELECTION SYSTEM

1. *Develop Competency Model(s) for the Target Job(s).* Methods for developing competency models have been described in Chapters 10 through 12. A good rule is to involve as many of the people who will use the model in the study as possible. Managers who have been trained in and conducted Behavioral Event Interviews (BEIs) and worked with researchers to identify competencies believe in the model and are much more likely to implement it.

The competency model dictionary defines the specific competency levels that predict threshold and superior performance in the jobs studied and becomes the template used to select or place employees.

2. *Select or Develop Assessment Methods.* Selection methods are chosen from the interview, test, assessment center, biodata, and rating methods (discussed in greater detail in the following section "Competency Assessment Methods") on the basis of cost-effectiveness,[3] administrative ease, and candidate acceptability. Valid methods (e.g., assessment centers) may be too costly and difficult to administer; others, such as tests, may be rejected by candidates or an organization's culture. The authors' experience is that the Behavioral Event Interview is the most cost-effective selection tool. It approaches the assessment center in validity[4] yet requires one to two hours instead of one to two days, is easy to administer, and is acceptable to almost everyone.

3. *Train Assessors in the Assessment Method.* Organization staff who will conduct assessments need to be trained to do the BEI, to administer tests, or to run an assessment center. Our experience is that most people can in two or three days learn to conduct and code a BEI with sufficient reliability to make effective selection decisions.

4. *Assess the Competencies of Candidates for Jobs.*

5. *Make Job–Person Match Decisions* for selection, placement, and promotion (discussed in greater detail in the section "Job–Person Matching Methods").

6. *Validate the Selection System* (optional but desirable). Whenever possible, organizations should track the performance of people selected using competency assessment methods to confirm the validity and return on investment in the method.

7. *Develop a Competency-Based Job and Person Data Base and Matching System*. Once more than a few jobs have been studied and people assessed, a computer is needed to keep track of job-competency requirements, employee competencies, and job–person match data. The design of competency-based human resource information systems is discussed in Chapter 23.

COMPETENCY ASSESSMENT METHODS

Assessment of candidates can involve a variety of methods: Behavioral Event Interviews; tests; assessment center simulations; biodata; review of performance appraisal reports; and superior, peer, and subordinate ratings. Recent reviews[5] list the following assessment methods in descending order of criterion validity correlations with job performance:

Assessment Method	*r*
Assessment centers	.65
Interviews (behavioral)	.48–.61
Work-sample tests	.54
Ability tests	.53
"Modern" personality tests	.39
Biodata	.38
References	.23
Interviews (nonbehavioral)	.05–.19

Table 18–1 shows the assessment methods we have used most frequently over the years to measure the core competencies described in Chapters 3 through 9. Assessment methods are grouped as:

- Behavioral Event Interviews (BEI), coded for competencies
- Tests, which measure one or more competencies, and are either *operant* (tests that ask the person being tested to generate behavior) or *respondent* (tests that ask the person being tested to choose one of several responses)
- Assessment Centers that provide simulation exercises requiring the test taker to generate behavior, usually in a situation with other people, coded for one or more competencies
- Biodata consisting of facts about a person's past life: education, family, work experiences, leisure-time activities, and so on, that provide evidence of competency expression
- Ratings of a person's competencies by people who have observed him or her (e.g.,"360 degree" ratings by the person's boss, peers, subordinates, customers, external experts, and even family members)

Table 18–1 Methods Used to Assess Core Competencies

Competency	Tests		Assessment Center	Biodata	Ratings
	Operant	Respondent			
1. Self-Control	Picture Story Exercise (activity inhibition)	CPI; Jackson, Edwards, 16 PF	"Stress" interview; exercises		
2. Self-Confidence	PSE (efficacy, helplessness scales)	Seligman	Presentation exercises		
3. Organizational Commitment		Strong-Campbell; Kuder Preference; Organizational climate; "citizenship"; job satisfaction			
4. Flexibility	Analysis of Argument		Bray Job Interview		
5. Expertise	Speed of Learning (savings score)	Knowledge content		Credentials	
6. Information Seeking			Bray job interview; "treasure hunt" exercises		
7. Analytical Thinking	Programmers Aptitude; Airline Scheduling Test				
8. Conceptual Thinking	Thematic Analysis; Analysis of Argument; WAIS; Rorschach; Programmed Cases	Watson-Glaser	"Strategic plan/vision speech" presentation exercise		

Table 18–1 (*Continued*)

Competency	Tests		Assessment Center	Biodata	Ratings
	Operant	Respondent			
9. Achievement motive values	Picture Story Exercise coded for n Ach; Airline Scheduling Test (efficiency)	Hay/McBer Behavioral Description Inventory; Jackson, Edwards, Cattell, 16 PF; CPI	Business production game (efficiency, quality, risk taking, innovation)		
10. Concern for Order	Army Alpha: attention to detail; Rorschach		Business production game (quality)		
11. Initiative	Rorschach		"Treasure hunt" exercises; business production game		
12. Interpersonal Understanding	Programmed Cases; Social Network Reasoning	Profile of Non-Verbal Sensitivity (PONS)	Counseling exercises (interpersonal understanding: accurate empathy, warmth, genuineness, initiation)		
13. Customer Service Orientation	PSE (helping motive profile: $n\,Ach_2\,n\,Aff_3\,n\,Pow_2$)	Hogan customer service scale; Strong-Campbell	Role plays (irate customer)		Customer service survey
14. Impact and Influence	PSE (n Power), Social Network Reasoning	Jackson, Edwards, Cattell 16-PF; CPI: dominance scales	Influence, negotiation, presentation exercises		SYMLOG (dominance scale); Managerial Style; Organizational Climate

Competency					
15. Organizational Awareness		Organization Climate (ideal scale); organization citizenship; Strong-Campbell, Kuder			
16. Relationship Building				No. of contacts, friends	
17. Directiveness	PSE (n Power)	Jackson, Edwards, Cattell 16-PF; CPI: Dominance scales	Influence, negotiation exercises		SYMLOG (dominance scale)
18. Developing Others			Counseling; coaching exercises		Managerial Style Inventory (coaching scale)
19. Teamwork and Cooperation	PSE ("integrator" motive profile: n Ach$_2$ n Aff$_3$ n Pow$_2$)		Leaderless group exercises		SYMLOG (positiveness, task scales)
20. Team Leadership	PSE (socialized power)	Jackson, Edwards, Cattell 16-PF; CPI dominance scales	Leaderless group exercises; "vision speech" presentation		SYMLOG (dominance, positive, task scales); Managerial Style Inventory; Organizational Climate subordinate surveys

The Behavioral Event Interview (BEI)

The Behavioral Event Interview, conducted properly, can be used as a psychometric instrument to assess individual competencies. Numerous studies have
shown the validity of structured "behavioral" interviews in which the interviewee is asked to describe what he or she actually did in critical job or life
situations.[6] For example, motive competencies coded in BEI transcripts of
Navy officers correlated $r = .60$ (36% of the variance) with the performance
criterion while a projective test measure of the same motives correlated at
only $r = .33$ (10% of the variance).[7] One explanation for this finding is that
while a projective test measures operant motives "globally," (i.e. in every area
of life), the BEI focuses on motives aroused in an individual's most critical *job*
situations (what psychologists call a specific "need press") and hence is a better predictor of performance on the job.

Individual assessment BEIs can be conducted in exactly the same way as the
open-ended research BEIs described in Chapter 11 (any success high points or
failure low points), or focused to give the interviewee an opportunity to
demonstrate a specific competency required by a job. For example, probes for
Achievement Drive include, "Tell me about a time you accomplished something on your own," ". . . about the most challenging situation you have faced
in your job," or ". . . about a time you did something new." Competency-
based selection projects often include development of focused BEI protocols
with questions for the interviewer to ask and competencies to listen for and
check off when heard.

An important aspect of this and other structured interview method is to be
sure that all people being assessed are asked the same questions and given
equal time to respond.

Individual assessment BEIs are coded for competencies in the same way as
the research BEIs described in Chapter 12. Coders can work from written
transcripts (the easiest), video- or audiotape recordings, or—if very experienced—in "real time" as they conduct the BEI.

Competencies can be coded in several ways:

- Nominal presence or absence (at any point on a competency scale); or
- At a specific interval level on a scale: (1) every time seen in an incident,
  (2) once per incident (scale high point or average of levels coded), or
  (3) per entire BEI transcript (scale high point or average levels coded).

Our experience indicates averaging the highest level of each competency
coded in three separate incidents provides the most stable data for making assessment decisions.

Interrater reliability can be calculated by:

1. Category agreement using nominal presence or absence data. Reliabili-
    ties of .80–.85 are fairly easily established using this method.[8]

2. Standard correlation coefficient if using scale interval data. Inter-rater reliabilities of .80 (Pearson's r) between trainee coders and experts were attained after 30 hours' training in a recent study. Selection validity can be improved by training interviewer/coders. Research indicates that trained coders can attain very high degrees of interrater reliability ($r = .95+$).[9]

3. Rank order correlation if comparing individuals on total competency score (e.g., using Kendall's tau; two coders' ranking of individuals) or coefficient of concordance (more than two coders).[10]

Rank order reliabilities (agreement on which of several individuals is highest, next highest, etc., in descending order) are easiest to establish and can be based on either nominal or interval data. In five studies conducted by the first author with interviewer trainees in Europe and Asia (many of whom did not speak English as a first language), one day of training was sufficient to achieve interrater reliabilities of $r = .85$ to 1.00 in ranking three applicants on five competencies coded from videotaped BEIs in real time.

Pooling of ratings—having several interviewers conduct BEIs with the same person and then share and reconcile or average their competency scores for the person—can also increase multiple coders' effective reliability when making election decisions.[11]

Tests[12]

Many standard work-sample, mental ability, and personality tests can be used to measure competencies. In addition, new tests of "practical intelligence"[13] have been developed to measure specific competencies not assessed by traditional psychological tests. Table 18–1 shows some of the tests used most often to measure competencies.

"Operant" tests, which require the test taker to act, measure behaviors that are very different from those measured by "respondent" tests, which ask the test taker to choose from a list of answers. For example, there is a big difference between the ability to choose which of a list of answers represents an effective argument and being able to stand up in a competitive group and argue effectively. We prefer operant tests such as *critical* work-sample tests, that require behavior as close to that needed in actual critical job incidents as possible. (Assessment centers work because they measure operant behavior in exercises similar to actual job tasks.) Despite this preference, some respondent tests are valid measures of competencies.

Operant competency tests include the following:

- *Picture Story Exercise (PSE).* This is a written Thematic Apperception Test (TAT) that can be coded for Achievement (nAch), Affiliation (nAff), and Power (nPow) Motives,[14] Self-Control, Efficacy (feeling capable of doing things, in control of one's life versus helpless or powerless),[15] "socialized" power (influence used to accomplish some common good greater than oneself or to empower: make *others* feel strong) versus "personalized" power (influence used for the person's self-aggrandizement, to make others feel he or she is strong).[16]

The PSE can provide a measure of competency motive "molecules," such as the managerial profile (high achievement, high power, affiliation lower than power: $n\text{Ach}_3 n\text{Pow}_4 n\text{Aff} < n\text{Pow}$) or the helping/service "integrator" motive profile (moderate achievement, moderate-high affiliation, moderate power: $n\text{Ach}_2 n\text{Aff}_3 n\text{Pow}_2$) known to predict success in these jobs.[17]

- *The Speed of Learning Test.* This open-book test requires people being tested to solve complex problems in a specific knowledge area (neuroanatomy, military tactics, computer troubleshooting). People with knowledge of the area being tested solve more of the problems faster because they know what to look for and how to look for relevant information. For example, a surgeon may not remember the name of an obscure nerve to be avoided in a complex operation, but will know it is there and be able to find it in a neuroanatomy textbook faster than someone who has not studied neuroanatomy.

- *The Test of Thematic Analysis.* Respondents receive two differing or conflicting sets of data about a topic (e.g., two opposing critiques of a work of art) and compare them. Responses are scored for compound comparison distinctions made, evidence cited, and statement of overarching themes.

- *Analysis of Argument.* Test takers are given a strong statement on one side of a controversial topic (e.g., abortion) and asked to write an essay arguing for or against it. Then they are asked to write a second essay taking the *opposite* side of the issue. Responses are scored for disciplined logic in exposing contradictions in the opposing side's arguments, creation of central organizing themes for attack or defense of positions, and intellectual flexibility under pressures of time and emotion.[18]

- *Programmer Aptitude Test.* Test takers are given a pseudocomputer language—a set of symbols, nouns, and verbs—and asked to write complex mathematical equations or simulated computer programs to process data. Responses are scored for use of abstract symbols, logic, proper time, and cause → effect sequences (i.e., Analytic Thinking).

- *Airline Scheduling Test.* People being tested are given an airline schedule and asked to plan a very complex itinerary. Answers are scored for efficiency: most direct routes, fewest hours wasted making connections, and lowest possible total fares (i.e., Achievement Orientation and Analytic Thinking). A variant is the *Planning and Scheduling Test,* which requires test takers to construct a complex Program Evaluation and Review Technique (PERT) chart with many dependencies to minimize time and cost to complete a project.

- *Weschler Adult Intelligence Survey (WAIS).* A classic intelligence test with some operant exercises that ask test takers to organize data (abstract shapes, cartoons) into meaningful patterns or sequences, for example, cartoons in an order that tells a story (conceptual thinking).

- *Rorschach.* Test takers are shown inkblot pictures and asked what they see—and why. Responses can be scored for statement of overall theme and supporting data (parts of the picture that add up to its whole), which indicates Conceptual or Analytic Thinking, and movement (whether test takers see human figures moving toward a goal), which may measure Initiative.[19]

"Respondent" competency tests include:

- *The Watson-Glaser Critical Thinking Appraisal.* This is a reading comprehension test that measures Conceptual Thinking competencies: inference, recognition of assumptions, deduction, interpretation, and evaluation of arguments. Some items are deliberately controversial to test whether respondents' attitudes or emotions reduce their ability to think critically (i.e., an interaction of Self-Control with Conceptual Thinking competencies).

- *The Seligman Attributional Style Questionnaire.* Self-confidence can be measured according to how people respond to failure: either pessimistically or in a "depressive explanatory style" (failures are global, enduring, and the result of a fundamental defect in one's personality: "I *always* mess up *everything* . . . it's me, *I'm* no good") or optimistically: ("I may have messed up *this once,* but I've learned and I'll do fine in the future").[20]

- *Strong-Campbell Vocational and Kuder Preference Inventories.* These are designed to measure values and preferred activities ("Which would you rather do: read a book or pick apples?") and relate those preferences to those of people who like and remain in different types of jobs.[21] "Occupation preference" is a self-concept competency: Effective and superior performers tend to like their jobs and be "business-minded."[22]

- *Knowledge Tests.* Traditional exams require test takers to choose a correct response: "Which of the following is the correct formula for sulfuric acid?" As noted, respondent content knowledge tests rarely distinguish superior from average performers.

- *Programmed Cases.* Test takers are presented with brief facts about a person's life, then are asked which of two behaviors the person will most likely have shown next (see, e.g., the case of "Bill" in Chapter 12). This tests for interpersonal understanding and conceptual thinking.

    Programmed Cases sequences can also test for prejudice or sensitivity versus insensitivity to foreign cultural cues. Almost all test takers become more accurate in predicting future behaviors as they get more information about a person; their "learning curve" accelerates. Test items can be introduced in the middle of a Programmed Cases sequence that give data about a person's race, sex, or culture. For example, after a number of items that indicate "James likes music," an item reveals that James is black. A subsequent item asks: "On his vacation, is it most likely that James went to Vienna to listen to opera or went to Las Vegas to watch a championship fight?" A prejudiced person might think in stereotypes: "A lot of prizefighters are black; not many blacks listen to classical music," and answer incorrectly. Research indicates that prejudiced people stop learning and make increasing numbers of errors after seeing a fact that triggers their prejudice or stereotypes.

- *Personality Tests.* These include the California, Edwards, Hogan & Hogan, Jackson, 16 PF, and so on. Personality Inventories measure such self-reported (self-concept) competencies as dominance (Impact and Influence), Achievement, sociability, aggression, impulsivity, order, cooperativeness, leadership, novelty seeking, self-confidence—even Customer Service Orientation.

  Self-concept measures can distinguish superior from average performers. For example, California Personality Inventory scores for superior software development managers as compared with superior programmers and systems analysts show managers are higher in "people-related" personality traits: dominance, sociability, extroversion, management and leadership potential.[23]

  The authors are testing a new personality test, the *Behavioral Description Index (BDI)* designed to measure all 20 core competencies.[24]

- *Social Network Reasoning Tests.* Test takers watch a videotape of a complex group process (e.g., the jury deliberations in the classic movie *Twelve Angry Men*). The videotape is stopped at various points and test takers are asked: "Who influences whom? How? If you wanted to influence Person *X*, what appeals would you use?" These tests measure (small) Organizational Awareness, Interpersonal Understanding, and Impact and Influence reasoning (if not actual behavior).

- *Ideal Organizational Climate Survey.* Test takers describe their ideal organizational work environment in terms of desired responsibility, standards, clarity, and team commitment (dimensions known to arouse achievement motivation).[25] The desired organizational climate of superior organizational consultants is significantly higher than that of average consultants. Surveys of organizational citizenship values (and behaviors) provide a measure of organization commitment and occupational preference competencies.

- *Profile of Nonverbal Sensitivity (PONS).* Test takers listen to brief tape recordings of speech (excerpted from psychotherapy sessions) that have been electronically filtered so the *tone of voice* can be heard but not the words. Test takers are asked to choose the emotion expressed in the tone of voice: sad, angry, and so on. Superior human-service workers, consultants, and diplomats are better able to hear the nonverbal content of others' speech.[26]

- *Nonverbal Cues Tests.* Test takers are asked to look at pictures of two people standing beside or opposite each other and answer which of the couples is involved in a relationship versus just posing together and which of the two is the supervisor (boss) and which the supervisee (subordinate). Nonverbal cues in the pictures include relaxation versus tenseness of posture, angle of bodies (leaning toward each other), distance between bodies, age, similarity or difference of clothing, amount of physical contact (touching or not), direction of gaze and eye contact. Persons high in Affiliation motivation and Interpersonal Understanding are better able to detect which couples are in love; people high in Power motivation (Impact and Influence competencies) are better able to identify supervisor–supervisee status relationships.[27]

Assessment Centers

Many standard assessment center exercises can be observed and coded for competencies:

- *In-Basket Exercises.* These present test takers with management problems, such as employee requests for time off, decisions about allocation of resources, conflicts among co-workers, threats from the union, and the like. Subjects' responses can be coded for information seeking (trying to get additional information before acting), analytic thinking (dealing with problems in priority and logical sequence order), concern for order, use of concepts (mentioning policies or decision rules being followed) or even concept creation (recognizes emerging patterns in problems being presented and develops an "overarching" strategy for dealing with them).

- *"Stress" Exercises and Interviews.* Subjects can be put in very stressful situations and intrusively questioned about their motives and behaviors. For example, in a well-known assessment center where spies were selected for work behind enemy lines, candidates were locked in a small room with one naked light bulb, then slipped a note that told them they had been captured in the middle of the night photographing documents in the enemy's headquarters. A few minutes later, the door was broken down by men dressed as enemy soldiers, who then forcefully interrogated the subject. These exercises test for self-control and influence skills under stress.

- *Presentation Vision/Strategy Speeches.* Subjects can be told they have an hour to prepare a presentation to the Board of Directors on (a) their organization's mission, vision, and strategy, and (b) their work group's mission and strategy in relation to it. Subjects are left in a room with overhead transparencies, flip charts, pens, and a variety of presentation materials. Their presentations are coded for preparation, oral presentation skills, Impact and Influence, and Team Leadership.

- *Job Interview.* Candidates are told they may be selected for any of three jobs and given fairly vague one-page descriptions of each job. The interviewer then asks: "What additional information would you like about any job?" Subjects' responses are coded for information seeking and clues to motivation: Do they ask about job security? Opportunities for advancement? A chance to innovate? Responsibility for managing others? After the subject has "run dry" of questions, the interviewer gives him or her more detailed (and surprising) information about each job, again asks the candidate which job he or she prefers now and if he or she has any additional questions. The subject's responses can be scored for flexibility and self-control.[28]

- *Leaderless Group Exercises.* Several subjects in a group are given one or more problems to solve that require input (and sometimes consensus) from all group members. Problems can be how to divide a limited budget, who to lay off, or which vendor to hire. Each subject may be given a role (e.g., "You are the production manager and you must get $50,000 to keep your plant running"). Subjects' responses can be coded for many competencies: information seeking, interpersonal understanding, impact and influence, teamwork and cooperation, and team leadership (e.g., who "moves into the vacuum" to assume the leadership position—and with how much success).

- *"Treasure Hunt" Exercises.* Subjects are given the task of getting unusual physical objects (e.g., a copy of John F. Kennedy's book *Profiles of Courage*) and facts (e.g., capital gains tax rates in Luxembourg) under severe time constraints. Subjects' behaviors are coded for initiative, information seeking, and self-confidence (willingness to make "cold calls" to strangers to ask silly questions).

- *Business Production Game.* Subjects are given roles as managers or workers in competitive business games requiring goal setting, efficient use of resources, and production of widgets to high-quality standards under time constraints and competitive pressures. "Managers" and workers are scored for Achievement Drive, Concern for Order, Initiative, Information seeking, Impact and Influence, Teamwork and Cooperation, and Team Leadership competencies.

- *Role Plays.* Subjects can be asked to role-play dealing with an irate customer, a poor-performing or distraught employee; influencing a sales prospect; or negotiating with a vendor, union representative, or government official. Role plays can be designed to measure many competencies: interpersonal understanding, customer service orientation, impact and influence, and teamwork and cooperation, in developing "win-win" solutions to conflicts.

■ *Peer Coaching and Counseling Exercises.* Subjects are given the role of counselor and asked to help a real colleague solve a problem or integrate assessment data about him- or herself. "Counselors" are scored for interpersonal understanding, impact and influence, directing and developing others' competencies.

A basic rule for assessment center design is that exercises should be as close as possible to the actual critical situations a subject will face on his or her job. (Behavioral Event Interview critical incidents are an excellent source for realistic exercises because BEIs focus on the most difficult situations an organization's best performers have to deal with now.) Assessment centers have the great advantage of requiring operant behavior. If the best predictor of future behavior is past behavior in similar situations, realistic assessment centers should provide "work sample" data that will predict actual job performance.

Biodata

Biographical data ("bio-data") can be used to predict some competencies. For example, competency assessment methods were used to study "overseas adjustment," the ability of executives sent to foreign countries to adapt to and become effective in a different culture. The criterion sample compared people who adjusted, were highly effective, and loved their foreign assignments with those who were ineffective, hated their overseas situation, and returned home. Unsurprisingly, some of the predictors of overseas-adjustment competencies included considerable voluntary travel when young (e.g., having "bummed" through Europe as a student), number of friends and contacts in different countries, speaking one or more foreign languages, and a stable family all of whose members (spouses and children) enjoyed travel adventures with a high degree of novelty.[29]

Ratings

Ratings of subjects by managers, peers, subordinates, customers, outside experts (human resources assessors), and even family members (often called "360 degree" ratings by people "all around" the person being assessed) are an increasingly popular method of measuring competencies.

Some of the rating methods used include:

■ *Competency Assessment Questionnaires.* These are survey instruments that ask knowledgeable observers to rate the subject on competencies important in a job. For example, the just-noticeable-difference competency scales can be used in a questionnaire that asks which level on the scale best describes how a particular subject typically behaves on the job.

- *Competency Q-Sort.* Competencies or behavioral indicator levels can be presented on index cards to an observer who is asked to sort the cards on a scale from "most characteristic" to "least characteristic" of the person being rated.

- *Customer Survey.* Customers or clients can be asked to rate supplier personnel on "customer service orientation" behaviors and related competencies: interpersonal understanding, initiative, developing others.

- *SYMLOG* (Systematic Multiple-Level Observation of Groups). Achievement, affiliation, and power (impact and influence), teamwork and cooperation and team leadership competencies can be rated using SYMLOG, a survey that measures Dominance, Positive versus Negative responses to others, and Task Orientation—and all possible combinations of these dimensions. Persons high in teamwork and cooperation competencies will be rated "positive" and "task-oriented"; effective team leaders will be rated "dominant, positive, and task-oriented," indicating active leadership toward common goals.[30]

- *Managerial Style.* A managerial style questionnaire that rates managers on coercive, authoritative, affiliative, democratic-participative, pacesetting, and coaching managerial styles provides a measure of effective influence and impact, team leadership ("authoritative"), teamwork and cooperation ("democratic-participative"), and developing others ("coaching") competencies—when ratings are made by the managers' *subordinates.* Managers' self-reports of their managerial style do not predict effective performance.[31]

- *Organizational Climate.* Ratings of the organizational climate created by managers in their work groups—again rated by subordinates—provide a good measure of team leadership competencies. Subordinates of more effective managers consistently report higher personal job satisfaction and morale.[32]

JOB–PERSON MATCHING METHODS

In competency-based human resource management systems, selection and placement decisions are based on the "fit" or "match" between *job* competency requirements and *person* competencies. The underlying premise is "the better the fit between the requirements of a job and competencies of a person, the higher the person's job performance and job satisfaction will be." High job performance and satisfaction in turn predict retention (1) because good performers need not be fired; and (2) because satisfied employees are less likely to quit.

As an example, Figure 18–1 shows the fit between the competencies of a technical professional and the competency requirements of his first job (new-hire industrial chemist) and his fourth job (manager of an oil refinery). This person can be seen to be a good match for his first job, which largely requires individual contributor competencies: achievement orientation, technical expertise and cognitive skills. However, he is not a good match for his fourth job:

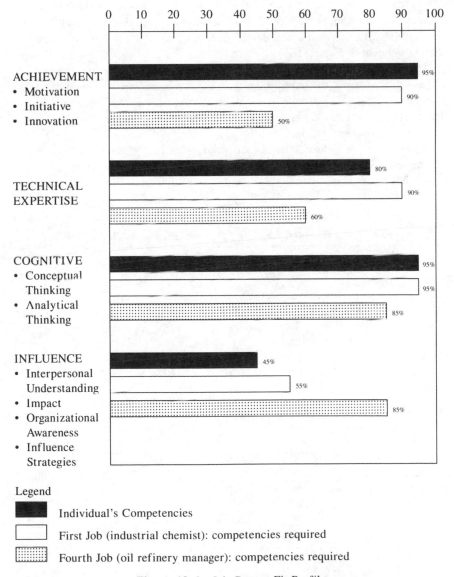

Legend

■ Individual's Competencies

☐ First Job (industrial chemist): competencies required

▦ Fourth Job (oil refinery manager): competencies required

Figure 18–1 Job–Person Fit Profile

His individual contributor skills exceed the managerial job's requirements, and he lacks the interpersonal and organizational influence skills needed to succeed in upper management.

Two quantitative job–person matching algorithms are the "weighted absolute difference" and "profile comparison" methods.[33] The weighted absolute difference method calculates how much a person differs from the competency requirements of the job on each competency, multiplies these differences by a weight based on the importance of each competency, and sums weighted differences for all competencies. Table 18–2 shows a "weighted absolute difference" calculation for the industrial chemist and oil refinery job–person matches shown in Figure 18–1.

The "weighted absolute difference" job–person matching algorithm uses the *absolute value* of person competencies and job competency requirements, for example, "level 2" versus "level 6" on the Achievement Orientation scale. The best candidate is the person with the lowest total difference from the competency requirements of the job.

Note that the weighted absolute difference method penalizes a person for having *more* of any competence than the job requires. Intuitively, it makes sense that more of one competence (e.g., very high achievement orientation)

Table 18–2   Weighted Absolute Value Job–Person Match Analysis

Competency	Job Required	Person Score	Difference Δ	Weight	Weighted Absolute Value Δ
FIRST JOB: INDUSTRIAL CHEMIST					
Achievement	90	95	5	3	15.0
Technical Expertise	90	80	−10	2	20.0
Cognitive	95	95	0	3	0
Influence	55	45	−10	1	10.0
Total	330				45.0

% MISMATCH (weighted absolute value/job total)   13.6%
% FIT (1 − % mismatch)   86.4%

	Job Required	Person Score	Difference Δ	Weight	Weighted Absolute Value Δ
FOURTH JOB: OIL REFINERY MANAGER					
Achievement	50	95	45	1	45.0
Technical Expertise	60	80	20	1	20.0
Cognitive	85	95	10	2	20.0
Influence	85	45	40	3	120.0
Total	280				205.0

% MISMATCH (weighted absolute value/job total)   73.2%
% FIT (1 − % mismatch)   26.8%

should compensate for lower competence than the job requires on some other competency: A very motivated person would be expected to develop a competency he or she lacked. The penalty for overqualification comes from evidence that people with more competence than a job requires will pay attention to the wrong aspects of the job. For example, a supervisory engineer too high in achievement orientation will spend his or her time solving interesting engineering problems instead of managing.

The Profile Comparison method[34] correlates the rank order of the competency requirements of a job (Q-sorted on the basis of "most important" to "least important" for performance) with the average rank order of a person's competencies (Q-sorted on the basis of "most descriptive" to "least descriptive" of the person by the person's self-report and by his or her manager and a peer). The best candidate is the person with the highest job–person rank order correlation.

Table 18–3 shows the rank order correlations between the person and the two jobs—entry-level industrial chemist and fourth-level oil refinery manager shown in Figure 18–1. This person is clearly a better match for the individual technical contributor job than for the managerial position.

The "profile comparison" method uses the *relative importance* of individual competencies compared with job competency requirements. The best candidate is the person whose competencies are most highly correlated with the competencies required by the job. Profile comparison job–person match correlations show criterion validities of .39–.98 with job performance, .22 with job satisfaction, and −.19 with turnover.[35]

A human resource manager might use these job–person match data in several ways.

Recruitment/Selection

The good job–person match between the person and the entry-level technical/professional individual contributor job shown in Figure 18–1 predicts superior performance and suggests the candidate should be hired.

Table 18–3 Profile Comparison (Correlation*) Method Job-Person Match Analysis

Competency	Person Rank	First Job Rank	Fourth Job Rank
Achievement	1.5	2.5	4
Technical Expertise	3	2.5	3
Cognitive	1.5	1	2
Influence	4	4	1
Person-Job Rank Order Correlation:		.85	−.55

*Spearman rank order correlation with ties in *Non-Parametric Statistics for the Behavioral Sciences,* by S. Siegal, 1956. New York: McGraw-Hill.

Competency-based recruiting and selection systems usually focus on screening methods that winnow a small number of strong candidates from large numbers of applicants quickly and efficiently. Assessing recruits involves special challenges: Recruiters must screen many applicants in a short period (30-minute interviews); applicants straight from college may have little work experience on which to base judgments, and so on. Competency-based recruiting systems therefore stress identification of a few (3–5) core competencies that meet the following criteria:

■ Competencies that applicants will have had the opportunity to develop and demonstrate in their lives to date (e.g., initiative)

■ Competencies that are likely to predict candidates' long-run career success and that are hard to develop through employer training or job experience. These include master competencies such as achievement orientation or concern with influence and impact, which are more cost-effective to select for than to develop. For example, a firm hiring technical individual contributors might want to recruit 10 percent of new hires for influence and impact competencies. By selecting some candidates who not only had good grades in the sciences but also were captains of sports teams or leaders in student organizations, the firm would have a pool of technical employees with the competencies to become managers in the future.

■ Competencies that can be reliably assessed using a short, targeted Behavioral Event Interview (BEI) developed for this purpose. For example, if "collaborative team leadership" is a desired competency, interviewees might be asked, "Tell me about a time when you got a group to do something." Their responses are then coded for consensus-building versus adversarial behaviors.

Succession Planning and Promotion

The poor job–person match between the person and the fourth-level managerial job shown in Figure 18–1 indicates that the candidate is unlikely to be successful in a managerial position and should *not* be promoted.

Competency-based job–person matching algorithms have many applications in succession planning. Candidates can be systematically compared on the basis of "goodness of fit" to jobs they might assume in the future. For example, a rule of thumb following from Weber's Law is that a 15 percent difference (plus or minus) between a person's competence and the competence requirements of the job will by definition be "just-noticeably-different" and should predict a successful promotion or placement. A job–person difference of 15 to 32 percent (two just-noticeable-differences) represents a challenging promotion (or significant demotion). Job–person matches greater than three just-noticeable-differences (32%–52%) will be "real stretches" for a person, with significant retention risks from failure if the job requirements exceed the person's competencies, or from boredom if the person's abilities exceed the job's requirements.

Development—Training and Career Pathing

Comparison of the person's competencies with the competency requirements of the fourth-level job shown in Figure 18–1 indicate that this person should be sent to interpersonal skills training, assigned to jobs that require interpersonal and influence competencies (e.g., a developmental job in human resources or labor relations), or seconded to a mentor who is known throughout the organization as a "master corporate politician."

> Competency-based career pathing and development (training and/or developmental assignments) programs are based on gaps between employees' competencies and the competency requirements of their present or future jobs, as defined by the competencies demonstrated by superior performers in these jobs. As shown in Figure 18–1, the competency requirements for a job define a "template" for development. Employees who are appraised as lacking in a specific competency can be directed to a specific developmental activity designed to teach them the missing competency, improve their performance in their existing jobs, or prepare them to advance to higher level jobs in the future.

Performance Management

This person should have specific objectives for development of interpersonal and influence competencies during each performance period, and should be assessed on development of these competencies at each performance appraisal.

Competency-Based Pay

This person should be rewarded for development of interpersonal and influence skills by providing merit "pay for skill" bonuses for development and demonstration of these competencies.

CASES: IMPACT OF COMPETENCY-BASED SELECTION ON PERFORMANCE AND RETENTION

Experiments that compared salespeople selected on the basis of competencies assessed using BEIs with a control group of persons selected using other methods indicate competency-based selection can show significant return on investment from increased performance and retention (decreased turnover), as shown in Table 18–4.

In the commercial sales case, 33 salespeople were hired using the BEI and a competency model; a control group of 41 was selected without behavioral interviews. In the following three years, five of the competency-selected group quit or were fired, compared with 17 turnovers in the control group.

Table 18–4   Impact of Competency-Based Selection on Performance and Turnover

	Performance			Turnover		
Sales Group	Control	Competency	Δ (%)	Control (%)	Competency (%)	Δ (%)
Commercial	10.5%	18.7%	+78	41	15	−63
Computer	NA	NA	(NA)	30	3	−90
Wholesale	Base	14%	+14	Base	−50	−50
Retail	$4,200/wk	$5,000/wk	+19	40	20	−50
Average			+37			−63

Competency-selected salespeople increased sales an average of 18.7 percent per quarter, compared with a 10.5 percent average increase for salespeople in the control group. On an annual basis, competency-selected salespeople sold $91,370 more than control group salespeople, a net revenue increase of $2,558,360 ($91,370 × 28 salespeople).

In the computer sales training case, a major computer firm decided to transfer several thousand senior staff ("overhead people who *cost* money" at an average yearly compensation of $50,000 each) to become salespeople who *make* money.

Not all staff "bureaucrats" have the competencies to be effective in sales: Initial attrition from sales training was 30 percent or 210 of 700 staff people sent for sales training each year. Sales trainees who failed three successive month-end tests were terminated after four months. In salaries alone, each failure cost the firm $16,667 × 210 failures = $3,500,000 per year. (This figure is conservative because trainee fringe benefits and the costs of training (instructors, materials, and overhead) were also lost.)

The firm developed a competency model for successful salespeople and used it to screen staff executives admitted to sales training. Attrition from the competency-selected group was 3 percent or 21 dropouts, a 90% reduction in costs worth $3,150,000.

In the retail sales case, 50 percent of 60 new hires were selected on the basis of competencies assessed using a Behavioral Event Interview and the other 50 percent were selected using traditional biodata criteria (one requirement was "10 years' sales experience," which essentially limited them to middle-aged white males, an affirmative action concern). In the year following selection, turnover in the competency-selected group was 20 percent (six people left) and average sales, $5,000 per week. Turnover in the control group was 40 percent (12 people left) and average sales, $4,200 per week. Benefits of the competency-based selection system were:

- Turnover cost avoidance—6 salespeople retained at a $20,000 per person replacement cost = $120,000

- Increased revenues—30 salespeople × $40K extra sales/year × 50% gross margin = $600K/year net increased contribution
- A total one-year benefit of $720,000

The return on $30,000 invested in the competency study and selection training was 2,300 percent. In addition, the competency-based selection system resulted in the hiring of more female and minority salespeople (without prior sales experience), solving the affirmative action problem.

NOTES

1. Caldwell, D. F., & O'Reilly, C. A. (1990), Measuring person–job fit with a profile-comparison process, *Journal of Applied Psychology, 75*(6), 648–657; Caldwell, D. F. (1991, April 12), *Soft skills, hard numbers: Issues in person–job/person–organization fit,* Paper presented at the Personnel Testing Conference of Southern California Spring Conference, Ontario, CA.

2. Locke, E. A. (1976), The nature and causes of job satisfaction in M. Dunette (Ed.), *Handbook of industrial and organizational psychology,* Chicago: Rand McNally, 1976, pp. 1328–30; Mowday, R. T., Porter, L. W., & Steers, R. M. (1982), *Employee-organization linkages: The psychology of commitment, absenteeism and turnover,* New York: Academic Press; Caldwell (1991), op. cit.

3. Cascio, W. F (1982), *Costing human resources: The financial impact of behavior in organizations,* Boston: Kent Publishing; Smith, M. (1988). Calculating the Sterling value of selection, *Guidance and Assessment Review, 4*(1), Leicester, UK: British Psychological Society, provide methods for calculating the cost-effectiveness of various selection methods given their costs of administration and criterion validity.

4. McClelland, D. C., & Boyatzis, R. E. (1982), The leadership motive pattern and long-term success in management, *Journal of Applied Psychology, 67*(6), 737–743. Also see Boyle, S. (1988), Can behavioral interviews produce results? *Guidance and Assessment Review, 4*(1), Leicester, UK: British Psychological Society.

5. Smith, M. (1988), Calculating the Sterling value of selection, *Guidance and Assessment Review, 4*(1). Leicester, UK: British Psychological Society; Boyle, S.(1988), Can behavioral interviews produce results? *Guidance and Assessment Review, 4*(1), Leicester, UK: British Psychological Society.

6. Janz, T. (1982), Initial comparisons of patterned Behavioral Description interviews versus unstructured interviews, *Journal of Applied Psychology, 67,* 577–580.

   Opren, C. (1985), Patterned behavior description interviews versus unstructured interviews: A comparative study, *Journal of Applied Psychology, 70,* 774–776.

   Latham, G. P., Saari, L. M., Pursell, E. D., & Campion, M. A. (1980), The situational interview, *Journal of Applied Psychology, 65,* 422–427.

   Latham, G. P., & Saari, L. M. (1984), Do people do what they say? Further studies on the situational interview, *Journal of Applied Psychology, 69,* 569–573.

   Latham and Saari report some success with a "fortune-teller" situational interview that asks interviewees what they *would* do in job situations; the right answer is what superior performers actually did in the test situation. McBer studies of U.S. Army junior officers and small-business entrepreneurs did not replicate Latham and Saari's findings. We continue to feel more confident about reports of actual behavior than hypothetical assertions of what an interviewee might do.

7. Winter, D. G., & Healy, J. M. (1982), An integrated system for scoring motives in running text: Reliability, validity, and convergence, Paper presented at the American Psychological Association, Los Angeles, 1981; Department of Psychology, Wesleyan University.

8. Category agreement

$$\text{reliability} = \frac{2 \times \# \text{ agreements (number of times the competency is scored by both coders)}}{\# \text{ scored by coder}_1 \text{ but not by coder}_2 + \# \text{ scored by coder}_2 \text{ but not by coder}_1}$$

Boyatzis, R. E. (1982), *The competent manager: A model for effective performance*, New York: Wiley; Atkinson, J. W. (Ed.), (1958), *Motives in fantasy, action and society*, Princeton, NJ: Van Nostrand.

9. Lawton, G. W., & Borman, W. C. (1978), Constructing stimuli with known true scores for determining validity of rating scales, *Proceedings: Sixth Annual Symposium on Psychology in the Department of Defense*, Colorado Springs: U.S. Air Force Academy Department of Behavioral Sciences and Leadership.

10. Siegal, S. (1956), *Nonparametric statistics for the behavioral sciences* (p. 229). New York: McGraw-Hill.

11. Rosenthal, R. (1973), Estimating effective reliabilities in studies that employ judges' ratings, *Journal of Clinical Psychology, 29,* 1–4.

12. A general reference for published tests is Mitchell, J. V. (1985), *The ninth mental measurements yearbook* (Vols. I and II), Lincoln, Nebraska: University of Nebraska Press. Information about competency tests not otherwise cited is available from McBer and Company.

13. Sternberg, R. J., & Wagner, R. K. (Eds.), *Practical intelligence,* Cambridge, UK: Cambridge University Press.

    Sternberg, R. J. (1986), *Intelligence Applied,* San Diego: Harcourt, Brace Jovanovich.

    Goleman, D. (1981, January), The new competency tests: Matching the right people to the right jobs, *Psychology Today,* 35–46.

14. Atkinson, J. W. (Ed.) (1958), *Motives in fantasy, action and society,* Princeton, NJ: Van Nostrand; Winter, D. G. (1973), *The power motive,* New York: Free Press.

15. Bandura, A. (1986), *Social foundations of thought and action: A social cognitive theory,* Englewood Cliffs, NJ: Prentice-Hall: "self-efficacy" coding system; Seligman, M. (1991), *Learned optimism,* New York: Knopf: "depressive explanatory style" coding system; Jacobs, R. (1991), *Moving up the corporate ladder: A longitudinal study of motivation, personality and managerial success in women and men,* doctoral dissertation, Boston University; Boston: McBer: "helplessness" (lack of power) coding system.

16. McClelland, D. C. (1975), *Power: The inner experience,* New York: Irvington.

17. Lawrence, P. R., & Lorsh, J. W. (1967, November–December), New management job: The integrator, *Harvard Business Review, 45*(6), 142–151; Kolb, D. A., and Boyatzis, R. E. (1970), On the dynamics of the helping relationship, *Journal of Applied Behavioral Science, 6*(3), 267–289.

18. Winter, D. G., McClelland, D. C., & Stewart, A. J. (1981), *A new case for the liberal arts,* San Francisco: Jossey-Bass.

19. Piotrowski, Z. A., & Rock, M. (1963), *The Perceptanalytic Executive Scale,* New York: Grune & Stratton.

20. Seligman, M. (1990), op. cit.

21. A good review of vocational interest inventories is Davis, R. (1991), Vocational interests, values and preferences, in M. D. Dunnette & L. M. Hough (1991), *Handbook of industrial and organizational psychology* (Vol. 2), Palo Alto, CA: Consulting Psychologists Press.

22. Theories of work adjustment suggest that vocational interest inventories should not relate to performance, as by definition, the performance of the criterion group of people remaining in

a job category is normally distributed. Our studies, however, have often found that superior performers have statistically significantly higher occupational preference scores than do average performers. Our hypothesis is that comparison samples of average performers include people not temperamentally suited for the job, who will not remain in it. These people depress the mean occupational preference scores for the average performer sample, producing statistically significant differences between the average and superior groups.

23. Wiley, R., (1990), MIS Managerial and technical jobs: measured competency differences, Boston: Hay Management Consultants.

24. Page, R. C., & DePuga, I. S. (1992, May 2), *Development and cross-cultural applications of a Competency Assessment Questionnaire,* Paper presented at the Seventh Annual Conference for Industrial and Organizational Psychology, Montreal, Quebec.

25. Litwin, G., & Stringer, R. (1968), *Motivation and organization climate,* Boston: Harvard Business School Research Press.

26. Rosenthal, R., Archer, D., Koivunmaki, J. H., DiMatteo, M. R. & Rogers, P. (1974, January), Assessing sensitivity to non-verbal communications: The PONS test, *Division 8 Newsletter,* Washington, DC: American Psychological Association.

27. In Sternberg, R. J. (1986), *Intelligence applied* (pp. 303–315), San Diego: Harcourt, Brace Jovanovich.

28. Bray, D. W. (1991, April 12), *Assessment center methodology in evaluating personal characteristics,* Paper presented at the Personnel Testing Conference of Southern California Spring Conference, Ontario, CA.

29. Mansfield, R. S. (1982), Review of empirical studies on overseas adjustment, in R. S. Mansfield (1982), *Advanced Intercultural Relations Workshop,* Boston: McBer.

30. Bales, R. F., & Cohen, S. P. (1979), *SYMLOG,* New York: Free Press.

31. McBer. (1991), *Managerial Style Inventory technical manual,* Boston: McBer. See also McClelland, D. C., & Burnham, D. H. (1976, March–April), *Power: The great motivator, Harvard Business Review,* 159–166,

32. McBer. (1991), *Organizational Climate Survey technical manual,* Boston: McBer. See also studies reported in McClelland, D., & Burnham, D. (1976) Op. cit.

33. Page, R. (1991), Job–person similarity, Minneapolis, MN: Hay Management Consultants. Page reviewed 16 job–person matching algorithms and concluded the "least differences" method produced results equal to more complex methods such as the Euclidean distance—D^2 approach—recommended in Cronbach, L. J., & Glesser, G. C. (1953), Assessing similarities between profiles, *Psychological Bulletin, 50,* 456–473.

34. Caldwell, D. F., & O'Reilly, C. A. (1990), Measuring person–job fit with a profile–comparison process, *Journal of Applied Psychology, 75*(6), 648–657; Caldwell, D. F. (1991, April 12), *Soft skills, hard numbers: Issues in person–job/person–organization fit,* Paper presented at the Personnel Testing Conference of Southern California Spring Conference, Ontario, CA.

35. Caldwell, D. F. (1991), Op. cit.

19

Performance Management[1]

DEFINITION

A Performance Management System (PMS) is the cycle shown in Figure 19–1 of managers working with subordinates to:

1. *Plan Performance.* Define job responsibilities and expectations, and set goals or objectives for a performance period

2. *Coach/Manage.* Offer feedback, support, and reinforce development throughout the performance period

3. *Appraise Performance.* Formally evaluate performance at the end of the performance period

Performance appraisal provides information for other personnel functions:

- *Compensation.* Determining fixed or performance-based pay
- *Succession Planning.* Identifying candidates to replace incumbents in other—usually higher—jobs
- *Discipline.* Probation or dismissal actions
- *Development.* Training, job assignments, or mentoring relationships that increase employee competencies
- *Career Pathing.* Planning future job assignments designed to give employees specific experiences and/or competencies

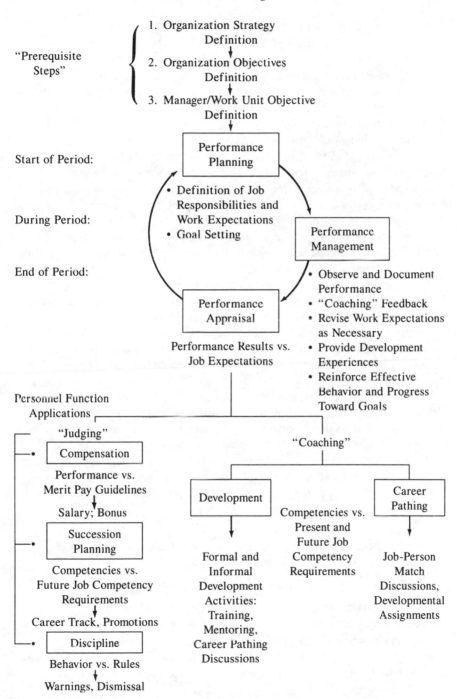

"Prerequisite Steps"

1. Organization Strategy Definition
2. Organization Objectives Definition
3. Manager/Work Unit Objective Definition

Start of Period:

Performance Planning

During Period:

- Definition of Job Responsibilities and Work Expectations
- Goal Setting

Performance Management

End of Period:

Performance Appraisal

- Observe and Document Performance
- "Coaching" Feedback
- Revise Work Expectations as Necessary
- Provide Development Experiences
- Reinforce Effective Behavior and Progress Toward Goals

Performance Results vs. Job Expectations

Personnel Function Applications

"Judging"

Compensation

Performance vs. Merit Pay Guidelines

Salary; Bonus

Succession Planning

Competencies vs. Future Job Competency Requirements

Career Track, Promotions

Discipline

Behavior vs. Rules

Warnings, Dismissal

"Coaching"

Development

Competencies vs. Present and Future Job Competency Requirements

Formal and Informal Development Activities: Training, Mentoring, Career Pathing Discussions

Career Pathing

Job-Person Match Discussions, Developmental Assignments

IMPROVEMENT OF ORGANIZATION PERFORMANCE

Figure 19–1 A Generic Performance Management System (PMS)

COMPETENCY-BASED PERFORMANCE
MANAGEMENT SYSTEMS

In recent years, the emphasis in PMS has been on *performance*—the "what" of behavior—the specific quantitative monetary, productivity, or quality results achieved in the recent *past*. The focus has been on *rewards* (performance-based bonuses, merit awards).

At present, many organizations are becoming interested in management and appraisal of *competence*—the "how" of performance. They are seeking more qualitative assessment, oriented to the *future* and focused on *development*.

A competency approach brings a different perspective to performance management. Performance is viewed in terms of the process competencies employees use to achieve their job results.

A PMS that combines planning, management, and appraisal of both performance results and competency behaviors is called a "mixed model" of PM or a "total PM" approach. Mixed models assess and reward both performance and competence, both what employees actually "delivered to the bottom line" in the past year and how they did it: the characteristics they showed that predict superior performance in their present job, or in future jobs.

Figure 19–2 shows how performance and competence are balanced in mixed models. In a line job, achievement of performance results may be weighted 90 percent and demonstration of competency behaviors only 10 percent. At the other extreme, an appraisal form for a service position might weight competence 100 percent. Performance objectives for a staff job might give equal weight to results and demonstration of competency behaviors.

In most mixed models, achievement of performance results is quantified, past oriented, and tied to unit goals, based on a short term, and used to make compensation decisions. Competency appraisal is more qualitative (although the JND scales proposed in Chapters 3 through 9 can measure competencies in numbers as well), longer range, future oriented, and used for employee development and career path planning.

In "Mixed Models," **Performance** *and* **Competencies** are considered
(50%–90%)   (10%–50%)

PERFORMANCE ("pay for results")	COMPETENCIES ("pay for skill")
• **"What"** of performance	• **"How"** of performance
• **Quantitative:** Tied to unit goals	• **More** qualitative
• **Short time frame:** One year, past performance	• **Longer time frame: Future** performance in present and future jobs
• **Reward oriented**	• **Development** (behavior change) oriented

Figure 19–2   Performance-Based and Competence-Based Appraisal Approaches

ORGANIZATIONAL ISSUES

Current problems that indicate a need for competency-based performance management include the following:

- Job performance standards and appraisal criteria are seen as unequal or unfair because:

  One group of workers must achieve at a higher level than other workers in equivalent jobs to receive a good evaluation or reward

  Workers are graded on a "bell curve," so that most workers are rated average or below average, regardless of the absolute level of their performance

  Expected results are not under the workers' control, (e.g., using a productivity index such as "tons of steel per secretary")

  Employees have little input into the performance goals set for them.

- Performance appraisal is seen by managers and employees as a bureaucratic "paperwork" exercise that they do not take seriously because it has little impact on employee performance or development.

- Employees see nothing in the PMS for them—performance appraisals do not address their questions about skill development or career advancement.

- The performance management system has little impact on actual management; it doesn't lead managers to do their jobs better or to develop or provide feedback to their employees.

- The performance management system does not reflect or reinforce the organization's strategy because it fails to focus employee behavior on strategic priorities such as quality or service.

- Performance ratings are inflated. If 95 percent of the workforce is rated "4 (very good)" on a scale of 1 to 5, employee ratings are not of any use for promotion decisions or succession planning.

"Mixed model" performance plus competency PMS are particularly appropriate for:

- *Uncertain Environments.* In uncertain and rapidly changing environments, where results are not under employee control, hard results objectives are often rendered irrelevant by external events (e.g., oil sales targets in a year when prices drop from $35 to $18 a barrel). In such situations, evaluation must be based on whether employees did everything they could, whether they demonstrated the right *behaviors* rather than achieving targeted results. The less control employees have over results, the more performance should be based on expression of competencies.

■ *Qualitative/Process Service Jobs.* In jobs with no measurable outcomes, qualitative skills—competencies—are the best indicators of employee performance. For an air cabin crew, competency behaviors, such as smiling and being unfailingly cheerful to tired, disgruntled passengers, or staying cool in emergencies, *are* the job output. The more subjective the job output, the more important it is to appraise competency behaviors.

■ *Self-Managing Teams.* In teamwork groups, individual results outputs may be less important than contribution to the group process. Teamwork and cooperation competencies, the ability to work well with different groups of people, are increasingly important in the diverse work forces of the global organization. Even in technical/professional individual contributor jobs, "organizational citizenship behaviors" predict superior performance. For example, in a study of computer programmers, three organizational citizenship behaviors (e.g., the willingness to stay after hours to help a colleague finish a project) accounted for 13 percent of the variance in dollar-valued work performance (10 measures of technical ability accounted for 63%–68% of the variance).[2] The more important team performance is, as opposed to individual performance, the more important it is to appraise teamwork and cooperation behaviors of individual workers.

■ *Jobs Intended for Development of Future Performance.* The more a job or organization's objectives for employees stress development of skills (e.g., management trainee positions), the more appraisal should be based on demonstrations of improved competence.

■ *Changing Organizational Strategy, Focus, or Markets.* In changing environments and organizations, employees' potential to contribute to the firm in the future may be more important than their past performance. For example, the ability to sell a firm's new products in the European Common Market may be more important than sales of older products in domestic markets. Most performance management systems are past oriented. The greater a firm's emphasis on future performance, the more its PMS should stress development and appraisal of competencies.

STEPS IN DEVELOPING COMPETENCY-BASED PERFORMANCE MANAGEMENT SYSTEMS

1. Identify competencies required for superior performance in present or future jobs (competencies needed to implement a desired strategic change). To add value, a PMS should motivate employees to do *better* than their current actual performance. Figure 19–3 shows a competency-based PMS matrix

	Results ←	Priority Tasks/ Behaviors ←	Competencies
Desired		• _____	• _____
(Superior: top 10%)	1.5x	• _____	• _____
Actual		• _____	• _____
(Acceptable)	x	• _____	• _____

Figure 19–3 Performance Management

that provides employees with a template for *superior* performance. This matrix compares the "actual" results, task priorities, behaviors, and competency levels of the employee being appraised with those of best performers ("desired") in the job.

2. Develop a "mixed model" performance management system for assessing both performance results and competency behaviors that predict performance in the job.

3. Train managers and employees in performance management (e.g., coaching for performance improvement). Performance coaching involves:

    a. Agreement between manager and employee on his or her "actual" levels of competence. An employee's competency levels are most easily assessed with "360 degree" ratings by colleagues "all around" the employee (i.e., by his or her boss, and a sample of peers, subordinates, and customers who know the employee's work well). The average of these ratings is compared with the employee's self-assessment of his or her competencies.

    b. The employee identifying the "desired" levels of competence he or she wants to develop *to meet his or her own performance or career advancement goals.*

    c. Agreement on a "contract" between employee and manager on

        • The employee's competency development goals and the action steps he or she will take to attain them

        • The help and support the manager will give the employee

This coaching approach uses the principles of "self-directed change" theory, which holds that adults change only when they

■ Feel it is in their own best interests to do so

■ Feel dissatisfied with their existing situation or level of performance ("actual")

- Are clear about a "desired" situation or level of performance
- Are clear about action steps they can take to move from the actual to the desired situation or level of performance

Competency-based PMS shift the emphasis of appraisal from organization results achieved to employee behaviors and competencies demonstrated. Diagnosis and problem solving to deal with poor performance takes this form: "If results are not at the desired level, give higher priority to these job tasks, demonstrate these behaviors more often, and develop these competencies" (i.e., model the task priorities, behaviors, and competency levels of the best performers in the job).

The addition of competencies to performance management systems has important implications for management. Managers explicitly commit themselves to provide employees with formal training, coaching, and other competency development activities during the performance period.

The most important factor in implementing a competency-based performance management system is training managers to provide this coaching and developmental assistance. (Studies of effective performance management systems consistently find training to be an important input.)[3] Employee training also helps employees understand how the PMS works, what their role is, how to assess themselves, and how to contract for competency development activities with their managers.

CASES

Flight Attendants

A European airline sought to develop a flight attendant competency-based PMS that captured the airline's best customer service practices. Eight competencies were identified: personal impact, customer care, resilience, efficiency, customer management, teamwork, and adaptability. Four-point, just-noticeable-difference scales were constructed for each competency from actual BEI incidents from superior and average flight attendants. Figure 19–4 shows the "customer care" scale.

Flight service managers and independent appraisers unknown to the flight attendants regularly travel as passengers to observe attendants and record critical incident interactions with customers. (Appraisers have the option of creating little assessment center situations, for example, bumping a flight attendant to spill coffee on themselves to see how attendants deal with a situation.)

The performance assessment form includes both the competency scale and a space to record critical incident evidence of ratings. Appraisers are trained to conduct the competency-based performance appraisal session, give feedback, and coach flight attendants to improve their performance.

Competency

Customer Care: A concern for providing prompt, courteous and attentive service to all customers, plus the ability to understand and interpret their concerns and feelings. Confidence in own abilities to provide that service.

1. Does not recognize customer needs, does not regularly demonstrate courtesy and cheerfulness to them, makes little effort to be responsive. May demonstrate an awkwardness or lack of confidence.

Typical Behavior	*Critical Incident Example(s)*
• Uses voice intonation that indicates own negative feelings, especially of anger, frustration, etc. • Allows personal feelings to overlap into job. • Gives negative answers to customers with no attempt to assist (e.g., "we have no hanging space"). • Provokes detrimental customer letters.	1. _____ _____ _____ _____ 2. _____ _____ _____ _____

2. Is consistently courteous and cheerful to customers, interprets obvious manifestations of their needs, and has confidence to assist and provide service to them.

Typical Behavior	*Critical Incident Example(s)*
• Likes to see happy customers. • Jokes with customers who do not mind (and is able to tell the difference). • Builds rapport with customers. • Reassures nervous customers. • Knows regular customers' preferences.	1. _____ _____ _____ _____ 2. _____ _____ _____ _____

Figure 19–4 Behavior-Anchored Rating Scales (BARS)
"Just Noticeable Differences" with Behavioral Examples

3. Is consistently polite and cheerful and makes a special effort to address customers' needs, can interpret nonverbal communication and diagnose customers' needs when not explicitly stated. Shows confidence in own ability in new nonroutine situations but is not overbearing or "showy."

Typical Behavior	*Critical Incident Example(s)*
• Explains everything in detail to frightened customers, sitting with them to reassure them.	1. _____ _____
• Returns regularly to check on certain customers.	_____ _____
• Looks at customers' faces for signs of anxiety, confusion, etc., during boarding.	2. _____ _____ _____

4. Is consistently courteous and cheerful to customers even when under pressure. Interprets nonverbal behavior from subtle cues and has a track record of successfully "reading people." Has complete confidence in own ability with a "can-do" attitude to challenging situations. Conveys enthusiasm about the job and the airline.

Typical Behavior	*Critical Incident Example(s)*
• Calms down irate customers, concluding by making them feel good about that flight.	1. _____ _____ _____
• Anticipates potential problems and takes precautionary action (e.g., goes out of way to arrange for unaccompanied minors to sit in flight deck); takes ring pulls from cans for old and arthritic customers; shows elderly customers where toilet facilities are and how they operate without being asked.	_____ 2. _____ _____ _____ _____
• Receives complimentary customer letters.	

Figure 19–4   *(Continued)*

Oil Company Technical Professionals and Managers

A large oil company that uses competency-based selection and training surveyed employees to determine what information they, the *employees,* wanted in their performance reviews. Employees requested data that would answer five questions:

1. What did I *accomplish* in the performance period; that is, what hard results outcomes did I achieve?

2. *How* did I do it; that is, what competencies did I demonstrate? What are my strengths and weaknesses?

3. *Where do I stand* vis-à-vis my peers in terms of performance and competence?

4. *Where am I going;* that is, what career path options do I have? Promotion chances? Lateral job moves or jobs I may be capable of performing in the next five years?

5. What do I need to *develop* in order to:

    a. perform better in my *current* job; and

    b. to prepare myself for *future* jobs?

The firm concluded, "If competencies are valid selection tools, they should be valid appraisal tools" and implemented a performance appraisal system designed to answer these five questions. Generic competency models were developed for technical/professional individual contributors and managers.

All individual contributors are appraised on six competencies: initiative, self-confidence, concern for effectiveness (i.e., achievement), teamwork, technical skills and knowledge, and "enthusiasm for work."

Managers are appraised on eight competency behaviors: sets high standards, supports risk taking, communicates openly, fosters teamwork, delegates and empowers, coaches and develops, recognizes and rewards, and manages diverse (minority and international) work groups effectively.

These competencies are selected for in-college recruiting, taught in training programs, reinforced in survey-guided organizational development interventions, and tracked in the firm's human resource management information system. All human resource programs (except compensation) are integrated, based on the competencies that the firm has chosen to change its culture from an authoritarian "command and control" environment to one empowering employees and encouraging innovation and entrepreneurial initiative.

Automobile Manufacturer

An automobile manufacturer implementing self-managing work groups sought to develop a PMS that appraised employees' teamwork and cooperation competencies. Key to the firm's strategy was eliminating its traditional adversarial relationship with its union and replacing it with a team-focused culture in which everyone worked together to make a world-class car. The firm decided to measure hard results outcomes (quality and productivity measures) on a work group rather than an individual basis, with 50 percent of an individual's appraisal based on three to five *peer* reviewers' ratings of his or her demonstration of five competencies:

1. *Practices Team Involvement.* Communicates with other team members, shares information, resolves conflicts, and develops other members' skills.

2. *Demonstrates Problem-Solving and Analytic Skills.* Analyzes situations, recognizes potential problems, generates alternative solutions, and reaches resolution.

3. *Demonstrates Intrapreneurial Behavior.* Takes calculated risks by deviating from traditional behavior and established methods when appropriate, adapts easily to change, defers immediate gratification to achieve long-term organization goals.

4. *Contributes to Organizational Competitiveness.* Acts to reduce costs, increase quality, and use technology to gain a competitive edge.

5. *Demonstrates Leadership Skills.* Provides "team leadership" direction to others, serves as a role model for others, influences others in a positive manner, facilitates the efforts of others to make a contribution to the organization.

In addition to these competencies, each employee identifies four to six responsibilities along with criteria for assessing performance on each one; these criteria are the basis for the remaining 50 percent of a person's appraisal.

This firm's performance management cycle has five steps:

1. Employees meet with their team coordinator (formerly "foreperson") and agree on the employees' four to six responsibilities and selection of two to four reviewers who become the employees' Evaluation Team. Reviewers can come from any part of the firm, and even from contractor, supplier, or customer organizations.

2. Reviewers complete appraisal worksheets on the employee being appraised.

3. The Team Coordinator convenes the Evaluation Team, and it reaches consensus on ratings of the employee on the five competencies and job responsibilities. The Coordinator records the final ratings and destroys individual reviewers' worksheets.

4. The Coordinator meets with the employee to discuss the reviewers' ratings. The Coordinator and employee sign and date the worksheet. Each receives a copy.

Team coordinators receive training on how to give effective feedback. The process guidelines emphasize the system's coaching intent: "This whole process is intended to provide you with the help and guidance you need to maximize your skills and perform at your best."

The unusual feature of this PMS is the use of peer ratings of competencies as a formal part of appraisal.

NOTES

1. Portions of this chapter first appeared in Spencer, L. (1991), Performance management systems. In M. Rock & L. A. Berger (Eds.), (1991), *The compensation handbook,* New York: McGraw-Hill.

2. Orr, J. M., Mercer, M., & Sackett, P. R. (1989), The role of prescribed and nonprescribed behaviors in estimating the dollar value of performance, *Journal of Applied Psychology, 74,* 34–40.

3. See review in Spencer (1991), op. cit.

20

Succession Planning

DEFINITION

Succession planning is an ongoing system of selecting competent employees ready to move into key jobs in the organization, should these become vacant. Job–person matches are made between existing employees and future jobs they might assume. Traditionally, these future jobs were usually higher level positions. In the current environment of downsizing and rapid organizational change, succession planning may be for key jobs above, at the same level, or even below the job an employee now holds. Increasingly, succession planning is for lateral job moves (e.g., to a different function, project team, or geography).

The usual criteria for a successful succession planning system include

1. One, preferably two, well-qualified internal candidates are identified as ready to assume any key job should it become vacant.

2. A record of successful promotions (or other job placements): Few people fail.

3. Few superior performers leave the organization because of "lack of opportunity."[1]

COMPETENCY-BASED SUCCESSION PLANNING

Competency-based succession planning systems identify the competency requirements for critical jobs, assess candidate competencies, and evaluate possible job–person matches. Career path "progression maps" identify key "feeder" jobs for lateral or higher level "target" positions within a job family or across job families.

Table 20–1 shows seven generic levels for line, staff function, and team/ project management used in the Expertise—B. Managerial Breadth competency scale.[2] Jobs at any given level are feeder positions for higher rungs on the job ladder, and for lateral moves to positions in other job families.

A competency-based succession planning system assesses how many employees in which feeder jobs have (or have the potential to develop) the competencies to perform well in key target jobs. There are two ways of doing this.

The first is to compare the competencies of people in the feeder job with the competency requirements of the target job, as was done in Figure 18–1 and Tables 18–2 and 18–3 for an industrial chemist's match to an individual contributor and business unit manager job.

The second is to compare the competency requirements of the feeder job and the target job using the weighted absolute difference or profile comparison

Table 20–1   Generic Organizational Structure: Feeder Jobs and Levels

Line	Staff	Team/Project
1. *Individual Contributor:* Seasoned professional New hire	1. *Individual Contributor:* Seasoned professional New hire	1. *Individual Contributor:* Seasoned professional New hire
2. *First Line Supervisor:* Homogenous work group	2. *Lead professional:* Integrates other professionals work	2. *Team/Project Leader:* without permanent reports
3. *Department:* Manages several work units managed by subordinate supervisors	3. *Function Manager:* (finance, human resources) for a small business unit	3. *Project Manager:* Coordinates Project/Team Leaders from several work groups
4. *Several Departments:* Manages plant, region, several departments, function managers	4. *Several Functions:* (e.g., finance and administration)	4. *Large Project Manager:* Manages other Project managers
5. *Business Unit:* President or General Manager	5. *Top Function Manager:* for a business: VP Finance, VP Marketing	5. *Major Product Manager:* Coordinates all functions—R&D, marketing, manufacturing, HR
6. *Division:* Manages many business units (e.g., Group VP of large firm)	6. *Corporate Executive VP:* (e.g., Chief Financial Officer)	6. *Mega Project Manager:* $100+ million (e.g., NASA, military weapons acquisition)
7. *Major Corporation CEO:* Large complex multi-division organization		

methods discussed in Chapter 18. Either method can be used to calculate a percentage or correlation statistic showing the similarity or difference in competencies required by the two jobs. For example, Table 20–2 shows the commonality between jobs at three levels in three-job families.

Several interesting observations can be made for these data. First, the first-level Technical Support job (the lowest status level-one position) is as good or better a match (hence competency development assignment) for second level Design, Program, and Project manager jobs as are the first-level jobs in these job families. (A reason for this finding: technical support people have more customer contact and are more service oriented, making them better design, program, and project managers.)

Second, second-level manager jobs in any job family are equally good matches, hence preparation, for third-level manager jobs in any job family.

Third, while there is a significant gap between the competencies required at levels one and two, there is very little difference between competency requirements at levels two and three. Are these really different jobs? When job profile comparison shows few differences among levels in an organization's job hierarchy, it suggests the organization has too many managerial layers.

Table 20–2   Profile Comparison of Competencies Required by Jobs at Three Levels in Three-Job Families

	Level Three		
	Design	Program	Project
Level Two			
Design	.77	.77	.75
Program	.72	.79	.71
Project	.79	.79	.82

	Level Two		
	Design	Program	Project
Level One			
Design	.54	.44	.56
Program	.53	.53	.64
Project	.39	.25	.50
Tech Support	.56	.60	.65

Overall Correlations by Level
Level One jobs with Level Two jobs: .69
Level Two jobs with Level Three Jobs: .92

Note: Adapted from D. F. Caldwell. *Soft Skills, Hard Numbers: Issues in Person–Job/Person–Organization Fit.* Paper presented at the Personnel Testing Conference of Southern California Spring Conference. Ontario, CA. April 12, 1991.

ORGANIZATIONAL ISSUES

The issues that indicate a need for competency-based succession planning systems include:

- Promotion or placement outcomes are poor; too many people promoted or transferred to new responsibilities fail or quit. Typical examples are promoting the best salesperson to sales manager or the best technical professional to supervisor and then finding he or she lacks essential interpersonal understanding and influence skills.

- There is a need to redeploy technical/professional staff people to marketing or line management jobs—or managers back to individual contributor roles in an organization that is cutting middle management. "Lean and mean" organizations offer fewer vertical promotional or career path opportunities, with the result that more succession planning is lateral. In downsizing organizations, the key placement question may be which managers have kept up with their technical and professional competencies so they are able to return to individual contributor roles.

- Organizational changes require employees with different competencies. Globalizing firms need employees with the competencies to function in different parts of the world. Privatizing organizations need to determine which government bureaucrats have enough achievement motivation to become entrepreneurs and businesspeople. Stagnant firms need employees with innovative and entrepreneurial competencies to survive in markets with shorter product life cycles and fast-moving foreign competitors. Downsizing firms need to decide who stays and who is let go, that is, which employees have the competencies to fill demanding "same amount of work with fewer people" jobs in the new, smaller organization.

- Mergers, acquisitions, and reorganizations require the surviving firm to decide which existing employees are needed for (which) jobs in the new structure. Mergers of similar firms often result in an organization with two marketing departments, two sales forces, duplicate staffs in many functions; merger efficiencies come from elimination of the double headcount. As with downsizing organizations, the question of who stays and who goes is determined by which employees have the competencies to succeed in the firm's future jobs.

STEPS IN DEVELOPING COMPETENCY-BASED SUCCESSION PLANNING PROJECTS

1. *Identify Key Jobs.* Identifying these jobs in the organization's structure—or the structure it wants for the future usually includes identifying the firm's strategy, its critical value-added target jobs, and key feeder jobs to these target jobs. Most organizations will have some variant of the seven levels shown in Table 20–1 for line, technical/professional, or functional staff, and team/project manager job families. Vertical progression in a job family is

a. *Individual contributor,* often divided into two subgroups: new hire and seasoned professional

b. *First-level functional supervisor,* managing a homogeneous group of individual contributors (e.g., a move from engineer to chief engineer or programmer to software development team leader). For functional technical/professionals and project job families, this level may be a lead professional who acts as a temporary team leader, assists and integrates other professionals' work, and mentors junior employees, but does not have any permanent reports.

c. *Department, function or project* managers, who manage supervisors or lead professionals of several work groups

d. *Multiple departments or functions* managers, who manage several other department, function, or project managers (e.g., a plant or regional manager, or director of finance and administration)

e. *Business unit* general manager, such as CEO of a small firm (less than $10 million in annual revenues); top functional manager, such as Marketing or Finance Vice President of a medium-size firm ($10–100 million revenues); or manager of a major project

f. *Division* general manager, such as CEO of a medium-size firm ($10–100 million revenues); top functional executive in a large firm ($100+ million revenues), or megaproject manager

g. *CEO of a large, complex multidivision organization*

2. *Develop Competency Models for Critical Target and Feeder Jobs.* Frequently this involves development of competency models for each of several steps in a job family ladder. BEIs conducted with four superiors and two averages at each level are analyzed to identify competencies required for a superior performance at the level and also to pinpoint how the competencies change or grow as an employee advances up the ladder.

3. *Assess Candidates (and Current Job Holders) Against Competencies for Target Jobs.* As in competency-based selection programs, substeps are (a) identify cost-effective assessment methods, and (b) train assessors to evaluate candidates for (and incumbents in) target jobs. Assessment for succession planning can require considerable resources. Each level down an organization goes in assessing people in feeder jobs increases the population to be assessed ((average span of control)$^{\#\ levels}$). For example, if span of control is seven employees in a feeder job to each higher level job, one level down requires 7 assessments, two levels: $7 \times 7 = 49$ assessments, and three levels: $7 \times 7 \times 7 = 343$ assessments.

4. *Make Decisions about Job Incumbents and Candidates.* Job incumbents are evaluated on their competence to do their jobs and potential to go higher in the future. People are usually classified as

    a. *Promotable,* either:

        (1) Ready now, or

        (2) Developable (i.e., could be ready in the future if they develop specific competencies to the level required by the future jobs for which they are candidates)

    b. *Not promotable*:

        (1) Competent in their current job, and/or

        (2) Have potential to transfer laterally to some other job

    c. *Not competent* in their current job and not a fit with other jobs in the organization as it will be in the future. These people are candidates for early retirement or outplacement.

If the organization finds there is no one promotable or developable for key jobs, the only alternative is to recruit new hires with needed competencies.

5. *Develop a Human Resource Management Information System.* Succession planning for more than a few positions all but requires a computerized human resource information system to keep track of the competency requirements of all jobs, competencies of these people assessed, and evaluation of possible job–person matches.

6. *Develop a Development/Career Pathing System (Optional).* Succession planning systems create demand for competency-based development and career pathing systems. Once employees understand the competency requirements for higher jobs and the gaps between their competencies and those required by the jobs they want, they ask for training or other developmental activities to close the gap. Similarly, once an organization is aware of the competencies it needs to be successful and the gaps between these needs and the capabilities of its existing or projected staff, it seeks selection or developmental programs to close these gaps.

CASE[3]

A regional insurance company with declining market share in a rapidly changing financial environment implemented a six-step succession planning program:

    1. Identify the strategic direction for the firm

    2. Identify the implications of the firm's strategy for its leadership

    3. Assess competencies the CEO (and owner) had—or did not have

4. Define the critical competency dimensions that other members of the top management team needed to have for the firm to succeed with its strategy

5. Assess the firm's top managers against these competencies

6. Action steps: Recruitment, development, and termination decisions

Strategic Direction

The firm's strategy was to grow and diversify the business, expanding beyond a regional property and casual company by:

- Designing new products and services to enhance market positioning
- Developing strategic alliances with similar firms in other parts of the United States and around the world to acquire and cross-sell new products and services

Leadership Implications

Implementation of this strategy required senior executives who were:

- *Market-Oriented and Market-Driven.* People who listened to customers to identify future needs, as opposed to "operations focused" processors of bids and claims
- *Innovative.* People who could imagine and develop new products and services
- *Relationship Builders.* People able to develop, manage, and nurture business alliances
- *Goal Oriented and Achievement Driven.* Hands-on executives who would act to implement the firm's strategy and improve its return on investment

CEO Assessment

The CEO was assessed as a "big picture type," high in conceptual thinking skills and good at strategic planning, but not "hands-on," or action oriented. The CEO accepted the idea that he needed executives with competencies complementary to his own, people who could translate his grand strategies into concrete action and make the strategy *happen.*

Definition of Competencies Needed in Top Managers

Seven competencies were identified as critical for the top management team: Self-Confidence, Achievement Orientation, Innovation, Initiative, Directing Others, Interpersonal Sensitivity, and Team Leadership.

Assessment of Existing Executives

Members of the top management team were assessed on each competency, with results shown on a scale in Figure 20–1 (letters A through K each represent an executive). A total competency score was calculated for all executives as shown in Figure 20–2. Executives A, B, and C scored positively at 3.5 to 4; F through I had some of the competencies; and G through K were at best questionable. The implication of this analysis: The firm could not implement its strategy with its existing top management team.

Initiative:
A tendency to act in a self-directed way, by taking action before being directed or forced by events; to seize opportunities, seek in-depth information, and do significantly more than is required.

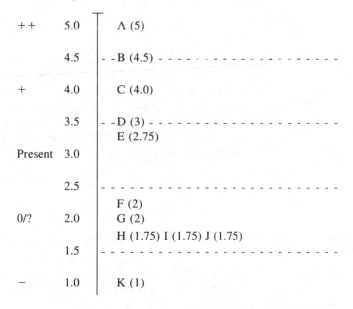

Key:

++	Maximum results are achieved when utilizing this competency
+	Successfully utilizes this competency in various situations
Present	Candidate will utilize this competency but not always effective
0/?	No indication whether or not the individual will utilize this competency
−	Resistant to the utilization of this competency

Figure 20–1   Executives' Ratings on Initiative

Overall Competency Level

```
++      5.0  ┬
             │
        4.5  │ - - - - - - - - - - - - - - - - - - - - - - - - -
             │ A (4.10)
 +      4.0  │ B (3.74)
             │ C (3.54)
             │
        3.5  │ - - - - - - - - - - - - - - - - - - - - - - - - -
             │ F (3.24)
             │ D (3.19)
Present 3.0  │ E (2.76)        OVERALL GROUP (2.80)
             │ I (2.52)
        2.5  │ - - - - - - - - - - - - - - - - - - - - - - - - -
             │ G (2.20)
 0/?    2.0  │ J (2.02)
             │ H (1.77)
             │ K (1.74)
        1.5  │ - - - - - - - - - - - - - - - - - - - - - - - - -
             │
 -      1.0  │
```

Key:
++	Maximum results are achieved when utilizing this competency
+	Successfully utilizes this competency in various situations
Present	Candidate will utilize this competency but not always effective
0/?	No indication whether or not the individual will utilize this competency
−	Resistant to the utilization of this competency

Figure 20–2 Executives' Ratings on Overall Competency Level

Action Steps

The succession planning analysis resulted in the following decisions:

- Invest in developing executives A, B, C, F, and D, identified as the top management team's key future players.
- Remove or replace executives K, H, J, and G.
- Use the competency model to recruit and select top executives from the outside who have the missing competencies.
- Assess managers in feeder jobs for the top management positions on the critical competencies and invest in developing candidates for strategic jobs most important to the firm's future: R&D, marketing, and human resources.

NOTES

1. See Mahler, W. R., & Drotter, S. J. (1986), *The succession planning handbook for the chief executive,* Midland Park, NJ: Mahler Publishing.

2. These levels parallel the seven strata Elliot Jacques argues are universally applicable to all organizations. Jacques differentiates levels the degree of cognitive complexity and the time horizon managers at each level must be able to deal with—see Jacques, E. (1989), *Requisite organization,* Arlington, VA: Cason-Hall.

3. Hofrichter, D., & Myszkowski, G. J.(1989), Developing managers who can implement the strategy: Competency-based succession planning. In H. E. Glass (Ed.), (1989), *Handbook of business strategy: 1898/1990 yearbook,* Boston: Warren, Gorham & Lamont; Hofrichter, D. (1990, April 1). *Comparative competency analysis and recommendations on XYZ Executive Assessments,* Paper presented at the 1990 Annual Conference of the Human Resource Planning Society, Naples, FL.

CHAPTER

21

Development and Career Pathing

DEFINITION

Competency-based training and development activities include formal training programs; development center feedback; self-development resource guides; computer and interactive video-assisted self-instruction; job assignments; mentoring relationships; and organizational structure, process, and culture interventions designed to increase individuals' competence.

COMPETENCY-BASED TRAINING AND DEVELOPMENT

Competencies can be taught. Evidence from many studies indicates that even core motive competencies such as achievement orientation[1] and traits such as self-confidence ("learned optimism,"[2] reduction in depressive explanatory style, and fear of failure,[3] "origin" vs. "pawn" self-concept)[4] can be modified.

A general method for teaching competencies has developed based on four theories of how people learn and change: (1) adult experiential education, (2) motivation acquisition, (3) social learning, and (4) self-directed change.

Adult Experiential Education Theory

Experiential education approaches[5] hold that adults learn best if they are exposed to the four inputs shown in Figure 21–1:

- *Abstract Conceptualization* (AC). A new theory, idea, or set of "how to" instructions

286

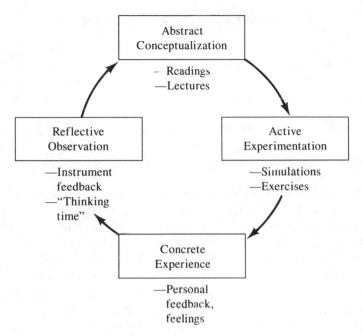

Figure 21–1   Adult Learning Styles

- *Active Experimentation* (AE). Actually trying out the abstract theory, idea, or instructions to do something
- *Concrete Experience* (CE). Feedback on the effects of one's experimental behaviors
- *Reflective Observation* (RO). Thinking about what happened, leading perhaps to a modification of a person's theory or ideas about how to behave in the future

Although people usually prefer one or two learning inputs over the others, adult learning is most efficient for everyone if all four inputs follow one another, as shown in the Figure 21–1 circle.

For example, to teach the competency Developing Others, the instructor could give a lecture on how to use a "coaching" managerial style (AC), then have learners try to use "coaching" behaviors in a simple business game where one person has to direct the other to do something, for example, build a tower using blocks (AE). Both "manager" and "worker" experience the effects of managerial behaviors that help or hinder completing the task (CE). After the simulation, learners reflect on what worked and what didn't (RO)—and on how they might improve their performance in a second round (AC). The learning cycle reinforces abstract concepts about how to develop another person's ability to perform a task and practical interpersonal skills for doing so.

McClelland's Theory of Motive Acquisition

In his well-known paper, "Toward a Theory of Motive Acquisition,"[6] David McClelland identifies 12 principles by which people can acquire or change core personality traits such as motives and self-concept. These principles can be summarized in five inputs:

1. *Conceptual Model.* Learners must be given a new conceptual framework for thinking about their behaviors and reasons to believe in this new model (research findings, prestigious references, trainer confidence, links to goals valued by the learner).

McClelland defines a motive as "an affectively-toned associative network," that is, a pattern of thinking with positive feelings attached. To instruct someone in achievement motivation, the teacher must tell the learner exactly what the achievement thoughts are—and associate thinking the 11 elements of achievement-motivated thought with pleasurable outcomes. Thinking these 11 thoughts makes the person higher in achievement motivation *by definition.*

2. *Self-Assessment.* Learners must receive feedback on how much of the competency they have and how this compares with the level of competence that will get them what they want in life (e.g., success in management).

3. *Practice.* Learners must practice using the new thoughts and behaviors, first in simulated activities and then increasingly in real life activities. For example, to help learn achievement motivation, learners can practice everything from cooking breakfast, tying their shoes, driving to work, and selling their next client assignment while thinking all of the 11 achievement thoughts.

4. *Goal Setting.* Learners must set goals and plan for use of the competency in important activities in their life. Consciously setting a goal and getting feedback from self and others strengthens motive thoughts and increases the likelihood of goal attainment.

5. *Social Supports.* Learners must have a socially "safe" and supportive environment in which to learn, experiment with, and practice new thoughts and behaviors. Learning is better maintained if, after training, learners receive support and coaching from valued others (e.g., a boss) and from a "reinforcing reference group" of fellow learners who can support and encourage one another to use the new competency. Ideally, training gives the learner membership in a prestigious new group that speaks a new common language, shares new values, and is committed to keeping members' learning alive.

Social Learning Theory

Social learning theory[7] holds that people learn interpersonal skills from "behavior role modeling": observing and imitating other people who demonstrate or model successful behavior in a situation. Behavior modeling methods show learners numerous live, film, or videotape examples of a person like the learner performing the specific competencies in a realistic situation. Learners are encouraged to imitate or role-play the model, for example, they say the same words, with the same intonation, said by an actor playing a manager conducting a performance appraisal. Managers learning how to make a charismatic vision speech can be shown tapes of great speakers (e.g., Winston Churchill's addresses to the British people during World War II, Martin Luther King's "I have a dream" speech, or John F. Kennedy's Inaugural Address). Learners then try to give a "vision speech" of their own, "hamming it up" (i.e., imitating or even exaggerating playing Churchill, King, or Kennedy). Exaggeration helps break inhibitions in trying new behaviors: Learners return to a more natural style in their jobs. Numerous studies have shown behavior modeling is effective in teaching hard-to-articulate interpersonal skills.[8]

Self-Directed Change Theory

Self-Directed change research holds that adults change their behavior when three conditions are present:

- Dissatisfaction with an existing condition ("Actual")
- Clarity about a desired condition ("Ideal" or goal)
- Clarity about what to do to move from the Actual to the Ideal ("Action Steps"):

Actual ←--------------→ Ideal
"Discrepancy:"
Energy and direction for change

People change only if they feel it is in their own best interests to do so. Adults cannot be "changed" except through a process that leads them to feel *personally* dissatisfied with their current competency, *personally* clear about what their *own* goals for competence are, and *personally* clear (and confident) about *how* to use new competency behaviors. Learners must feel a gap or discrepancy between their current and a desired level of competence: It is this gap that provides the energy and direction for change.

A corollary of self-directed change theory is that people cannot be changed against their will. Early efforts to teach achievement motivation to stimulate economic development in Third World countries were criticized as "brainwashing." Critics felt psychologists had no right to "muck about with people's minds" by teaching achievement thinking to subsistence farmers. (In the ideological language of that time, "achievement motivation" was equated with "ruthless capitalism.") These critics were assured that in fact, a person's motivation cannot be changed unless the person really sees it in his or her self-interest to change. Brainwashing does not work: Competency learners must want and work hard to develop new competencies.

These four theories led to a general strategy of six steps for design of competency learning experiences: recognition, understanding, self-assessment, skill practice, job application, and follow-up support.

1. *Recognition.* The objective of Step 1 is to get learners to convince themselves that the competencies to be taught do exist and are important to being able to do their jobs well.

Two ways learners can be led to this recognition are "compare-and-contrast" cases and hard simulations. A compare-and-contrast case gives learners critical incidents from a superior performer and an average performer in the learners' job. Learners are asked: What is the difference between these two people? Who is the superstar and who is the average performer—and why? What is the superstar doing that the average performer is not doing? Learners are essentially asked to do a thematic analysis as described in Chapter 12. Learners will observe, for example, "The woman who's the success thinks about doing better and takes many more action steps when she's blocked." They infer and demonstrate to themselves the importance of achievement motivation and initiative.

A second way to stimulate recognition is to involve learners in a hard simulation. The simulation should be a situation or problem that feels very real to participants and is sufficiently challenging for them not to be able to solve easily. The intended learner response is: "Yes, this is the kind of situation I encounter on my job, and no, I don't know how to do it well . . . *[hence] I have something to learn.*"

Compare-and-contrast cases and recognition simulations are designed to establish credibility for the competencies and create an "actual–ideal discrepancy" for learners that motivates them to want to learn.

2. *Understanding.* Step 2 explains the new competency concept. Learners are taught exactly what the competency is and how to do it. Readings and lectures provide the conceptual model for the competency, for example, the 11 elements of achievement-motivated thought or behavioral indicators and methods for direct persuasion. Live or video demonstrations provide modeling examples of the competency in use in a job situation.

3. *Self-Assessment.* Step 3 gives learners feedback on their own levels of competence against the levels that predict superior performance. Usually a graph like that shown in Figure 21–2 is used to highlight the gaps between the learner's actual competence and the ideal shown by superior performers in the job. Learners identify for themselves the biggest discrepancy they feel and the competencies they have the most energy and interest in learning.

4. *Skill Practice/Feedback.* In Step 4, learners practice the competency behaviors in realistic simulations, compare their performance with the standard for superior performance, and get coaching feedback on how to do better. Learners repeat as much practice/feedback as they need to reach the superior standard.

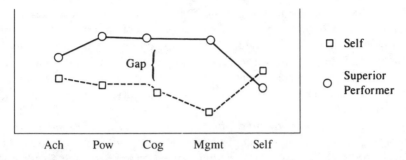

Figure 21–2 Individual Feedback—Competency Gaps

5. *Job Application Goal-Setting.* In Step 5, learners set goals and develop action plans for exactly how they are going to use new competency behaviors in their real jobs. Research shows that goal-setting increases the likelihood of goal accomplishment from between 5 and 20 percent to between 60 and 70 percent.[9] Goal-setting results in an average increase in productivity of 19 percent.[10] Effective goals are specific, measurable, challenging but with moderate risk, and time phased. Learners may also anticipate the resources and obstacles that may help or hinder them in goal accomplishment; this "reentry" planning seems to help people survive initial setbacks.

6. *Follow-Up Support.* Follow-up and support activities include:

- Sharing competency goals and plans with supervisors, and contracting with them for feedback and coaching assistance in use of new behaviors.
- Rewarding initial experimentation with use of new competency behaviors.
- Holding "goal progress review meetings" at which learners hold a reunion, report progress on attaining their goals, share what has worked and has not worked, get additional ideas from the trainers, and generally support and encourage one another.
- Establishing reinforcing reference groups of competency-trained people, that is, a "critical mass" of people in each work group who speak the same language and can encourage one another.

Measuring and Credentialing Competencies

John Raven[11] has observed that educating for competencies has been retarded by the difficulty of measuring and credentialing competencies learned. For competency-based management training programs developed for the American Management Association, three criteria were used to measure and credential competence: performance on an operant test, demonstration of the competence in an assessment center simulation, and documentation of performance on the job.

For example, a learner was certified "passed" in achievement motivation after he or she had (1) written an action plan containing all 11 elements of achievement-motivated thought; (2) observed acting to improve efficiency or quality, to innovate, or to outperform a competitive team in a business simulation; and (3) documented having originated and sold a new product, process, or procedure that increased revenues, efficiency, quality, or productivity in his or her organization.

Competency-based training programs can include "bottom-line learning projects" in which learners set goals to undertake to demonstrate use of one or more competencies, perform their jobs better, or improve their firm's operating results. Learners are not certified as having completed the training or checked off on the competencies until they submit the results of their project.

Benefits of Competency-Based Training

Meta-analysis of management training evaluation studies permits an estimate of behavior change and added value that competency-based training can produce. Burke and Day[12] found behavior-modeling training can change behavior .78 of a standard deviation and shift the bell-shaped curve of bottom-line results as much as .64–.67 of a standard deviation, as shown in Figure 21–3. If one standard deviation represents 48 percent higher performance in a complex job as discussed in Chapter 2, training can result in significant productivity increases (.64–.67 (48%) = 29%–32%). The highest payoffs are offered by

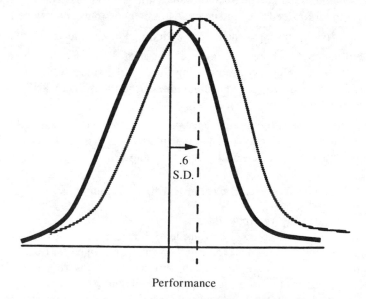

.6
S.D.

Performance

Training can shift curve as much as .6 S.D., worth .6 × 40% salary = 24% salary

Figure 21–3   Value Added by Competency-Based Training

performance management and general management training. These results, as well as the literature on goal-setting interventions, indicate that competency-based training will be most effective when it includes goal-setting to improve bottom-line performance.

ORGANIZATIONAL ISSUES

The following issues indicate a need for competency-based training:

- A straightforward need to increase performance: "Our salespeople are being outsold by our competitors' salespeople: We've got to give them better selling skills to get them selling more."
- A desire to reducing learning curve time from job entry to full productivity: "It takes our new hires too long to get up to speed."

OBJECTIVES

1. Minimize learning-curve time to 100% productivity (average productivity of experienced people in the job)

   and/or

2. Increase productivity above current "100%" baseline: performance level of *superior* people in the job

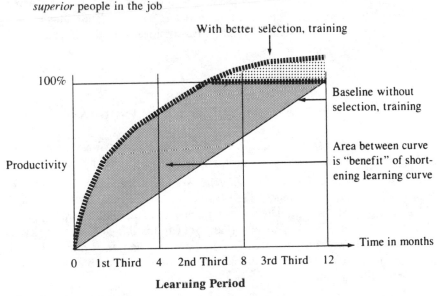

- Professionals average:
  —12 months to become fully (100%) productive
  —50% productivity in their first year.

Figure 21–4 Professional Development Learning Curve

Figure 21–4 shows a typical learning curve for a technical/professional job. Without formal training (on-the-job training only, the control condition), new hire professionals take an average of one year to become fully productive (with 100% productivity defined as the average performance of an experienced employee). New hires average 50 percent productivity during their learning curve period.[13]

It can be argued that there are only two reasons to do training: to get people to get up to speed (100% productivity) faster or to get them up to higher speed (i.e., increase productivity above existing average performance).

Competency-based training designed to teach new hires all the algorithms superior performers use to do the job well and the competencies underlying superior performance can reduce learning curve times by a third to a half and result in higher average performance. Because competency-based training teaches to the template for *superior* performance, trainees' performance can be significantly increased (see Figure 21–3).[14]

- A need to communicate, teach, or reinforce skills needed to implement an organization's (new) vision, strategy, or philosophy, such as Total Quality Management (TQM).

- A need to provide employees with the feedback they need to make development or career path decisions. For example, feedback that compares competencies likely to be required in future jobs with individuals' current levels of competence can motivate employees to identify needs for personal development.

STEPS IN DEVELOPING
A COMPETENCY-BASED TRAINING PROGRAM

1. *Development of a Competency Model.* Such a model must specify the competencies needed for superior performance in a present or future job.

2. *Identification of Which Competencies Are Cost-Effective to Train versus to Select For.* Core competencies and traits like achievement motivation and initiative can be trained, but it may be more cost-effective to hire a person who already has these competencies than to try to instill achievement motivation in someone who does not have it. The rule is: Selection is prepotent over training (or, more colloquially, you can teach a turkey to climb a tree—but it is easier to hire a squirrel).

3. *Select Most Cost-Effective Development Options.* Competency-development options include formal competency-based training; development center feedback; self-development resource guides; computer- and interactive video-assisted self-instruction; job assignments; mentoring relationships;

and organizational structure, process, and culture interventions designed to increase individuals' competence.

Competency-Based Training Programs. Formal competency-based training programs are designed and conducted as one-day or two-week classroom courses led by a stand-up trainer and using all adult experiential learning inputs: reading, lectures, live or video demonstrations, instrumented feedback, role plays and simulations, and self-assessment reflection exercises.

Development Centers. Development centers are one-day to two-week assessment centers in which participants take tests and are observed in various exercises (presentations, leaderless group discussion, role plays, competitive business or negotiation simulations), and then are given feedback on the competencies they have demonstrated.

Development centers differ from assessment centers in that their purpose is to develop participants rather than to provide the organization with data on which to make hiring, placement, or promotion decisions. They are based on the premise that self-assessment alone may be enough to motivate feedback recipients to develop competencies about which they feel deficient on their own.

Self-Development Resource Guides. Self-development resource guides are "read these books, take these courses, engage in these activities, seek these assignments, do a developmental rotation in these jobs, work for these mentors" prescriptions for development of specific competencies. These guides are usually custom-developed to reference an organization's training offerings, career path opportunities, and courses available at local universities. Chapter 23 shows how resource guides can be computerized and programmed to generate development advice for any job–person match competency gap.

Computer- and Interactive Video-Assisted Training. Computer- and interactive video-assisted self-instruction systems can teach even interpersonal competencies using behavioral modeling techniques.[15] These systems follow the recognition, understanding, self-assessment, skill practice/feedback and follow-up support approach. For example, an interactive video disk system used to teach sales presentation skills consists of a computer screen that presents situations and a television camera that records the learner's responses. The system presents the following inputs:

- *Recognition.* The learner is shown a brief video of a tough customer prospect who asks, "Just what are your qualifications?" and a number of other hard questions about the salesperson's firm, product, support policies, and the like. The attached camera records the novice salesperson's halting responses.

- *Understanding.* The learner is shown an experienced salesperson answering each of the customer's tough questions. The lesson explains exactly what to say and why; it is a conceptual model of how to handle the sales presentation, complete with a script: "If the customer says 'X,' you can say 'Y.'"

The learner is further taught a coding system for scoring videotaped responses for presentation skill competencies. The learner watches a presentation, enters on the computer the level of competence he or she scored it for, and gets immediate feedback on the right score. The computer continues competency scoring skill practice/feedback exercises until the learner can score a presentation accurately. This process reinforces the learner's mastery of the behavioral indicators that define the competency.

- *Self-Assessment.* The learner is presented with another tough customer and records his or her sales presentation and answers to questions. Then the learner scores his or her presentation for the sales presentation competencies, that is, critiques and gets feedback on his or her own performance. The computer keeps track of the learner's progress and presents him or her with more challenging situations as his or her competence increases.

- *Skill Practice/Feedback.* The learner repeats skill practice/feedback exercises until he or she scores his or her performance as meeting the standard for fully competent sales presentation performance. The learner then takes the tape to the course supervisor or his or her manager to be certified competent on the simulated task.

- *Job Application.* The learner experiments with using competencies learned in a joint sales call with the course supervisor or his or her manager. The supervisor or manager certifies the learner on competencies demonstrated in the on-the-job situation.

- *Follow-Up Support.* The learner can return to the computerized learning system at any time to brush up on skills. A "help system" version of the program may be installed on employees' personal computers to provide behavior modeling examples of how to handle specific situations. For example, a manager in doubt about how to conduct a confrontation session with an employee suspected of having a drug problem can call up on his or her computer and see a role play (with script) of an actor-manager confronting a drug abuser.

Computer interactive video-training systems are expensive ($150,000 to $1 million) but can be cost-justified where large numbers of employees need to be trained and course curricula are standard for all trainees.

Developmental Job Assignments. Learners can be given job assignments designed to help them develop specific competencies. For example, in a large oil firm, a competency model found that superior engineers not only were good engineers, they also were good presenters. They literally could knock the mud off their boots in Sumatra, get on a plane, fly halfway around the world to the firm's New York headquarters, and give a presentation skillful enough to convince a roomful of financial executives to give them another $200 million for developing a new oil field.

To develop technically competent junior engineers who lacked presentation skills, the firm offered job assignments as trainers or public relations staff spokespersons. It figured a year or two giving daily training presentations or press briefings can teach even the most inarticulate engineer how to talk.

Developmental career paths put employees in a series of developmental jobs in succession, to give them foreign experience, staff experience at corporate headquarters, then hands-on line management experience in a manufacturing plant.

Mentors. Learners can be assigned to work for a senior manager who is a widely acknowledged master of a competence the learner needs to develop. For example, if someone lacks organization awareness or use of influence strategy competencies, he or she could be assigned to work for someone known to be a "political animal" with the explicit expectation that the master corporate politician will coach the learner in political sensitivity and maneuvering. Firms may lend aspiring executives who lack political skills to a national politician's presidential campaign for a year to absorb political skills, make contacts, and build relationships with influential figures.

External Development Activities. Learners may be encouraged to develop competencies in volunteer or even moonlighting jobs outside the work environment. Research indicates that technical and scientific personnel frequently have learned managerial competencies in off-job leadership roles such as coaching children's sports teams or leading marriage encounter sessions for their church.[16]

Organizational Structure, Process, and Culture Interventions. Organizational structure, process, and culture interventions can be designed to increase employees' competence, for example, programs[17] designed to increase achievement motivation, innovation, and entrepreneurship in staid firms.

- *Structure.* Formation of small, autonomous "new venture teams" in "incubator" or "greenhouse" structures separate from a firm's traditional businesses and administrative practices, yet supported by marketing, finance, and manufacturing function experts.

- *Process.* Specific programs that encourage employees with new ideas to submit them to an internal venture capital group which identifies ideas and people for further development, then trains and supports entrepreneurs and new venture teams from product development to market introduction.

- *Climate and Culture.* An organizational environment that values new ideas, supports calculated risk taking, gives employees sufficient responsibility and clarity, and rewards entrepreneurial efforts—all factors shown by Litwin and Stringer[18] to arouse achievement motivation in employees.

The most powerful competency-based development programs coordinate all of these training and coaching options in a systems intervention where all inputs complement and reinforce one another.

4. *Develop Assessment Methods and Training Curricula* (where applicable). Development center assessment instruments, training, and self-development resources are developed following the methods outlined earlier for teaching competencies.

5. *Train Trainers* (where applicable). When stand-up trainers will be used to deliver competency-based training, these trainers are taught competency content and the competency development process skills. Trainer training is itself a competency-development process: Trainers are prepared using a competency model based on the behaviors of superior adult educators.[19]

6. *Train Learners*

7. *Evaluate Training Results.* Evaluation of competency-based training programs should include assessment of on-the-job behavior change and "hard" results outcomes (increase in revenues, productivity or quality, or client service measures; reduction in turnover, grievances, and other "people problems") whenever possible. Evaluation studies indicate 60 to 70 percent of competency-based training programs show positive cost-benefit ratios and returns on investment if properly designed and conducted.[20]

CASES

Achievement Motivation Training for Small Business

The best evidence that competencies can be taught and that competency-based training generates attractive returns on investment comes from studies of achievement motivation training for small business entrepreneurs.

For example, minority entrepreneurs in 10 cities in the United States attended an eight-day achievement motivation course:[21] one five-day session, followed by one-day "goal progress review meetings" three, six, and nine months after the initial training.

The initial five-day session taught the elements of achievement-motivated thought:

- Concern with performing better and more efficiently
- Comparison of results attained against an internal standard of excellence
- Innovation
- Development of long-range plans
- Statement of a strong need for goal attainment
- Estimation of the probabilities of success and failure
- Anticipation of personal and external obstacles

- Initiative (propensity to act)
- Use of help

Case studies of successful and unsuccessful entrepreneurs were used to illustrate how these thoughts led to such entrepreneurial behaviors as:

- Setting challenging but moderate risk goals
- Spotting opportunities
- Taking calculated risks
- Assuming personal responsibility for task accomplishment
- Seeking and using feedback from experts to improve performance

Learners practiced these behaviors in realistic business simulations, receiving feedback on competency expression, quality, and economic outcomes: sales and profits. At the conclusion of the course, participants set goals and developed action plans to improve their businesses.

At the one-day follow-up goal progress review meetings, trainees reported their progress against the goals set in the five-day session. They discussed what had worked, what had not worked, and got help and support from the instructors and fellow participants. These review meetings were designed to provide a reference group that would reinforce the lessons of the five-day session.

Table 21–1 shows cost–benefit ratio and return on the U.S. Small Business Association's $287,500 investment in the program. Compared with a control group of untrained small business owners, achievement-trained entrepreneurs generated 227 additional jobs producing additional employees' income of

Table 21–1 Benefits of Achievement Motivation Training

OBJECTIVE: Increase minority entrepreneurship income, jobs, tax revenues
PROGRAM: Achievement Motivation Training in 10 cities cost: $287,500
RESULTS: Trainees versus control group (small business averages) increased

Jobs (32%): 227

Income		Tax Rate	Revenues
Business	$615,000	22%	$ 189,900
Proprietors	484,000	20%	97,400
Employees	651,100	11.5%	75,000
			362,300 (Year 1)
			705,000 (Year 2)
			$1,067,300

Payback: 9.5 months
C/B (1 year): 1: 1.26   ROI: 26%
      (2 years): 1: 3.71   ROI: 271.%

$651,100; $615,000 more business profits, and $484,000 additional personal income. Assuming the lowest marginal tax rate, incremental taxes on additional income alone returned the U.S. government's investment in achievement-motivation training in 9.5 months. Two-year return on investment was 271 percent.[22]

U.S. Navy Leadership and
Management Education and Training (LMET)

Over 14 years (1976–1990), the U.S. Navy trained more than 200,000 people in leadership and management competencies identified in a double cross-validation study of superior versus average officers and enlisted leaders in submarine, surface, and air commands in the Atlantic and Pacific Fleets.[23]

Table 21–2 shows the design of a two-week competency-based leadership and management course. The first course module introduced the U.S. Navy competency model, measured trainees' preferred learning style and the principles of experiential education, and gave them feedback on their competencies against the model for superior Navy leaders.

The second module focused on achievement-motivation-related competencies: setting standards and goals, increasing efficiency and effectiveness, planning and monitoring to improve military quality and productivity measures (e.g., operational readiness rates and technical inspection scores).

To ensure relevance, underlying competencies such as achievement motivation were taught in the context of practical management methods (e.g., total quality management (TQM) and productivity improvement techniques). First the underlying competency was taught, then the management methods in which the competency could be demonstrated.

The reason for this approach is as follows. One can teach a quality improvement method alone, for example, statistical process control; but unless the learner is motivated, he or she is unlikely to use the method. Quality and productivity *improvement* are totally about achievement motivation: doing better against standards of excellence (quality) or existing efficiency (productivity). Use of quality and productivity methods is most likely if achievement motivation to use them is aroused. Teaching the underlying motive with managerial techniques makes abstract competencies concrete and practical and arouses motivation to use management methods.

The third module of LMET courses taught interpersonal attending, listening, and responding skills. A surprising finding of the Navy competency research was that Navy officers spent as much as 50 percent of their time counseling teenage crew members. Superior officers had good coaching and counseling skills. The LMET course taught practical interpersonal understanding and responding: accurate empathy, nonpossessive warmth, genuineness, and problem-solving help with love, money, drugs and alcohol, and related adolescent problems. Trainees practiced counseling "subordinates in

Table 21-2 Design of a Two-Week Competency-Based Leadership and Management Course

Introduction	Achievement	Interpersonal	Power	Cognitive	Integration	Application
Contracting	Competencies	"Helping Motive Profile" competencies	"Influence" competencies	Competencies	"Combination" cases, simulations	Planning: Goal setting, commitment
Learning style: "Learning to learn"	Goal setting Planning Monitoring Productivity, quality, innovation, and entrepreneurship modules	Counseling Coaching	Presentation Management Networking	Analysis Diagnosis Conceptualization Problem solving		
Competency feedback: Self vs. superstar						

distress" in role plays drawn from actual counseling incidents reported in the research study.

The fourth LMET module dealt with use of power and influence competencies: giving direct orders, assertive persuasion, presentation skills, networking, and political maneuvering in complex military organizations.

The fifth module taught cognitive (analytical and conceptual) thinking competencies through learning and practice of rational data gathering, diagnosis, alternatives identification, and criteria-based decision-making methods.

The sixth module, "Integration," presented participants with complex cases and simulations that required them to identify, analyze, and solve problems using all competencies learned. For example, a preparation for a major inspection exercise involved planning equipment, material, and human resources; coaching and counseling key crew members; negotiation with shipyard repair facilities; intelligence gathering about inspectors' "hot buttons"; and overall leadership of many people with conflicting interests under demanding time pressures.

The final job application exercise gave trainees all available data on the ship they would be assigned to next. Trainees had to evaluate ship performance measures (combat preparedness inspection scores, operational readiness rates, and equipment maintenance records) and human resource statistics: morale, AWOL rates, disciplinary infractions, and retention rates. Based on their analysis, they had to identify their priorities for their command tour: ship performance and human resource problems and opportunities to focus on. Then they prepared their "coming-on-board speech," in which a new commanding officer addresses the ship's crew and states his or her mission and objectives.

Trainees practiced giving their speech to peers in the course. Speeches were videotaped and coded for clarity, charisma, and "empowering" impact on their audience. At the end of the course, officers set goals and developed action plans for the steps they would take to improve their ship's performance in their first three months in their new jobs.

NOTES

1. McClelland, D. C., & Winter, D. (1971). *Motivating economic achievement,* New York: Free Press; Miron, D., & McClelland, D. C. (1979), The Effects of achievement motivation training on small business, *California Management Review, 21*(4), 13–28.; Heckhausen, H., & Krug, S. (1982), Motive modification, in A. Stewart, (Ed.), *Motivation and society,* San Francisco, CA: Jossey-Bass.; Varga, K. (1977), Who gains from achievement motivation training? *Vikalpa: The Journal for Decision Makers,* Ahmedabad, India: Indian Institute of Management, 2, 187–200.

2. Seligman, M. (1991), *Learned optimism,* New York: Knopf.

3. Heckhausen & Krug, op. cit.

4. deCharms, R. (1968), *Personal causation,* New York: Academic Press.

5. Adult experiential education ("andragogy") principles are summarized in Knowles, M. (1971), *The modern practice of adult education: Andragogy versus pedagogy,* New York: Association Press. Research on the four learning inputs is discussed in Kolb, D. (1984), *Experiential Learning,* Englewood Cliffs, NJ: Prentice-Hall.

6. McClelland, D. C. (1965), Toward a theory of motive acquisition. *American Psychologist,* 1965, *20,* 321–333.

7. Bandura, A. (1969), *Principles of behavior modification,* New York: Holt, Rinehart & Winston.

   Bandura, A. (1977), *Social learning theory,* Englewood Cliffs, NJ: Prentice-Hall.

8. Latham, G. P., & Saari, L. M. (1979), Application of social learning theory to training supervisors through behavior modelling, *Journal of Applied Psychology, 64,* 239–246; Burke, M. J., & Day, R. R. (1986), A cumulative study of the effectiveness of managerial training, *Journal of Applied Psychology,* 1986, *71,* 232–245. Also see review in Goldstein, I. L. (1991), Training in work organizations. In M. D. Dunnette & L. M. Hough (1991), *Handbook of industrial and organizational psychology,* Palo Alto, CA: Consulting Psychologists Press.

9. Kolb, D. A., & Boyatzis, R. E. (1967), Goal setting and self-directed behavior change, *Human Relations, 23*(5), 439–457.

   Meyer, Herbert H., Kay, Emanuel, & French, John R. P., Jr. (1964), Split roles in performance appraisal, *Harvard Business Review, 43,* 124–129.

10. Latham, G. P., & Locke, E. A. (1979; Autumn) Goal setting: A motivational technique which works, *Organizational Dynamics,* 68–80.

11. Raven, J. (1977), *Education, values and society: The objectives of education and the nature and development of competence,* London: H. K. Lewis; New York: Psychological Corp.

12. Burke, M. J., & Day, R. R. (1986), A cumulative study of the effectiveness of managerial training. *Journal of Applied Psychology, 71,* 232–245. These results may represent the best training can do, because failures rarely are reported: Only training programs that work get written up, published, and meta-analyzed. But enough studies show results of these magnitudes are possible for them to represent standards that human resources professionals should strive for.

13. Spencer, L. M. (1986), *Calculating human resource costs and benefits* (pp. 106–109), New York: Wiley.

14. Burke, M. J., & Day, R. R. (1986), A cumulative study of the effectiveness of managerial training, *Journal of Applied Psychology, 71,* 232–245.

15. Lambert, C. (1990 November–December), The electronic tutor, *Harvard Magazine,* 42–51.

16. Dreyfus, C. (1990), Scientists and engineers as effective managers: A study of the development of interpersonal abilities, unpublished doctoral dissertation, Case Western Reserve University Weatherhead School of Management Department of Organizational Behavior, Cleveland, OH.

17. Spencer, L. (1989), Stimulating innovation and entrepreneurship in mature organizations, Boston: McBer.

18. Litwin, G., & Stringer, R. (1968), *Motivation and organizational climate,* Boston: Harvard Business School Research Press.

19. McBer (1991), Competency-based Training Seminar, Boston: McBer.

20. Spencer, I. M. (1986), *Calculating human resource costs and benefits,* New York: Wiley.

21. A detailed description of an achievement motivation training program appears in McClelland, D. C., & Winter, D. (1971), *Motivating economic achievement,* New York: Free Press. Also see McClelland, D. C. (1965, November –December), Achievement motivation can be developed. *Harvard Business Review,* 3–20.

22. Miron, D., & McClelland, D. C. (1979), The effects of achievement motivation training on small business, *California Management Review, 21*(4), 13–28.

23. Spencer, L. M. (1978, April), The Navy Leadership and Management Training Program; A competency-based approach, *Proceedings for the Sixth Symposium: Psychology in the Department of Defense,* Colorado Springs: U.S. Air Force Academy Department of Behavioral Sciences and Leadership. Also see McBer, (1987), *A History of the U.S. Navy Leadership and Management Education and Training Program,* Boston: McBer.

22

Pay

A man is worth as many men as languages he speaks.
—William Shakespeare

DEFINITION

Compensation systems refer to methods used to set fixed and variable pay for the jobs in an organization. These methods can be arrayed on a continuum from unstructured to highly structured:

- *Unstructured "Free Market" Nonsystems.* All pay is set by one-off negotiations between employer and employee. "Free market" pay negotiations are often found in "star" occupations such as rock music, professional sports, and investment banking.

- *Whole Job Ranking and Paired Comparison Systems.* Jobs are ranked on their difficulty or importance to the organization, and employees in "bigger, harder, more valuable" jobs receive higher pay.

- *Classification Systems.* Jobs are rigidly classified, and the people holding them are paid by level and grades within level (e.g., all "Level 14, grade 3" employees receive the same pay).

- *Highly Structured Factor Comparison Systems.* Jobs are analyzed in terms of their knowledge and skill requirements, and the amount of responsibility or "accountability" employees in them assume. Knowledge, skill, and accountability factors are measured on specific scales, with each scale level worth a certain number of job measurement points. The sum of these factor points gives a point total for the job. The point totals for all jobs in an organization are related to pay by multiple linear regression statistics.

With the exception of the pure "free market" negotiation approach, compensation systems attempt to quantify and set pay for the competency requirements of *jobs*—although it is not *jobs* but *people* who are paid.

COMPETENCY-BASED PAY

Competency-based pay is compensation for *individual* characteristics, for skills or competencies over and above the pay a *job* or organizational role itself commands. Individual characteristics that merit higher pay may be demographic factors (seniority, minority status) or competencies (experience, potential, creativity, entrepreneurial initiative, loyalty, institutional memory, portability, or fluency in other languages).

Many compensation experts are wary of pay for competence, believing, "As soon as a firm begins paying for 'nice to have' characteristics divorced from job accountabilities that measure value added to the firm, it loses control of its compensation system . . . that way lies corruption."

Problems with the pay for competence concept include internal equity and the potential for misuse. How is one competency to be valued against another? The fear is that the "the loudest voices—the most influential or best-organized groups of workers" will see that their characteristics are most highly valued. Pay for education systems reward employees with the most seniority, "the ones who have been with the company long enough to attend the most courses." Frequently these courses do not teach skills relevant to improved organizational performance.[1]

ORGANIZATIONAL ISSUES

The following issues may indicate the need for a competency-based pay system:

- Inability to attract "good" (i.e., more competent than average) employees
- The perception that people with certain competencies add more value to the firm than those without them in identical jobs (the person "worth as many people as languages he [or she] speaks")
- The perception that job-based pay systems are inappropriate when change is so fast that the very concept of a (stable) "job" may have lost its meaning. In these situations, a person either has many "jobs" or roles or the "*person* makes the job": the value added to the firm is a function of the individual's competencies rather than a hard-to-define position.

- The need for incentives to motivate employees to maintain and enhance state-of-the-art skills, (e.g., where an employee's development and potential future value are worth more than his or her present position or performance)

- A traditional job evaluation system that appears to reward "empire building" with the very things the firm is trying to avoid: managing many employees, big budgets, or large asset bases because these are worth more "accountability" factor points that can justify higher pay

- The need to justify compensation of knowledge workers who don't manage many people or assets, for example:

Before our "rightsizing" campaign eliminated his division, Bob used to manage 450 people and a $25 million business. Now he's got one third of a secretary . . . *But* he's the only person who knows reinsurance laws in Luxembourg in 1992 (and other expertise key to our business) . . . how do we pay him enough to keep him, now that he no longer has the "accountability" points to justify his salary?

- Highly structured compensation systems that are expensive to develop and maintain

- The perception that highly structured compensation systems promote bureaucracy: rigid hierarchies, narrow job descriptions, and restrictive job classifications, which reduce organizational flexibility, and are incompatible with the "flat" structures and "empowered" employees organizations are moving to in the future. Many organizations are experimenting with "broad banding": ranges of pay for a given job or job family of 50 to 100 percent of the minimum pay for the position.

- The perception that job-based pay systems treat employees as "commodities" instead of valuing individual differences, inhibiting employee initiative and creativity. Advocates of competency-based pay hope to place a higher value on the "intellectual assets" that are increasingly important in an information economy, and reward individual development as well as competencies such as willingness to collaborate in teams and flexible attitudes toward change.

STEPS IN DEVELOPING COMPETENCY-BASED COMPENSATION SYSTEMS

1. *Identify Key Factors.* Identify *job* role requirements, *person* competencies that predict performance, and *performance* results for each level in a job family. Bases for compensation can be diagrammed on two axes, as shown in Figure

External Market

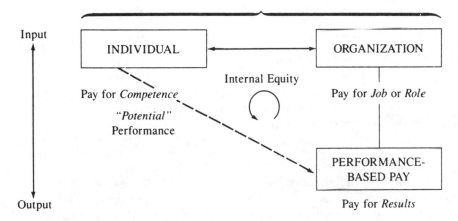

Note. Variation on a diagram proposed by David Fitt. In H. Murlis & D. Fitt, "Job evaluation in a changing world." *Personnel Management,* May 1991; and H. Murlis & D. Fitt, *Evaluating skills, competencies and jobs.* London: Hay Management Consultants, (1991).

Figure 22–1   Compensation System Variables

22–1. One axis is "individual to organization" and the other is "input to output." Traditional compensation systems pay for an organizational job or role: *organizational input* requirements such as technical knowledge, problem solving, and accountability (number of people and dollar value of assets managed.)

Performance-based pay systems supplement base salary determined by organizational role with additional pay for *organizational outputs:* actual performance results, economic benefits brought into the firm. Examples of pure performance-based pay systems include piecework and full commission sales: Employees get paid only when they perform and in direct proportion to their productivity.

Competency-based pay systems pay for *individual input* characteristics, for the ability to add economic value to the firm at some future point in time. Note that this is essentially the definition of an *asset.*

Organizational job, performance, and individual competence pay decisions are further subject to *external market* and *internal equity* variables. Individual characteristics (e.g., an MBA from an elite business school) may have higher external market prices. Internal equity (e.g., to MBAs hired in previous years) may limit the price a firm is willing to pay.

The key to rational competency-based pay is the clarity about the dashed diagonal between individual competency inputs and organizational outputs shown on Figure 22–1. A clear economic relationship should exist between the competency paid for and the economic value to the firm.

This relationship can be expressed in an equation:

$$E(v) = A * p * DF$$

where

$E(v)$ = the *expected value* of a candidate in dollars
A = the *amount* of economic value in dollars an individual's
       competency may bring the firm
p = the *probability* that the firm will get the amount; and
DF = the *discount factor* used to find the present value of a benefit
       received at some future point in time.

Amount (A) represents economic benefit the competency will provide; probability (p), the *likelihood* that the firm will get the benefit; and the discount factor (DF), *when* the firm will get the benefit. An example is the calculation a professional sports team makes in a contract with a star athlete. The team must estimate the additional revenue the star will bring in box office and media receipts, when and for how long the team will receive this stream of earnings, and the probability that the star will play for the length of the contract (e.g., not be injured or otherwise unable to perform). A decision to pay for a person's "portability," "innovativeness," or "entrepreneurship," represents a similar investment analysis—or should.

Management–labor agreements on "multiskilling" provide a simple example of competency-based pay based on economic value analysis. Traditional practice in an European water authority required four craftspeople to install a water meter: A laborer dug a hole for a new water meter, a mason bricked in the hole, a plumber connected the pipes to the water meter, and an electrician connected the wires to the meter. The mason then finished bricking in the hole and the laborer shoveled dirt back into the hole.

Under the multiskilling agreement, meter installers were cross-trained in all four crafts. After training, one worker dug the hole, bricked it in, connected the pipes, connected the wires, finished the brickwork, and shoveled the dirt back into the hole.

A cost–benefit analysis of the dollar value of this multiskilling example is shown in Table 22–1. Before multiskilling, four workers took three hours to complete a meter installation (for most of the three hours, three workers stood around looking into the hole while one person worked), a total of 12 person-hours. After multiskilling, one worker completed the entire installation in four hours, a savings of eight person-hours worth $85 per installation. A worker with multiple skills clearly has an economic value to the organization, even if paid more: At $20 per hour, the multiskilled worker still saves the utility 52 percent per installation.

More complex competency-based pay systems can be developed using regression equations. Multiple regression equations can include job size, competencies, and performance factors:[2]

$$Y = \alpha + \beta_1(x_1) + \beta_2(x_2) + \beta_3(x_3) + E$$

where

Y = pay in dollars
α = y intercept
$\beta_1(x_1)$ = job size
$\beta_2(x_2)$ = competence
$\beta_3(x_3)$ = performance
E = error variance

Use of competencies in pay formulas requires precise measurement of these competencies. The just-noticeable-difference scales presented in Chapters 3 through 9 provide one method of quantifying competency measurements for use in regression equations.

Figure 22–2 shows a regression analysis with job size on the horizontal axis and pay and competence on the vertical axis. A given job is represented by a box bisected by the regression line relating salary to job size. Jobholders' competence varies in a bell-shaped distribution around the regression line. A person less competent than average should be paid less—and either trained or redeployed. A person more competent than average should be paid more or promoted to a larger job (the dashed box on Figure 22–2) that pays more—assuming there is a next job.

The upper and lower boundaries of the job box represent the "broad band" minimum-to-maximum pay rates for the job. Data cited in Chapter 2 for the economic value of superior performance suggest that these pay boundaries should be 19 percent, 32 percent, and 48 percent for simple, moderately complex, and complex jobs.

Table 22–1   Cost-Benefit Justification of Pay for Multiskilling:
Installing Water Meters

Laborer: digs $10/hour	
Mason: bricks in $15/hour	Multiskilled worker does all tasks
Plumber: connects pipes $15/hour	
Electrician: connects wires $15/hour	
4 workers for 3 hours = 12 person-hours	1 worker for 4 hours = 4 person-hours (200% productivity increase)
12 hours @ avg. $13.75/hour = $165/job	4 hours @ $20/hour = $80/job (52% cost reduction)

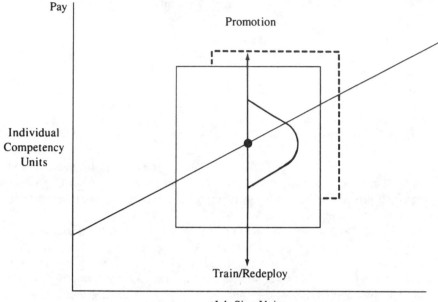

Note. Variation of a figure developed by Douglas O'Donnell, Hay Management Consultants, Glasgow Scotland.

Figure 22–2   Job Size and Competency Unit Axes

Boundaries in competency-based pay systems are very important to prevent "bracket creep": increasing numbers of workers who are paid more than they contribute to the organization in increased revenues or more employees who are paid at a level of competence than the organization has actual jobs requiring that competence.

For example, a firm implemented a competency-based pay system with six broad pay levels or "bands"—technical, professional, supervisor, manager, executive, and senior executive—and stated its intention to pay employees at their competency level irrespective of the job they were in. An executive without subordinates or executive accountabilities continued to be paid at the executive level.

Employees immediately demanded that competencies be defined precisely and that there is "equality of development opportunities." More technical and professional employees met the paper competency requirements for managerial jobs—and demanded to be paid as supervisors or managers—than there were such jobs. The firm's compensation structure quickly became uncompetitive vis-à-vis its competitors.

The problem with this firm's "pay for competence" system was that the input "competencies" (completion of business school courses) it rewarded were not linked to performance results outputs: increased revenues or profits from higher productivity that could be used to pay for more competent workers.

2. *Determine Relative Percentages.* Decide the relative percentages of total compensation the organization wants to pay for *job* role, *person* competence, and *performance* results. Competency-based pay systems usually include all three basic factors: base pay based on organization job or role, plus additional pay for person competencies, either brought to the job or acquired or demonstrated in it, plus pay for individual, team, or organization performance results, and shown in Figure 22–3. Fixed pay (salary) is set by base pay for the job, plus additional pay based on the competencies a person brings to the job that predict better than average performance. Variable pay can include additional compensation for competencies demonstrated on the job or acquired while in it ("pay for skill"), and for actual performance by the person, his or her team, or profit sharing based on the organization's economic results.

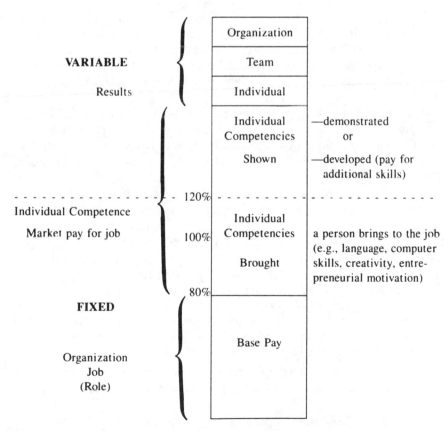

Figure 22–3 Job, Person Competencies, and Results
Components of Pay

A general trend in compensation is to increase the variable components of pay, for example, to put 20 to 100 percent of pay "at risk," conditional on demonstration of competence and results.[3]

CASES

Hiring a Consultant with Marketing and Sales Competencies

New hires in professional service firms rarely sell any work during their first two or three years. An unusual consultant candidate opened her hiring interview with the statement:

> I am working in 50 Fortune 500 companies. Only two of them overlap with those your firm is now working with: General Electric and Mobil. I can get you into at least 10 others in the coming year. This is how I'm going to do it . . .

This candidate provided persuasive evidence that she had unusual entrepreneurial initiative and selling competencies. (Needless to say, the interviewer did not believe the candidate until she described in a Behavioral Event Interview how she in fact *had* developed work in several major corporations.) However, the candidate wanted $35,000 more in starting salary than the consulting firm usually paid new hires.

The hiring firm had to answer the pay-for-competence question: What is entrepreneurial sales competence worth? A rule of thumb in professional service firms is that a professional must bring in three times his or her salary to cover base pay, fringe benefits, and overhead (i.e., in this case, an additional $105,000 in a year).

The consulting firm would much rather have offered to pay the consultant a $35,000 bonus *after* she had actually billed the additional $105,000. (Pay for performance is always preferable to pay for competence because it is risk free.) In this case, however, external market conditions did not permit the pay for performance approach. The candidate knew her market worth and could command the $35,000 premium from any of several firms.

The hiring firm's competency-based pay calculations were as follows:

- How much is the candidate's entrepreneurial sales competence worth? Assuming a 25 percent yield on her sales efforts and an average sale size of $100,000, presentations to 10 companies should yield $250,000.

- When would the firm get this increased revenue? Assuming a sales cycle of six months, within the first year—eliminating the need to use a discount factor.

- What is the probability of the new consultant delivering this increased revenue? The firm estimated 50 percent, recognizing that some of the risk had been accounted for in assuming only a 25 percent yield on sales efforts. Fifty percent of $250,000 is $125,000—above the $105,000 break-even point for this investment in entrepreneurial competence.

The consulting firm hired the candidate at the $35,000 premium. (And she generated revenues of more than $700,000 in her first year.)

Automobile Manufacturer

A complex base salary pay for role, pay for competence, pay for team performance, and organizational gain sharing is shown in Figure 22–4. An automobile manufacturer (see the competency-based performance management system case discussed on pages 273–275) wanted its employees to have a significant portion of their compensation "at risk" to motivate their collaboration as team members in making the enterprise a success. The firm decided to divide employee compensation into four different factors:

1. *Base Pay for Job Role* (organizational input).
2. *Individual Competence* (inputs). Specifically team collaborative competencies as rated by a "review committee" composed of an employee's team coordinator and peers, and completion of skill development training programs.

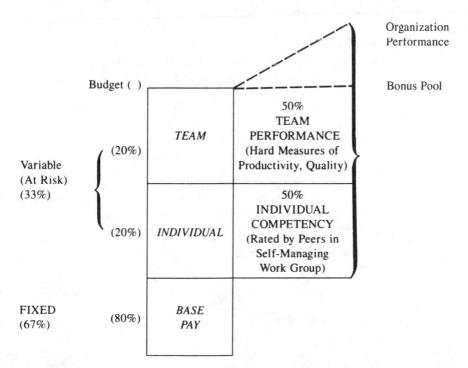

Figure 22–4 Competency, Team, and Organization Performance-Based Pay

3. *Team Performance* (performance outputs). Based on hard measures of team productivity and quality, such as the number of good cars or car parts produced by the team at standard cost.

4. *Overall Organization Results* (performance outputs). Whether or not the firm made money selling automobiles.

As shown in Figure 22–4, base pay is set at 80 percent of the market rate (100%). The bonus pool is dependent on the overall organization's budgeted level of performance. If the firm meets its performance goals, a worker can earn up to 120 percent of the market rate, or an additional 50 percent of base salary, *if* his or her individual competencies are rated 100 percent by his or her team *and* the team meets 100 percent of its productivity and quality goals. At the firm's expected level of performance, 67 percent of pay is fixed or guaranteed and 33 percent is variable or at risk, based on individual competence, team performance, and organizational profits.

If the overall organization does better than expected, the bonus pool and variable pay can be larger; if the firm does not meet its goals, variable pay will be less. The test of this compensation system will come when the firm does not meet its goals and worker compensation falls below 100 percent of the market rate.

The "entrepreneurial consultant" case provides an example of competency-based pay included in base salary. The automobile manufacturer case is an example of competency-based pay as part of a variable performance-related bonus. This variable pay for *demonstrated* competence is somewhere down the diagonal between competence as an input, a potential for or predictor of future performance, and individual performance that adds value to the firm.

NOTES

1. Dufetel, L. (1991, July), Job evaluation still at the frontier, *Compensation and Benefits Review,* New York: American Management Association.

2. In this equation, job size is a fixed effect, and competence and performance are variable effects—pay for a job changes only gradually over time as labor conditions change. Job holders can earn more money by being promoted to a larger job, by demonstrating more competencies, or by producing more performance results. Competence and performance bonuses are merit pay that are not added to a worker's base salary. Pay for the job would not change unless the job itself did. Bonus pay for increasing competence rewards a person for gaining depth in a job, or "inward mobility . . . in a world with overpopulated senior populations, recognition for inward mobility would seem desirable." O'Malley, M. (1991), *Integrating competencies into compensation planning and salary administration,* Stamford, CT: Hay Management Consultants.

3. See Boyett, J. H., & Conn, H. P. (1991), *Workplace 2000* (Chapter 5), New York: Dutton.

23

Integrated Human Resource Management Information Systems

DEFINITION

An integrated human resource management information system (IHRMIS) is a data base shared by all human resource functions that provides a "common language" and integrates all human resource (HR) services.

COMPETENCY-BASED IHRMIS

The concept of an integrated human resource information system is shown in Figure 23–1.[1] A data base nucleus containing information about the competency requirements of jobs and competencies of people is used by all human resources functions: recruitment, selection, placement, compensation, performance management, succession planning, and training and development. All functions use the common language of competencies. Recruiters recruit and select for competencies required by jobs. Training and development is focused on those competencies that lead to superior performance in jobs. Succession planning is done by comparing employees' competencies with the competency requirements of future jobs. Compensation includes competency-based pay elements to encourage employees to develop needed competencies. The performance appraisal system assesses employees' competencies at least yearly and inputs these data to the data base to be sure that the system has up-to-date assessments of individuals' competencies.

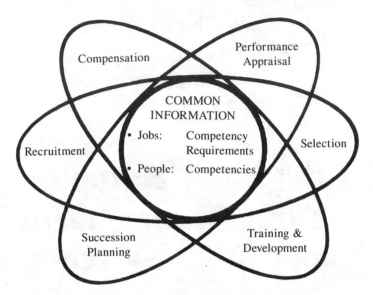

Figure 23–1   Integrated Uses of a Competency Data Base

An integrated human resource integration system includes:

1. *Organizational Chart.* An organizational charting function creates a data-base record "file folder" for each job in the firm. Managers can see, create, and delete jobs as needed. The firm's organization chart is updated instantly and is always current.

2. *Job Description and Analysis.* The system asks questions and lets users input data to develop job descriptions, competency model profiles of the requirements for jobs, and job-measurement points for compensation planning.

Job Description. A computer-generated job description includes:

a. Job title (and identifying information; e.g., a job number referencing the job's level, numbering from the CEO down, or the lowest job level up, and the job family function or track)

b. Job content: Tasks and Responsibilities

c. Job accountabilities: Performance standards or objectives and measures for the job

d. Job measurement data: Used to set compensation for the job

e. Competency requirements: Definition of the skills and characteristics required for adequate and superior performance in the job

Job Competency Requirements Analysis. A job competency analysis expert system asks a series of "branching" questions, for example, "Does this job require dealing with people (beyond simply giving and receiving instructions and information)?"

A "yes" to this question triggers a series of additional questions. For example, "Does this job involve cooperating in a team? Dealing with conflict? Influencing others? Selling? Teaching or training?" If these questions are answered "yes," Interpersonal Understanding and Impact and Influence competencies are flagged as being required by the job.

For a "no" answer to the "dealing with people" question, the program eliminates many interpersonal skill-related questions and branches to the next core question: "Does this job require accomplishing objectives?" A "yes" answer triggers further questions, for example: "Does the job require . . . developing new products and services? Accomplishing challenging goals, i.e., doing better than has been done before or making continual efficiency and productivity improvements? A "yes" answer to any of these questions flags achievement orientation at the level required by the job task.

This "job competency requirements analyzer" (also described in Chapter 10) uses a data base of many competency models and competency → task relationships to construct a complete competency model profile for the job.

3. *People Assessment.* A similar process can be used to assess employees or competencies. The system can ask questions about the extent to which a person demonstrates each of the competencies required by a given job. These questions can be formatted as a "focused" behavioral event interview protocol (described in Chapter 18) or as a competency-based performance appraisal form (see Chapter 19).

Assessment Advisor. An "assessment advisor" function can also recommend other assessment methods, for example: tests, application form items, or assessment center exercises and suggest which can be used to assess a candidate or employee on specific competencies required by a job.

Performance Management Advisor. A "performance management advisor" can generate performance appraisal forms with scales for key competencies required by the job, and can advise managers on coaching observations and instructions that help an employee develop these competencies.

The system records and evaluates data from all assessment methods and appraisal forms to develop (or update) individual competency profiles, which can be compared with competency requirements profiles for various jobs.

4. *Job–Person Matching.* An expert system built into the integrated human resource information system can also be used to assess the match between a given job's competency requirements and an individual's competencies. Using the pattern-matching algorithms discussed in Chapter 18, a user can give the computer a list of individuals and have the computer find the person(s) best matched to a given job. This job–person matching system can be used for selection job placement, promotion decisions, and succession planning.

5. *Development Advice.* The job–person matching system can also be used for development planning. A person can be matched to a job and the gaps between his or her competencies and the job competency requirements identified. The system can then reason, "*If* there is a gap in competency *X, then* the person should develop this competency by reading these books, taking these training courses, working for these mentors, or working in these developmental jobs, . . ." Figure 23–2 shows a computer-generated development guide for increasing Impact and Influence competencies.

The "development advisor" expert system can prepare and print a complete development plan for employees, either to improve performance in their current job or to prepare for a future job.

6. *Training Needs Assessment.* The employee competence data base can be queried about the levels of competence in a multiple-incumbent job, a department, or other component of the organization. For example, the data base can answer queries such as "How many salespeople in our high tech sales force have Customer Service Orientation competence at Level 5 or above?" or "How many employees in corporate accounting have the competence to move up to comptroller jobs in our subsidiaries?" These data can be used for training needs assessment (e.g., if few salespeople have the desired level of customer service orientation, the training department is alerted to develop training for this competency).

7. *Development and Career Path Manager.* An IHRMIS can include and track employee progress against development and career advancement plans: training courses enrolled in and completed successfully, and developmental job assignments and projects completed that certify employees have attained a given level of competence.

8. *Administration.* IHRMISs can provide administrative assistance, record keeping, program management, on-screen testing and reports generation, and competency-based training.

ORGANIZATIONAL ISSUES

The issues addressed by integrated human resource systems include:

- *Fragmentation.* In many organizations, disparate human resource functions and services use different and often conflicting languages and systems. Recruiters recruit for one set of characteristics. Performance appraisals appraise another set of characteristics. The training department trains yet a third set of knowledge and skills.

- *Inefficient Use of Resources.* Fragmentation results in inefficient use of resources: duplicated computers and data bases, duplicate staffs, and excessive head count. It also confuses human resource system clients.

- *Confusion and Conflicting Messages.* Managers and employers must master the several different languages and may receive conflicting

Illustrative Example: "Mary"

Development Goal			Development Actions	Time Target

Competency Area: Concern for Impact

Job Rating: 4	Development Rating: 2	Overall Time Goal: 6/92

SPECIFIC OBJECTIVE

Increase my daily involvement and influence behavior with others outside the unit, especially people who are current or potential users of the unit's services.

Illustrations: I would initiate several meetings a week with department heads and supervisors for the purpose of improving our service and working relationship. I would get involved in committee and task force groups and work to positively influence policy and operating management recommendations.

POTENTIAL OBSTACLES

1. Preference for working on tangible, practical tasks. These are present at all times within the unit and are easy to focus on.

2. Lack of confidence and skill in persuading and influencing others who aren't subordinates.

3. Reluctance to delegate responsibility to subordinates with only periodic review of progress and results.

PRACTICAL ACTION STEPS

Your Own:

1. Using a weekly planning calendar, schedule at least five meetings each week with other managers and supervisors. Will write a brief agenda for each meeting noting my goals and areas of mutual business interest. — **7/15/91**

2. To gain some good ideas about influencing others, will read *The Power Handbook: A Strategic Guide to Organizational and Personal Effectiveness.* Will summarize main points that are especially relevant to my style and development needs. — **10/31/91**

3. Will attend one internal or external training seminar aimed at skill building in persuasion and personal influence. Will get assistance from my development coach to identify the right resource. — **11/1/91**

4. Will join one special task force that will provide a regular opportunity to present ideas and recommendations to a group. Will plan specific influence actions and seek feedback from group. — **1/1/92**

Others:

Boss: Discuss observations about strengths and weaknesses in the area of influencing others. Review action plan, provide suggestions, and participate in follow-up discussions reviewing progress. — **7/10/91**, **Quarterly**

Development Coach: Assist in identifying skill-building seminar and making arrangements. Review development action plan and make suggestions. Participate in behavior practice sessions to increase comfort and skill development. — **7/7/91**, **8/23/91**, **10/9/91**, **2/7/92**

Figure 23–2 Development Planning Worksheet

319

messages about what is important. Messages given by different functions and services at best do not reinforce one another, and at worst, directly conflict.

STEPS IN DEVELOPING INTEGRATED HUMAN RESOURCE MANAGEMENT INFORMATION SYSTEMS

1. *Identify Key Jobs.* Critical or benchmark jobs are identified to be entered in the IHRMIS, using the defining process described in Chapter 19. The case examples in this chapter suggest that organizations do not implement IHRMIS for the total organization at one time. Rather, an IHRMIS is implemented in one function (e.g., do 40 job analyses for a new marketing unit in Europe), or to solve a specific problem (e.g., provide succession planning data for the top 100 jobs and 200 people in the firm).

2. *Analyze the Competency Requirements of Key Jobs.* The expert system job analyzer and/or other competency analysis methods, for example, behavioral event interviews, are used to develop competency models for the key jobs in the system. Usually an organization will want to conduct more in-depth BEI or other competency modeling studies for key "benchmark" jobs and use these to calibrate the expert system to the organization. The expert system is valid when it gives the same competency profile for a job that human competency model experts get.

3. *Assess the Competencies of Key People.* Competency data for candidates or for employees performing key jobs are developed, using the expert system person assessor.

4. *Develop Human Resource Management Applications.* The expert system job–person matcher is configured to generate selection, placement, succession planning, individual and group training needs assessment, and development recommendations using the client organization's resources such as training courses offered internally or offered by external vendors.

CASES

Nationwide Insurance

Published examples of IHRMIS are heavily oriented to job analysis for purposes of job description, classification, and evaluation for setting compensation. Nationwide Insurance Companies[2] has developed an integrated, four-phase, personnel system.

Phase 1. Job Analysis.   A computerized job analysis questionnaire was used to collect data on 10,000 positions. Each job was described using six job factors: managerial plans, managerial actions, financial responsibility, human resource responsibility, knowledge and contacts, and decision-making responsibilities. Job factors measured the extent to which the job involved various task activities:

- *Managerial Actions.* Counseling, legal/regulatory affairs, supervision
- *Decision-Making Responsibilities.* People planning, corporate policy
- *Financial Responsibilities.* Capital expenditures, profit and loss objectives
- *Knowledge Areas.* Property and casualty insurance, corporate relations

Phase 2. Development of Human Resource Management Applications.   These job analysis data were used to develop employee assessment methods for:

- *Selection.* Supervisor ratings, assessment center scores, interview guides, tests
- *Performance Appraisal.* Performance evaluation and employee development reviews
- *Compensation.* Job grading and merit pay administration
- *Training and Development.* Needs analysis, course delivery, assessment center scores, and training evaluations

Phase 3. Manpower and Succession Planning.   Employee data collected by HR applications were aggregated to provide organization-wide human resources planning information: entry, turnover, and retirement data and successor availability for key jobs.

Phase 4. Strategic Business Planning.   Human resources data were integrated with the organization's mission and strategy planning. For example, the HRMIS could assess whether Nationwide Insurance had the human resources to implement a strategic new sales initiative.

The Nationwide Insurance integrated personnel system is not explicitly competency-based as competencies are defined in this book, although "planning," "supervision," and counseling task activities can be employee capabilities as well as job requirements. In scope and intent, however, the Nationwide system is the best published example of an IHRMIS.

U.S. Computer Company

A major U.S. computer company adopted a strategy of moving from selling hardware to selling system integration consulting. Its salespeople and technical consultants needed to know:

1. *Hardware and Software Platforms.* Not only the firm's but also those of 100 other manufacturers—and how to link all these systems together in local and wide area networks.

2. *Vertical Market Applications.* How system integration could be used in banking, insurance, local government, manufacturing, and other industries to improve customer productivity.

3. *Consulting Competencies.* Especially team collaboration in multidisciplinary work teams with members of the firm, competing firms, third-party vendors, and client reengineering teams.

The firm developed a data base with these three sets of competencies: technical, industry (vertical application), and interpersonal. An expert system job–person matcher enabled sales and project managers to find consultants who had the combination of technical, industry, and interpersonal skills to work on complex projects.

For example, one project involved the merger of two major banks in the southeastern United States. The resulting megabank faced the integration of two MIS departments using different computers and software and numerous line operations in conflict over how their future merged system would operate. Appropriate consultants needed to (1) know how to interface two computer communications LANs; (2) know how imaging systems can be used to speed transaction processing in banks; and (3) have the interpersonal skills to consult in a highly politicized environment.

Finding one or more consultants who fit this complex job profile is a job made for an IHRMIS. The computer firm's system can access its 1000-plus sales and technical consultants and identify employees with competencies that match the job's requirements. Multinational organizations in a diverse and rapidly changing environment will need IHRMISs to staff the multidisciplinary teams that will do much of the "knowledge work" of the future.

NOTES

1. Our colleague Ron Page has helped us develop these concepts—see Page, R., & Van De Voort, D. M. (1989), Job analysis and HR planning. In W. Cascio (Ed.), *Human resource planning, employment and placement,* Washington, DC: BNA Books.

2. Avner, B. D., & Williams, J. E. (1986, December 1), Career directions: An integrated personnel system, in *Prentice Hall Personnel Management: Policies and Practices Service,* pp. 985–992.

24

Societal Applications

This chapter describes the use of competency methods by states and the U.S. Department of Labor for workforce planning, and discusses implications of this research for education, training, and child rearing.

COMPETENCY-BASED WORKFORCE PLANNING

Competency-based workforce planning includes motive, self-concept, and cognitive and interpersonal competencies with traditional demographic and skill variables in forecasting labor markets.

ISSUES

State and national agencies, like businesses, try to identify the kinds of jobs their economies will offer in the future and plan education and training to prepare their citizens for these future jobs. Economic issues driving labor market studies include:

- Fundamental change from an industrial to an information, "knowledge worker" economy, causing the decline of old industries and the rise of new businesses
- Increasing competition from other states and countries for these new business opportunities (e.g., traditionally, location of new manufacturing plants, but in the future, new service and information firms)
- Rapid technological change
- Demographic shifts, presenting new populations to be educated

■ Changes in business structure and organizational values toward greater worker participation, responsibility, and initiative

All these factors require workers with new knowledge, skills, and competencies.

STEPS IN DEVELOPING SOCIETAL APPLICATIONS

Competency-based workforce planning includes the following steps:[1]

1. *Project Employment.* Project jobs likely to be lost and created in the next 10 to 20 years. Complex economic models take into account long-term economic growth trends, patterns of new business formation, growth and decline in all industrial sectors, and unemployment rates to forecast the number of jobs in each sector and occupational group.

2. *Project Future Labor Force Supply.* Create projections from census data, demographic forecasts, and projected graduates from state educational institutions.

3. *Profile Skills and Competencies Required by Each Occupation.* Competencies are classified in six groups:

   a. *Psychomotor:* Use of tools or processes to complete tasks

   b. *Factual Knowledge:* Breadth and depth of knowledge needed to perform effectively. Psychomotor and knowledge content competencies are grouped together as "technical skills."

   c. *Intellectual/Cognitive:* Thinking and reasoning

   d. *Interpersonal:* Ways in which workers must interact with others to complete a job

   e. *Motivational:* The nature and level of motivation required to do the job

Just-noticeable-difference scales for each competency group are shown in Table 24–1.[2]

Interviews, panels, and mailed surveys ask a broad sample of business, education, government, and education leaders about the competency requirements of each occupation. For example, Figure 24–1 shows new jobs projected for the state of Connecticut by interpersonal impact level. Forecasts for each occupation and industrial sector are summarized for the entire state economy. For example, Figure 24–2 shows changes in the number of jobs by competency level required for Connecticut from 1984 to 1995.

4. *Assess Current Education and Training Programs.* Educators, business executives, union leaders and community groups are surveyed on their current education and training offerings, and the degree to which these programs develop specific competencies.

Table 24–1 Competency Scales for Workforce Planning

I. PSYCHOMOTOR

1. Perform bulk movement of goods.
2. Manipulation of goods requiring eye-hand coordination.
3. Manipulation of goods with eye-hand coordination under time pressure.
4. Precision manipulation of goods *or* monitoring several physical events *or* several coordinated precision movements under time pressure.
5. Precision manipulation of goods under time pressure responding to unpredictable situations.

II. FACTUAL KNOWLEDGE

1. No particular factual knowledge.
2. Some specialized knowledge in a particular field.
3. In-depth knowledge in a field or a body of information.
4. In-depth knowledge in several fields or bodies of information.

III. INTERPERSONAL

1. Work alone.
2. Work with others on tasks.
3. Work with others: Influencing individuals to do something.
4. Work with others: Influencing strangers or a group in an established pattern of activities.
5. Work with others: Influencing a group of people as a whole.

IV. INTELLECTUAL/COGNITIVE LEVEL

1. Rote memory.
2. Diagnostic use of concepts: Application and interpretation.
3. Diagnostic use of concepts: Application and interpretation requiring perception of causation.
4. Systematic thinking: Perception of multiple causal relationships.
5. Synthetic reasoning: Concept formation through pattern recognition.

V. MOTIVATION

1. Security: Subsistence, money.
2. Affiliation: Desire to be/work/interact with others on other than task-related matters.
3. Precision: Desire to be accurate, give attention to detail.
4. Integration: Desire to coordinate, orchestrate the work of others.
5. Entrepreneurial: Desire to do new and innovative things, start businesses.
6. Influence: Desire to lead, inspire others to act.

5. *Analyze Mismatches between Future Job Requirements and Workers' Likely Competencies.* Competency requirements of jobs in each industrial and occupational group are compared with projected worker competencies. Gaps or mismatches between job requirements and worker competencies are identified and used to plan education and training programs to develop competencies employees will need in the future.

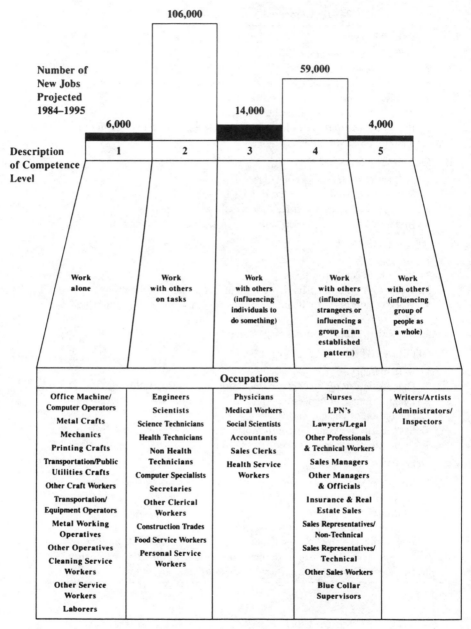

Source: McBer and Company © *Executive Report of Jobs for Connecticut's Future,* January, 1986—Third Printing, March, 1986.

Figure 24–1   New Jobs by Interpersonal Level

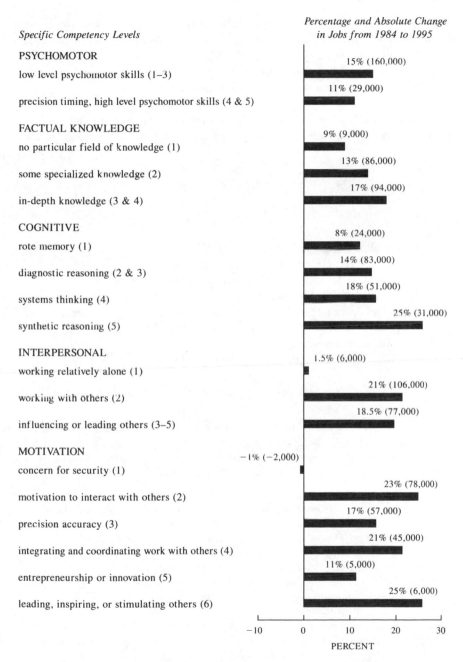

Specific Competency Levels

Percentage and Absolute Change in Jobs from 1984 to 1995

PSYCHOMOTOR

low level psychomotor skills (1–3)
15% (160,000)

precision timing, high level psychomotor skills (4 & 5)
11% (29,000)

FACTUAL KNOWLEDGE

no particular field of knowledge (1)
9% (9,000)

some specialized knowledge (2)
13% (86,000)

in-depth knowledge (3 & 4)
17% (94,000)

COGNITIVE

rote memory (1)
8% (24,000)

diagnostic reasoning (2 & 3)
14% (83,000)

systems thinking (4)
18% (51,000)

synthetic reasoning (5)
25% (31,000)

INTERPERSONAL

working relatively alone (1)
1.5% (6,000)

working with others (2)
21% (106,000)

influencing or leading others (3–5)
18.5% (77,000)

MOTIVATION

concern for security (1)
−1% (−2,000)

motivation to interact with others (2)
23% (78,000)

precision accuracy (3)
17% (57,000)

integrating and coordinating work with others (4)
21% (45,000)

entrepreneurship or innovation (5)
11% (5,000)

leading, inspiring, or stimulating others (6)
25% (6,000)

−10   0   10   20   30

PERCENT

Source: McBer and Company, 1985 © *Executive Report of Jobs for Connecticut's Future,* January, 1986—Third Printing, March, 1986.

Figure 24–2   Jobs by Required Competency Levels for the State of Connecticut

6. *Recommend Ways to Develop, Strengthen, or Expand Education and Training Programs to Teach Competencies Needed in the Future.* Curricula are recommended for key parts of the state's education delivery system: public and private schools and universities, employer training programs, private training firms, and community organizations.

Steps in state or national workforce planning follow closely the job–person matching approach described for single jobs and individuals in Chapter 18.

CASES

State of Connecticut

A workforce planning project supported by 50 Connecticut business firms and foundations surveyed 200 companies and 1,000 education, business, labor, and government leaders on competency requirements for future jobs.

Economic studies forecast a 15 percent decline in manufacturing jobs offset by a 45 percent increase in clerical, technical, professional, managerial, and human service jobs in high tech, trade, finance, office services, health care, education, and personal service sectors.

The Connecticut competency study concluded:

Occupations requiring high levels of cognitive and interpersonal competencies are growing most rapidly.

Six of the ten fastest growing occupations require high levels of cognitive and interpersonal competencies. Occupations requiring such higher order cognitive skills as systems thinking (lawyers, technicians) and synthetic (conceptual) reasoning (doctors, computer specialists) are growing substantially more than average.

Jobs demanding interpersonal skills—ranging from working with to managing others—are also increasing rapidly . . . interviews with employers indicate that, in the future, productivity will increasingly depend on teams of people working together. This includes doctors and nurses and other medical workers providing patient care, lawyers and paralegals analyzing cases, and groups of people working together on the plant floor to control and maintain machines will replace the assembly line. *The Connecticut workforce needs help in developing these competencies.* Employers . . . report general satisfaction with their workers current levels of technical skills—i.e., factual knowledge and psychomotor coordination. Employers express concern, however, over employees' current and future levels of cognitive, interpersonal skills. A significant number (45%) . . . anticipate that workers will need higher-level cognitive skills by 1995. More than one-third felt that employees currently lack the necessary levels of interpersonal skills . . . increasingly important factors (making the) difference between average and superior job performance.

Fully one-half of those interviewed reported that employees are not appropriately motivated. Two out of five also anticipated that motivational demands will be significantly different in the future. . . . fewer than one half of responding employers and educators rated students as adequate in their ability to interpret and synthesize information and solve problems. Graduates were also given low marks for motivation (defined as "desire to exert extra effort").[3]

One employer summarized his observations about the cognitive, interpersonal and motivational competencies of recent employees: "They can read, write and figure OK—the problem is, they can't think (if they get hit with something new), can't get along with others, and don't give a damn!"

Connecticut's educational system was judged inadequate to respond to the state workers' needs for increased competence.

Connecticut teachers focus more on teaching subject matter mastery than problem-solving, "critical thinking," or interpersonal skills. . . . fewer than one in five (of a sample of 484 educators) volunteered concern about such cognitive skills as students' ability to think logically or independently, support an argument, or make decisions and conclusions.

Only 8 percent of educators included encouraging communications skills as an objective; only 3 percent mentioned students' future interaction with their co-workers as a subject for teachers' concern.[4]

Employer-based training programs reach fewer than 20 percent of workers each year. (Nationally, less than one-tenth of the total work force receive training each year.) Skilled technical, professional, and managerial employees receive a disproportionate share of training. Training tends to be narrowly focused on specific companies' current work and products rather than on competencies more broadly applicable to future jobs (see Table 24–1). Community programs focus on such educational needs as "English as a second language." Unions offer apprenticeship programs and explicit training in negotiation and arbitration competencies but reach only about 500 workers a year.

The Jobs for Connecticut's Future recommends "improving the teaching of interpersonal, cognitive, and motivational competencies in all education/training settings."

Similar competency assessments have been conducted for the states of Arkansas, Colorado, Indiana, Mississippi, and Missouri with essentially similar findings:

In Missouri and Colorado, firms consistently complained about deficiencies in "new basic skills . . ." For all occupations, from manager down to semi-skilled worker, firms wanted to see better communication, problem-solving, computer and teamwork skills, as well as the ability to set and meet priorities. Training in these higher order skills were deemed top priority by firms for all types of workers . . .[5]

United States Department of Labor

In 1991 the U.S. Department of Labor published, "What Work Requires of Schools: A SCANS (Secretary's Commission on Achieving Necessary Skills) Report for America 2000."[6] The SCANS report summarizes research leading to what amounts to a national competency model for U.S. workers.

Economic Trends. SCANS researchers first summarized trends in the U.S. economy and anticipated changes in U.S. jobs. Relevant economic trends include declining productivity, stagnant worker earnings and income, and a massive shift from manufacturing jobs (paying an average of $10.84 per hour) to service and retail jobs (paying 9% to 37% less). Table 24–2 shows expected changes in jobs as U.S. workplaces move from a traditional to a high-performance model.

Competencies. SCANS researchers surveyed business owners, public employees, union officials, educators, workers, and students to define knowledge, skills, and competencies needed to perform jobs in the future. The Commission

Table 24–2 Characteristics of Today's and Tomorrow's Workplace

Traditional Model	High-Performance Model
STRATEGY	
Mass production	Flexible production
Long production runs	Customized production
Centralized control	Decentralized control
PRODUCTION	
Fixed automation	Flexible automation
End-of-line quality control	On-line quality control
Fragmentation of tasks	Work teams, multi-skilled workers
Authority vested in supervisor	Authority delegated to worker
HIRING AND HUMAN RESOURCES	
Labor-management confrontation	Labor-management cooperation
Minimal qualifications accepted	Screening for basic skills abilities
Workers as a cost	Workforce as an investment
JOB LADDERS	
Internal labor market	Limited internal labor market
Advancement by seniority	Advancement by certified skills
TRAINING	
Minimal for production workers	Training sessions for everyone
Specialized for craft workers	Broader skills sought

Source: "Competing in the New International Economy." Washington: Office of Technology Assessment, 1990.

further developed competency models using "critical incidents" and illustrative tasks and tools used on the job.[7] Models were developed for 15 jobs in 5 job families:

1. Restaurant and accommodations (chefs, front desk clerks, assistant housekeepers)
2. Manufacturing and construction (electricians, numeric control drill operators, offset lithographer press operators)
3. Office and finance (bank tellers, underwriter assistants, secretaries)
4. Health and human services (medical record technicians, registered nurses, teacher's aides)
5. Trade and communications (truck drivers, retail salespeople, inside equipment technicians)

These models were meta-analyzed to identify generic competency clusters broadly applicable across many jobs and occupations. Table 24-3 shows the three foundation skills and personal characteristics and five competencies that were identified.

SCANS further defined proficiency levels (just-noticeable difference scales) for each competency for each job. For example, resource scheduling has five levels:

1. *Preparatory.* Scheduling oneself
2. *Work-Ready.* Scheduling a small team
3. *Intermediate.* Scheduling a production line or substantial construction project
4. *Advanced.* Developing roll-out schedule for new product or production plant
5. *Specialist.* Develop algorithm for scheduling airline

Table 24-4 shows the "work-ready" levels of proficiency for a chef on the five SCANS competencies.

Coding the SCANS basic skills and competencies on the scales described in Chapters 3 to 9 indicates considerable convergence. In declining order of frequency, the SCANS skills and competencies code for:

1. Analytic Thinking: 7
2. Concern for Order/Accuracy/Quality: 7
3. Achievement: 6
   A. Orientation: 5
   C. Innovation: 1

  4. Conceptual Thinking: 5

  5. Developing Others: 4

  6. Teamwork and Cooperation: 4

  7. Customer Service Orientation: 3

  8. Interpersonal Understanding: 2

  9. Information Seeking: 2

  10. Impact and Influence: 3

  11. Organizational Commitment: 3

  12. Organizational Awareness: 1

  13. Initiative: 1

  14. Self-Confidence: 1

"Unique" competencies mentioned include Accurate Self-assessment (1), Honesty/Integrity (1), Working with Cultural Diversity (1), and specific knowledge areas (e.g., uses computers and other technologies).[8]

SCANS estimates that fewer than 50 percent of U.S. high school graduates have even the basic reading and writing skills needed for "work-ready" proficiency. Nonacademic competencies are not measured, so graduates' proficiency on the five SCANS competencies is unknown.

Implications for Learning

SCANS concludes with observations about how schools must change to develop competencies. These changes are summarized in Table 24–5. Five core subjects (English, mathematics, science, history, and geography) are to be taught in ways that develop problem-solving and interpersonal skills in the context of real-life and work problems. A sample assignment could be to:

> Develop a plan to show how a production schedule can be maintained while a staff is trained in a new procedure. Estimate the number of additional employees or extra overtime required. Prepare charts to explain; make a presentation to other team members.[9]

SCANS recommends development of measures for "formal, nationally comparable assessments made in the 4th, 8th, and 12th grades" of all U.S. schoolchildren's proficiency in the SCANS competencies. More radically, SCANS calls for *certifying* that the competencies have been developed.

> SCANS aims to promote the development and use of assessments that can provide the basis for a new kind of high school credential which would

Table 24–3 Competencies and Foundation Skills

FIVE COMPETENCIES

1. **Resources.** Identifies, organizes, plans, and allocates resources:
   - *Time.* Selects goal-relevant activities, ranks them, allocates time, and prepares and follows schedules.
   - *Money.* Uses or prepares budgets, makes forecasts, keeps records, and makes adjustments to meet objectives.
   - *Material and Facilities.* Acquires, stores, allocates, and uses materials or space efficiently.
   - *Human Resources.* Assesses skills and distributes work accordingly, evaluates performance, and provides feedback.
2. **Interpersonal.** Works with others:
   - *Participates as Member of a Team.* Contributes to group effort.
   - *Teaches Others New Skills*
   - *Serves Clients/Customers.* Works to satisfy customers' expectations.
   - *Exercises Leadership.* Communicates ideas to justify position, persuades and convinces others, responsibly challenges existing procedures and policies.
   - *Negotiates.* Works toward agreements involving exchange of resources, resolves divergent interests.
   - *Works with Diversity.* Works well with people from diverse backgrounds.
3. **Information.** Acquires and uses information:
   - *Acquires and Evaluates Information*
   - *Organizes and Maintains Information*
   - *Interprets and Communicates Information*
   - *Uses Computers to Process Information*
4. **Systems.** Understands complex interrelationships:
   - *Understands Systems.* Knows how social, organizational, and technological systems work and operates effectively with them.
   - *Monitors and Corrects Performance.* Distinguishes trends, predicts impacts on system operations, diagnoses systems' performance, and corrects malfunctions.
   - *Improves or Designs Systems.* Suggests modifications to existing systems and develops new or alternative systems to improve performance.
5. **Technology.** Works with a variety of technologies:
   - *Selects Technology.* Chooses procedures, tools, or equipment including computers and related technologies.
   - *Applies Technology to Task.* Understands overall intent and proper procedures for setup and operation of equipment.
   - *Maintains and Troubleshoots Equipment.* Prevents, identifies, or solves problems with equipment, including computers and other technologies.

Table 24–3   *(Continued)*

A THREE-PART FOUNDATION

1. **Basic Skills.** Reads, writes, performs arithmetic and mathematical operations, listens, and speaks:
   * *Reading.* Locates, understands, and interprets written information in prose and in documents such as manuals, graphs, and schedules.
   * *Writing.* Communicates thoughts, ideas, information, and messages in writing; and creates documents such as letters, directions, manuals, reports, graphs, and flow charts.
   * *Arithmetic/Mathematics.* Performs basic computations and approaches practical problems by choosing appropriately from a variety of mathematical techniques.
   * *Listening.* Receives, attends to, interprets, and responds to verbal messages and other cues.
   * *Speaking.* Organizes ideas and communicates orally.
2. **Thinking Skills.** Thinks creatively, makes decisions, solves problems, visualizes, knows how to learn, and reasons:
   * *Creative Thinking.* Generates new ideas.
   * *Decision Making.* Specifies goals and constraints, generates alternatives, considers risks, and evaluates and chooses best alternative.
   * *Problem Solving.* Recognizes problems and devises and implements plan of action.
   * *Seeing Things in the Mind's Eye.* Organizes and processes symbols, pictures, graphs, objects, and other information.
   * *Knowing How-to-Learn.* Uses efficient learning techniques to acquire and apply new knowledge and skills.
   * *Reasoning.* Discovers a rule or principle underlying the relationship between two or more objects and applies it when solving a problem.
3. **Personal Qualities.** Displays responsibility, self-esteem, sociability, self-management, and integrity and honesty:
   * *Responsibility.* Exerts a high level of effort and perseveres toward goal attainment.
   * *Self-Esteem.* Believes in own self-worth and maintains a positive view of self.
   * *Sociability.* Demonstrates understanding, friendliness, adaptability, empathy, and politeness in group settings.
   * *Self-Management.* Assesses self accurately, sets personal goals, monitors progress, and exhibits self-control.
   * *Integrity/Honesty.* Chooses ethical courses of action.

Table 24–4 Services Know-How:
Levels of Competence Expected for Entry on a Career Ladder

Accommodations and Personal Services

Chef

Competencies	Examples of Work-Ready Levels
Resources	Develop cost estimates and write proposals to justify the expense of replacing kitchen equipment. Develop a schedule for equipment delivery to avoid closing restaurant. Read construction blueprints and manufacturers' installation requirements to place and install equipment in the kitchen.
Interpersonal	Participate in team-training and problem-solving session with multicultural staff of waiters and waitresses. Focus on an upcoming Saturday night when a local club has reserved the restaurant after midnight for a party. Three people cannot work and the team has to address the staffing problem and prepare for handling possible complaints about prices, food quality, or service.
Information	Learn how to use a spreadsheet program to estimate the food costs of alternative menus and daily specials. Make up weekly menu and print it with desk-top publishing software.
Systems	Analyze "system" that determines the average and maximum wait from the time customers sit down until they receive the appetizer and then the entree. Modify system to reduce both the average and maximum waiting time by 20 percent. Determine expected increase in the number of customers served.
Technology	Read the specifications and listen to salespeople describe three competing ovens for the kitchen. Write a report evaluating the ovens and making a recommendation. Set the automatic controls on the chosen oven to prepare a sample dish.

Table 24–5 Characteristics of Today's and Tomorrow's Schools

Schools of Today	Schools of Tomorrow
STRATEGY	
Focus on development of basic skills	Focus on development of thinking skills
Testing separate from teaching	Assessment integral to teaching
LEARNING ENVIRONMENT	
Recitation and recall from short-term memory	Students actively construct knowledge for themselves
Students work as individuals	Cooperative problem solving
Hierarchically sequenced—basics before higher order	Skills learned in context of real problems
MANAGEMENT	
Supervision by administration	Learner-centered, teacher directed
OUTCOME	
Only some students learn to think	All students learn to think

measure mastery of specific, learnable competencies. This approach is intended to renew the dignity of the high school diploma, giving it real meaning as a mark of competence.

Certifying the five competencies can serve several purposes not now being achieved. They will link school credentials, student effort, and student achievement; they will provide an incentive for students to study; and they will give employers a reason to pay attention to school records. Finally, they will provide a clear target for instruction and learning. Assessment can thus help improve achievement, not simply measure it.[10] (See Table 24–3.)

Great Britain's development of competency-based National Vocational Qualifications (NVQs); NVQ training and certification through firms, unions, and educational and training organizations; and a national data base of NVQs for several hundred occupations provides a model for the implementation of SCANS in the United States.[11]

SUMMARY:
IMPLICATIONS FOR EDUCATION AND PARENTING

The research reported in this book, and in the preceding state and national studies, suggests that a relatively small number of competencies predict success at work and in life:

- *Achievement Orientation.* The desire to attain standards of excellence and do better, improve performance
- *Initiative.* Acting to attain goals and solve or avoid problems before being forced to by events
- *Information Seeking.* Digging deeper for information
- *Conceptual Thinking.* Making sense of data and using algorithms to solve problems
- *Interpersonal Understanding.* Hearing the motives and feelings of diverse others
- *Self-Confidence.* A person's belief in his or her own efficacy, or ability to achieve goals
- *Impact and Influence.* A person's ability to persuade others to his or her viewpoint
- *Collaborativeness.* Working effectively with others to achieve common goals

If these findings are true, the obvious implication for education and parenting is to develop these competencies explicitly, as part of a conscious, goal-directed curriculum.

Schooling

Proven methods for teaching competencies exist and have been extensively documented.[12] A few examples include:

1. *Mastery Learning.* This educational method assumes "what any person in the world can learn, almost all persons can learn if provided with appropriate prior and current conditions of learning"; that is, most children and adults can learn anything if they are provided with individualized instruction and allowed to proceed at their own pace. With a supportive environment, 95 percent of learners can reach a given criterion if allowed 10 to 20 percent more time. Learners are measured against objective standards of excellence (e.g., solving arithmetic problems of a certain difficulty, *never* on a curve, which defines most students as mediocre and some as failures).[13]

Mastery learning curricula are fundamentally structured and imbued with achievement motivation. Learners repeatedly set goals, take initiative, assume responsibility for their own learning, and use feedback on performance to improve against the objective standard.

2. *Discovery Learning.* This educational approach involves many research projects where learners must repeatedly seek information and organize or conceptualize data to discover principles or draw conclusions.

Discovery learning curricula implicitly and explicitly teach information seeking, analytic and conceptual thinking required of knowledge workers in an information economy.

3. *Interpersonal Skills Training.* This method explicitly teaches interpersonal understanding competencies, not in oft-ridiculed "touchie feelie" sessions but as objectively measurable skills. An example is peer counseling training in which learners are scored on JND scales of accurate empathy, warmth, genuineness, and initiation skills.[14]

Another example is the interpersonal understanding and collaborative competencies explicitly taught in Quaker schools. (The authors' children attend a Friends school, affording frequent opportunities for field observation.) Friends' tradition prizes the facilitation of genuine group consensus "freely arrived at." Children are explicitly taught from kindergarten to understand others' feelings and reach consensus in resolving conflicts. Five-year-olds' fights are stopped and the children are asked: "What is (the other child) feeling right now? What does he or she want? What are you feeling? What do you want? What can you suggest that will get both of your needs met?"

These interpersonal understanding and conflict resolution methods are hardly revolutionary or unique to Friends schools. What *is* different is that Friends' schools *explicitly* teach interpersonal understanding, teamwork, and cooperation, and conflict resolution skills as part of their formal curricula.

Children receive hundreds of mini-competency-based training sessions, with opportunities to practice and get feedback, each year from kindergarten through high school.

4. *Cooperative Learning.* In this educational approach, learners work in teams on learning assignments, and/or teach or tutor other children. Most "real world" work involves work in teams and the concept that asking a co-worker for information or help in solving a problem is "cheating" is counterproductive if not absurd.

Cooperative learning curricula explicitly teach teamwork, collaboration, and developing others' competencies. Opportunities for leadership via socialized power—influence used to help a group achieve a common goal are many, if not formally designated.

5. *"Adult" Education and Training.* The methods and exercises (described in Chapter 21) that typify this method, such as role playing, leaderless group, and business game simulations, require the use of many workplace competencies.

The SCANS report appears almost to call for secondary schooling organized around an "industrial engineering" curriculum: "Look at this workflow process. How can you improve it, make it more efficient? How will you convince your co-workers to go along with your suggestions?" There is no reason why the many hundreds of business games and adult learning exercises developed by industrial trainers and consultants specifically to teach workplace competencies cannot be used in elementary and secondary schools.

6. *Apprenticeships and Internships.* Education based in the workplace, using basic skills and competencies to do real work, solves real problems.

None of these methods are new, but few are available to most children in the United States today.

The logical question is "why?" John Raven[15] suggests that while the inability to measure, and hence to credential, nonacademic competencies has prevented their adoption in formal curricula, the real problem is the lack of shared values about what schools should teach. For example, parents support the idea of teaching "critical thinking"—until the first time a child critically questions a parent's beliefs about religion, politics, or sexuality. Many parents espouse the development of initiative and independence, when what they really want is deference and obedience.

There seems to be a generalized reluctance in public schools to teach anything that might involve "mucking about with children's minds," brainwashing, or inculcating "secular humanism." Motive, trait, and self-concept competencies are felt to be the business of the family or church, not public education.

Competency-based education also faces opposition at the college and graduate school level. Repeated attempts to measure and base accreditation on outputs (what students can actually do) have been rejected by faculty who do not want to be held accountable.

For example, the American Association of Collegiate Schools of Business (AACSB) proposed testing students and accrediting business schools on their ability to develop "non-cognitive skills, such as leadership and the ability to cope with stress.[16] The AACSB identified 19 competencies in six categories: administrative skills (decision-making ability), performance stability (tolerance of uncertainty), work motivation (energy level), interpersonal skills (leadership), values of business (ethics), and general mental ability (conceptual thinking). This proposal was vetoed by traditional business school faculty who wanted to continue to teach content knowledge but not the actual skills of management.

A few business schools (Case Western Reserve's Weatherhead School of Business is one) have adopted a competency value-added approach. Students are assessed on competencies during the first two weeks of their first year, then again at the end of their second year. MBA recipients are credentialed not just on having passed accounting, marketing, and production courses, but also on self-confidence, achievement motivation, and leadership competencies.[17]

The problems of teaching, measuring, and credentialing nonacademic competencies objectively are essentially solved. Evidence that these competencies predict success in work and life is abundant. The challenge is to change the attitudes of educators and the public to accept and value competencies as nonideological, objectively measurable, and teachable skills needed for success in life. Competencies such as achievement motivation and collaborativeness should be seen as subjects no different from reading and arithmetic. The Jobs for the Future and SCANS reports are a step toward this end.

Parenting

Most educators accept the primary role of parents and family in children's cognitive and affective development.[18] Studies of how motives are learned[19] suggest methods parents can use to develop competencies in their children. For example, child-rearing practices that produce children high in achievement motivation include allowing the child a large (but not unrealistic) "life space" and providing children with units of "microcoaching."

Life space is the distance a child is allowed to go from a parent's body or sight at various ages. Children high in achievement motivation are found to have parents who encouraged them at every age to have the largest life space the child could realistically handle. (Allowing a child to take unrealistic risks—wander into a street or across town—does not produce achievement motivation). These children were expected to walk to school, take (realistic) risks in sports or hobbies, and take responsibility for chores by themselves earlier than most children. Microcoaching refers to little incidents of teaching a child to master some aspect of his or her environment. Studies of mothers of poor children who performed as well as middle-class students in school found that these mothers provided many more coaching interactions, with causal explanations, than did mothers of less successful children.

For example, in one videotaped incident, a mother notices her toddler groping at a handle to a dresser drawer. She walks over, kneels down next to the child, helps the baby grasp the handle, then with her hand on the baby's, slides the drawer in and out a couple of times. The mother releases the child's hand the instant the child "gets it," when the baby's face lights up with obvious joy at having mastered this little task. The toddler repeatedly slides the drawer in and out, in and out. The mother backs off, careful not to rob her baby of the "win."

In another example, two mothers are compared in the way they tell a child not to go outside without shoes on. Both children ask "Why?"

One mother responds: "'cause if you do, I'll whump ya!"

The other mother explains: "*If* you go outside without your shoes on, *then* you are likely to step on a piece of broken glass and get an owie . . . and if you get an owie, *then* I will have to take you to the doctor . . . and *if* you go to the doctor, (*then*) she may have to give you one of those shots you hate . . ." This mother repeatedly coaches her child in if → then causal reasoning.

Mothers of achievement-oriented children are observed to microcoach their children from 30 to as many as 100 times a day. This use of "developing others' competencies" resembles the coaching managerial style used by effective supervisors to arouse achievement motivation in employees.

The competency movement has seen the recent publication of books designed to help parents develop their children's competencies. For example, Dorothy Rich's *MegaSkills,*[20] provides many exercises for teaching 10 core competencies: self-confidence, motivation, effort, responsibility, initiative, perseverance, caring, teamwork, common sense, and problem solving. Rich calls, as do the Jobs for the Future and SCANS reports, for more explicit measurement and teaching of motive, self-concept, cognitive, and interpersonal skills.

NOTES

1. Abstracted from steps used in studies conducted by McBer and Company and Jobs for the Future for the State of Connecticut. Jobs for the Future (1986), *Executive report of jobs for Connecticut's future,* Somerville, MA: Jobs for the Future.
2. Boyatzis, R. E. (1984), Identification of skill requirements for effective job performance, Boston: McBer.
3. Jobs for the Future. op. cit. pp. 23, 25.
4. Jobs for the Future, op. cit. p. 33.
5. Pennington, H., Austin, J., & Flynn, E. (1991), Creating a market in education and training: The case of missing demand. Somerville, MA: Jobs for the Future.
6. Secretary's Commission on Achieving Necessary Skills (SCANS) (1991), *What work requires of schools: A SCANS report for America 2000,* Washington, DC: U.S. Department of Labor.

7. SCANS, op. cit., Appendix D, Jobs Analysis, p. D-1.

8. Coded from competencies listed on pp. 2-4 to 2-7, Secretary's Commission on Achieving Necessary Skills (SCANS) (1991), *Skills and tasks for jobs: A SCANS report for America 2000,* Washington, DC: U.S. Department of Labor.

9. SCANS, *Skills and Tasks,* op. cit., p. 21.

10. SCANS, *Skills and Tasks,* op. cit., p. 30.

11. General information and numerous publications on Great Britain's NVQ initiatives are available from the National Council for Vocational qualifications, 222 Euston Road, London NW1, UK.

12. Examples of teaching achievement motivation in the schools are in Alshuler, A. S. (1973), *Developing achievement motivation in adolescents,* Englewood Cliffs, NJ: Education Technology Publications; deCharms, R. (1976), *Enhancing motivation: Change in the classroom,* New York: Irvington; McClelland, D. C. (1972), What is the effect of achievement motivation training in the schools? *Teachers College Record, 74,* 129–145.

13. See Block, J. H. (Ed.) (1971), *Mastery learning: Theory and practice,* New York: Holt, Rinehart & Winston; and Bloom, B. S. (1976), *Human characteristics and school learning,* New York: McGraw-Hill.

14. See Carkhuff, R. R. (1973), *The art of helping,* Amherst, MA: Carkhuff Associates; and Carkhuff, R. R., & Berenson, B. G. (1976), *Teaching as treatment.* Amherst, MA: Human Resource Development Press.

15. See Raven, J. (1981), The most important problem in education is to come to terms with values, *Oxford Review of Education, 7,* 3; and Raven, J. (1987, Fall). Values, diversity and cognitive development, *Teachers College Record, 89,* 21–38.

16. A plan to rate B-schools by testing students (1979, November 19), *Business Week,* 171–174.

17. See Boyatzis, R. E., Cowen, S. S., & Kolb, D. A. (1992, May), Implementing curriculum reform in higher education: Year one of the new Weatherhead MBA program, *Selections;* Boyatzis, R. E. (in press), Developing the whole student: An MBA required course in managerial assessment and development, *Journal of Management Education;* Boyatzis, R. E., (1979) The impact of an MBA programme on managerial abilities, *Journal of Management Development, 8,* 66–76.

18. See Goodson, B., & Hess, R. (1975), *Parents as teachers of young children: An evaluative review,* Palo Alto, CA: Stanford University Press; Clark, R. (1983), *Family life and school achievement: Why poor black children succeed or fail,* Chicago: University of Chicago Press.

19. Rosen, B. C., & D'Andrade, R. G. (1959), The psychological origins of achievement motivation, *Sociometry, 22,* 185–218. Also see McClelland, D. C. (1989), *Human motivation,* Cambridge, UK: Cambridge University Press.

20. Rich, D. (1988), *MegaSkills,* Boston: Houghton Mifflin.

25

Competency-Based Human Resource Management in the Future

Most observers agree that the future business environment will include:

- An ever-increasing pace of technological and societal change
- A further shift to an information economy requiring highly skilled knowledge workers
- Intensifying global competition
- Fragmentation of markets into specialized niches
- Diversity—employees and customers from every race, sex, country, and culture in the world

Simultaneously, the United States labor force will be

- *Less* educationally well-prepared for technical information economy jobs[1]
- *Less* committed to work and more concerned about a "balanced life style" that emphasizes family and leisure

These trends will create a tight labor market for the most needed knowledge workers.

Organizations will need to respond to these changes by innovating more rapidly, continually improving service, quality, and productivity, and marketing to, managing, and motivating more diverse kinds of people. Successful organizations will be flatter and leaner (have fewer managerial levels and fewer middle managers); responsibility and decision making will be pushed down to workers closest to customers and production. Much work will be done by empowered knowledge workers in temporary multidisciplinary teams.

COMPETENCIES IMPORTANT IN THE FUTURE

Competencies that the authors[2] and other researchers[3] see as increasingly important for executives, managers, and employees of these "organizations of the future" include:

For Executives:

- *Strategic Thinking.* The ability to understand rapidly changing environmental trends, market opportunities, competitive threats, and strengths and weaknesses of their own organizations, to identify the optimum strategic response
- *Change Leadership.* The ability to communicate a compelling vision of the firm's strategy that makes adaptive responses appear both feasible and desirable to its many stakeholders, arousing their genuine motivation and commitment; to act as sponsors of innovation and entrepreneurship; and to allocate the firm's resources optimally to implement frequent changes
- *Relationship Management.* The ability to establish relationships with and influence complex networks of others whose cooperation is needed for the executive's organization to succeed and over whom he or she has no formal authority: product champions, customers, stockholders, labor representatives, government regulators at all levels (local, state, and federal), legislators, interest groups—in many countries[4]

For Managers:

- *Flexibility.* The willingness and ability to change managerial structures and processes when needed to implement their organization's change strategies
- *Change Implementation.* "Change leadership" ability (similar to that of executives) to communicate the organization's needs for change to coworkers; and "change management" skills: communication, training, group process facilitation, needed to implement change in their work groups
- *Entrepreneurial Innovation.* The motivation to "champion" new products, services, and production processes
- *Interpersonal Understanding.* The ability to understand and value the inputs of diverse others

- *Empowering.* Managerial behaviors—sharing information, participatively soliciting co-workers' ideas, fostering employee development, delegating meaningful responsibility, providing coaching feedback, expressing positive expectations of subordinates (irrespective of diversity differences), rewarding performance improvement—that make employees feel more capable and motivated to assume greater responsibility

- *Team Facilitation.* Group process skills needed to get diverse groups of people to work together effectively to achieve a common goal: establishing goal and role clarity, controlling "overtalkers," inviting silent members to participate, and resolving conflicts

- *Portability.* The ability to adapt rapidly to and function effectively in any foreign environment so that a manager is transferable to positions in Nairobi, Jakarta, Moscow, or anywhere else in the world. Research indicates this competency is correlated with such competencies as liking for travel and novelty, resistance to stress, and cross-cultural interpersonal understanding.[5]

For Employees:

- *Flexibility.* The predisposition to see change as an exciting opportunity rather than a threat, for example, adoption of new technology as "*getting to play* with new gadgets, the latest and best!"

- *Information-Seeking Motivation and Ability to Learn.* Genuine enthusiasm for opportunities to learn new technical and interpersonal skills (e.g., the secretary who, when asked to learn to use a spreadsheet program and take over department accounting, welcomes this request as "job enrichment" rather than seeing it as an additional burden). This competency transcends computer literacy and other specific technical skills future workers are believed likely to need; it is the impetus for life-long learning of *any* new knowledge and skill required by the changing requirements of future jobs.

- *Achievement Motivation.* The impetus for innovation and "kaizen," the continuous improvement in quality and productivity needed to meet (or better, lead) ever-increasing competition

- *Work Motivation under Time Pressure.* Some combination of flexibility, achievement motivation, stress resistance, and organizational commitment that enables individuals to work under increasing demands for (new) products and services in ever shorter periods of time—often expressed as "I work best under pressure—the challenge really gets my juices flowing!"

- *Collaborativeness.* The ability to work cooperatively in multidisciplinary groups with diverse co-workers: positive expectations of others, interpersonal understanding, organizational commitment

■ *Customer Service Orientation.* A genuine desire to be of help to others; interpersonal understanding sufficient to hear customers' needs and emotional state; sufficient initiative to overcome obstacles in the employee's own organization to solve customer problems

FUTURE DIRECTIONS FOR COMPETENCY RESEARCH

Future competency research will be accelerated by at least four developments:

1. *Rapid Growth of the Worldwide Competency Data Base.* This will produce more precise generic models for superior performance in more economically important jobs and more detail about cultural differences in competency expression.

2. *Advances in Measurement.* More precise scaling of competencies and more operant tests of nontraditional abilities should produce more and better methods of assessing and credentialing competencies.

3. *Better Understanding of Competency—Situational Interactions and Combinational Rules.* Psychologists, like physicists and chemists, have long looked for a "periodic table" of the core "elements" of personality.[6] We have found an atomic model useful in thinking about competencies.

Behavioral indicators, the smallest useful unit of observation of a competency, correspond to "atoms." As shown in the discussion of the Competency Dictionary earlier in this book, behavioral indicators can be scaled in order of increasing intensity or completeness of action, much like orbital electrons at lower to higher levels of energy.

Competencies correspond to "elements" composed of or described by several behavioral indicators. For example, Achievement Orientation has eight "intensity," seven "impact," and five "innovation" behavioral indicators.

Competencies can also be "molecules": a combination of several competencies. For example, the "leadership motive profile," a competency that predicts long-term managerial success in business, consists of two motives, high Achievement motivation and Power motivation (higher than Affiliation motivation), and a trait, Self-Control.[7] This competency could be described in a "chemical" formula:[8]

$$n\,\mathrm{Ach}_3\,n\,\mathrm{Pow}_4(n\,\mathrm{Aff}_{<4})\mathrm{SCT}_{2+}$$

where

n Ach = Achievement motivation
n Pow = Power motivation
n Aff = Affiliation motivation
SCT   = Self-control

and subscripts 0 to 4 represent amount or energy level on a scale: 0 = none, 1 = low-moderate, 2 = moderate, 3 = moderate-high, 4 = high.

Competency *clusters* correspond to "macromolecules" or chemical families: competencies that often are used together, or that share a common level. For example, three competencies (Directing Others, Developing Others, and Team Leadership) usually appear together in studies of managers, so are discussed together as a Managerial competency cluster. Motives and traits can be grouped together as deep characteristics of people that drive and direct behavior and are relatively hard to teach or change.

More precise measurement of both competencies and situational contexts will provide more algorithms, that is, IF job situation S_1, THEN use of competencies C_1, C_2, and C_3 (or the combined "molecule" of competencies $C_1C_2C_3$) is most likely to result in superior performance. Several research studies are underway to develop a topology or periodic table of job situations, investigate how competencies are expressed in different situational contexts, and identify algorithms and combinational rules.

4. *Increased Use of Competency-Based Selection with Diverse Populations.* Better competency assessment methods will better reveal what people *can* do—regardless of race, age, sex, formal education, credentials, or previous work histories.

For example, a 15-year experiment funded by the Fund for the Improvement of Post-Secondary Education (FIPSE) and conducted by the Center for Adult Experiential Education (CAEL) has tested the use of competencies to select nontraditional students (poor minorities, older women returning to education after raising families) on the basis of competencies assessed using the Behavioral Event Interview. Competencies predict success in college, account for variance in performance not predicted by traditional college admissions tests, do not discriminate on the basis of age or sex, and cause less adverse impact on the basis of race.[9]

CAEL is now experimenting with an "Employee Potential Program" that uses competencies to select "underclass" youth with few formal work or educational qualifications into jobs and remedial education programs to prepare for employment. Based on the Student Potential Program, competencies employers should look for in selecting potential employees from disadvantaged populations include:

- *Motivation to Learn.* Achievement motivation and initiative
- *Tenacity.* The perseverance and ego strength needed to complete remedial education and/or job training programs
- *Organizational Commitment.* Motivation to fit in (adopt prevailing business dress and work behaviors, e.g., punctuality) and stay with the organization that has invested in the employees' training rather than using their new skills to get a job elsewhere

- *Interpersonal Skills.* Understanding, flexibility, collaborativeness, and customer service orientation sufficient to work effectively with co-workers and customers who may represent very different cultural and behavioral norms; and socialized power and influence skills needed to confront and change organizational attitudes or practices when mutual accommodation is required

5. *Use of Computers and Artificial Intelligence Programs.* These will evolve into "integrated human resource information systems" that will help

- Determine the competency requirements of jobs
- Assess employees' competencies (e.g., advances in voice recognition "natural language" computer linguistics may enable a computer to "listen to," score—and perhaps even conduct—Behavioral Event Interviews in real time)
- Make optimum job–person matches using increasingly sophisticated pattern-matching algorithms
- Provide development advice or actual training based on assessed gaps between competencies people have and those needed to perform their jobs well
- Provide "help screen" information and assistance, including "modeling" examples of how to handle any of many difficult interpersonal situations

These services will all be on line and instantly available to managers and employees wherever they are. Computers will keep up-to-date inventories of the competencies of all people in an organization, so that it can instantly know what and where its human assets are to respond to any opportunity or change in its environment.

CONCLUSION

Human resources management adds value when it helps individuals and organizations do *better* than their present level of performance. The competency methods described in this book focus on identifying those measurable and developable human characteristics that (with good job–person matches) predict *superior* job performance and satisfaction—without race, age, gender, culture, or credential bias. The competency approach is fairer, freer, and more effective. Competencies provide a common language and method that can integrate all human resource functions and services—selection, performance appraisal, career and succession planning, training and development, and compensation—to help people, firms, and even societies be more productive in the challenging years ahead.

NOTES

1. Johnson, W. B., & Packer, A. E. (1987), *Workforce 2000: Work and workers for the 21st century*, Indianapolis: Hudson Institute.

2. Spencer, L. M. (1991), Job competency assessment, in H. Glass (Ed.), *Handbook of business strategy*, Boston: Warren, Gorham & Lambert.

3. Naisbitt, T., & Aburdene, P. (1985), *Reinventing the Corporation*, New York: Warner Books, (see especially Chapter 4, The Skills of the New Information Society, pp. 119f.); Howard, A. (1991, April 12), New directions for human resources practice. In D. W. Bray, (Ed.), *Working with organizations and their people: A guide to human resources practice*, New York: Guilford Press; and Howard, A. (1991), *Personal characteristics for a post-industrial society*, Paper presented at the Personnel Testing Conference of Southern California Spring Conference, Ontario, CA.

4. As anticipated by Kotter, J. (1985), *Power and influence*, New York: Free Press.

5. Mansfield, R. S., & Mumford, S. (n.d.), A competency-based approach to intercultural relations, Boston: McBer.

6. The idea of "atoms" (things that cannot be cut or divided) of the human mind is a tradition in Western philosophy dating at least from Democritus (c. 420 BC). It is echoed in John Stuart Mills' division of the mind into thinking, feeling, and doing faculties, and Sigmund Freud's id, ego, and superego. Perhaps best known is the German philosopher Gottfried Liebnitz's concept of "monads": absolutely simple entities, ultimate units of being, of which human minds and souls are made. Liebnitz believed monads developed independently and any inter-relations among them resulted from coincidental "harmonies," not causal interactions. Our view is more "chemical" and socio-biological. Competencies group logically to cause behaviors which have adaptive value: help people act effectively to survive and prevail.

7. McClelland, D. C. (1975), *Power: The inner experience*, New York: Irvington; McClelland, D. C., & Boyatzis, R. E. (1982), The Leadership Motive Pattern and long term success in management, *Journal of Applied Psychology, 67,* 737–743.

8. The idea of expressing competencies in "chemical" formulas we owe to John Raven, PhD.

9. Austin, A. W., Inouye, C. J., & Korn, W. S. (1986), *Evaluation of the CAEL Student Potential Program*, Los Angeles: University of California, Los Angeles.

Bibliography

Alshuler, A. S. (1973). *Developing achievement motivation in adolescents.* Englewood Cliffs, NJ: Education Technology Publications.

Argyris, C., Putnam, R., & Smith, D. M. (1987). *Action science.* San Francisco: Jossey-Bass.

Argyris, C., & Schon, D. A. (1974). *Theory in practice: Increasing professional effectiveness.* San Francisco: Jossey-Bass.

Atkinson, J. W. (Ed.). (1958). *Motives in fantasy, action and society.* New York: Van Nostrand.

Austin, A. W., Inouye, C. J., & Korn, W. S. (1986). *Evaluation of the CAEL Student Potential Program.* Los Angeles: University of California, Los Angeles.

Avner, B. D., & Williams, J. E. (1986, December 1). Career directions: An integrated personnel system. In *Prentice Hall Personnel Management: Policies and Practices Service.* Englewood Cliffs, NJ: Prentice-Hall.

Bales, R. F., & Cohen, S. P. (1979). *SYMLOG.* New York: Free Press.

Bandura, A. (1969). *Principles of behavior modification.* New York: Holt, Rinehart & Winston.

Bandura, A. (1977). *Social learning theory.* Englewood Cliffs, NJ: Prentice-Hall.

Bandura, A. (1986). *Social foundations of thought and action: A social cognitive theory.* Englewood Cliffs, NJ: Prentice-Hall.

Barrett, G. V., & Depinet, R. L. (1991). A reconsideration of testing for competence rather than intelligence. *American Psychologist, 46,* (10), 1012–1024.

Bellak, A. O. (1981). The Hay Guide Chart-Profile Method of Job Evaluation. In M. Rock (Ed.), *The compensation handbook* (2nd ed.,) New York: McGraw-Hill.

Block, J. H. (Ed.) (1971). *Mastery learning: Theory and practice.* New York: Holt, Rinehart & Winston.

Bloom, B. S. (1976). *Human characteristics and school learning.* New York: McGraw-Hill.

Boyett, J. H., & Conn, H. P. (1991). *Workplace 2000*. New York: Dutton.

Boyatzis, R. E. (1972). *A two factor theory of affiliation motivation*. Unpublished doctoral dissertation, Harvard University.

Boyatzis, R. E. (1973). The need for close relationships and the manager's job. Boston: McBer.

Boyatzis, R. E. (1982). Competence at work. In A. Stewart (Ed.), *Motivation and society*. San Francisco: Jossey-Bass.

Boyatzis, R. E. (1982). *The competent manager: A model for effective performance*. New York: Wiley.

Boyatzis, R. E. (1984). *Identification of skill requirements for effective job performance*. Boston: McBer.

Boyatzis, R. E. (1989) The impact of an MBA programme on managerial abilities. *Journal of Management Development, 8,* 66–76.

Boyatzis, R. E. (in press). Developing the whole student: An MBA required course in managerial assessment and development. *Journal of Management Education*.

Boyatzis, R. E., & Burruss, J. A. (1977). *Validation of a competency model for alcoholism counsellors in the U.S. Navy*. Boston: McBer.

Boyatzis, R. E., Cowen, S. S. & Kolb, D. A. (1992, May). Implementing curriculum reform in higher education: Year one of the new Weatherhead MBA program. *Selections, 8*(1), 27–37.

Boyle, S. (1988). Can behavioral interviews produce results? *Guidance and Assessment Review, 4*(1), 4–6. Leicester, UK: British Phychological Society.

Bray, D. W. (1991, April 12). *Assessment center methodology in evaluating personal characteristics*. Paper presented at the Personnel Testing Conference of Southern California Spring Conference. Ontario, CA.

Buchhorn, D. (1991). *Behavioral Event Interview quantitative results*. New York: L'Oreal Corporation.

Burke, M. J., & Day, R. R. (1986). A cumulative study of the effectiveness of managerial training. *Journal of Applied Psychology, 71,* 232–245.

Caldwell, D. F. (1991, April 12). *Soft skills, hard numbers: Issues in person–job/person–organization fit*. Paper presented at the Personnel Testing Conference of Southern California Spring Conference. Ontario, CA.

Caldwell, D. F., & O'Reilly, C. A. (1990). Measuring person-job fit with a profile-comparison process. *Journal of Applied Psychology, 75,* 648–657.

Carkhuff, R. R. (1969). *Helping and human relations* (Vols. I & II). New York: Holt, Rinehart & Winston.

Carkhuff, R. R. (1973). *The art of helping*. Amherst MA: Carkhuff Associates.

Carkhuff, R. R., & Berenson, B. G. (1976). *Teaching as treatment*. Amherst, MA: Human Resource Development Press.

Cascio, W. F. (1982). *Costing human resources: The financial impact of behavior in organizations*. Boston: Kent Publishing.

Clark, R. (1983). *Family life and school achievement: Why poor black children succeed or fail*. Chicago: University of Chicago Press.

Crane, D. (1972). *Invisible colleges*. Chicago: University of Chicago Press.

Cronbach, L. J., & Glesser, G. C. (1953). Assessing similarities between profiles. *Psychological Bulletin, 50,* 456–473.

Davis, R. (1991). Vocational interests, values and preferences. In M. D. Dunnette and L. M. Hough, (Eds.), *Handbook of industrial and organizational psychology* (Vol. 2). Palo Alto, CA: Consulting Psychologists Press.

deCharms, R. (1968). *Personal causation.* New York: Academic Press.

deCharms, R. (1976). *Enhancing motivation: Change in the classroom.* New York: Irvington.

Dreyfus, C. (1990). *Scientists and engineers as effective managers: A study of the development of interpersonal abilities.* Unpublished doctoral dissertation, Case Western Reserve University Weatherhead School of Management, Department of Organizational Behavior, Cleveland, Ohio.

Dufetel, L. (1991, July). Job evaluation still at the frontier. *Compensation and Benefits Review.* New York: American Management Association, July-Aug. 1991, 53–67.

Fallows, J. (1985, December). The case against credentialism. *The Atlantic Monthly,* 49–67.

Fischer, K. W., Hand, H. H., & Russell, S. (1984). The development of abstractions in adolescence and adulthood. In M. L. Commons, et al. (Eds.), *Beyond formal operations: Late adolescent and adult cognitive development.* New York: Praeger.

Flanagan, J. C. (1954). The critical incident technique. *Psychological Bulletin, 51,* 327–358.

Ghiselli, E. E. (1969). *The validity of occupational aptitude tests.* New York: Wiley.

Glaser, B., & Straus, A. (1967). *The discovery of grounded theory.* Chicago: Aldine.

Goldstein, I. L. (1991). Training in work organizations. In M. D. Dunnette & L. M. Hough (1991). *Handbook of industrial and organizational psychology.* Palo Alto, CA: Consulting Psychologists Press.

Goleman, D. (1981, January). The new competency tests: Matching the right people to the right jobs. *Psychology Today,* 35–46.

Goodson, B., & Hess, R. (1975). *Parents as teachers of young children: An evaluative review.* Palo Alto, CA: Stanford University Press.

Guion, R. M. (1991). Personnel assessment, selection and placement. In M. D. Dunnette & L. M. Hough (Eds.), *Handbook of industrial and organizational psychology.* Palo Alto, CA: Consulting Psychologists Press.

Harris, M. M. (1989). Reconsidering the employment interview: A review of recent literature and suggestions for future research. *Personnel Psychology, 42,* 4 (Winter), 691–726.

Hay Systems. (1988). *Strategic management simulations.* Washington DC: Hay Systems Inc.

Heckhausen, H., & Krug, S. (1982). Motive modification. In A. Stewart (Ed.), *Motivation and society.* San Francisco, CA: Jossey-Bass.

Hofrichter, D. (1990, April 1). *Comparative competency analysis and recommendations on XYZ Executive Assessments.* Paper presented at the 1990 Annual Conference of the Human Resource Planning Society, Naples, FL.

Hofrichter, D., & Myszkowski, G. J. (1989). Developing managers who can implement the strategy: Competency-based succession planning. In H. E. Glass (Ed.), *Handbook of business strategy: 1898/1990 yearbook.* Boston: Warren, Gorham & Lamont.

Hogan, R. T. (1991). Personality and personality measurement. In M. D. Dunnette & L. M. Hough (Eds.), *Handbook of industrial and organizational psychology.* Palo Alto, CA: Consulting Psychologists Press.

Howard, A. (1991). New Directions for human resources practice. In D. W. Bray (Ed.), *Working with organizations and their people: A guide to human resources practice.* New York: Guilford Press.

Howard, A. (1991, April 12). *Personal characteristics for a post-industrial society.* Paper presented at the Personnel Testing Conference of Southern California Spring Conference. Ontario, CA.

Hunter, J. E., Schmidt, F. L., & Judiesch, M. K. (1990). Individual differences in output variability as a function of job complexity. *Journal of Applied Psychology, 75*(1), 28–42.

Jacobs, R. (1991). *Moving up the corporate ladder: A longitudinal study of motivation, personality and managerial success in women and men.* Doctoral dissertation, Boston University. Boston: McBer.

Jacques, E. (1989). *Requisite organization.* Arlington, VA: Cason Hall.

Janz, T. (1982). Initial comparisons of patterned Behavioral Description interviews versus unstructured interviews. *Journal of Applied Psychology 67,* 577–580.

Jobs for the Future. (1986). *Executive report of jobs for Connecticut's future.* Somerville, MA: Jobs for the Future.

Jobs for the Future. (1991). *Economic change and the American workforce.* Somerville, MA: Jobs for the Future.

Johnson, W. B., & Packer, A. E. (1987). *Workforce 2000: Work and workers for the 21st century,* Indianapolis: Hudson Institute.

Kane, J., & Lawler, E. (1979). Methods of peer assessment. *Psychological Bulletin, 85*(3), 555–586.

Kelner, S. P. (1991). Interpersonal motivation: Positive, cynical and anxious. *Unpublished doctoral dissertation,* Boston University.

Knowles, M. (1971). *The modern practice of adult education: Andragogy versus pedagogy.* New York: Association Press.

Kobasa, S. C., Maddi, S. R., & Kahn, S. (1982). Hardiness and health: A prospective study. *Journal of Personality and Social Psychology, 42,* 168–177.

Kolb, D. (1984). *Experiential learning.* Englewood Cliffs, NJ: Prentice-Hall.

Kolb, D. A., & Boyatzis, R. E. (1967). Goal-setting and self-directed behavior change. *Human Relations, 23*(5), 439–457.

Kolb, D. A., & Boyatzis, R. E. (1970). On the dynamics of the helping relationship. *Journal of Applied Behavioral Science, 6*(3), 267–289.

Kotter, J. (1982). *The general managers.* New York: Free Press.

Kotter, J. (1985). *Power and influence.* New York: Free Press.

Lambert, C. (1990, November–December). The electronic tutor. *Harvard Magazine,* 42–51.

Landa, L. (1974). Algorithmization in learning and instruction. Englewood Cliffs, NJ: Learning Technology Publications.

Latham G. P., & Locke, E. A. (1979, Autumn). Goal setting: A motivational technique which works. *Organizational Dynamics,* 68–80.

Latham, G. P., & Saari, L. M. (1979). Application of social learning theory to training supervisors through behavior modelling. *Journal of Applied Psychology, 64,* 239–246.

Latham, G. P., & Saari, L. M. (1984). Do people do what they say? Further studies on the situational interview. *Journal of Applied Psychology, 69,* 569–573.

Latham, G. P., Saari, L. M., Pursell, E. D., & Campion, M. A. (1980). The situational interview. *Journal of Applied Psychology, 65,* 422–427.

Lawrence, P. R., & Lorsh, J. W. (1967, November–December). New management job: The integrator. *Harvard Business Review, 45*(6), 142–151.

Lawton, G. W., & Borman, W. C. (1978). Constructing stimuli with known true scores for determining validity of rating scales. *Proceedings: Sixth Annual Symposium on Psychology in the Department of Defense.* Colorado Springs: U.S. Air Force Academy Department of Behavioral Sciences and Leadership.

Lewin, A. Y., & Zwany, A. (1976). *Peer nominations: A model, literature critique, and a paradigm for research.* Springfield, VA: National Technical Information Service.

Litwin, G., & Stringer, R. (1968). *Motivation and organizational climate.* Boston: Harvard Business School Research Press.

Livingston, J. S. (1969, July–August). Pygmalion in management. *Harvard Business Review,* 81–89.

Locke, E. A. (1976). The nature and causes of job satisfaction. In M. Dunnette (Ed.), *Handbook of Industrial and Organizational Psychology* (pp. 1328–1330). Chicago: Rand McNally.

Mager, R. F. (1982). *Troubleshooting the troubleshooting course.* Belmont, CA: David Lake Publishers.

Mahler, W. R., & Drotter, S. J. (1986). *The succession planning handbook for the chief executive.* Midland Park, NJ: Mahler Publishing.

Mansfield, R. S., McClelland, D. C., Spencer, L. M., & Santiago, J. (1987). *The identification and assessment of competencies and other personal characteristics of entrepreneurs in developing countries.* Final Report: Project No. 936-5314, Entrepreneurship and small enterprise development, Contract No. DAN-5314-C-00-3065-00. Washington, DC: United States Agency for International Development; Boston: McBer.

Mansfield, R. S., & Mumford, S. (1982). A competency-based approach to intercultural relations. In R. S. Mansfield (Ed.), *Advanced intercultural relations workshop design.* Boston: McBer.

Mansfield, R. S. (1982). Review of empirical studies on overseas adjustment. In R. S. Mansfield, *Advanced intercultural relations workshop.* Boston: McBer.

Mayfield, E. C. (1964). The selection interview: A re-evaluation of published research. *Personnel Psychology, 17,* 239–249.

McBer. (1986). *Entrepreneurship and small-enterprise development: Second annual report.* Washington, DC: United States Agency for International Development; Boston: McBer.

McBer. (1987). *A history of the U.S. Navy Leadership and Management Education and Training Program.* Boston: McBer.

McBer. (1981, 1991). *Interviewing for competence.* Boston: McBer.

McBer. (1991). *Managerial Style Inventory technical manual.* Boston: McBer.

McBer. (1992). *Competency-based training seminar.* Boston: McBer.

McClelland, D. C. (1965). Toward a theory of motive acquisition. *American Psychologist, 20,* 321–333.

McClelland, D. C. (1972). What is the effect of achievement motivation training in the schools? *Teachers College Record, 74,* 129–145.

McClelland, D. C. (1973). Testing for competence rather than for intelligence. *American Psychologist, 28,* 1–14.

McClelland, D. C. (1975). A competency model for human resource management specialists to be used in the delivery of the human resource management cycle. Boston: McBer.

McClelland, D. C. (1975). *Power: The inner experience.* New York: Irvington.

McClelland, D. C. (1976). *The achieving society.* New York: Irvington.

McClelland, D. C. (1976). *A guide to job competence assessment.* Boston: McBer.

McClelland, D. C. (1978). Entrepreneurship and management in the years ahead. In C. A. Bramlette & M. H. Mecon (Eds.), *The individual and the future of organizations* (Vol. 7). Atlanta: Georgia State College of Business Administration. Also reprinted in McClelland, D. C. (1984). *Motives, personality and society.* New York: Praeger.

McClelland, D. C. (1978). *Guide to behavioral event interviewing.* Boston: McBer.

McClelland, D. C. (1984). *Motives, personality and society.* New York: Praeger.

McClelland, D. C. (1989). *Human motivation.* Cambridge, UK: Cambridge University Press.

McClelland, D. C. (in press). The knowledge testing-educational complex strikes back. *American Psychologist.*

McClelland, D. C., Atkinson, J. W., Clark, R. A., & Lowell, E. L. (1953). *The achievement motive.* New York: Appleton-Century-Crofts.

McClelland, D. C., & Boyatzis, R. E. (1982). The leadership motive pattern and long-term success in management. *Journal of Applied Psychology, 67*(6), 737–743.

McClelland, D. C., & Burnham, D. H. (1976, March–April). Power: The great motivator. *Harvard Business Review,* 159–166.

McClelland, D. C., & Dailey, C. (1972). Improving officer selection for the foreign service. Boston: McBer.

McClelland, D. C., & Dailey, C. (1973). Evaluating new methods of measuring the qualities needed in superior foreign service information officers. Boston: McBer.

McClelland, D. C., Davis, W. B., Kalin, R., & Wanner, E. (1972). *The drinking man: Alcohol and human motivation.* New York: Free Press.

McClelland, D. C., & Fiske, S. T. (1974). *Report to the Executive Office of Manpower Affairs on validation of a human service worker test.* Boston: McBer.

McClelland, D. C., Klemp, G. O., Jr., & Miron, D. (1977). Competency requirements of senior and mid-level positions in the Department of State. Boston: McBer.

McClelland, D. C., Koestner, R., & Weinberger, J. (1989). How do self-attributed and implicit motives differ? *Psychological Review, 96,* 690–702.

McClelland, D. C., & Winter, D. (1971). *Motivating economic achievement.* New York: Free Press.

McClelland, D. C., & Winter, D. G. (1978). Thematic analysis: An empirically derived measure of the effects of liberal arts education. *Journal of Educational Psychology, 79*(1), 8–16.

McGraw, K. L., & Harbison-Briggs, K. H. (1989). *Knowledge Acquisition: Principles and Guidelines.* Englewood Cliffs, NJ: Prentice-Hall.

Meyer, Herbert H., Kay, Emanuel, & French, John R. P. Jr. (1964). Split roles in performance appraisal. *Harvard Business Review 43:* 124–29.

Miller, G. A. (1956). The magical number seven, plus or minus two: some limits on our capacity for processing information. *Psychological Review, 63,* 81–97.

Miron, D. & McClelland, D. C. (1979). The effects of achievement motivation training on small business. *California Management Review,* 1979, *21*(4), 13–28.

Mischel, W. (1968). *Personality and Assessment.* New York: Wiley.

Mitchell, J. V. (1985). *The Ninth Mental Measurements Yearbook,* Vols. I and II. Lincoln, Nebraska: University of Nebraska Press.

Mowday, R. T., Porter, L. W., & Steers, R. M. (1982). *Employee-Organization Linkages: The psychology of commitment, absenteeism and turnover.* New York: Academic Press.

Murlis, H., & Fitt, D. (1991, May). Job evaluation in a changing world. *Personnel Management.*

Murlis, H. & Fitt, D. (1991). Evaluating skills, competencies and jobs. London: Hay Management Consultants.

Naisbitt, J., & Aburdene, D. (1985). *Re-inventing the Corporation.* New York: Warner Books.

Nowlen, P. M. (1988). *A new approach to continuing education for business and the professions: The performance model.* New York: Macmillan.

O'Malley, M. (1991). Integrating competencies into compensation planning and salary administration. Stamford, CT: Hay Management Consultants.

Opren, C. (1985). Patterned behavior description interviews versus unstructured interviews: A comparative study. *Journal of Applied Psychology, 70,* 774–776.

Orr, J. M., Mercer, M., & Sackett, P. R. (1989). The role of prescribed and nonprescribed behaviors in estimating the dollar value of performance. *Journal of Applied Psychology, 74,* 34–40.

Page, R. C. (1991). *Job–person similarity.* Minneapolis, MN: Hay Management Consultants.

Page, R. C., & DePuga, I. S. (1992, May 2). *Development and cross-cultural applications of a Competency Assessment Questionnaire.* Paper presented at the Seventh Annual Conference for Industrial and Organizational Psychology, Montreal, Quebec.

Page, R. C., & Van De Voort, D. M. (1989). Job analysis and HR planning. In W. Cascio (Ed.), *Human resource planning, employment and placement.* Washington, DC: BNA Books.

Pelz, D. C., & Andrews, F. M. (1976). *Scientists in organizations.* Ann Arbor, MI: Institute for Social Research, University of Michigan.

Pennington, H., Austin, J., & Flynn, E. (1991). Creating a market in education and training: The case of missing demand. Somerville, MA: Jobs for the Future.

Perkins, D. N. (1981). *The mind's best work.* Cambridge, MA: Harvard University Press.

Perkins, D. N. (1986). *Knowledge as design.* Hillsdale, NJ: Lawrence Erlbaum.

Piaget, J. (1965). *The child's conception of the world.* Totowa, NJ: Littlefield, Adams.

Piotrowski, Z. A., & Rock, M. (1963). *The Perceptanalytic Executive Scale.* New York: Grune & Stratton.

A plan to rate B-schools by testing students. (1979, November 19). *Business Week,* 171–174.

Primoff, E. (1973). *How to prepare and conduct job element examinations.* Washington, DC: U.S. Civil Service Commission.

Raven, J. (1977). *Education, values and society: The objectives of education and the nature and development of competence.* London: H. K. Lewis; New York: The Psychological Corp.

Raven, J. (1981). The most important problem in education is to come to terms with values. *Oxford Review of Education, 7*(3), 253–272.

Raven, J. (1987, Fall). Values, diversity and cognitive development. *Teachers College Record, 89,* 21–38.

Rich, D. (1988). *MegaSkills.* Boston: Houghton Mifflin.

Rondina, P. (1988, October 27–28). *Impact of competency-based recruiting techniques on dropout rates in sales training programs.* Paper presented at the McBer 25th Anniversary Symposium. Boston: McBer.

Rosenthal, R. (1973). Estimating effective reliabilities in studies that employ judges' ratings. *Journal of Clinical Psychology, 29,* 1–4.

Rosenthal, R. (Ed.). (1979). *Skill in non-verbal communication.* Cambridge, MA: Oelgeschlager.

Rosenthal, R., Archer, D., Koivunmaki, J. H., DiMatteo, M. R., & Rogers, P. (1974, January). Assessing sensitivity to nonverbal communications: The PONS test. *Division 8 Newsletter.* Washington DC: American Psychological Association.

Rosenthal, R., & Jacobson, L. (1968). *Pygmalion in the classroom.* New York: Holt, Rinehart & Winston.

Secretary's Commission on Achieving Necessary Skills (SCANS). (1991). *What work requires of schools: A SCANS report for America 2000.* Washington, DC: U.S. Department of Labor.

Secretary's Commission on Achieving Necessary Skills (SCANS). (1991). *Skills and tasks for jobs: A SCANS report for America 2000.* Washington, DC: U.S. Department of Labor.

Seligman, M. (1991). *Learned optimism.* New York: Knopf.

Shapero, A. (1989). *Managing professional people: Understanding creative performance.* New York: Free Press.

Siegel, S. (1956). *Nonparametric statistics for the behavioral sciences.* New York: McGraw-Hill.

Sloan, S., & Spencer, L. M. (1991, February 28). *Participant survey results: Hay Sales-force Effectiveness Seminar.* Atlanta: Hay Management Consultants.

Smith, M. (1988). Calculating the Sterling value of selection. *Guidance and Assessment Review, 4*(1). Leicester, UK: British Psychological Society.

Spangler, W. D. (1992). The validity of questionnaire and TAT measures of need for achievement: Two meta-analyses, *Psychological Bulletin, 112*(1), 140–154.

Spencer, L. M. (1978, April). The Navy Leadership and Management Training Program: A competency-based approach. *Proceedings for the Sixth Symposium: Psychology in the Department of Defense,* Colorado Springs: U.S. Air Force Academy Department of Behavioral Sciences and Leadership.

Spencer, L. M. (1983). *Soft skill competencies.* Edinburgh: Scottish Council for Research in Education.

Spencer, L. M. (1986, April 1). *An update on achievement motivation theory and entrepreneurship.* Paper presented at the Séminaire Entrepreneurship, École des Hautes Études Commerciales, L'Université de Montreal, Boston: McBer.

Spencer, L. M. (1986). *Calculating human resource costs and benefits.* New York: Wiley.

Spencer, L. M. (1989). Stimulating innovation and entrepreneurship in mature organizations. Boston: McBer.

Spencer, L. M. (1991). Job competency assessment. In H. Glass (Ed.), *Handbook of business strategy.* Boston: Warren, Gorham & Lambert.

Spencer, L. M., McClelland, D. C., & Spencer, S. M. (1990, August). *A history and state of the art of job competency assessment methods.* Paper presented at the American Psychological Association Annual Conference, Boston: McBer.

Sternberg, R. J. (1986). *Intelligence applied.* San Diego: Harcourt, Brace Jovanovich.

Sternberg, R. J., & Wagner, R. K. (Eds.). *Practical intelligence.* Cambridge, UK: Cambridge University Press.

Stewart, A. (Ed.) (1982). *Motivation and society.* San Francisco: Jossey-Bass.

Straus, A., & Corbin, J. (1990). *Basics of qualitative research: Grounded theory procedures and techniques.* Newbury Park, CA: Sage.

Streufert, S., & Swezey, R. (1986). *Complexity, managers and organizations.* New York: Academic Press.

Uniform Guidelines on Employee Selection Procedures. (1978). *Federal Register, 43*(166), 38290–38309.

Varga, K. (1977). Who gains from achievement motivation training? *Vikalpa: The Journal for Decision Makers.* Ahmedabad, India: Indian Institute of Management, 2, 187–200.

Wiley, R. (1990). MIS managerial and technical jobs: Measured competency differences. Boston: Hay Management Consultants.

Winter, D. G. (1973). *The power motive.* New York: Free Press.

Winter, D. G., & Healy, J. M. (1982). *An integrated system for scoring motives in running text: Reliability, validity, and convergence.* Paper presented at the American Psychological Association, Los Angeles, 1981. Department of Psychology, Wesleyan University.

Winter, D. G., & McClelland, D. C. (1978). Thematic analysis: An empirically derived measure of the effects of liberal arts education, *Journal of Educational Psychology,* *70*(I), 8–16.

Winter, D. G., McClelland, D. C., & Stewart, A. J. (1981). *A new case for the liberal arts.* San Francisco: Jossey-Bass, pp. 32–35.

Zullow, H. M., Oettingen, G., Peterson, C., & Seligman, M. E. (1988). Pessimistic explanatory style in the historical record. *American Psychologist, 43*(9), 673–682.

Index

References to tables and figures are set in **boldface**.

A

Accountability:
  future jobs and, 110
  identification of, 100
Achievement and action cluster:
  Achievement orientation, 25–29, **26–27**
  Concern for order, quality and accuracy,
    29–31, **30**
  Information seeking, 34–36, **35**
  Initiative, 31–34, **32**
Achievement motivation:
  future research in, 344
  generally, 22
  self-directed change and, 289
  training in, see Achievement motivation
    training
Achievement Motivation Training:
  benefits of, 299, **299**
  process of, 298–299
Achievement orientation (ACH):
  common behaviors, 28
  defined, 25
  dimensions of, 25, 28
  entrepreneurial risk taking and, 21, 29
  examples, 28–29
  in executives, 214–215
  in factory workers, 28
  in general managers, 66, 214
  generic models and, 160
  in human service professionals, 197
  in janitors, 28
  links with other competencies, 29, 31, 43,
    58, 60–61, 66–67, 77
  in management:
    generally, 203–204, 211, 213
    research and development, 218
  in researchers, 164
  in salespeople, 172, 176–177, 184, 213
  scales of, 22, **26–27**
  in scientists, 164
  significance of, 336
  in technical/professionals, 162, 164, 170, 214
  titles for, 25

Acquisition of (technical) expertise (EXP C):
  generally, 73, 77
  links with other competencies, 36
Acquisitions, succession planning and, 279
Action behaviors, 12, 21
Adult education/training, 338
Affiliation, motivation by, 22
Affiliative interest:
  in client relationship manager, 88
  interpersonal understanding and, 189
  in teachers, 88, 192
  uniqueness of, 88
Airline scheduling test, 248
Alcoholism counselors:
  competency of, 191
  competency identification in, 137
  developing others in, 198
  developmental skills in, 188
  flexibility in, 196
  performance criteria, 96
  professional expertise in, 193
  self-control in, 193
Algorithms, 126, 145, 147, 155
American Association of Collegiate Schools
    of Business (AACSB), 339
American Management Association, 291
Analysis, thematic, see Thematic analysis
Analytic thinking, 11
Analytical Thinking (AT):
  behavioral indicators, 68–69
  defined, 68
  dimension of, 68
  examples, 69–70
  in human service professionals, 194–195
  links with other competencies, 29, 31, 34,
    36, 43, 72–73, 77
  in management, 205–206
  in salespeople, 181
  scale, **69**
  in technical/professionals, 164–166
  titles for, 68
Anecdotes, in competency reports, 154
Apprenticeships, 338–339

Argument, analysis of, 248
Argyris, Chris, 115
Army officers, *see* Military officers
Army soldiers, direct observation of,
    103–104
Artificial intelligence programs, in future
    research, 347
Assessment centers, 242, 251–253
Assessors, assessment method training, 241
Authoritative managerial, links with other
    competencies, 86
Automobile manufacturer:
    compensation system case study, 313–314
    performance management case study,
        273–275

B

Bank managers, unusual competencies in, 89
Bank trust officers:
    cognitive competencies in, 67
    performance of, 137
Behavioral codebook, *see* Competency
    codebook
Behavioral Description Index (BDI), 250
Behavioral Event Interview (BEI):
    advantages of, 98–99
    analysis of:
        confirmation of, 151
        thematic, *see* Thematic analysis
    behavioral events:
        key questions, 124
        problems/solutions, 129–131
        technique pointers:
            don'ts, 127–129
            do's, 124–127
            generally, 129
    career path, 122
    characteristics needed for job:
        objectives of, 131–132
        problems/solutions, 132
        technique pointers, 132
    conclusion, 132–134
    confidentiality of, 120
    development of, 5, 97–98
    disadvantages, 99
    discrepancies in, 151
    dramatic dialogue form, 126
    evidence, checking on, 103
    explanation and introduction:
        problems/solutions, 121–122
        purpose of, 119
        technique pointers, 121
    "focused," 125, 127
    interpretation, 133–134
    job responsibilities:
        problems/solutions, 123–124
        questions regarding, 122
        technique pointers, 122–123
    outline of, 119

preparation for, 118–119
    reinforcement, 127
    in selection process, 246–247
    short competency model, role in, 108
    spreadsheets, 151, **152, 154**
    summary, 132–134
    tape-recording of, permission for, 120–121
    transcripts, coding of:
        example, **143–144**
        significance of, 135–136, 145
        types of, 143
Behavioral indicators:
    function of, 19–20
    future research and, 345
    See also specific competencies
Biodata, 242, 253
Boss-to-subordinate relationship, 58
Boyatzis, Richard, 19, 199
Brainstorming, 169
Brainwashing, 289
Business managers, performance criteria for,
    94
Business-mindedness, links with other
    competencies, 43
Business production game, 252
Business situations exercise, 231, 236

C

California Personality Inventory, 250
Career paths:
    job-matching and, 259
    progression maps, 276
    system development, 281
    See also Succession planning
Case Western Reserve Weatherhead School of
    Business, 339
Causal relationships:
    causal flow models, 12, **13**
    defined, 9
Center for Adult Experiential Education
    (CAEL), 346
Change implementation, future trends and,
    343
Chief engineers, performance of, 129
Children, competency development in:
    parent's role in, 339–340
    school's role in, 335–339
Churchill, Winston, 289
Classical competency studies:
    criteria sample, identification of, 96–97
    data analysis, 104–105
    data collection:
        behavioral event interviews, 97–99
        computer-based expert systems,
            101–102
        direct observation, 103–104
        expert panels, 99–100
        job/function analysis, 102–103
        surveys, 100–101

model:
    applications preparation, 106
    development, 104–105
    validation of, 105–106
performance effectiveness criteria, 94, 96
process, **95**
Client-relationship managers:
    affiliative interest in, 88
    customer service orientation in, 43, 51
    unique competencies in, 88
Clusters:
    future research in, 346
    identification of, 19
    See also specific competency clusters
Coast Guard officers:
    cognitive competencies in, 67
    unusual competencies in, 89
Coding, methods of, 143
Cognitive competencies:
    Analytical Thinking, 68–70, **69–70**
    Conceptual Thinking, 70–73, **71**
    function of, 67
    technical/professional/managerial expertise,
        73–77, **74–76**
Collaborativeness:
    future trends and, 344
    significance of, 336
College deans, articulateness of, 141
College teacher, competency model for,
    148–149, **149**
Combinational rules, future research of, 345
Commercial loan officers, cognitive
    competencies in, 67
Communications:
    concrete style of, 88
    LANS, 322
    management-employee, 318, 320
    upward, 88
Compensation systems, defined, 304–305
Competency, defined, 9
Competency Assessment Questionnaire,
    253–254
Competency-based pay, job-matching and,
    259
Competency characteristics, development of,
    5
Competency codebooks:
    development of, 105
    function of, 149
    preparation of, 151
    refinement of, 150
Competency dictionary:
    caution regarding, 23–24
    generic levels, 148
Competency model reports, format options,
    153–155
Competency Q-Sort, 254
Competency studies, design of:
    classic studies, 94–109

preparatory work, 93–94
    See also Classical competency studies
Competition, future trends and, 342
Computer-assisted training, 295
Computer-based expert systems:
    advantages of, 102
    disadvantages of, 102
    expert panel members and, 108
    function of, 101
Computer professionals, technical expertise
    in, 168
Computer programmers, competency
    identification in, 137
Computer software professionals:
    achievement orientation in, 213
    impact and influence in, 164
    technical expertise in, 168
Computers, future research and, 347
Concept formation, 104
Conceptual Thinking (CT):
    behavior descriptions of, 71
    defined, 11, 70
    dimensions of, 70–71
    examples, 72
    in human services management, 195, 218
    links with other competencies, 29, 34, 36,
        43, 57, 72–73, 77, 86, 88
    in management, 210
    in salespeople, 72, 182
    scale, **71**
    significance of, 336
    in technical/professionals, 164–165
    titles for, 70
Concern for order, quality and accuracy
    (CO):
    defined, 29
    dimensions of, 30
    examples of, 31
    executives and, 215
    links with other competencies, 31
    in management:
        in armed forces, 219
        generally, 211, 213
        in military officers, 219
    scale of, **30**
    in technical/professionals, 167–168
    titles for, 29–30
Concurrent construct validation, 106
Concurrent cross-validation, 105–106
Confidentiality, significance of, 120
Conflict resolution, 23, 169, 205
Connecticut, competency study in, 328–329
Consultant(s):
    achievement orientation in, 197
    compensation system case study, 312–313
    competency identification in, 137–138
    customer service orientation in, 193–194
    developing others in, 188
    flexibility in, 196

Consultant(s) *(Continued)*
  impact and influence in, 47
  interpersonal understanding in, 189–190
  nonverbal cues and, 251
  organizational awareness in, 50
  outcomes, 140
  self-confidence in, 81
  teamwork and cooperation in, 194
  technical knowledge of, 193
  thoughts, 138
Content analysis of verbal expression (CAVE), 5
Cooperative learning, 338
Cost-benefit analysis:
  management goal-setting and, 204, 215
  multiskilling, 308
  training and development, 294
Counselors:
  affiliative interest in, 192
  analytical thinking in, 195
  initiative in, 195
Creative designers, competency identification
    in, 138
Criterion reference:
  defined, 9
  significance of, 13–15
Criterion samples, use of, 3
Criterion validity, emphasis on, 7
Critical incidents, 5, 98, 112, 123–125. *See
    also* Behavioral Event Interview (BEI)
Critical jobs, 94
Cross-cultural entrepreneurship competency
    study:
  assessment methods, development of:
    business situations exercise, 231
    criteria used, 228–229
    interview(s):
      focused, 229–230, 232, 234, 236
      information, 229
    picture story exercise, 231–233, 236
    pilot of, 232–233
    self-rating questionnaire, 230–231, 236
    SYMLOG (Systematic Multiple Level
        Observation of Groups), 230,
        232–234, 236
    validation samples, 232–234
  background questions, 221
  behavioral event interview method, 221–222
  business data included in, 221
  competency scores, factor analyses of, 226
  conclusions, 227, 238
  discriminant function analysis, 225
  generic competency model, **222–224**
  regression analyses, 225
  sample for, 220–221
  scores:
    differences among, 234
    relationship among, 234–235
    SYMLOG, 235
  t-tests, 224–225, 234

Cross-cultural interpersonal sensitivity:
  significance of, 37
  study of, 5
Cross-cultural sales, 174
Culture interventions, training and, 297
Customer Service Orientation (CSO):
  in client relationship manager, 43, 51
  defined, 40
  dimensions of, 41
  examples of, 43
  future trends in, 345
  in human service professionals, 192–194
  links with other competencies, 34, 36, 40,
      43, 53, 58, 73, 85
  in management, 214, 216–217
  in religious leaders, 40
  in salespeople, 178–181
  scale of, **41–42**
  in teachers, 40, 193–194
  in technical/professionals, 169
  titles for, 40
  "total quality" managers and, 155
  typical indications of, 41, 43
Customer Survey, 254

D

Data base, application of, 20
Deckhands, unusual competencies in, 89
Developing Others (DEV):
  common behaviors, 55, 57
  defined, 54
  dimensions of, 55
  examples of, 57
  in human service professionals, 188–189,
      192
  links with other competencies, 31, 34, 40,
      57
  in management:
    in armed forces, 219
    first-line supervisors, 213–214
    generally, 206–207, 211
    production management, 218
    sales managers, 184, 216
  in military officers, 57, 219
  scale, **55–56**
  in supervisors, 55
  in technical/professionals, 169
  titles for, 54–55
Development and career path manager, 318
Development centers, 295
Differentiating competencies, defined, 15
Diplomats:
  competency identification in, 137
  competency model for, 110
  Foreign Service Information Officers, 4–7,
      104–105
  nonverbal cues and, 251
  performance analysis of, 104–105
  physical appearance of, 141

Direct observation:
advantages of, 103–104
disadvantages of, 104
process of, 103
Direct persuasion:
management and, 202
in technical/professionals, 164
Directiveness: Assertiveness and Use of
Positional Power (DIR):
defined, 57–58
dimension of, 58
examples of, 60
in human service professionals, 196–197
links with other competencies, 31, 60–61, 80
in management:
executives, 215
generally, 58, 209, 215
research and development, 217
in salespeople, 58, 183–184
scale, **59**
in secretaries, 58
in technical/professionals, 169
titles for, 58
typical behaviors, 58, 60
Discovery learning, 337
Distribution of Expertise (EXP D), 73, 77
Downsizing, succession planning and, 279

E

Economics, effect on, 14–15
Ecuador, entrepreneurship study of, *see*
Cross-cultural entrepreneurship
competency study
Effective performance, defined, 13
Effort, amount of, 22
Employee Potential Program, 346
Employees, future research of, 344–345
Empowerment:
future trends and, 344
interview techniques for, 121, 124
significance of, 168
Engineers:
achievement orientation in, 162
self-confidence in, 167
Entrepreneurial innovation, future trends
and, 343
Entrepreneurial risks, management and, 21,
29, 204
Entrepreneurs:
cross-cultural study of, *see* Cross-cultural
entrepreneurship competency study
small-business:
actions, 140
motivation, 139
Environmental influences, 254, 323, 342
Executives:
achievement orientation in, 214–215
concern for order, quality and accuracy in,
215

directiveness: assertiveness and use of
positional power in, 215
future trends for, 343
organizational awareness in, 214–215
relationship building in, 214–215
self-control in, 215
Experiential education theory:
defined, 286
inputs, **287**
principles of, 286–287
Expert panels:
advantages of, 99
disadvantages of, 99–100
functions of, 99
future jobs and, 110
short competency model, role in, 108
Expert system, BEI analysis and, 151, 153

F

Fact finder, interview strategy, 117
Factory workers, achievement orientation in,
28
Failure, dealing with, 22, 81, 208
Feedback:
performance management and, 274
significance of, 184, 189
Feeder jobs, succession planning and, 280
First-line supervisors:
generally, 213
of hourly workers, 213
of technical/professional workers, 213–214
Fischer, K. W., 68
Flanagan, J. C., 5, 98
Flexibility (FLX):
behavioral indicators, 84
defined, 83–84
dimension of, 84
examples of, 84–85
future trends and, 343–344
in human service professionals, 196
links with other competencies, 29, 40,
85–86
in military officers, 84–85
scale, 85
in technical/professionals, 167, 169
titles for, 84
Flight attendants, performance management
case study, 270
Foreign Service Information Officers
(FSIOs), 4–7, 104–105
Fortune-teller, interview strategy, 117
Fragmentation, 318
Fund for the Improvement of Post-Secondary
Education (FIPSE), 346
Future jobs, approaches to:
expert panels and, 110
known job elements, correlation with, 110
present job analysis, 110–111
superior performance and, 111

Future trends:
  business environment, 342
  employee competencies, 344–345
  executive competencies, 343
  labor force, 342
  management competencies, 343–344
  research, 345–347

G

Generic models:
  coding models:
    indicators, interpretation of, 160–162
    procedure for, 159–160
  function of, 159
Government officials, articulateness of, 141
Graphs, in competency reports, 155
Group Management competency, 160

H

Helping and human service cluster:
  achievement orientation in, 197
  affiliative interest in, 192–193
  analytical thinking in, 194–195
  conceptual thinking in, 195
  competency cluster, 37
  customer service orientation in, 193–194
  developing others in, 188–189
  directiveness/assertiveness in, 196–197
  flexibility in, 196
  impact and influence in, 186, 188
  initiative in, 195–196
  interpersonal understanding and, 189–190
  management of, see Human services
      management
  occupational preference and, 191
  organizational commitment and, 191
  personal effectiveness cluster and, 185
  professional expertise in, 193
  self-assessment in, 191
  self-confidence in, 190–191
  self-control in, 191
  teamwork and cooperation in, 194
  workers, generic model of, **186–187**
  See also specific competencies
Hospitals, management of, 218–219
Human Resource Management Information
    System, development of, 281
Human resource planning, 11
Human resource professionals, single-number
    job competency studies, 111–113
Human service management:
  competencies in, 186, 197–198
  conceptual thinking in, 195
  future of, 342–347
  organizational commitment in, 218
  organizational strategy of, 94
Human service workers:
  achievement orientation in, 213
  analytical thinking in, 194–195

  customer orientation in, 192–194
  developing others in, 188–189, 192
  directiveness: assertiveness and use of
      positional power in, 196–197
  flexibility in, 196
  impact and influence in, 186, 188
  initiative in, 195–196
  interpersonal understanding in, 189–190
  nonverbal cues and, 251
  performance:
    actions and, 140
    criteria for, 96
  self-confidence in, 190–191
  self-control in, 191
  team leadership in, 218
  teamwork and cooperation in, 194
Hypothesis generation, 104

I

Iceberg model of central and surface
    competencies, **11**
Ideal Organizational Climate Survey, 250
Imagery, eliciting, 100
Impact, Achievement B subscale, 27
Impact and influence (IMP):
  common indicators, 45
  in consultants, 47
  dimensions of, 45
  examples of, 45, 47
  function of, 44
  in human service professionals, 186, 188
  links with other competencies, 34, 40,
      45, 47–48, 53, 64, 66–67, 73,
      80, 86
  in managers, 202–203, 215
  Managerial competencies and, see
      Managerial competencies
  in salespeople, 172, 174–176
  scale of, **46–47**
  significance of, 336
  in software engineers, 164
  in technical/professionals, 164–166
  titles for, 45
Impact and influence cluster:
  impact and influence, 44–48, **46–47**
  organizational awareness, 48–50, **49–50**
  relationship building, 50–53, **52**
In-Basket Exercises, 251
India, entrepreneurship study of, see
    Cross-cultural entrepreneurship
    competency study
Industrial psychology, traditional, 7
Influence cluster, 44. See also specific
    competencies
Information Seeking (INFO):
  defined, 34
  examples of, 35–36
  links with other competencies, 29, 36–38,
      43, 50, 72, 77

in management, 209–210, 213–214
in researchers, 168
in salespeople, 182–183
scale of, **35**
significance of, 336
in technical/professionals, 168
titles for, 34
Information-Seeking Motivation, future
trends in, 344
Initiative (INT):
characteristics of, 33
defined, 31
discretionary effort, 33
examples of, 33–34
in human service professionals,
195–196
links with other competencies, 29, 34,
36, 61, 67
in management, 31, 33, 206, 214
in researchers, 166
in salespeople, 177–178
scale of, **32**
significance of, 336
in technical/professionals, 166
time-span and, 33
titles for, 31
Innovation (ACH C), links with other
competencies, 27, 29, 57, 77
Integrated human resource management
information system (IHRMIS):
administration, 318
cases:
Nationwide Insurance, 320–321
U.S. Computer Company, 321–322
compensation system, 315
defined, 315
development:
advice, 317–318
planning worksheet, **319**
steps for, 320
as development and career path manager,
318
integrated usage of, **314**
job description/analysis, 316–317
job-person matching, 317
organizational chart, 316
organizational issues, 317, 320
people assessment, 317
performance appraisal system, 315
recruitment, 315
succession planning, 315
training and development:
assessment of, 318
job performance and, 315
Intellectual Initiative, 34
IQ scores, significance of, 12
Intent, 12
Interactive video-assisted training, 295–296
Internships, 338–339

Interpersonal skills:
in disadvantaged populations, 346
training in, 337–338
Interpersonal Understanding (IU):
defined, 37
dimensions of, 38
examples of, 38
future trends and, 343
in human service professionals, 189–190
links with other competencies, 36, 38, 40,
43, 47, 53, 57, 64, 85
in management, 203–204, 208–209, 214,
216
in salespeople, 178, 184
scale, **39**
significance of, 336
in technical/professionals, 167
titles for, 37–38
Interrater reliability, 105
Interviewing methods:
competency approach to, basic principle of,
115
traditional:
candidate motives and abilities, 115
examples of, 115–117
problems with, 117–118
See also Behavioral Event Interview (BEI)

J

Jacques, Eliot, 33
James, William, 13
Janitors, achievement orientation in, 28
Job assignments, developmental, 296–297
Job candidates:
overqualified, 23
succession planning and, 280–281
Job-competency approach, function of, 7–8
Job Competency Assessment (JCA) methods:
managers and, 199
short process, expert panels and, 107–109
Job Interview, selection test, 252
Job mismatches, 325
Job-person matching methods:
absolute value analysis, **256**
algorithms and, 256
career pathing, development of, 259
competency-based pay, 259
decisions, 241
generally, 254–257
integrated human resource management
information system, 317–318
job-person fit profile, **255**
management role in, 204
performance management, 259
Profile Comparison, 257
recruitment/selection, 257–258
succession planning/promotion, 258
training, development of, 259
Jobs for Connecticut's Future, 329

Job size, significance of, 67
Job task/function analysis:
    advantages of, 102–103
    disadvantages of, 103
    process, 102
Just-noticeable-difference (JND) scales:
    competency reports and, 154
    complexity, 21
    development of, 7, 20–21
    effort, amount of, 22
    impact, size of, 21
    intensity/completeness of action, 21
    new competencies, treatment as, 147–148
    unique dimensions, 22

K

Kennedy, John F., 289
King, Martin Luther, 289
Knowledge, significance of, 10–12
Knowledge engineering, 110–111, 127
Knowledge tests, 249

L

Labor force, future trends in, 342
Leaderless group exercises, 252
Leadership changes, future trends in, 343
Learning, concrete style of, 88
Learning ability, future trends and, 344
Learning motivation, in disadvantaged
    populations, 346
Litwin, G., 297

M

Macromolecules, 346
Malawi, entrepreneurship study of, see
    Cross-cultural entrepreneurship
    competency study
Management, failure of, 10, 81
Management-labor agreements, multiskilling,
    308
Managerial competencies:
    developing others, 54–57, **55–56**
    directiveness/assertiveness and use of
        positional power, 57–61, **59**
    support for, 67
    teamwork and cooperation, 61–64, **61–62**
    team leadership, 64–66, **66**
Managerial style, 254
Managers:
    achievement orientation in, 66, 203–204,
        211, 213–214
    analytical thinking in, 205–206
    in armed forces, 219
    behavioral event interview tips, 131
    competency clusters in, frequency of, **200**
    computer-based expert systems and, 101
    conceptual thinking in, 210
    concern for order in, 211
    credibility, establishment of, 211
    customer orientation in, 214, 216–217
    dealing with failure, 208
    developing others in, 206–207
    directiveness/assertiveness in, 58, 209
    direct persuasion, 202
    feelings, 139
    function models, 215–218
    future trends for, 343–344
    generic model of, **201**
    in human services, see Human service
        managers
    impact and influence in, 202–203, 215
    information seeking in, 209–210, 213–214
    initiative in, 31, 33, 206, 214
    interpersonal understanding in, 203–204,
        208–209, 214, 216
    levels of:
        executives and general managers,
            214–215
        first-line supervisors, 212–214
        middle management, 214
        types of, generally, 201
    marketing managers, 216–217
    motivation, 139
    organizational awareness in, 211, 214
    organizational commitment in, 214, 218
    outcomes, 140
    performance criteria of, 96
    production managers, 218
    relationship building in, 211, 214
    research and development managers,
        217–218
    sales managers, 216
    self-confidence in, 81, 207–208, 214
    self-control in, 78–79
    superior, 199
    team leadership in, 66, 210–211, 213
    teamwork and cooperation in, 63, 204–205,
        213
    technical, organizational strategy of, 93
    technical expertise in, 211–212, 217
    "total quality," 155
Manufacturing managers:
    physical setting and, 141
    thoughts, 138
Marketing managers, competencies in,
    216–217
Mastery learning, 337
McClelland, David C., 67–68, 97, 288
Measurement, advances in, 345
Mentors, significance of, 297
Mergers, succession planning and, 279
Microcoaching, 339
Middle management, 214
Military officers:
    behavioral event interview, sample of,
        116–117
    concern for order, quality and accuracy in,
        219

developing others in, 57, 219
on expert panels, 99–100
feelings, 139
flexibility in, 84–85
good criteria for, 96, 99
interviews with, 116–117
as managers, 219
motivation, 139
organizational awareness in, 219
performance criteria for, 96
physical setting and, 141
self-confidence in, 219
team leadership in, 219
thoughts, 138–139
unusual competencies in, 89
Molecules, 145, 345-346
Motive Acquisition, Theory of, 288
Motive competencies, 9–12

N

National Vocational Qualifications (NVQs),
    workforce planning system, 336
Nationwide Insurance, human resource
    management case study, 320–321
Navy officers:
  on expert panels, 99–100
  organizational commitment, 87
  performance criteria, 97
  superior performers, 98
Networking, 169, 180, 215
New competencies, treatment of, 147-148
Nonverbal cues tests, 251
Nurses:
  achievement orientation in, 197
  affiliative interest in, 192
  competency of, 191
  conceptual thinking in, 195
  developing others in, 188
  directiveness/assertiveness in, 196
  flexibility in, 196
  initiative in, 196
  professional expertise in, 193
  self-control in, 191
  technical knowledge in, 193
  unusual competencies in, 89

O

Observation data, BEI analysis and, 151
Occupational preferences, 88
Oil company technical
    professionals/managers, performance
    management case study, 272–272
Operations management, performance of, 128
Organizational Awareness (OA):
  in consultants, 50
  defined, 48
  dimensions of, 49
  examples of, 50
  in executives, 214–215
    in general managers, 211, 214
    indicators of, 49–50
    in management:
      in armed forces, 219
      generally, 211
    in military officers, 219
    links with other competencies, 40, 48, 50,
        66
    scale of, **49**
    in technical salespeople, 50
    titles for, 48–49
Organizational change:
    and selection, 240–241
    succession planning and, 279
Organizational climate, effect of, 254
Organizational Commitment (OC):
    behavioral indicators, 86
    defined, 86
    dimension of, 86
    in disadvantaged populations, 346
    examples of, 87–88
    links with other competencies, 88
    in management:
      generally, 214, 218
      in human service management, 218
      research and development management,
          218
    in navy officers, 87
    in researchers, 87
    scale, **87**
    titles for, 86
Organizational development consultants:
    conceptual thinking in, 195
    development skills in, 188
    directiveness/assertiveness in, 196
    function of, 23
Organizational psychology, traditional, 7
Organizational strategy, defining, 93–94
Organizational structure/design:
    competency model development and, 94
    training and development, 297
Organizational understanding, links with
    other competencies, 43

P

Panel, BEI analysis and, 151, 153
Parents, role of, 339–340
Pay, competency-based:
    base pay, 313–314, **313**
    boundaries, 310
    cases:
      automobile manufacturer, 313–314
      consultant, hiring of, 312–313
    cost-benefit justification, **309**
    defined, 305
    development steps:
      key factors, identification of, 306–310
      relative percentages, determination of,
          311–312, **311**

Pay, competency-based *(Continued)*
  input competencies, 307, 310
  need indications, 305–306
  output competencies, 307
  performance-based, 307
  system variables, **307**
Peer Coaching/Counseling Exercises, 253
Peer ratings:
  performance management and, 275
  significance of, 96
Performance:
  improvement of:
    method, 15
    obstacles to, 155
  as selection factor, 240
  See also specific careers/occupations
Performance appraisal, function of, 264
Performance Management System (PMS):
  behavior-anchored rating scales (BARS),
    271–272
  case studies:
    automobile manufacturer, 273–275
    flight attendants, 270
    oil company technical
      professionals/managers, 272–272
  competency-based:
    development steps, 268–270
    generally, 266, **266**
  defined, 264
  generic, **265**
  job-matching and, 259
  "mixed model" performance, 267, 269
  motivation and, 268
  organizational issues of, 267–268
  "self-directed change" and, 269–270
Personal effectiveness competencies:
  characteristics, generally, 88–89
  flexibility, 83–86, **85**
  organizational commitment, 86–88, **87**
  self-confidence, 80–83, **82**
  self-control, 78–80, **79**
  unusual competencies, 89
Personality tests, in selection process, 250
Peterson, C., 81
Physicians:
  competency of, 191
  conceptual thinking in, 195
  expertise in, 193
  initiative in, 196
  performance criteria, 96
  self-confidence in, 190
  self-control in, 191
Picture Story Exercise (PSE), 176, 231–232,
    236, 247–248
Pilots, thoughts of, 138
Planning and scheduling test, 248
Police captains, physical appearance of, 141
Populations, future research of, 346
Portability, future trends and, 344

Positive affiliation, in human service
    professionals, 192
Positive expectations of others, in human
    service professionals, 6, 105, 192
Power:
  in management, 203
  motivation by, 22
  need for, 44, 76
  See also Empowerment
Predictive validity, 106
Presentation vision/strategy speeches,
    251–252
Presidents, articulateness of, 141
Production managers, competencies in, 218
Professional expertise, in human service
    professionals, 193
Profile of Nonverbal Sensitivity (PONS), 7,
    250–251
Program Evaluation and Review Technique
    (PERT), 248
Programmed cases, 249
Programmer aptitude test, 248
Promotion:
  job-matching and, 258
  succession planning and, 279
Pygmalian effect, 193

Q

Questionnaires:
  Competency Assessment Questionnaire,
    253–254
  Self-rating questionnaire, 230–231, 236
  Seligman Attribution Style Questionnaire,
    249

R

Raven, John, 291
Recommendations, in competency report, 155
Rejection, fear of, 89
Relationship Building (RB):
  behavior indicators of, 51–52
  defined, 50
  dimensions of, 51
  examples of, 50–53
  in executives, 214–215
  in general managers, 214
  links with other competencies, 34, 40, 43,
    48, 50, 53, 66
  in management, 211
  in salespeople, 180–181
  scale of, **52**
  in technical/professionals, 169
  titles for, 51
Relationship management, future trends
    and, 343
Religious leaders, customer service
    orientation in, 40
Repair technician, high tech equipment,
    superior vs. average, 145–146, **146**

Research:
  future trends in, 345–347
  methods of, significance of, 3
Research and Development managers,
    competencies in, 217–218
Researchers:
  achievement orientation in, 164, 213
  computer-based expert systems and, 101
  information seeking in, 168
  initiative in, 166
  organizational commitment in, 87
Research scientists:
  performance criteria for, 94
  unusual competencies in, 89
Resources, inefficient use of, 318
Restricted range effect, 12
Rich, Dorothy, 340
Role plays, 252–253
Rorschach Test, 249

S

Sales managers:
  achievement orientation in, 214
  behavioral event interview, sample of, 115
  developing others in, 184, 216
  directiveness: assertiveness and use of
      positional power in, 184
  generally, 184
  interpersonal understanding in, 184
  teamwork and cooperation in, 216
Salespeople:
  achievement orientation in, 172, 176 177,
      184, 213
  analytical thinking in, 181
  behavioral event interview tips, 131
  "cold call," self-confidence in, 147
  competency model for, 110
  conceptual thinking in, 72, 182
  customer service orientation in, 178–181
  directiveness/assertiveness in, 58, 183–184
  on expert panels, 100
  failure in, 179
  feedback and, 184
  financial sales and, 171, 180–181, 183
  generic model of, 173
  impact and influence in, 172, 174–176
  information seeking in, 182–183
  initiative in, 177–178
  interpersonal understanding in, 178, 184
  interview strategy, 118
  job task/function analysis of, 103
  manager of, see Sales managers
  networking, 180
  Organizational awareness in, 50
  rejection and, 179
  relationship building in, 180–181
  retail sales, 176
  sales cycles and:
    intermediate, 171, 177, 181–182

long:
    characteristics, 172
    Conceptual thinking in, 182
    defined, 171
    strategies for, 175–176
    technical sales and 178–179, 181
  short:
    characteristics, 172
    defined, 171
  strategies for, 174
  self-confidence In, 81, 83, 179–180
  situation and, 137
  superior, 171
  surveys and, 100
  technical expertise in, 183
SCANS (Secretary's Commission on
    Achieving Necessary Skills) report,
    workforce planning system:
  competencies, 330–331, 333, 334–335
  economic trends and, 330, 334 336
  education:
    characteristics of, 335
    implications for, 336–339
    foundation skills, 334
    learning implications, 335–336
    parenting, implications for, 339–340
  proficiency levels:
    defined, 331
    "work-ready" levels, 335
School principals, unusual competencies in,
    89
Schools:
  education implications, 336–339
  management of, 218–219
  role of, 335–336
Scientists, achievement orientation in,
    164
Secretary, Directiveness: Assertiveness
    and Use of Positional Power in, 58
Selection, competency-based methods:
  assessment methods:
    assessment centers, 251–253
    Behavioral Event Interview (BEI),
        246–247, 258
    biodata, 253
    functions of, 242, 243–245
    ratings, 253–254
    tests:
      operant, 247–249
      respondent, 249–251
  case study of, performance and retention,
      259–261
  defined, 239
  development steps, 241–242
  job-person matching methods, see
      Job-person matching methods
  organization issues of, 240–241
Self-assessment, accurate, 88
Self-concept competencies, 10–12

Self-Confidence (SCF):
  behavioral descriptions, 81, 83
  in consultants, 81
  dealing with failure and, 22, 81, 147
  defined, 80
  dimension of, 81
  in engineers, 167
  examples of, 83
  independence variable of, 80–81
  in human service professionals, 190–191
  links with other competencies, 60, 64, 83,
    88
  in management:
    in armed forces, 219
    generally, 81, 207–208, 214
  in military officers, 219
  in salespeople, 81, 83, 179–180
  scale, **82**
  significance of, 336
  in technical/professionals, 167
  titles for, 81
Self-Control (SCT):
  behavioral indicators, 79–80
  defined, 78–79
  dimension of 79
  examples of, 80
  executives and, 215
  in human service professionals, 191
  links with other competencies, 80
  in management, 78–79
  scale, 79
  titles for, 79
Self-development resource guides, 295
Self-Directed Change Theory, 289–291
Self-rating questionnaire, 230–231, 236
Seligman, S., 81
Seligman Attributional Style Questionnaire,
  249
Short competency assessment (JCA):
  behavioral event interviews, 108
  data analysis, 109
  expert panels role in, 108
  model, development and validation of, 109
  process of, **107**, 113
Single-incumbent jobs, studies of, 111–113
Situational interactions, future research of,
  345
Skills:
  significance of, 11–12
  workforce planning and, 324
Social learning theory, 288–289
Social network reasoning tests, 250
Speed of learning test, 248
Spreadsheets, 151, **152**, **154**
Stamp, Gillian, 33
Standard deviation, 14
Statistical analysis, 19, 97
Stewart, A. J., 67–68

Strategic thinking, future trends in, 343
"Stress" exercises and interviews, 251
Stringer, R., 297
Strong-Campbell Vocational and Kuder
  Preference Inventories, 249
Student Potential Program, 346
Succession planning, competency-based:
  case study, insurance company:
    existing executives, assessment of,
      283–284
    strategies of, 281–284
  defined, 276
  development of, 279–281
  generally, 276–278
  generic organizational structure, **277**
  job families, vertical progression, 280
  job-matching and, 258
  jobs at three levels, competencies required,
    278
  organizational issues, 279
  as selection factor, 240
Superior performance:
  defined, 13
  value of, **14**
  See also specific careers/occupations
Surveys:
  advantages of, 101
  BEI analysis and, 151, 153
  development guidelines, 101
  disadvantages of, 101
  function of, 100–101
SYMLOG (Systematic Multiple Level
  Observation of Groups), 230, 235, 254

T

Tables, in competency reports, 155
Target job:
  competency model development for, 241
  succession planning and, 280
Teachers:
  achievement orientation in, 197, 213
  affiliative interest in, 88, 192
  analytical thinking in, 195
  customer service orientation in, 40,
    193–194
  developing others in, 188–189
  developmental skills in, 189
  directiveness/assertiveness in, 196–197
  flexibility in, 196
  initiative in, 195–196
  interpersonal understanding in, 38, 190
  occupational preference in, 191–192
  organizational commitment in, 191–192
  professional expertise in, 193
  self-confidence in, 191
  teamwork and cooperation in, 194
  unique competencies in, 88
Teaching methods, 337–339

Team facilitation, future trends and, 344
Team leadership (TL):
  defined, 64
  dimensions, 64
  examples of, 66
  in human service management, 218
  in management:
    in armed forces, 219
    generally, 66, 210–211, 213
    production management, 218
  links with other competencies, 34, 50, 61,
    66, 77, 86
  in military officers, 219
  scale, **65**
  in technical/professionals, 169
  titles for, 64
  typical behaviors, 64–65
Teamwork and cooperation (TW):
  defined, 61
  dimension of, 61, 63
  examples, 63
  in human service professionals, 194
  in management:
    generally, 63, 204–205, 213
    production management, 218
    research and development, 217
    sales managers, 216
  links with other competencies, 40, 50, 61,
    64, 80
  scale, **61–62**
  in technical/professionals, 168
  titles for, 61
  typical behaviors, 63
Technical managers, organizational strategy
  of, 93
Technical/profession/managerial expertise
  (EXP):
  behavioral indicators, 76
  in computer professionals, 168
  defined, 73
  dimensions of, 73
  examples, 76–77
  links with other competencies, 34, 36, 43,
    73, 77
  in management, 211–212, 217
  in salespeople, 183
  scale, **74–76**
  in software professionals, 168
  in technical/professionals, 168–170
  titles for, 73
Technical/professionals:
  achievement orientation in, 162, 164, 170,
    214
  analytical thinking in, 164–166
  brainstorming, 169
  conceptual thinking in, 164–165
  concern for order and quality in, 167–168
  customer service orientation in, 169

  defined, 161–162
  developing others in, 169
  directiveness/assertiveness in, 169
  direct persuasion in, 164
  expertise in, 168–170
  flexibility, 167, 169
  function of, 162
  generic competency model for, **163**
  impact and influence in, 164–166
  information seeking in, 168
  initiative in, 166
  interpersonal understanding in, 167
  managers of, 170
  networking, 169
  relationship building in, 169
  self-confidence in, 167
  team leadership in, 169
  teamwork and cooperation in, 168
Tenacity, in disadvantaged populations, 346
Test of thematic analysis, 248
Tests, in selection process, 242, 247–251
Thematic analysis:
  competency identification:
    actions, 139–140
    articulateness, 141
    cognitive/intellectual, 141
    feelings, 139
    interpersonal, 142
    involvement of, 137
    motivation, 138–139, 142
    outcomes, 140
    physical appearance, 141
    situation and, 137
    team approach:
      BEI sample:
        coding of, 151
        statistical analysis, 150–151
      coding:
        codebook preparation, 151
        preliminary testing of, 149–150
        process of, 143
        reconciliation of, 150
      competencies defined, 147
      formation of, 142–143
      interview analysis, individual, 143
      questions for, 148
      statistical analysis, 151
      thoughts, 137–138
      validation steps, 149
  concept:
    creation, 136
    use of, 135–136
  defined, 104
  organization of, 137–142
Thematic Apperception Test (TAT), 5, 98,
  231–232, 247
Theme Log, 145
Theorist, interview strategy, 117

Therapist, interview strategy, 117
Thinking, complexity and, 21
Threshold competencies, defined, 15
Total quality management (TQM), 155
Training:
  entry-level, 106
  job-matching and, 259
  need for, as selection factor, 241
Training and development, competency-based:
  adult experiential education theory,
      286–287
  benefits of, 292–293
  "bottom-line learning projects," 292
  case studies:
    achievement motivation training, small
        business, 298–300
    U.S. Navy Leadership and Management
        Education and Training (LMET),
        300–302, **301**
  defined, 286
  design steps of, 290–291
  development steps, 294–298
  measurement/credentials of, 291–292
  motive acquisition theory, 288
  organizational issues, 293–294
  professional development learning curve,
      293
  self-directed change theory, 289
  social learning theory, 288–289
  value added by, **292**
Trait competencies, 10–12
"Treasure Hunt" Exercises, 252
Trust, establishment of, 119
Trust officer:
  directiveness: assertiveness and use of
      positional power in, 183–184
  initiative in, 177
Turnover/retention rate, as selection factor,
    240

U

Underlying characteristics, defined, 9
Uniform Guidelines on Employee Selection
    Procedures, 102
Unique competencies, 22, 88–89, 147,
    216–217, 335

United States Agency for International
    Development (USAID), personal
    entrepreneurial characteristics
    cross-cultural study by, 220
U.S. Computer Company, human resource
    management case study, 321–322
U.S. Navy Leadership and Management
    Education and Training (LMET),
    300–302, **301**
U.S. Small Business Association, 299
U.S. State Department Foreign Service
    Information Officers, study of (FSIOs),
    4–7, 105
Unusual competencies, 89
User friendliness, significance of, 106

V

Validity, 7, 105–106, 109
Visioning, 88

W

Watson-Glaser Critical Thinking Appraisal,
    249
Weschler Adult Intelligence Survey (WAIS),
    249
Winter, D. G., 67–68
Work motivation, future trends and, 344
Workforce planning:
  business structure changes, 324
  cases:
    Connecticut, state system, 328–329
    United States Department of Labor
        (SCANS), report 330, 334–336
  competency scales, **325**
  competition, 323
  demographics, 323
  economic environment and, 323
  job changes, expected, **330**
  jobs by required competency levels, **327**
  new jobs by interpersonal level, **326**
  societal applications, development steps,
      324–325, 328
  technological change and, 323
Worldwide Competency Data Base, growth
    of, 345
Writing skills, 88